THE GUN DIGEST BOOK OF 9mm HANDGUNS

*By Dean A. Grennell
and Wiley Clapp*

DBI BOOKS, INC.

About Our Covers

In the world of 9mm pistols, the name "SIG-Sauer" is about as familiar to handgunners as the name "Jaguar" is to car owners. It's that simple.

On our front cover you'll see (to the left) a SIG-Sauer P225 in experimental satin nickel, complete with SIGARMS' new, optional checkered walnut grip. (The P225 is an abbreviated version of the SIG-Sauer P226, seen on the right.) When it comes to compactness of carry, the P225 should get the nod from those who want a lightweight 9mm and are content with 8 rounds in the mag and one up the spout.

Need more ammo? Take a closer look at the P226 — the magazine holds 15; and with one more in the chamber the total adds up to a sweet 16. Depending upon your politics, you might find it noteworthy that the SIG-Sauer P226 came in "second" (some say "first") during the U.S. Army's recent pistol trials.

On our back cover you'll find, to the left, a P226 dressed in satin nickel with an in-the-blue P225 hovering just above.

Both the P225 and P226 have SIG-Sauer's patented firing pin safety block and frame-mounted de-cocking lever. The P226 comes in blue, only, while the P226 is available in blue, optional satin nickel or the new "X-finish," a bonded synthetic that's impervious to saltwater corrosion.

Want more? See pages 138, 207, and 209 — you won't be disappointed. Everything you see on our covers is from SIGARMS, Tysons Corner, VA.
Photos by John Hanusin.

Produced by

GALLANT CHARGER PUBLICATIONS

PUBLISHER
Sheldon Factor

EDITORIAL DIRECTOR
Jack Lewis

PRODUCTION DIRECTOR
Sonya Kaiser

ARTISTS
June Armstrong
Denise Comiskey
Gary Duck

PRODUCTION COORDINATOR
Gerry Del Ré

COPY EDITOR
Shelby Pooler

CONTRIBUTING EDITOR
Chuck Karwan

PHOTO SERVICES
C'est DAGuerre Labs

ISBN: 0-910676-97-6   Library of Congress Catalog Card Number: 86-071043

CONTENTS

CHAPTER FOURTEEN: NINEFIRING ALL AVAILABLE 9mmP HANDGUNS
Shooting An Even Fifty Handguns, All That We Could Find **170**

CHAPTER FIFTEEN: NINEFIRING CONCLUDED
Commenting On The Lessons Learned From All That Shooting **222**

CHAPTER SIXTEEN: COMMERCIAL AMMUNITION COMPARED
Conducting Firing Tests Of Available Commercial 9mmP Ammo **230**

CHAPTER SEVENTEEN: THE NICER NINES OF BAR-STO
Giving Typical 9mmP Autos An Edge In Accuracy **246**

MANUFACTURER'S DIRECTORY **252**

ACKNOWLEDGEMENTS

After fighting my way through the complexities of assembling the best part of this, my first book, I am struck with the thought that the easiest part of writing a book is writing it. We have relied heavily on the camera to tell you the story of 9mmP handguns. The overwhelming majority of photos in this book were taken by co-author Dean Grennell. In this area of journalistic skill, Dean Grennell has no peer. Because of Dean's photographic skills, you will come to understand 9mmP handguns not only more quickly, but also more completely. I am eternally grateful that he was here to offer this valuable talent.

Other people helped out, too. Bill Haynes, the artful craftsman at the Gallant/Charger photolab, more than once brought tone and contrast to my otherwise murky negatives. Even the sometimes overprogrammed and distraught staff at C'est DAGuerre Labs made a big contribution. You can't leave the discussion of photography without mentioning John Hanusin, whose cover photography has graced DBI books for a number of years. I've yet to meet this man as this is written and I haven't even seen the covers of this book, but I'm betting that they are his usual first-rate effort.

Words are needed to make a book a book. You would be enormously amused to see our words in their original form. But by the time that they have been edited by the bear at the end of the hall, Jack Lewis; then set error-free in type by Shelby Pooler or Gerry Del Re; artfully "laid down" with pictures on story boards by Denise Comiskey, Gary Duck or June Armstrong...well, then they begin to look pretty nifty.

Still, the one person most responsible for making it all come together, creating and designing the ambience and character of the volume you hold in your hand, is Production Director Sonya Kaiser. We will be eternally grateful for the talented effort of this super lady, a person who must certainly hold the patent rights to patience.

Chuck Karwan contributed more than the several chapters under his by-line. He sent along some of his own personal firearms for the Ninefiring chapter. Further, he was always ready with a quick answer to a technical question or a protracted discussion of 9mmPs in general. In more than just direct ways, Chuck helped to shape the character of the book, and we owe him.

We got lots of help from people in the industry. Bob Valentine at SIGARMS was lots of help, as was Bob Magee at Interarms, Herb Belin at Smith & Wesson, Bob Platkin at Colt, and a host of others. We're indebted to Winchester, Remington and Federal for sizeable quantities of 9mmP ammunition and to Winchester, Hodgdon, Du Pont and Hercules for powder. Locally, the guys at S&S Precision bullets were always good for a few more boxes of their excellent cast bullets. Ditto for Hornady, Nosler, Sierra and Speer for their jacketed ones.

Special thanks go to two guys in particular. Irv Stone at Bar-Sto Precision was generous with his time and talent, making it possible to tell the story of those incredible barrels. And finally, there's Jon Maxwell, who cheerfully handed me about six grand worth of collector-grade handguns, a couple of them mint and unfired, doing so with the cheery admonition to "...go ahead and shoot 'em as much as you need to!" Friends like that make the job a lot easier.

Personally, I'm indebted to Chris Weare and Joe Boyd, who helped with certain specific portions of the book, but who also were consistently inquisitive and unfailingly enthusiastic about my efforts to turn out a quality product. Thanks, guys.

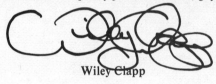

Wiley Clapp

First, I'd like to say thanks to my wife, Jean, for putting up with the production pangs of yet another DBI book. If you didn't know, C'est DAGuerre Labs is the darkroom — all fourteen square feet of it — in the corner of my shop at home and the considerable bulk of all the photos in the book came out of its constricted confines. That involved a lot of mornings when Jean came out to find the kitchen littered with film tanks and reels, or the living room floor carpeted with drying prints. In spite of that, she has not complained — hardly at all — and I'm grateful.

Next, thanks to colleague and collaborator Wiley Clapp, whose contribution to the volume at hand is indeed substantial. In many areas of 9mm lore, Wiley's expertise is leagues ahead of my own. He can identify any of the numerous models of SIG-Sauers from across a crowded room; to me, they all look pretty much the same and I'm a little awed by his ability. At his request, I gave him a cram course in my somewhat maverick photographic approach, involving single-lens reflex view cameras and provided him with an example of same. He took several of the photos that appear here and, if you can tell his from mine, you've a keener eye than I have.

I'll second the motion on thanks to the folks that Wiley named and add: Dave Andrews, Ken Alexander, Dick Lee, Steve Langford, Betty Millett, Bill Siems, Steve Hornady, Dick Placzek, Mike Wright, Bob Ellison, Jim Hull, James and Wayne Gibbs, Del Shorb, Fred and Buzz Huntington, Walt and Anne Stephenson, the Hodgdon clan, Dave Corbin, Warren Center, Richard and Sherri Beebe, Marty Liggins, Dick Dietz, Kevin Parsons, Johnny Falk, Tony Sailer, Harband Singh, Dan Bechtel, Sid Bell, John Bianchi, Rudy Herman, Ken Ramage, Neale Perkins, Mike Bussard, Bob and Barbara Hayden, Tim Pancurak, Bob and Frank Brownell, Stan Newman, Tim Lasater, Diane McCarthy, Becky Bowen, Bob Ruch, Bill Ruger, Steve Vogel and Al Benson. If I missed anyone who thinks their name belongs here, they can letter it in the margin and I'll endorse the entry with apologies.

Back in Northbrook, Illinois, Sheldon Factor and Bob Anderson performed their usual and extremely helpful chore of reading the book as it went together, pointing out areas for correction, clarification and so on.

As always, I close by expressing special thanks to the gun-loving, book-buying public, without whose encouragement and support, none of this would be possible. Hope you enjoy!

Dean A. Grennell

The outstanding virtue of the 9mmP is its ability to deliver high-velocity shots without an undue amount of recoil to disturb the sight picture. Here, Roger Combs executes a fast "Double-Tap" with a Llama Model XI-B and the muzzle is not uptilted appreciably. It becomes progressively more difficult to do this with guns of larger caliber.

THE NINE-MILLIMETER PARA-WHAAT?

YOU HAVE here an entire book, nominally and essentially devoted to a funny but fierce little old cartridge, as well as to the firearms designed to employ it. Most if not all of the discussion will be concerned primarily with the autoloading or semi-automatic firearms, along with revolvers. In addition to these, there are machine pistols, also known as submachine guns, doing their noisy and boisterous thing with the same cartridge, perhaps modified slightly in loading specifications and general ballistics. We may touch upon

such things, occasionally, but the publisher of the book at hand has also brought forth a companion volume on assault weapons, including full-auto guns chambered for the 9mm cartridge. There seems little point to conduct exhaustive explorations of the myriad burpguns taking the 9mm cartridge when they are covered in the contemporary book. There is more than ample discussion on the non-full-auto 9mm guns to fill a book of the envisioned size and that is what we propose to do.

The cartridge under discussion has been around for

nearly all of the century now a-dwindle. It has been known by many different names and terms, including 9mm Luger, 9mm Parabellum, 9x19mm and 9mmP. For the sake of uniformity, we will adhere to the 9mmP designation, fairly consistently. The 9mm Luger designation is commonly used in the USA on boxes of the ammunition and, less frequently, on the firearms, themselves. Many ammomakers brand the cartridges as 9mm Luger (Parabellum). There is

Discussing the Origins, Antiquity, Wherefors And How-Comes Of This Book's Basic Topic

one specific auto pistol known as the Luger, likewise as the *Pistole* '08 by reason of its adoption by the German Army or *Wehrmacht* in 1908. It's named for its designer, one Georg Luger — sometimes mentioned as George Luger — active in the late Nineteenth and early Twentieth Centuries. Luger refined and developed his design from the earlier, much more cumbersome and unwieldy Borchardt. Both pistols employ the same basic principle of operation, a delayed-blowback involving a toggle that is kicked up or broken at a certain point in recoil.

In many parts of the world, however, reference to a Luger is apt to draw little but blank stares of incomprehension and Parabellum or some local equivalent is the commoner term. That, in turn, has caused some amount of local confusion as to the meaning and derivation of Parabellum.

The basic Luger pistol was designed by Georg Luger, above, in the closing portion of the nineteenth century and early twentieth century. (K. Ryan drawing.)

For an elegantly clarifying explanation of all that, we are indebted to a British firearms authority, one Major Geoffrey Boothroyd, author of *The Handgun* and other erudite works. He also lent a guiding hand to the late Ian Fleming, creator of the ever popular James Bond, aka Agent 007, making earnest efforts to spare knowledgeable Bond fans their pained winces at inadvertent gaffes stemming from Fleming's unfamiliarity with the operation of handguns. As the series went on, the discussion of guns became more credible and all credit for that is due to Boothroyd, mentioned as official armourer for the double-nought section. (Or is it the double-ought?)

On pages 413-414 of *The Handgun,* Boothroyd provides about as much background details on the Parabellum business as most might feel any urgent need to absorb and acquire. According to Boothroyd, the Parabellum designation was first applied to the slightly longer, bottlenecked cartridge with a nominal bullet diameter of 7.65mm, often

The Luger, or Pistole '08, has a novel delayed blowback action in which the action recoils for a short distance, following which the toggle is "broken" to eject the empty case, as illustrated in this photo.

WINCHESTER. *Western.*

X30LP

30 Luger
(7.65mm)

93 gr.
Full Metal Case

50 Pistol-Revolver Cartridges

Companion cartridge of the 9mmP, the .30 Luger, is rarely designated as a Parabellum. Still loaded by Winchester, its case is slightly longer than that of the 9mmP, shown in an enlarged view at right, with typical bullet design.

termed the caliber .30 Luger. That was a turn of the century effort, the cartridge, like Luger's pistol, a more graceful and sophisticated refinement of the Borchardt and its cartridge.

Luger worked for the Ludwig Loewe firm during the interlude when they moved from the manufacture of sewing machines to firearms. As they went along, they acquired ammunition manufacturing interests and eventually became the *Deutche Waffen-und Munitions-fabriken AG,* familiarly and more comfortably abbreviated as DWM, as it will be termed for the remainder of the book. AG is for *Aktiengesellschaft* or *Aktien Gesellschaft,* a joint-stock company.

Actually, Luger was modifying the Borchardt pistol and cartridge in the closing years of the Nineteenth Century and submitted his 7.65 mm version of the Borchardt-Luger for trials held by the Swiss at Berne in 1899. The cartridge, essentially identical to the modern .30 Luger round, was called the 7.65 mm Parabellum and the gun was known as the *Pistole Parabellum.*

All of this stems from the Latin phrase, *"Si Vis Pacem Para Bellum,"* and Boothroyd translates that to, "If you want Peace, prepare for War." In German, the same slightly cynical observation becomes — again, according to Boothroyd: *"Bereite Den Krieg vor Parabellum."* Krieg, in German, means war or at war, according to my well-

Winchester's usual practice is to term it the 9mm Luger (Parabellum) and Smith & Wesson rollmarks the barrel of their Model 669 as in the photo at right. Use of Luger and/or Parabellum follows no set pattern.

thumbed Langenscheidt's English/German dictionary/ *worterbuch*. Being rather rampantly unilingual, I cannot elucidate the intricacies, much beyond that.

You are free, however, to formulate your own translations and approximations to personal taste. If you try to equate it to some other word, such as paramedic, you are apt to call down caustic showers of opprobrium upon your bloody but unbowed head, as I can ruefully testify, having done just that. Anyone who has taken the considerable bother to become fluidly fluent in Latin, let alone German,

is apt to be stridently unforgiving of minor discrepancies, as I've learned in perusing occasional letters dripping with vitriol; both blue and green.

With all that noted, understood and at least tacitly accepted, I almost hate to go on and dig for an English/ Usanian translation of Luger. A double dot over a letter, the u in this example, is termed an *umlaut* and often is transmuted to English by adding a letter e after the umlauted letter: thus, ue, in this instance. Most typesetting facilities in the USA do not boast umlauts and similar dia-

Colt, on the other hand, favors 9mm Luger as the designation on pistols made for that cartridge.

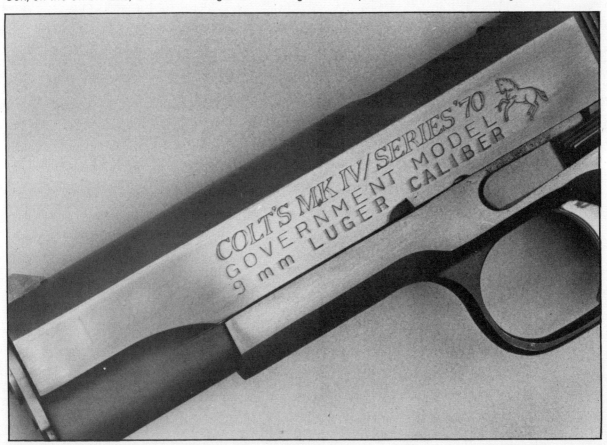

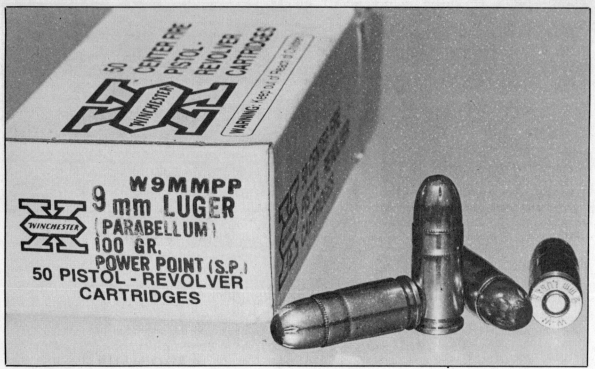

Although the traditional 9mmP bullet is a full metal jacket/round nose (FMJ/RN) design, many current ammomakers offer loads with bullets designed to deliver expansion on impact, such as this one.

Basic specifications of the 9mmP are shown in this dimensional drawing by one of the authors. The case tapers from .394" at the rim to .380" at the mouth and that introduces a few problems, as will be discussed here, later.

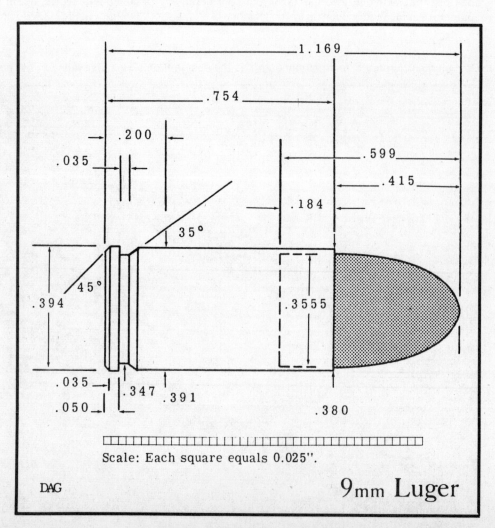

Scale: Each square equals 0.025''.

DAG

9mm Luger

critical marks such as the tilde and all the rest. The u in Luger is rarely if ever given an umlaut. The only instance I recall, offhand, was in *Anatomy of a Murder*.

According to the faithful, if somewhat scanty Langenscheidt's, there is no precise cognate for Luger/luger. The closest approach is luge — meaning lie, as in falsehood — and (their upper-case): Lugner, meaning liar; an umlaut over the u in both instances.

As I've mentioned in other books, I prefer not to say American as opposed to English because it causes our good neighbours in Canada to take umbrage at the unwarranted assumption that we're the only Americans on the North American Continent. I think they have a valid point there. To be more specific, I've coined the term, *Usanian,* which you've already encountered. In Usanian vocalizing, Luger is pronounced with a long u: Looger or perhaps Lewger. The precise voicing by a practicing Teuton may vary a bit and, for all I know, might come out Luhrger. At any rate, as I've decided long ago, umlauts can be slippery little rascals. As H. Allen Smith once observed, "Many of us consider gerbils to be harmless little rodents, but we must never forget that one once became propaganda minster of the Third Reich!"

Boothroyd reports that the first pistols were chambered for the 9mm Parabellum — as opposed to the 7.65mm Parabellum — in 1902, making it roughly nine years older than the .45 ACP (Automatic Colt Pistol) cartridge for the Colt Model 1911 pistol, which may or again may not have made its primal debut in 1911. We have, after all, the anomaly of the Springfield Model 1903 rifle that fires the caliber .30/'06 (i.e., 1906) cartridge. Contemplation of the fact that the hoarily traditional U.S. service pistol and its ludicrously ancient cartridge were finally superseded in 1985 by the even more antediluvian 9mmP is a thought at which some may find difficulty in stifling the odd smirk. So it sometimes goes.

There is, however, no gainsaying that the 9mmP has fairly well taken over the world as the most popular and widely employed pistol/submachine gun cartridge for military use and — to a somewhat lesser extent — for police use.

In translating between English (inch/foot) units of length and the Metric System, the usual conversion factors are .03937 and 25.4000508: millimeters times the former become inches and inches times the latter become millimeters, pretty close.

If there is any area of human endeavor where designations are more imprecise and bewildering than in the nomenclature of cartridges, I am unaware of it and, come right down to it, I don't think I'd even care to hear about it. Nine millimeters, by the regimen just cited, comes out to .35433-inch. The customary diameter for jacketed bullets to be used in 9mmP firearms is .355-inch; .356-inch for cast bullets. If we multiply .355 times 25.4000508, we get 9.017018034mm. As we've noted, the same cartridge is sometimes termed the 9x19mm, meaning its cartridge case is 19mm in length. Nominally, it's .754-inch and that works out to 19.1516383mm. In point of fact, as we'll discuss, later on, it is a great and notable rarity to encounter a 9x19mm case that is, by actual measurement, a full .754-inch in length, but we'll burn that bridge when we come to it.

It would be a plausible and hopeful, perhaps even wistful assumption that a 9mmP is a 9mmP, wherever the sun may shine or the waves may break. In the phrase of George Gershwin, it ain't necessarily so. Sporting arms and ammunition for use in them, in the USA, fall under the guiding specifications of the Sporting Arms and Ammunition Manufacturers Institute — SAAMI, as it will be termed, henceforth — and they have laid down dimensions and other particulars for the cartridge. Quite a bit of the domestic production of 9mmP ammo adheres fairly close to the dimensions in the accompanying drawing; others vary to greater or lesser extents and as to overseas production, varying degrees of departure may be encountered and, quite probably *will* be encountered.

I tend to think/I incline to believe/I dare to hope that things are gradually trending toward a state of stasis or galactic entropy with the 9mmP cartridge. A decade or two ago, I used to have to maintain at least three different shell holders in order to reload the 9mmP. Some case heads just wouldn't go into some shell holders and if you put other cases into other holders, the fit would be so loose they would not be plucked free of the dies. Another dimensional variation that can be and often is a real bugaboo in cases/reloads for auto pistols is the matter of brass thickness at the case neck. Some cases, resized, would not grasp some bullets with sufficient tenacity to hold them securely in place. Other bullets, put into other cases, would cause a bulge at the case mouth that prevented the resulting reload from chambering, in at least some pistols.

Suffice to say — as will be discussed to greater depth when we get to reloading the cartridge — it was, is and probably will remain a good idea to sort cartridge cases by headstamp when reloading the 9mmP. Along the way, be sure to sort out and segregate those Berdan-primed cases of foreign extraction. It is, at least theoretically, possible to reload a Berdan-primed case but it is monstrously impractical and unrewarding in terms of the time and special equipment and components it requires.

Apart from dimensions, the bedrock ballistics of the 9mmP vary quite a bit in various corners of the world. As made up to SAAMI specifications in this country, the absolute maximum peak chamber pressure is given as 35,700 copper units of pressure — abbreviated henceforth as c.u.p. — and that tends to be somewhat diffident by overall global standards, particularly since most loads fall well short of that figure. If you happen to have access to one of the fabled and legendary P'08 Lugers, you may find, as many have found, that domestic ammo does not muster enough pizzazz to function through the action. Judicious forcefeeding may be required, but it had better be damned judicious, rather than berserkly, gung-ho intrepid. It is possible to blow up a P'08 by overenthusiasm and the consequences are not a pretty sight.

In the meantime, the seeming diffidence of the domestic 9mmP is by no means the painful handicap one might casually assume it to be. SAAMI knows what it's doing and should be applauded, not booed. Take a moment to contemplate a photo or two that should appear nearby. These are not from injudicious reloads, but from factory loads of irreproachable credentials. They were fired in an early prototype of a small autoloading pistol, nominally chambered and suitably rollmarked for the 9mmP cartridge. I fired them, myself. I fired quite a few rounds through the small pistol, then paused to police up the spent

As discussed in adjacent text, the 9mmP operates at fairly high pressure levels and, at times, special conditions can and may boost pressures well above normal. Arrow in the photo at right indicates signs of a chamber irregularity.

brass, took a closer look at some of it and came about as close as I've ever gotten to a coronary seizure.

The alarming symptoms stemmed from two conditions: The prototype had an unduly lengthy protrusion of the unsupported case head over the feed ramp and it had, for good measure, rather chintzily-scant bore dimensions.

A tight bore, in itself, offers greater frictional resistance and that, in turn, boosts the peak working pressures, which result in higher velocity — provided the bullet gets out of the barrel without blowing the gun apart and portions of the shooter with it. Chronographing bullets out of this particular pistol, I got substantially higher velocities than I'd obtained with the same loads — factory loads, not wildeyed reloads! — out of another 9mmP pistol with a substantially longer barrel.

It's readily apparent what happened: The unsupported lower portion of the brass case bulged downward in a manner pregnant — and I use the word advisedly — with

grounds for extreme concern. It was awfully close to letting go and, when the head blows on a round in an auto pistol, it provides the shooter with a lot of adventure far better avoided.

I am not going to identify that particular pistol because the makers were advised of the state of things, muttered the caption of Peter Arno's immortal cartoon ("Well, back to the old drawing board!") and took great pains to rectify the situation. Later production of the same pistol does not pose comparable problems. In the meantime, the experience had modified my own *modus operandi* a little: Now, when I try out a new autoloader, I take pains to retrieve and inspect the first one or two empty cases ejected from its action. As an ongoing matter of personal philosophy, I prefer to never make the same mistake, even once.

As was noted earlier, the 9mmP has found greater favor among the military than among law enforcement groups. The reason for that lies in a basic dichotomy of outlook between the two organizations. Police rely upon the handguns as the absolute last-ditch tool for coping with situations beyond control by any other means. If an anti-

The Glaser Safety Slug, here in 9mmP, carries a novel bullet that encases a quantity of shot pellets inside a jacket. It is intended to rupture on impact for greater shock effect.

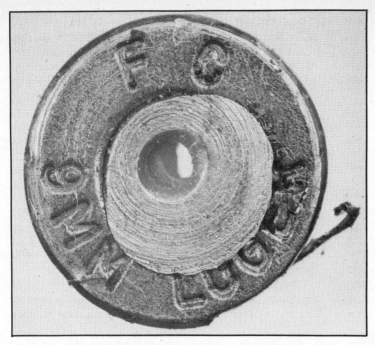

Another spent case, from a reputable factory load, as were examples on facing page, shows the extreme pressures that may develop when bore or chamber dimensions vary.

social type is manifestly about to kill or cause grievous bodily harm to the police officer or to a blameless third party, the policeman fires to prevent that from taking place. What is needed — urgently! — is a gun and load that will incapacitate the lawbreaker with absolute minimal delay.

The military situation is quite a different matter, entirely. Much of the time, anyone wearing the uniform of enemy forces can be and is to be potted with the gun at hand. If killed, the deceased enemy will take up no more than a small amount of time and effort from the burial detail con-

cerned. If, however, the enemy can be given a disabling wound, it will take up a lot of time, effort and personnel on the part of enemy forces to nurse the fallen foe back to recovery and, possibly, return to duty. Hence, from the military viewpoint, a wound has much greater strategic value than a lethal shot. Viewed from that highly specialized and somewhat cold-blooded standpoint, the 9mmP cartridge has few if any equals. Viewed as a decisive factor in typical police confrontations, it is by no means the same manifest leader of the pack.

The pair of 9mm bullets at left are Speer's TMJ design, for Totally Metal Jacketed. Same maker's jacketed hollow point (JHP) bullets for the .45 ACP are at right. As you might suppose, latter have more impact effect.

The fact remains, ineradicably: The 9mmP is a little tiny cartridge. It operates at fairly exalted levels of peak pressure and, if you take the muzzle velocity and the bullet weight, you can arrive at a figure for the nominal muzzle energy of the bullet in foot-pounds of energy (fpe). The energy of most 9mmP loads exceeds the energy of most .45 ACP loads. Respectively, the bullet diameters are .355-inch and .452-inch, with frontal areas of .099 and .1605 square inch. The area of the .45 bullet is about sixty-two percent greater than that of the 9mm bullet. When it comes to transferring kinetic energy to the target, frontal or cross-sectional area is an important factor.

It would help, of course, if the bullet could increase its frontal area upon impact with the target, thereby accelerating the transfer of kinetic energy, which is the primary purpose of any bullet, with the possible exception of those used in target practice.

Bullets capable of expanding upon impact cause all sorts of eyebrows to oscillate frantically, "Oh, you mean 'dum-dums'," the objectors babble, "but those are *outlawed by the Geneva Convention!*"

George Gershwin's weary voice, again. Huh-uh, folks, no truth in that, at all. "The Geneva Protocol 'for the prohibition of the use in war of asphyxiating, poisonous, or other gases, and of bacteriological methods of warfare,' signed on 17 June, 1925, on behalf of the United States and many other powers (...), has been ratified or adhered to by and is now effective between a considerable number of states. *However, the United States Senate has refrained from giving its advice and consent to the ratification of the (Geneva) Protocol by the United States, and it is accordingly not binding in this country."* That is a direct quote, with emphasis added, from the Dept. of the Army Field Manual #FM27-10, page 19, July, 1956, edition.

The Hague Convention No. IV, of 18 October, 1907 and its annex of regulations states, "It is especially forbidden (...) to employ arms, projectiles, or material calculated to cause unnecessary suffering." (HR, article 23, paragraph e.)

India's Dumdum Arsenal, located in or near the city of the same name, usually is given credit or blame for production of the first expanding-bullet ammunition for military

As quoted in the text, Army Field Manual FM27-10 spells out details of the so-called "Geneva Convention," which really had nothing to do with expanding bullet design.

The Wilkinson Linda is one of several examples of 9mmP pistols with remarkably generous magazine capacities. The one shown holds thirty-two rounds, in a staggered column. The Linda, here carrying a 2.5X Bushnell Phantom scope sight, is powerful and accurate but, as pointed out in the text, it is a mistake to assume that a high-capacity magazine can take the place of accurately aimed fire in a fight.

smallarms, hence the customary designation. Somewhere about the shop, I have part of a box of .22 Hornet ammunition, issued by the U.S. government in WWII for use with a survival rifle in that caliber and it is printed with the urgent admonition that it is not, under any circumstances, to be employed against enemy troops, due to the fact that the small bullets are of the jacketed hollow point (JHP) design. Given a hard choice, I think I'd rather be shot with a JHP from a .22 Hornet than with an armor-piercing incendiary (API) bullet in .30/06 — fully legal, sanctioned and often used in that war. But, you see, the JHP Hornet bullet is one of those nasty dumdums and, as the popular mass media likes to put it, "outlawed by the Geneva Convention!" Birdlime and brickdust; likewise, roach-milk!

Traditional military bullets of modern times, for use in handguns, rifles, carbines, machine guns and anything short of artillery, carries an FMJ bullet, either round nosed or Spitzer pointed. Enemy troops and/or non-combatants can be flash-fried with napalm or converted to radioactive cinders by nuclear bombs and it's all part of the grand old game. Exploding artillery shells are perfectly cricket and

kosher: always have been, probably always will be. A foeman struck with a round of high-explosive 155mm or vaporized by the blast of a 2000-pound blockbuster bomb is rightfully and properly overkilled. If, however, he is pinked with the JHP bullet from a .22 Hornet survival rifle, that constitutes a heinous war crime.

The logic behind all that may strike you as a little elusive. Candidly, it strikes me about the same way. It may make a slight amount of sense in terms of the military penchant to wound, rather than kill, even though the disparity between the message delivered to Hiroshima by the *Enola Gay* and a round of .22 short rimfire, with unclad lead bullet in either solid or hollow point may seem difficult to reconcile in terms of right versus wrong.

Be all that as it confusingly may, however. The strictures set up at the Hague Convention of 1907, proscribing expanding bullets — for smallarms, not for artillery! — apply to open warfare between major states/nations. They are not binding upon police and suspects when involved in exchanges of ballistic dialog. No police department in the known universe is or was a signatory to the Hague Convention of 1907 and thus is not bound to observe its proscription of expanding projectiles. The same applies to homeowners resisting criminal invasion of their domiciles and to a great many other hypothetical instances.

The 9mmP and the .45 ACP cartridges, among many other examples of handgun ammo, have at least one thing in common: They are usually fired from fairly short barrels of four or five inches, sometimes less and rarely more. Accordingly, the ammunition is loaded with a powder charge intended to provide optimum performance in a short barrel. Standard handgun ammo, in longer barrels, tends to show a diminishing-returns effect, rather quickly as the length of bore increases.

The average 9mmP load, in the equally average 9mmP firearms, is not overly noted for stunningly brilliant accuracy. In all honest candor, much the same can be observed about the .45 ACP cartridge and the guns that fire it. If rated by the typical military issue handgun — "goose-loose" is the customary term, meaning that, if you grab it by the handle and shake it, you get a merry tinkle of casually associated parts — you will be lucky to keep all hits in an area the size of a pie-plate, about ten inches in diameter, when fired with care from a steady rest at twenty-five yards. The groups may be considerably larger and often are.

With either cartridge, exceptional specimens may perform a whole lot better. One minute of angle represents a maximum spread between centers of about 1.05 inches at a distance of one hundred yards, proportional for other distances. It's abbreviated as one MOA and is considered pretty doggoned good for the better rifles. A handgun that will beat the MOA plateau is pretty scarce and memorable. I've managed to do that, a few times and have — just once! — dotted in a five-shot group with a reload in 9mmP that went precisely .250-inch between centers at twenty-five yards: just barely inside the magic MOA. That, however, was with the Marlin 9mm Camp Carbine, not with a handgun. With my 9mmP Colt, packing its Bar-Sto barrel and fitted with a scope sight, I've gotten down to around 1.5 inches between centers at twenty-five yards and down to about an inch of spread with a .45 auto and open iron sights, but that was not a .45 ACP, but a Detonics Score-

master in .451 Detonics magnum: the same basic case, with a slightly greater case length and beefed-up construction of the case head to cope with stiffer pressures.

As we'll be discussing in greater detail, in later chapters, the 9mmP is a rather trying and pestiferous case to reload, but it can be done. With the flexibility reloading brings, you can select judicious powder charges that boost the ballistics considerably from longer barrels.

In the words of an old song, (you) may have been a bringdown, but you never were a bore. That fairly well sums up my attitude toward the 9mmP. It's just about always a challenge to make the wee beastie perform, but when you succeed in that, it sort of makes you glow in the dark with gratification. A lot of the cartridges that were contemporaries when the 9mmP was fresh off the drawing board — such as the 7.65mm Parabellum and 7.62 Mauser — are seldom seen these latter days, but the 9mmP is doing well and making progress, all the while.

Let us now proceed to deal with the details of the spunky little cartridge and the guns that make it go snap-crackle-pocketa-pocketa. — *Dean A. Grennell*

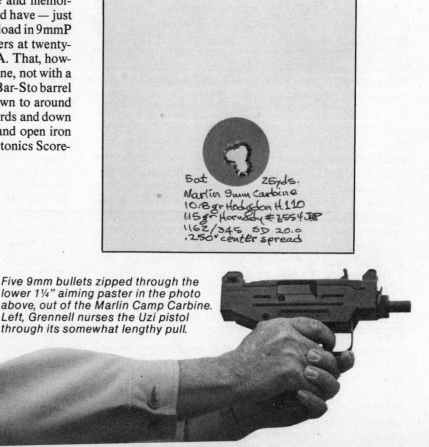

10.8gr H110
130gr Sierra #8345
FMJ 1166/393 SD 3.3

5 at   25yds.
Marlin 9mm Carbine
10.8gr Hodgdon H110
115gr Hornady #3554 JHP
1162/345 SD 20.0
.250" center spread

Five 9mm bullets zipped through the lower 1¼" aiming paster in the photo above, out of the Marlin Camp Carbine. Left, Grennell nurses the Uzi pistol through its somewhat lengthy pull.

An uncommonly neat, capable and handy pistol for the 9mmP is the ASP. It is converted from S&W Model 39 pistol by Armament Systems and Procedures of Appleton, Wisconsin.

CHAPTER 2

THE 9mmP CARTRIDGE

Moving Briskly Toward Its Ninetieth Birthday, This Remarkable Round Has Never Been Commonplace!

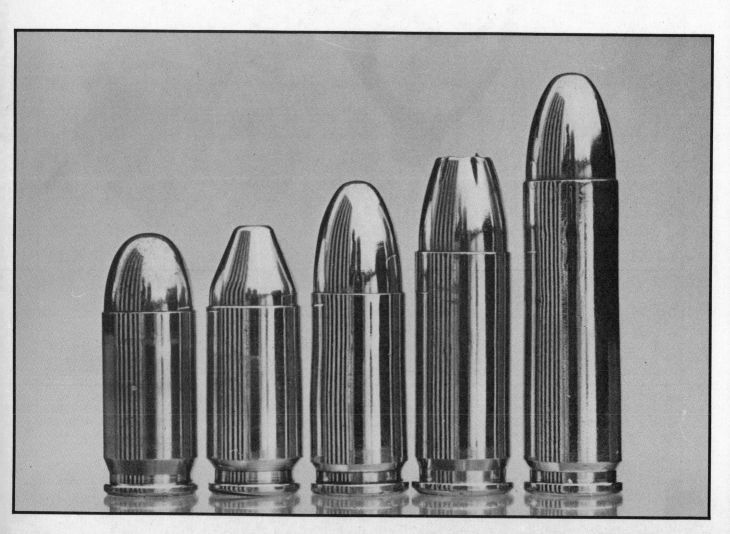

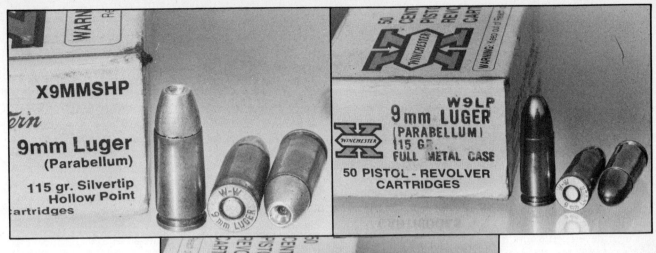

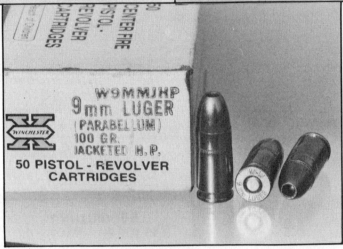

Three factory 9mmP loads from Winchester: The #X9MMSHP carries the Silvertip hollow point bullet that has a jacket of aluminum alloy, with lubricant in a cannelure near the base. The lubricant is necessary because aluminum alloy jackets tend to foul the bore objectionably without it. The Silvertip bullets tend to expand better than the one in the #W9MMJHP.

THE INTRODUCTION of nitrocellulose-based powders — often termed smokeless — set the field of firearms development on its collective ear and triggered a quantum leap forward in firearms capability, to which nothing else compares, even remotely. The technology of earlier days may have been capable of designing and producing autoloading pistols, but the original black gunpowder simply would not function in an auto pistol for more than a few shots before bore fouling became a serious problem.

Those must have been exciting times for anyone connected with research and development in firearms. Smokeless powders made auto pistols practicable, along with machine guns and assorted other developments. As with the appearance of nuclear devices, half a century or so later, it made the world a different place; not necessarily better, but indubitably different. There was no returning to earlier times and there still is not.

Development of the machine gun turned such stirring spectacles as cavalry charges into nothing more than an uncommonly picturesque form of suicide: a hard fact of life that cavalry enthusiasts were extremely loathe to accept and one that cost the life of many a brave man...and noble steed.

At about the same time, Georg Luger's new pistol and its cartridge were giving the humble sidearm most of the velocity and a good percentage of the punch that had represented a fairly decent rifle in the black powder era. Luger's approximate contemporary, Gabbett-Fairfax, was refining an auto pistol called the Mars, with ballistic capabilities that were hardly matched until Harry Sanford brought out his Auto-Mag pistol in the early '70s. Gabbett-Fairfax's design was, to put it charitably, an engineering nightmare while Luger's was respectably sound, by just about any standard you care to specify.

Now, the better part of a century later, we are still waiting — with understandably mounting impatience — for the next roaring breakthrough that will give the technology another comparable shot in the arm.

Ask yourself: How many artifacts of the 1902 era remain fairly well king of the mountain, right on down to the here and now, as well as the hazily visible tomorrows, up ahead? Give some contemplative thought to a 1902 automobile, a 1902 camera, a 1902 refrigerator, a 1902 locomotive or just any old 1902 marvel you'd care to suggest. How many of them survive, intact and thriving in the brave new, post-'84 world? I suggest that very few do. Now, do you begin to appreciate the singular genius of Georg Luger, John M. Browning and a few other giants of that receding day? Are we breeding innovative supernovas of comparable caliber today? Well, I wish I could suggest even one, in that particular field.

Luger developed a tiny little cartridge, capable of operating at peak pressures up to somewhere around 35,700 copper units of pressure (c.u.p.) and he did it and made it work, quite well, in a day when metallurgy was still in its squalling infancy, by contemporary standards. Thirteen years later, when the U.S. entered WWI, the need for service handguns was partially filled by turning forth Colt and Smith & Wesson revolvers to handle the domestic service

pistol round. Some years after the war, a rimmed version of the .45 Automatic Colt Pistol (ACP) cartridge was developed for convenient use in such revolvers. Mindful that the .45 ACP operates at a maximum pressure of 19,900 c.u.p., as well as the fact that such revolvers were made to use the .45 ACP, by means of a half-moon clip, the Sporting Arms and Manufacturers Association (SAAMI) decrees that the rimmed revolver round, the .45 Auto Rim (AR) must stay below 16,900 c.u.p. — a ton and a half lower than the .45 ACP! Differences in innate case strength between the two cartridges may account for this puzzling anomaly.

The figures for maximum SAAMI-specified pressures are given in the tenth edition of the *Speer Manual*. In point of fact, factory loads are made up to peak pressures well below the maximum figures. Elsewhere here, you will find discussions and illustrations to suggest that even sub-SAAMI-maximum pressures are a lot more than the occasional gun design can handle with aplomb. The 9mmP cartridge, by no means, has this problem all to itself. I propose to crank in, at about this point, a photo of three .45 ACP cases, cruelly abused and offering food for thought. These, if you please, did not start out as some wild-eyed reload. On the contrary, they were factory loads, of impeccable credentials, but they were fired in a gun that was

"Good grief — Gesundheit!" By way of demonstrating that the 9mmP is not alone in occasionally producing weird empty cases, these .45 ACP specimens were factory loads of reputable make, having been fired in a gun of dubious design. As text notes, peak .45 pressures are below 9mmP.

hamstrung to the hilt and beyond by teeming design flaws. These things can happen to any cartridge, even to one normally functioning at pressure levels far below those of the 9mmP.

For a cartridge nicely into its eighth decade, the 9mmP is doing remarkably well. It ranks as the number-one military handgun cartridge in the world and it's also in widespread use for submachine guns/machine pistols. For the cartridge collector, it must be a severely taxing challenge, because a near endless number of variations of the cartridge have been made at one time or another, somewhere.

The funny looking round at left is not a shot cartridge. Shown next to a conventional 9mmP load, the one with the crimped mouth is a blank, designed to feed out of the magazines of typical autoloading pistols for film use.

The movie and television industry uses a lot of 9mm blanks in routine operation, but these are difficult for the average person to obtain. The one illustrated comes with a star-crimped nose approximating the contours of a regular bullet, thus enabling it to feed out of most magazines. Such blanks usually work fairly well in gas-operated systems, although some modification may be required. If the auto-loader works by recoil, it's usually necessary to install a bushing in the bore to restrict the gas and simulate the effect of a launched bullet. Careful precautions must be taken to prevent the firing of conventional loads in guns thus converted for use with blanks.

Samson ammunition, made by Israel Military Industries (IMI), produces a special 9mmP load for use in carbines and submachine guns. A coat of black lacquer is applied to the tip of the bullets to distinguish them from other ammo,

Samsom ammo, from Israeli Military Industries, is available as a standard 9mmP and as a special load for carbines and submachine guns.

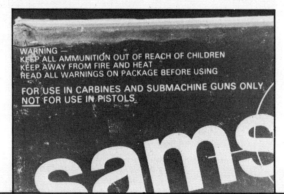

9mmP submachine guns come in many makes and designs. One of the rarest is the familiar Thompson, usually in .45 ACP. A few were made in 9mmP, with curved magazine and this one, serial S-1, is from the collection of J. Curtis Earl, 5512 North Sixth Street, Phoenix, Arizona 85012. Earl is a machine gun dealer, but I doubt if he's overly anxious to dispose of this one.

once out of the box and the headstamp likewise identifies the carbine load. The IMI carbine ammo box bears the warning: "For use in carbines and submachine guns only, *not* for use in pistols."

My semi-auto Wilkinson Linda pistol is also made in a version capable of full-auto fire so I reasoned that made it a sort of burpgun with a speech impediment. At any rate, I used the Linda, with its 7⅝-inch barrel, to chronograph some of the IMI carbine ammo. Average ballistics on five shots came to 1318/445 — by no means the highest I've clocked out of that gun. I've a dwindling, though seldom-used supply of some 9mmP with 90-grain JHP bullets, turned out by Super Vel when they were in Shelbyville, Indiana, that average 1789/640 out of the Linda. In an Uzi semi-automatic carbine, with a 16.1-inch barrel, the same load averaged 1953/762 and the standard deviation was a robust 147.7 fps. One round of the five turned in a velocity of 2123.1442 fps on the chronograph. That would have been good for 901 fpe: better than twice the usual performance of the 9mmP in handguns!

The special requirements of submachine guns dictate all manner of specialized 9mmP ammo. A few years ago, one of the leading bulletmakers produced a custom lot of 9mm FMJ/RN bullets at a weight of 145 grains. They were going into some subsonic loads for use in suppressed submachine guns — silenced, in the commoner term. The speed of sound, in air, is 1086 fps at 32°F and increases about 1 fps/degree F from that point. Thus, it would be about 1126 fps at 72°F and so on. If a moving object exceeds the speed of sound, it creates the sonic-boom effect with which many of us have become familiar. A supersonic bullet cannot be silenced or suppressed because of the noise it makes in going through the air and quite a few 9mmP loads operate at or above MACH I velocities.

Super Vel was a pioneer in the field of extra-performance ammunition and bullets capable of expanding on impact.

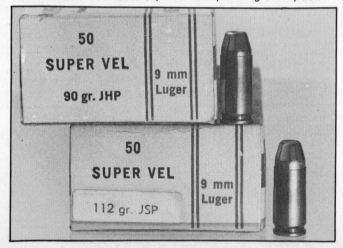

Curiously enough, the 9mmP seems to have been a cartridge ignored or overlooked by the wildcatting fraternity. There have been various wildcats — i.e., non-factory cartridges — created by necking the .45 ACP down to accept smaller bullets. The .38-45 Clerke is but one example and it's of interest because it used 9mm (.355-inch) bullets, making it an unusual hybrid between the two traditional arch-rival rounds.

John A. "Bo" Clerke developed the .38-45 to provide owners of the Model 1911-type pistols with an inexpensive conversion to the smaller bullet diameter. Being made from the .45 ACP case, it feeds out of the unmodified .45 magazine. Carrying somewhat lighter bullets, the battering recoil of the .45 ACP is reduced considerably. That is not the unalloyed asset you might suppose. The M1911 is a recoil-operated design and you need some minimal amount of push-back to operate the system. It doesn't help to install a weaker recoil spring because you need about as much spring-power as the standard spring delivers, just to move the slide forward and chamber the round properly.

Any attempt to generate enough recoil by boosting the bullet weight and/or powder charge runs into the hard fact that the .45 ACP case — and any wildcat produced from it — is tethered to a maximum pressure of 19,900 c.u.p., by SAAMI decree. I have sometimes observed that, if people enjoy doing crossword puzzles in obscure dialects of Sanskrit, endeavoring to isolate good loads for the .38-45 should afford them endless happy diversion.

A European cartridge, rarely encountered in the U.S., is the 9x18mm Ultra. It is just a tiny bit longer than the .380 ACP *aka* 9mm Corto, 9mm Kurz, et al. It seems to represent a response in certain European countries where use and possession of guns and cartridges of recognized military calibers — such as the 9mmP — are more or less forbidden. The 9x18mm Ultra is not quite a 9x19mm Parabellum and thus it evades the restriction.

A 9mmP, at left, lends perspective to the round of .38-45 Clerke at right. Latter is a hybrid of the 9mmP and .45 ACP and, like a four-footed hybrid, is mulishly reluctant to perform in the manner hopefully envisioned by the shooter.

The 9x18mm Ultra is just 1mm shorter in case length than the 9mmP and it is rarely encountered in the USA. Text discusses the probable reason for its existence in the grand scheme of things.

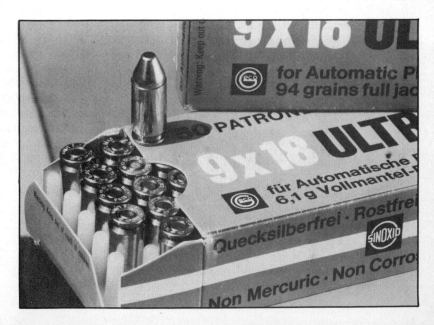

The .38 Colt Super cartridge is somewhat longer than the 9mmP and it is a modification of the older .38 ACP cartridge. The .38 Super was developed in the Twenties for use in a modification of the Model 1911 pistol and its dimensions are identical with those of the older .38 ACP round; the difference is that the .38 Super operates at significantly higher pressures. The SAAMI maximum for the .38 Super is the same as for the 9mmP, namely 35,700 c.u.p.

Curious as to the performance level of current .38 Super ammo, I clocked five apiece through my five-inch Government Model Colt and got:

LOAD	5-shot average	MAKER'S LISTING
Remington 115-grain JHP	1250/399	1300/431
Winchester 125-grain Silvertip	1186/390	1240/427
Remington 130-grain FMJ/RN	1163/391	1215/426
Winchester 130-grain FMJ/RN	1143/377	1215/426

There has been quite a bit of argument as to the comparative effectiveness of the 9mmP vs. the .38 Super, somewhat obscured by the fact that 9mmP loads commonly are tested through four-inch barrels and .38 Super through five-inch barrels. As I happen to own a five-inch Government Model Colt in 9mmP, it seemed like a pertinent procedure to put a few factory loads and reloads through it for purposes of objective comparison. I hoped that would bypass the plums-versus-kumquats aspect of the discussion. In the five-inch barrel, the quoted 9mmP loads went:

Federal 115-grain	1118/319
Hornady/Frontier 115-grain FMJ	1218/379
Win. 115-grain Silvertip JHP	1253/401
Fiocchi 115-grain FMJ	1276/416
Geco 123-grain FMJ	1258/432

You may draw such conclusions as you may feel inclined, from the foregoing. I should note that both of the test guns carried Bar-Sto barrels. All of the .38 Super loads were fired at the same mark from a distance of thirty-five yards — not twenty-five — and the extreme spread, center-to-center for the twenty-shot group was a fairly decent 4.864

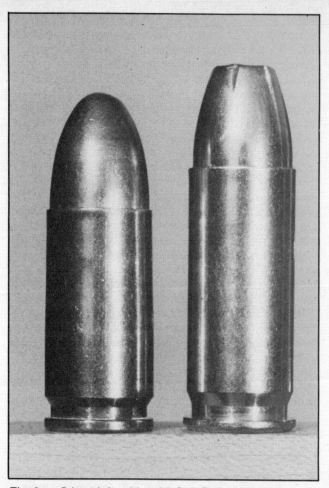

The 9mmP is at left, with a .38 Colt Super carrying a 125-grain Silvertip bullet by Winchester. Both cartridges operate at the same maximum pressure levels. Current factory loadings of .38 Super are comparable to the 9mmP in muzzle energy when both are fired from barrels of the same length. Refer to the text at left of the photo here.

inches, with rear sight left unchanged. Mr. Stone makes pretty nice barrels, out there in XXIX Palms.

As will be dwelt upon elsewhere, there are a great many different domestic and foreign loads available commercially for the 9mmP and I'm much more familiar with some than with others. Probably, my all-time favorite is the Federal #9BP load, with its 115-grain JHP bullet. This is not necessarily the hottest 9mmP load going but it has the undeniable virtue that its accuracy is quite apt to be gratifying, no matter from what it may be fired. For reasons that strike me as ample and sufficient, the Federal #9BP load has come to be the yardstick by which I measure other ammo of the same caliber.

At one time, Smith & Wesson produced ammunition and one of their 9mmP loads carried this unusual SWC bullet.

The Federal #9AP load, with its 123-grain FMJ/RN — Federal calls it metal case — bullet is no slouch, when it comes down to that. Some time back, I was doing tests to write up the Weaver Nighthawk semi-auto carbine in 9mmP and, in that particular gun, the #9AP outgrouped the #9BP, plumb croggling me with astonishment. Both grouped quite well, I should add.

There have been many strange and compellingly memorable bullets dreamed up for use in the 9mmP, down the several decades of its career. One of the more unusual was a 115-grain FMJ semi-wadcutter (SWC) design that was offered by Smith & Wesson during that fairly brief interlude when they ventured into the arena of ammomaking. This was actually a pretty good bullet; it fed admirably enough and it often grouped well, meanwhile cutting fairly clean holes in target paper and, one presumes, performing adequately on live targets.

Back about the time the Sixties were merging into the Seventies, Dr. Paul J. Kopsch of Lorain, Ohio, was working upon designs for a metal-piercing bullet of exceptional capability. He worked with a pair of local associates whose last names began with T (for Turcus) and W (for Ward). With Kopsch's last initial, that inspired the KTW brand name. It was put up in small, five-cartridge packs, prominently labeled, "FOR POLICE USE ONLY," and distribution was carefully limited to law enforcement personnel, plus a few small test samples to gunwriters of acceptable credentials.

The KTW ammo really did have the ability to penetrate all manner of resistant materials. Initially, the cores wre produced of a tungsten alloy — called *kennametal*, if memory serves — with a gilding metal base jacket to engage the rifling of the bore. Specific gravity of tungsten is 19.3, compared to 11.4 for lead. Thus, a tungsten bullet of a given volume would weigh about sixty-nine percent more than the same bullet would, if made of lead.

Tungsten is many times harder than lead, enabling it to resist deformation much better. A lot of fuss has been made

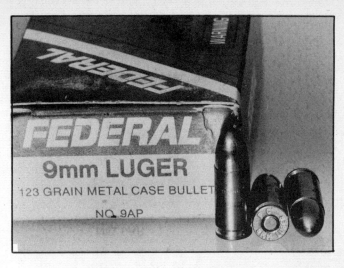

Federal's #9AP load is a duplication of the typical military round and serves quite well when such performance is desired. Feeding reliability is excellent, expansion is about non-existent, penetration is fine and accuracy is generally acceptable. The Federal #9BP, on the other hand, has a JHP bullet and sacrifices some reliability in some guns. It is quite apt to be uncommonly accurate and its capacity for expansion on impact is excellent.

The KTW bullet, here in 9mm, originally was made of tungsten, coated with teflon and with the copper jacket to ease passage up the bore. Later, they switched to bronze in place of the tungsten. See text for details.

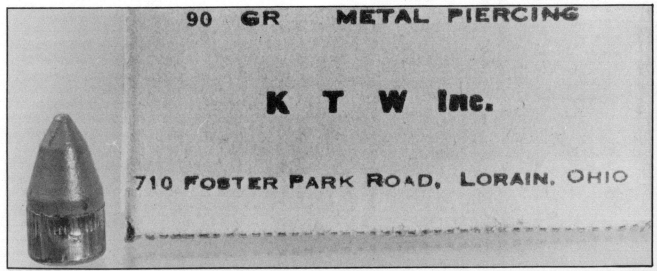

Above, from left: 9mmP; .380 ACP; .32 ACP and .25 ACP. In such company, the 9mmP is potent, indeed. Upper left, from left: 9mmP; .38 Special and .357 magnum. Despite its larger size, the .38 Special is less powerful than the 9mmP and the .357 magnum is only moderately more so. Lower left, the 9mmP looms huge, next to the .22 long rifle rimfire cartridge and performance is proportional.

about the teflon coating over the hard inner core. There's no doubt that the teflon helped to some extent, but tungsten bullets can do a lot of penetrating, even if entirely un-coated. KTW loaded their ammo in many different calibers, all the way from the humble .25 ACP up through .44 magnum and perhaps beyond that. In time, they shifted from the tungsten to bronze cores, finding performance was about the same, while the cost of raw material was reduced substantially.

Some say KTW never figured in a law enforcement situation. That is not necessarily true. It is, however, true that situations in which it did figure have been publicized little, if at all.

There was, for example, an incident in a European country that prefers to remain anonymous and shall, for that reason. A gang of terrorists had been engaged in some deed of dark dastardy and, hotly pursued, barricaded themselves inside a railway car they'd had the foresight to armor with steel plates of substantial thickness.

When the authorities arrived, they opened fire upon the car, using standard military 5.56mm hardball ammo in M-16s. The slugs bounced off the steel plate, without having any useful effect.

Some of the officers, however, had Uzi submachine guns, loaded with 9mmP KTW and that proved to be a horse of iridescently different color. What it did, actually, was to turn the terrorists into what one might term *good* terrorists.

You probably remember what happened, some while after that. One of the more hysterical television networks got wind of KTW and staged a breast-beating special to acquaint the whole world with the facts that: (1) Many police wore bullet-resistant garments and (2) bullets coated with nasty Teflon would go through such protective garb. In hardly a fraction of a trice, Teflon-coated bullets were re-christened as "cop-killer bullets."

From left: the 8mm Nambu; 9mmP and 10mm Auto, as used in the Bren Ten autoloading pistol. The 10mm takes bullets of .400-inch diameter and its probable long-term career and acceptance remains open to doubt at present.

Above right, from left: 9mmP; 7.65mm or .30 Luger and the 8mm Nambu. As you'll note, the .30 Luger is not just a necked-down 9mmP, but has a somewhat longer case. Lower right, the 9mm Winchester magnum is highly similar to the 9mmP, with about half-again as much case length and its safe to say that it will be an awfully long time before production of the tall one exceeds 9mmP!

For many years, up to that point, it had been a gentleman's agreement among the firearms press and its contributors to downplay and soft-pedal any discussion of the growing use of ballistic garments in law enforcement. If the bad guy knows about the vest, he aims for the head. Just that painfully simple. Once the coverage of the entire matter hit the screens of the nation's boob-tubes, in prime time, the damage was done and all hell was out for noon.

Even now, some while later, it's debatable if any sworn officers have been killed by bad-hats using Teflon-clad slugs but — thanks to that idiot network's rabid blabbermouthing — some number of officers are dead because their adversaries took pains to aim for their head instead of the temptingly large target of the torso, which might be protected by a ballistic vest. Meanwhile, gibbering lawmakers have ramrodded laws onto the books making possession and/or use of armor-piercing ammo a big, bad no-no.

For the sake of fairly full coverage, I include a photo of 90-grain KTW bullet, in all its apple-green splendor. Note please that it is a bare bullet, not part of a loaded round. In their day, they worked and worked with notable effect, but the idiot media shot them down...with electronic bullets that remain unregulated, down to the wincing present. So it sometimes goes.

Walk around it. Kick the tires thoughtfully. By any standard, viewed from any direction, the 9mmP is a remarkable cartridge, even after all this time. — *Dean A. Grennell*

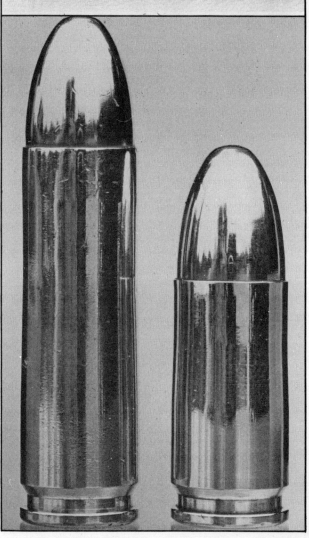

CHAPTER 3

RELOADING THE 9mm

Not Exactly The Reloader's Dream Cartridge, But It's Possible To Reload It Successfully And Here Are Some Tips, Kinks And Wrinkles!

AS CARTRIDGES go, the 9mmP offers a little more challenge than a great many reloaders are apt to feel they really need. There are several reasons for that state of affairs. To list some — not necessarily all — of them: The basic cartridge is quite small, taxing the manual dexterity of almost anyone. Ideally, reloading of the 9mmP should be performed by a highly trained squirrel, perhaps with a burly badger to work the handle on the loading press. Human fingers usually prove to be oversized, cumbersome and unwieldy for steering the bullet into the case mouth.

The 9mmP case is tapered, slightly. The sides of the full-diameter portion of the bullet, at a nominal diameter of .355-inch for jacketed or .356-inch for cast bullets, are parallel. For that obvious reason, the bullet walls are gripped only by a small portion of the case neck and therein lies a major segment of the problem.

Victor Borge, the Danish comic, used to favor a routine in which he started out by saying, "The trouble with pancakes is, in the first place, they should be waffles." In somewhat the same vein, it would make things simpler, to a most helpful extent, when reloading the 9mmP if, in the first place, it was a .38 Colt Super.

By the time you ram the base of the bullet down into the case mouth, you take up a lot of desperately needed powder space and powder space is one of the cartridge case virtues the 9mmP lacks to an uncommonly severe extent.

The 9mmP operates at fairly exalted pressures, for an auto pistol cartridge; 37,700 c.u.p., according to SAAMI spec's. That, it should be noted with all decent haste, is the absolute maximum and, in normal practice, commercial ammo is loaded lower than that pressure, by some given percentage. The .38 Colt Super operates to precisely the same ceiling. Due to the slightly greater capacity of the latter, it can drive a bullet of the same weight to somewhat higher velocities, out of barrels five or more inches in length. If you trim down to four-inch barrels, the edge of the .38 CS over the 9mmP is not overly great.

The maximum length overall (LOA) of the 9mmP may vary slightly from gun to gun, due to slight dimensional variations in magazines. The loaded cartridge has got to be of a length that enables it to be stuffed down into the magazine and, even more importantly, of a length that lets

Peter Kirker, (130 E. Vista Way, Vista, CA 92083), operating his automated Star press that is fitted with auto feed for bullets and cases. Most presses are simpler, less expensive.

I prefer to drop powder charges into cases held in a loading block and inspect the charge level visually before going on to seat the bullets.

The 9mmP, left, next to a .38 Colt Super. Latter has straight case walls, rather than tapered ones.

Some listed loads call for about as much powder as you can coax into the 9mmP case, as here.

Three different shapes of FMJ bullets for the 9mmP. As a rule, these feed more reliably than soft points.

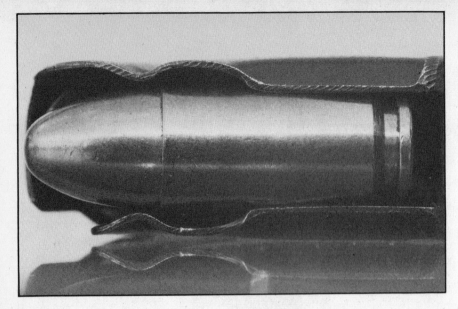

it feed back up out of the magazine without a hitch or snag.

The tension of the frictional engagement between the case neck and the bullet base is a critically important one. It must be tight enough to resist deeper seating of the bullet as the cartridge is stripped from the top of the magazine and slammed up into contact with the feed ramp and on up into the chamber. The bullets of the loaded cartridge want to remain stubbornly in place, throughout the feeding cycle. If one gets seated deeper than the rest, by reason of feeding stresses and a loose hold by the case mouth, the resulting peak pressures at the time of firing will be higher; substantially higher. The velocity will be higher and that particular shot may not group too close to the rest of them. The resulting higher pressures of the bullet that gets seated deeper in the course of feeding can and may damage the gun.

Examining factory ammunition, you'll note that some have a *cannelure,* which is a shallow circular indentation in the cartridge case, about where the base of the original bullet ended up. That is intended to hold the bullet in place and well may have done so, on the original loading.

At the time of original firing, nearly nineteen tons per square inch of pressure probably will have erased most if not all of the cannelure. You can still see it, but it will not provide much support, even if the base of the bullet ends up at that point.

Tools are available for executing fresh cannelures. Corbin makes one and so does C-H Tool & Die Corp. They can be used to put a cannelure in jacketed bullets, as made up by the swaging process, or they can put a cannelure in the cartridge case at any desired point, by means of suitable adjustment. A minor problem of such tools is that they leave the bullet and/or case slightly out of round and that may or may not be a serious matter. The primary purpose of canneluring tools is to provide an indented area around a jacketed bullet so the case mouth can be crimped into it. It is not a widespread custom to cannelure the case to provide support for the bullet base. It could be done, but it isn't done overly often.

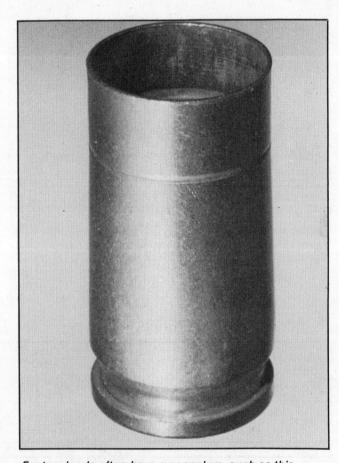

Factory loads often have a cannelure, such as this shallow groove near the case mouth, to hold bullet against rearward movement. Usually, as here, the cannelure is all but lost in firing and cannot be relied upon to perform the same function on reload.

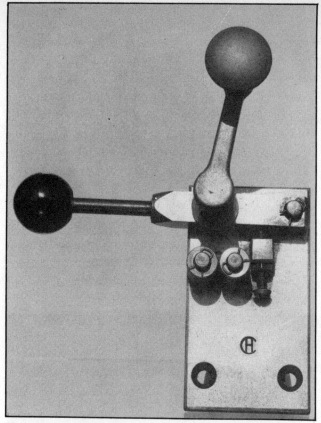

C-H Tool & Die, (106 N. Harding, Owen, WI 54460), makes this canneluring tool that can be adjusted for position and depth, handling all of the calibers.

The preferred and more popular approach is to resize the case mouths down just a little bit too small and then expand them back up with a straight-sided expander plug. In so doing, it provides a moderate length of uniform inside diameter at the case mouth and, if that is two or three thousandths (.002-.003-inch) smaller than the bullet base,

you end up with an acceptably tight hold on the bullet.

As is mentioned elsewhere, brass cases in 9mmP tend to vary in dimensions, especially in thickness of the brass at the case neck. Such variation is minimal to non-existent in cases of the same make and type, making it an excellent practice to sort the cases by headstamp, either before or

It is an excellent practice to sort empty 9mmP cases by headstamps, for the sake of uniform performance of the reloaded cartridges. The 9mmP tends to differ (often dramatically) between various makers.

The RCBS sizing die at left is the standard type of hardened steel and you must apply sizing lube to the cases before resizing. Same maker's tungsten carbide sizing die, right, does not require lubrication of cases.

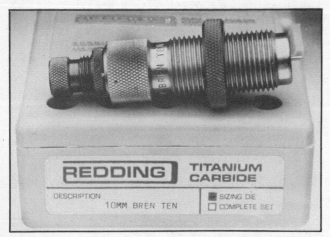

Instead of tungsten carbide, Redding uses titanium carbide, left, serving the same purpose but with some gain as to lubricity. Right, Lee Precision's tungsten carbide die for the 9mmP.

Left, viewed from the business end, here is the Lee Precision 9mm t-c die, showing the cemented insert of carbide at the mouth. Right, the carbide insert in a 9mmP sizing die from Hornady.

The RCBS Sidewinder case tumbler is a highly satisfactory device for cleaning and/or polishing empty cases. Don't use it for loaded ammo! Below, left, a closer look at their liquid cleaning concentrate and timer dial. Lower right, label markings on Hornady and RCBS die sets.

after putting them into load-ready condition. Only by so doing can you feel reasonably assured of uniform performance when fired.

As the 9mmP case is tapered, a much longer section of tungsten carbide is required for making up tungsten carbide resizing dies and the resulting die is somewhat more expensive than a die for .38 Specials and other straight-sided cases. In spite of that, a 9mmP carbide sizing die is an excellent investment, assuming you propose to reload the cartridge in reasonable quantity and frequency. The reason, of course, is that there is no need to apply case resizing lubricant to the brass when using a carbide die. When using a resizing die of hardened steel, you must apply sizing lube before sizing and it is fairly well mandatory to get it back off the cases before going on to complete the reloading operation. If lube is left on the cases, the tapered case tends to put a cruel and damaging amount of back-thrust against the action of the gun.

One of the more practical methods of applying resizing lube is to put a thin coating of it on an uninked stamp pad, rolling a batch of the cases across it before resizing. While it's possible to put the resized cases onto a K-Spinner, one at a time, to wipe the lube off with a rag or paper towel, it is a time-consuming chore. When working with a large number of cases, the lube is removed more easily by putting them into a case tumbler capable of working with liquids, adding a moderate amount of suitable detergent to the liquid medium. The RCBS Sidewinder tumbler works particularly well for such purposes, as does the case-cleaning concentrate RCBS supplies. After such treatment, the cases must be thoroughly air-dried, preferably under moderate heat, such as in a closed automobile on a warm, sunny day.

With a carbide resizing die, all of the foregoing folderol is neatly bypassed. The case goes in dry, comes out dry and is ready for further operations, as of that moment. With that considered, the higher price tag of the carbide sizer may seem a lot more bearable.

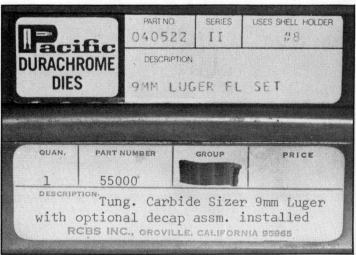

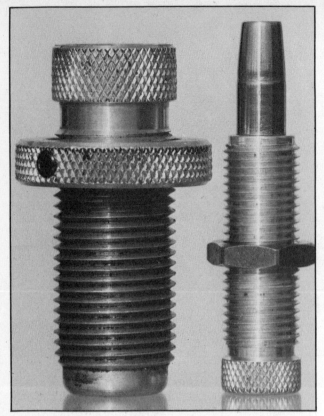

Lyman's M die for case neck expanding, here with a homemade plug, custom-turned for the 9mmP.

A closer look at that custom 9mmP plug: It is designed to flare the case mouth just enough to get the bullet seated, without weakening the grip of the mouth against the bullet base, as noted.

Here's the case mouth expander die from the RCBS set, fully assembled. Refer to the photos below.

In the matter of expander dies for the 9mmP, I've come to prefer Lyman's M-type die, with its series of contoured steps that permit adjustment so that a cast or even jacketed bullet can be put into the case neck for a short distance prior to seating the bullet. Properly done, cast bullets will be seated smoothly, without gouging metal off the bases and jacketed bullets equally so.

In point of fact, if you have access to a metal lathe and some modest amount of expertise in its use, it is possible to make up custom-tailored expander plugs for the Lyman M-die that function even better. It requires a threaded

shank with 10-32 NF thread and if you don't have the knack of cutting such threads on an integral shank, the easy way out is to drill and tap a hole in the top of the plug, cut and insert a suitable piece of 10-32 threaded rod and secure it in place with a drop of Stud N' Bearing grade Loctite. If all that is not readily feasible, just use the plug that Lyman supplies on their M-die for 9mmP.

When working with cases you've fired previously, sorting by headstamp is about all that's required. If you gain access to a supply of 9mmP brass from other sources, it's well to inspect each case keenly, so as to sort out and dis-

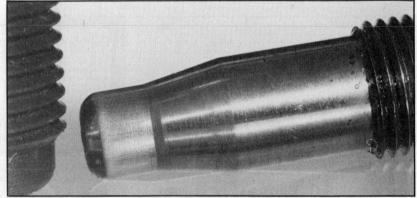

Business end of the RCBS 9mmP expander shows straight section and taper.

Cross-section of a Berdan-primed 9mmP case shows two flash holes and integral anvil.

Inside view of a Berdan-primed 9mmP case: The two flash holes are distinctive in appearance from the single flash hole of a Boxer-primed case.

card those cases with Berdan-type primers. They are readily identifiable by the presence of two small, off-center flash holes instead of the larger, central flash hole of the Boxer-type cases.

Attempts to deprime a Berdan case with conventional, Boxer-type dies usually results in a broken decapping pin; a nettlesome source of delay and frustration. My colleague, Wiley Clapp, offers a universal law that governs in such instances: the number of Berdan-primed cases encountered will exceed your supply of spare decapping pins by at least one. As observations go, I think that carries more truth than ironic humor.

Reclaimed military 9mmP cases, apart from the occasional, lurking Berdan type, may have stamp-crimped primers. If of the Boxer persuasion, those usually are punched out by conventional decapping pins with no futher problems, but it will be necessary to bevel or otherwise chamfer the edges of the primer pocket before you can seat a new primer into place.

Various makers of reloading equipment offer assorted types of swaging punches to handle the chore, or rotary reamers to serve the same purpose. In a pinch, if nothing else is available, it works reasonably well to use the pointed end of an inside/outside case neck deburring tool to cut away the stamped crimp and leave a slight chamfer around the primer pocket. If you have a crank-operated holder for the tool, such as the one Forster Products makes, that will save a lot of time and effort.

Flash hole of a Boxer-primed 9mmP case: This is the type customarily used for reloading. If a Berdan case gets to the press it may break the decapping pin if you don't notice it in time.

Forster's inside/outside case neck deburring tool and the small operating stand from the same maker. This works well for removing stamped crimp from around primer pockets, as shown.

To the best of my fairly certain knowledge, all Boxer-primed 9mmP cases use the smaller — .175-inch — diameter of primers and pistol primers rather than rifle primers. If the reloads are made up to sensible pressures, below the SAAMI ceiling, as they certainly should be, the small pistol primers will give you no trouble. In view of the small amount of powder space in the 9mmP case, I customarily use the standard small pistol primers, rather than the magnum types, regardless of the powder being employed.

To assure reliable functioning, primers need to be seated into the pockets gently but firmly, so as to pre-stress the wafer of priming mixture moderately. At the same time, they should not be seated with such an excessive degree of force as to distort the exposed portion of the primer cup visibly. To do so is to risk fracturing the wafer of primer mixture, perhaps resulting in a misfire or hangfire.

Most of the suitable charges of most powders are apt to bring the level of the powder charge up fairly close to the case mouth and some may leave the powder somewhat mounded up above the mouth, posing problems in getting the bullet base seated without spilling any of the powder.

If you are using some manner of automated or progressive reloading equipment, it may prove a considerable challenge to prevent spilling powder as the operation proceeds. Personally, I prefer to resize the cases, expand the mouths, seat the primers and then place the load-ready cases into a cartridge loading block before going on to drop the powder charges into the cases. In so doing, you have a good opportunity to inspect the comparative level of each and every powder charge keenly before going on to seat the bullets. In the stubby 9mmP cases, any discrepancy of charge volume will stand out quite clearly, as will missing charges.

Not all reloaders subscribe to identical attitudes and philosophies as regards the different steps of the operation. For my part, use of the loading block, followed by attentive inspection after dropping the powder charges, leaves me with total certainty that there is exactly one charge — no more, no less — in each and every case and I regard that as usefully reassuring, whether I'm the one who'll fire the resulting loads or not. If possible, I like to start the base of a bullet into the neck of each charged case and then go on to seat the bullet.

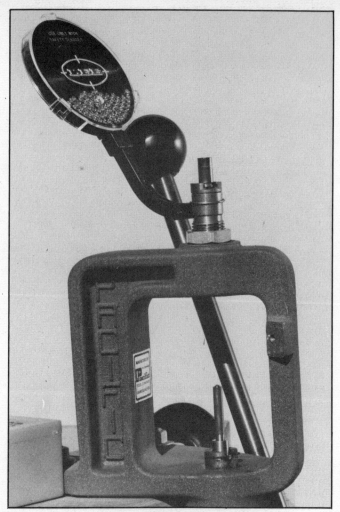

The Auto-Prime II, from Lee Precision, here set up in a Hornady/Pacific press. Primers are fed into place by gravity, helping to speed the job.

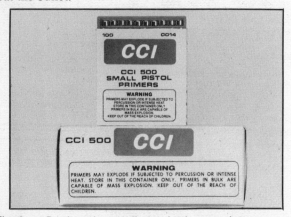

The 9mmP takes the small pistol primer, as here. Note and heed the warnings about safety measures.

The primer in a Winchester factory load, left, shows nicely radiused edges. Fired primer, per Federal case at right, may show flattening and drag-marks from the firing pin, as this one does.

When it comes to setting up and adjusting the bullet seating die, a system that works quite well is to take a factory load, perhaps with a FMJ/RN bullet, put it into the shell holder and run the ram to the top of its stroke. Holding it there, back the seating stem out of the seating die generously and turn the die body down until it makes firm contact with the case neck, locking it in that setting by tightening the locking ring against the top of the press. Then turn down the seating stem until that, in turn, makes firm contact with the tip of the bullet and lock that in its setting with the smaller locking ring. By such an approach, the bullet will be seated in approximate duplication of a typical factory load and it will work out well if the bullet you're using is of about the same size, design and type as the bullet in the cartridge used for setting the die. You will, of course, have to exercise some amount of judgment if you are using bullets of different design. The approach just outlined, for but one example, would not work well with the 88-grain Speer JHP, as it is considerably shorter than typical FMJ/RN bullets in the 115-125-grain weight class.

It is a good idea to make up a few loads on a one-at-a-time basis by way of assuring that you've provided the proper amount and degree of neck-flare for the bullets being seated. It's frustrating to drop the powder charges into fifty or a hundred cases, only to discover the case necks will not accept the bullet bases, making it necessary to dump all the charges back into the measure, re-flare the necks and do it all over again.

Depending upon the make, design and dimensions of the loading dies in use, you may have a trifling amount of neck flare remaining after the bullet has been seated. Unlike typical die sets for reloading revolver cartridges, dies for the 9mmP perform little if any crimping of the case mouth. In most instances, they will restore the profile at the neck to a straight line.

While you're still conducting your shakedown of the initial operations, along with assuring the neck flare is sufficient to accept the bullet base, it's a good idea to verify that the reloaded round will chamber without resistance or difficulty. You can remove the barrel from the pistol, hold it muzzle-down and see if the loaded round drops fully into place by its own weight. If you try the first few loads in the fully assembled pistol, it is of the greatest urgency that you observe suitable safety precautions to guard against inadvertent firing and the unpleasant consequences thereof.

The possible alternative to such inspection is to get a large batch of reloads made up and, when the time comes to fire them, make the discovery that hardly any of them will quite go into the chamber. The undesirability of such a *contretemps* is quite obvious.

Case mouth should be flared just enough so the bullet base can be started, as here.

Two of the so-called Hornady/Air Force FMJ bullets are at left and center, compared to conventional round nose. The flat tip often delivers better accuracy of the two.

POWDERS FOR THE 9mmP

Naturally enough, your choice of powder will be governed to some extent in light of the gun in which you propose to fire the reloads. The best powders for the ASP are not necessary ideal for use in the Marlin Camp Carbine or the Wilkinson Linda and the converse is equally true. In the shorter barrels, you need the faster-burning powders, such as Hercules Bullseye, Du Pont 700-X, Hodgdon HP38, Accurate Arms #7 or the like. Although AA-7 was designed specifically for use in the 9mmP, the shorter barrels may perform better with a slightly faster propellant such as Accurate Arms #5.

For the longer barrels, including the Uzi carbine, powders such as Bullseye may burn out and start losing their steam with the bullet about halfway to the muzzle, ringing in the law of diminishing returns. For the longer barrels, I have had some amounts of success with powders as slow in burning rate as Hodgdon H110 or Winchester 296; many claim those two are essentially identical, showing only the normal variation from lot to lot. Powders slower than H110 or 296 are apt to prove disappointing, regardless of barrel length.

My own personal favorite powder for the 9mmP, in barrels out to about six inches, is Hercules Herco, with a few qualifying comments. Hercules produces Herco primarily as a propellant for use in shotshells and tests it at typical shotgun pressure levels, which are typically about one-third the pressures generated in the hotter 9mmP loads. At 9mmP pressures, the variation from lot to lot of Herco may prove a bit erratic. Each time you get a new can of Herco, you need to start at a fairly light charge and work the weights up gradually and cautiously, ever alert for signs that it has approached or gone beyond the back-off point.

Bullseye is an excellent and highly satisfactory 9mmP powder in the shorter barrels to about four or five inches. Hercules Red Dot is nominally rated as slightly slower than Bullseye in burning speed, although I sometimes feel inclined to question that. I have sometimes used Red Dot with good success for extremely light loads in the .45 ACP, but I have never favored it for use in the 9mmP at the higher pressures that are fairly necessary for the smaller cartridge.

Nominally designed for use in shotshells, these three Du Pont powders work quite well in 9mmP.

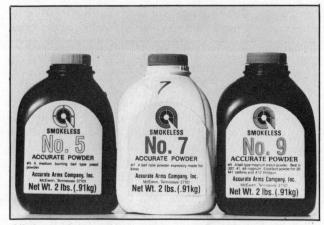

All three of these Accurate Arms powders can be used with 9mmP, although No. 7 is best choice.

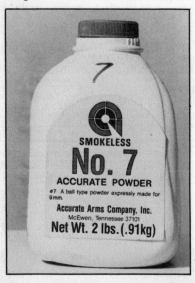

Accurate Arms No. 7 powder was developed expressly for use in the 9mmP and works quite well in it.

These fast-burning powders work superbly in the 9mmP, but must be used with strict regard to load data from reliable data sources.

Four other Hercules powders, all suited for use in the 9mmP, here arranged in order of burning speed, left to right, the fastest through slowest.

Hercules Green Dot, on the other hand, often can be used in the 9mmP to good advantage. Again, as with Herco, work the loads up for the given lot and start all over again when you pick up a fresh can. Consider buying it by the larger containers to minimize such research chores.

Hercules Unique can be used in the 9mmP and many reloaders stoutly swear by it. For some reason I cannot fully explain nor justify, I have sort of drifted away from using Unique extensively in handgun reloading, tending to prefer Herco in its stead. If you are one of those reloaders who favor Unique, use it, by all means.

For the lighter bullets in short barrels and for bullets of any practical weight in long barrels, Hercules Blue Dot is the propellant that really has a great deal to offer. As a usual rule, its accuracy is up among the finest of any and its upper velocities tend to be among the best obtainable with this cartridge.

Hercules 2400 is not overly well suited for use in the 9mmP, not even in carbine barrels.

Among the Du Pont powders, 700-X works quite well in pistols, often with outstanding accuracy and decent ballistics. Another Du Pont powder I've long favored in the 9mmP is their PB and I've heard from occasional 9mmP buffs who also profess to be partial to its use. Moderation is the key to contented and successful use of PB in the 9mmP. Resist the temptation to go overboard in rationing out the charges of it. Adhere to Du Pont's recommendations as to charges for the given bullet weights. The accuracy obtained with PB in this cartridge may surprise and delight you, depending upon the tastes and prejudices of the given gun.

With the longer barrels, some degree of success may be obtained with Du Pont 800-X. Although it's been on the market for two or three years at date of writing, I still do not feel I've worked up the degree of intimate familiarity with 800-X I really would've wished. Research time is endlessly in acutely short supply: an explanation, not an excuse.

Winchester 231 powder is well suited to use in the 9mmP, as used in accordance with their load data recommendations.

Norma R-1 and R-123 powders probably can be used in the 9mmP but their loading characteristics are somewhat in a state of flux at the present and reliable load data for their use is not readily available, just now.

The current — #24 — Hodgdon Manual lists data for their HS6, Trap 100 and HP38 powders for bullet weights from 90 to [good grief!] 160 grains. It is my personal hunch that their HS7 might also be employed to useful effect but, lacking their firm word on the matter, I hesitate to offer recommendations for its use. At the same time, I'd like to urge caution on the part of overly intrepid experimental ballisticians in exploring the possibilities of its use.

Accurate Arms imports powders manufactured by Israeli Military Industries (IMI) in Israel, including AA-7 which, as was noted, was especially formulated for use in the 9mmP cartridge. Depending upon the barrel length, bullet weight and similar pertinent factors, AA-5 and/or AA-9 may work acceptably well.

As always, it is a question of judiciously tailoring the propellant to the specific application at hand and that can call for some adroit amount of doing.

BULLETS FOR THE 9mmP

In an earlier time and place, the old Super Vel operation out of Shelbyville, Indiana, once produced an 80-grain JHP bullet for use in the 9mmP and .380 ACP. It had a concave base, to shave the weight down and wasn't very long at all. To the best of my knowledge, it was the lightest jacketed bullet produced to date in this diameter.

The 88-grain Speer #4000 is the lightest 9mm jacketed bullet in current production, as far as I know. There are various 90-grainers and the heaviest nominal 9mm currently offered is Sierra's 130-grain FMJ/RN #8345, developed for purposes of duplicating the traditional .38 Colt Super factory load, but usable in the 9mmP, as well. Jacketed bullets of heavier weights are apt to be of .357-inch diameter, rather than of the .355-inch diameter nominally intended for use in the 9mmP, thereby partially justifying my startled comment at the 160-grain maximum weight listed in the #24 Hodgdon Manual.

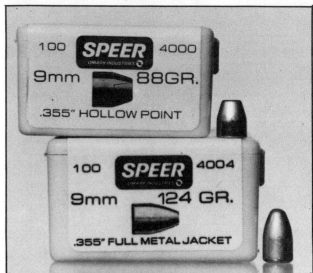

Speer's 88-grain JHP is probably the lightest readily available jacketed bullet for reloading the 9mmP. Lower bullet has jacket put on by electroplating, totally metal jacketed or TMJ.

When it comes down to cast bullets, rather than jacketed types, so far as I know, the Bantamweight crown is worn, and jauntily, by the Hensley & Gibbs #333, at a fighting weight of about 66.5 grains, depending upon the alloy. A stubby wadcutter, it is not a reliable feeder in most autoloaders, although it can be hand-chambered to occasional good effects. Curiously enough, my $268 presentation Colt will feed loads with this bullet, most of the time, and will group them quite well, although I really do not recommend it for use in autos. In the S&W Model 547, it really comes into its own and performs quite notably.

Cast bullets for the 9mmP customarily are lube/sized to diameters on the order of .3565-inch or so, although diameters to .358-inch may be at least marginally usable. If larger diameters are used, judicious care is a must in selection of the powder charge.

Lyman has, in the past, offered mould designs that let quite a bit of bullet nose project ahead of the case mouth, meanwhile, without a lot of bullet base occupying critical space down inside the case. Most if not all such have been eliminated in the recurring *putsches* that take place, from time to time, in the Lyman catalog listing of still-current mould designs. Lyman has discontinued more good mould designs than most other mouldmakers ever offered in the first place and yes, I continue to regard that as a deplorable state of affairs.

The H&G No. 307 is a superb feeder and often gives gratifying accuracy. It can also be sized to .358-inch for use in the .38 Special, right.

You would hardly expect this Hensley & Gibbs No. 333 bullet, at 66.5 grains, to feed in any auto, but it does surprisingly well in my Colt and in the ASP; likewise in revolvers, too.

Lyman's prime entry for use in the 9mmP was, has been and continues to be their #356402, a truncated-cone design that feeds quite well, usually groups a bit casually and offers a capable appearance when put up in 9mmP brass. I'd be the last to suggest that it's impossible to put the Lyman #356402 into a good load for some given pistol. It is just that, to the present moment, I've never been able to bring it off. I'm still trying.

The only RCBS bullet mould for 9mm that I've used to date is their #09-115-RN. It comes out weighing close to the rated 115 grains in typical casting alloys and I have been exceptionally well satisfied with its overall performance. It feeds with a high degree of reliability and its accuracy is practically always up there with the best of them. Except for the radiused nose, it is close to the general size and shape of the Lyman #356402.

In addition to the Hensley & Gibbs (H&G) #333, mentioned earlier, I've also worked with their #264 and #307 moulds. The #264 has a substantial wadcutting shoulder and a beveled base. It comes out of the mould just barely large enough to permit sizing it to .358-inch diameter for use in the .38 Special or .357 magnum and it often performs with exceptional accuracy in the .38 Special, as it also does in the 9mmP, making it an attractively versatile cast bullet design.

The SAECO No. 371 follows the Hornady/Air Force nose-form and is a good performer in the 9mmP, likewise feeding quite reliably.

The Hensley & Gibbs #307 has a single grease groove — as does the #264 — and a fully conical nose of about 65° included angle. It is one of a series of H&G designs with the conical nose, similar to the H&G #938, a 172-grain number for the .45 ACP. All of the work I've done with these bullets to the present indicates a highly encouraging amount of promise. They nearly always feed with outstanding reliability and they tend to deliver about the best accuracy of any cast bullet design. At the same time, they offer uncommonly favorable performance in penetrating hard targets and the conical points manifest what I tend to term the "snowplow effect" in yielding media. That is, they set the media into violent lateral motion and create impressively large impact cavitation. As with the #264, the #307 can be sized to .358-inch diameter for use in the .38 Special, .357 magnum, .357 Remington Maximum and perhaps in various rifle cartridges, as well.

In jacketed bullets, Speer recently introduced a line of totally metal jacketed (TMJ) bullets, in which the jacket metal is deposited upon the core by means of electroplating. I have found these to be exceptionally satisfactory in the various weights. They feed flawlessly and group right in there with the best.

Back in 1982, I bought one of the S&W Model 539 autos — made entirely of blued steel, rather than the aluminum alloy framed 439 or the stainless steel 639 — and had it fitted with a Bar-Sto barrel from Bar-Sto Precision. With the Speer 88-grain JHP bullet ahead of 6.9 grains of Herco, fired from a machine rest, that load went

Remarkably reliable and satisfactory, in my experience, Hornady's No. 3554, a 115-grain JHP design, is pictured here in its current form. See photo, next page.

Bullet at left is the original version of the Hornady No. 3554; it expanded well, but sometimes was reluctant to feed. So they changed it to the form in the center, which fed better but not perfectly. This bullet now is made in the form at the right, with the edges of the cavity rolled inward. This makes it feed better, accuracy is as good as ever, if not better and expansion is still quite good at 9mmP velocities.

In the course of sorting 9mmP cases by headstamp, and culling out Berdan-primed cases of foreign extraction, keep a watchful eye for split cases. Ones such as these should not be reloaded!

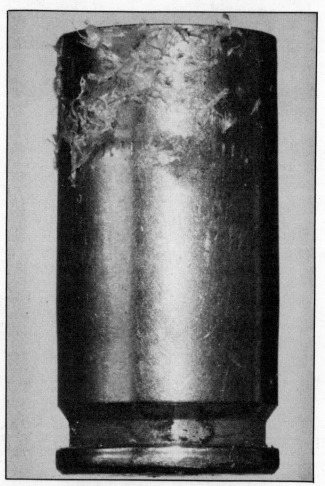

Souvenir of an experiment that flopped: We tried to catch the empties with a piece of thin plastic tarp and the sizzling-hot cases melted their way through. The plastic adheres with incredible tenacity and you can just barely get if off with acetone. Another example of, "Back to the old drawing board"...

Sierra imprints this customary note on their bullet boxes and it's excellent advice to follow.

into less than 1½ inches of spread at a distance of fifty yards.

Another reliable favorite is Hornady's 115-grain JHP, which has gone through at least three modifications, improving its performance each time and it was a pretty good bullet to start with. This is one of a small group of bullets I've come to regard as reliable wonder-workers. If the gun doesn't perform decently with such bullets, the odds against its performing well with any load seem unattractive. When testing reloads in the Marlin 9mm Camp Carbine, I used the 115-grain Hornady JHP to dot in a tight cluster at twenty-five yards, measuring precisely .025-inch between centers to bring the group slightly below one minute of angle (MOA).

SUMMING UP

Sort and inspect the empty cases, watching out for Berdan primers and foreign matter such as dead bugs that crawled into the case mouth and couldn't get back out.

Resize the case full-length, every time. The 9mmP does not usually respond well to neck-resizing only.

Expand the case mouths so that the base of the given bullet can be started into the mouth for perhaps 1/16-inch or a trifle less.

After seating the bullet, check to make certain the round will chamber easily. If it does not, you might try taper-crimping the case mouth by using the full-length resizing die, minus the decapping stem, adjusting it so it just puts a touch at the top of the ram stroke and trying the resulting reloads in the chamber to make sure you've got them right.

Make sure the loaded round will load into and come back out of the magazine. With the shorter bullets, you may have to seat them out a fair distance to assure reliable feeding.

Test the grip of case mouth against bullet base by putting a sample round, base-down, on a bathroom scale and pressing down with a piece of wood against the tip of the bullet until you run up twenty-eight pounds or so on the scale dial (that's two stone, if your bathroom scale is of British origin). Under that much pressure, the bullet should not slip back into the case, as checked against an untested load. If it does, correct the situation by sizing the case mouth smaller and/or using an expanding plug of smaller diameter. If that fails, try other makes of cases until you find one that passes the bathroom scale test successfully.
— *Dean A. Grennell*

The Major Handgun Bulletmakers, With Details On Their Offerings.

A representative sampling of factory bullets from makers such as Hornady, Norma, Nosler, Sierra and Speer. At one time, ammo makers such as Winchester and Remington offered bullets, but they have discontinued that practice and do not plan to resume it.

FOR THOSE who wish to reload the 9mmP cartridge but feel disinclined to personally produce the bullets — either by casting or swaging — the obvious alternative is to buy bullets over the counter. At one time, both Remington and Winchester marketed the same bullets they used for their loaded ammunition, but both have discontinued the sale of bullets. They, along with Federal, continue to offer empty, unprimed cases, however.

There are four major bulletmakers in this country — Hornady, Nosler, Sierra and Speer — plus the Swedish firm of Norma, represented by a U.S. distributor. We will discuss all five and their offerings, in alphabetical order.

HORNADY

Based in Grand Island, Nebraska, Hornady currently catalogs six jacketed bullets for the 9mmP, plus a round nosed design swaged of lead. All are of the usual .355-inch diameter. In the jacketed line, with index numbers in parentheses, there are:

90-grain JHP (3550)
100-grain FMJ (3552)
115-grain JHP (3554)
115-grain FMJ/RN (3555)
124-grain FMJ/FP (3556)
124-grain FMJ/RN (3557)

Hornady #3550 at 90 grains, is that maker's lightest.

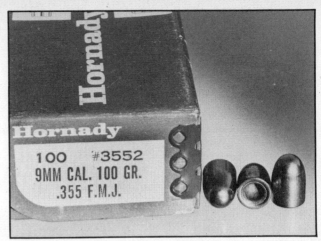

Hornady #3552 is a 100-grain FMJ with hollow base.

Above, Hornady #3554 is one of my all-time favorites, here in its latest configuration. Below, Hornady #3556 is sometimes called the Hornady/Air Force design, having been jointly developed to feed and group well.

You'll note that the full metal jacket (FMJ) designs are qualified as round nose (RN) and FP for flat point. The latter is often termed the Hornady/Air Force design, as Hornady developed it in cooperation with the USAF. The FMJ/FP feeds well in most autos, usually delivers good accuracy and has a moderately better impact effect in comparison to FMJ/RN designs. Hornady also offers the round nose (RN) designs for those who prefer them and they may be more reliable feeders in the fussier guns.

Hornaday's lead bullet for the 9mmP is a 124-grain RN design with a novel feature: The full-diameter portion of the base is knurled to retain the lubricant and the bullets are swaged from an alloy containing ninety-five percent lead and five percent antimony. The index numbers of this bullet change to reflect the number of bullets in the package. In lots of one hundred, it's #3567, at $5.75/box, as of the 1986 catalog and #1005 for the bulk-pack of one thousand, at $45.75 in the same source. That compares to prices ranging from $9.15 to $10/100 for the jacketed Hornady bullets. Prices are subject to change, of course and are quoted solely as a general guideline.

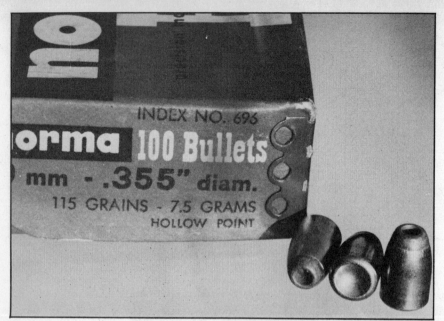

These two boxes of Norma bullets are of the type with cuprous-clad steel jackets, but that does not pose a problem with expansion of the #696 JHP design at left.

The Norma #557 is a FMJ design with concave base. Edges of the exposed jacket are rolled to help resist distortion on being fired.

A similar rolled edge can be seen on the base of the jacket on these Nosler 115-grain FMJ bullets.

NORMA

This maker offers four different bullets for the 9mmP, all in jacketed designs. Due to a shift and changeover in distribution channels, Norma components have not been in plentiful supply with local dealers for some time, but that state of affairs could improve and we hope it will. At one time, Norma made most of their bullets with steel jackets, clad in a cuprous alloy to resist corrosion. They may still do so and it takes but the touch of a magnet to find it out. Such bullets are not significantly harder on bores than are bullets jacketed with conventional gilding metal. Often, the older Norma bullets offered excellent accuracy and, one presumes, the current production will do the same. There are FMJ/RN designs in weights of 96 and 116 grains, with respective index numbers of 69031 and 69010. Numbers 69021 and 69026 weigh 115 and 116 grains; presumably, one is JSP, the other JHP, not necessarily respectively. The Norma catalog sheet does not specify that particular detail.

NOSLER

This is an old-line bulletmaker that has concentrated its attention upon rifle bullets until quite recent times. Their rifle bullets are highly regarded by many reloaders and

Sierra's 90-grain #8100 is their lightest bullet in .355-in. diameter.

Sierra 115-grain jacketed hollow cavity (JHC) is made so the cavity is larger in diameter than that of the hole in the point. This is intended to improve expansion upon impact.

shooters. There is reasonable basis to believe that the Nosler bullets for handguns will perform equally well. The sole Nosler entry for the 9mmP, to the present, is a 115-grain FMJ/RN, of .355-inch diameter.

SIERRA

This is a bulletmaker that works hard to come up with new ideas and stay ahead of the game. You want the bullet to expand? Very well, they'll provide bullets that expand with uncommon enthusiasm. The first such example, long since established in the state of the art is the JHC, standing for jacketed hollow cavity. Instead of the usual conical nose cavity, the one in the JHC is sort of flask-shaped and yes, they certainly do expand.

A newer Sierra design innovation is the Power Jacket, available in several numbers, including two for the 9mmP. It does not have the bulbous cavity of the JHC, but the jack-et carries six equidistant creases, about halfway down the ogive — that being the portion of any bullet of less than full bullet diameter; in a word, the nose. The creases pre-stress portions of the jacket and, upon impact, cause the nose to peel back like a truly shameless banana. We will refer to such entries as JHP/PJ.

The earlier 90-grain and 115-grain JHC Sierras have been replaced by the new JHP/PJs of the same weight. Index numbers, respectively, are 8100 and 8110.

Four FMJ designs round out the current Sierra line. There is a 95-grain FMJ/FP (#8105); a 115-grain FMJ/RN (#8115); a 125-grain FMJ/RN (#8120) and a 130-grain FMJ/RN (#8345). The two hollow points are termed *Sports Masters* and the four FMJs, *Tournament Masters*.

The 130-grain Tournament Master is noteworthy in being the heaviest 9mmP bullet readily available today. It was introduced primarily for purposes of enabling reloaders to duplicate the traditional factory load for the .38

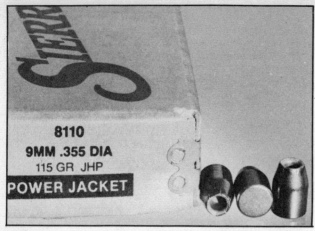

A recently introduced Sierra design, the #8110 has six creases in the jacket at the nose, intended to help assure a symmetrical rupturing of the jacket to assist expansion.

In close-up photo of the Sierra #8110 bullet, appearing at left, the details of the creased jacket nose can be seen more clearly. Sierra refers to this as their Power Jacket.

Sierra 125-grain #8120 is a full metal jacket, with round nose and flat base, intended for duplicating typical military 9mmP loads. While not apt to expand, it feeds reliably.

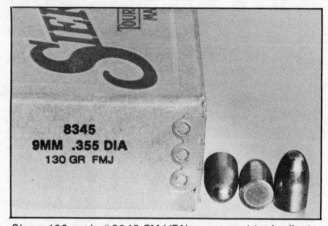

Sierra 130-grain #8345 FMJ/RN was meant to duplicate the typical factory load in .38 Colt Super, but it can be used in the 9mmP, as well. Sierra can supply load data.

Colt Super, but it works well in the 9mmP, as well. Sierra can furnish load data for its use in that cartridge. The 130-grainer is a promising possibility when working with the longer-barreled pistols and carbines in 9mmP although, as you'd logically suppose, its potential for expansion is doodley-zilch. It is, however, a formidable penetrator, especially if lofted to the more ambitious velocities.

SPEER

Up along the banks of Idaho's Snake River, breathing shallowly when the shifting winds waft picturesque breathing media from the sulfite paper mills, they have a really dedicated interest in providing a variety of bullets for resurrecting defunct 9mmP brass. Omark/Speer offers no less than seven different jacketed designs, plus an all-lead

At 88 grains, Speer's #4000 is the lightest 9mm bullet currently on the market. Capable of high velocities with the right loads, it feeds well in many guns and expands.

Speer's 100-grain #3983 JHP is one of the more reliable feeders among hollow points and, like the Hornady #3554, often delivers expectionally fine accuracy and expansion.

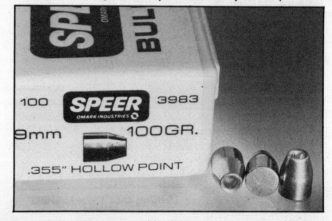

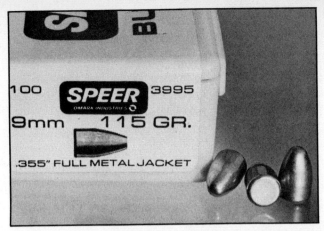
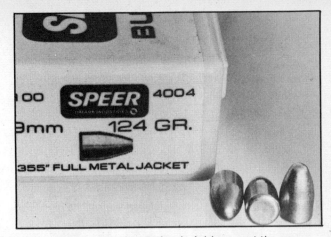

Speer's #3995 and 4004 are produced by a manufacturing process perfected by that maker in fairly recent times. The jackets are applied to the lead alloy core by means of electroplating and totally enclose the core, even on the base. They are sometimes termed TMJ for totally metal jacketed and they are capable of superb accuracy.

number, for good measure. One might wish they could find it in their hearts to break down and offer even one decent bullet for the .41 magnum, but that has yet to come to pass. The high brass at Omark continue to cling to their wistful hope that, if they only ignore the .41 mag for a long enough while, the presumptuous little upstart will vanish from the scene. But that is, admittedly, neither Damon nor yet Pythias for the current discussion.

The unjacketed Speer 9mmP bullet is their #4601, available in hundred-packs or bulk packs of five hundred. It weighs 125 grains, has a round nose and external lubricant that functions surprisingly well.

Their jacketed numbers are:

        88-grain JHP #4000
        95-grain FMJ+ #4001
       100-grain JHP #3983
       115-grain FMJ+ #3995
       115-grain JHP #3996
       124-grain FMJ+ #4004
       125-grain JSP #4005

The 88-grain JHP retains the distinction of being the lightest bullet readily available in this particular diameter, down to the present. In the days when Lee Jurras ran the Super Vel operation out of Shelbyville, Indiana, they offered an 80-grain JHP bullet with a concave base that retains the all-time title, even though decades out of production.

There are three designs termed FMJ+ and we need to discuss those. They have jackets that are deposited by electroplating and the jackets cover every visible portion of the bullet, including the base. These have also been termed totally jacketed bullets, or TMJs. I am not privy to the fine details of production used in their manufacture, but I can testify to one thing: These little bullets work just great and

shoot even better! That is somewhat curious because another outfit attempted to produce bullets, presumably by a comparable process and their TMJ bullets were among the poorest performers I have ever tested. But Speer seems to have isolated and eliminated the problem bug in the operation.

As with the 115-grain Hornady JHP, the 100-grain Speer JHP is one of those bullets for which it is a taxing challenge to find a really bad load. If you happen to own and operate a Colt Python, try either of these in the .357 magnum case and brace yourself for pleasant surprises. Meanwhile they do nothing but great in the 9mmP and, for good measure, in the .38 Colt Super as well as other rounds.

The Speer 125-grain JSP continues to exist as a sort of living anachronism. If you succeed in getting it out the muzzle, it *will* expand and with uncommon vigor. If, on the other hand, you own an autoloader capable of reliable feeding with this bullet, congratulate yourself because it will probably feed everything and anything at all.

There are many other makers, some of them quite good, but you won't find their output on shelves from Meddibemps, Maine, to Oceanside, California, and points in between. At least, not yet but, perhaps, one day — ? — *Dean Grennell*

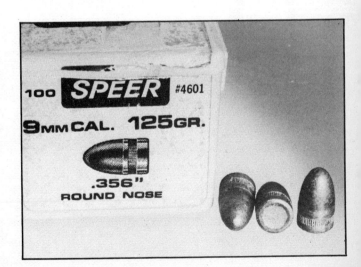

Speer's 125-grain #4601 is in lubricated lead alloy to offer a capable bullet for casual plinking at reduced cost.

MAKING 9mm BULLETS

CHAPTER 4

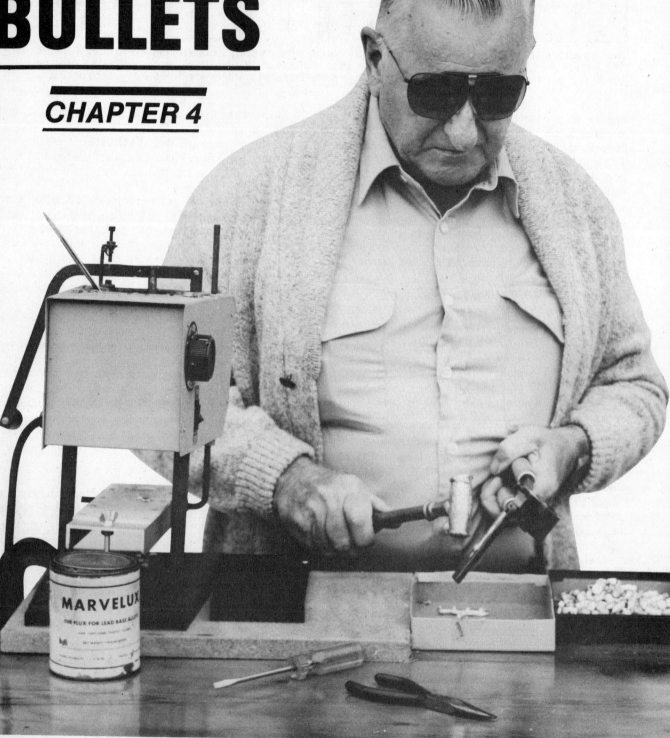

Casting bullets: Eye protection should be regarded as absolutely mandatory, to avoid danger from flying droplets.

MARVELUX
THE FLUX FOR LEAD BASE ALLOYS

Extensive Notes On a Process That Offers Bottomless Supplies Of Bullets At Modest Cost

PRODUCING BULLETS by melting a lead alloy and pouring it into moulds is just about the oldest form of projectile production — junior only to walking along and keeping an eye peeled for handy-sized rocks. Despite the undeniable antiquity of the process, it remains one of the simplest, most economical and best.

There are a few essential items of equipment. First and foremost, you need a mould, consisting of a set of metal blocks, with handles. The number of cavities may range from one to ten or more, with two and four as typical numbers.

You will need facilities for making up a suitable casting alloy. While muzzleloading firearms usually require projectiles of dead-soft, pure lead, that is not the ideal material for making bullets to use in centerfire firearms powered by smokeless (nitro) powders. You will also need facilities to melt and dispense the resulting alloy and, in virtually every instance, you can make up the alloy in the same pot you use for the final casting operations.

You will need a non-marring mallet to knock the sprue cutter aside and a couple of boxes — cardboard works well — in which to catch the sprues and finished bullets.

Likewise mandatory is some manner of arrangement for putting bullet lube into the grooves provided in all moulds for cast bullets. If you try to fire cast bullets without lube in those grooves, you will come to regret it, as I discovered, long ago. If you neglect the lube, the lead alloy sticks to the inside of the rifled bore and causes a ghastly mess.

Mindful that a lot of reloaders have to start at a fairly humble level — just as I did in the early '50s — I will try to discuss these basic aspects on a few different plateaus.

THE MOULDS

Several different firms produce bullet moulds today and some say they make molds. The spelling is a matter of personal taste. Actually, mould, with the extra u, is the preferred British spelling and the customary Usanian spelling omits the surplus letter. For the gathering years of my gunwriting career, I've hewn to the mould for making bullets and reserved mold for the green stuff that turns up on bread that's kept on hand too long. It is my private revolt against identical words with two or more meanings. You're welcome to spell the word, in either context, any way you wish.

From the viewpoint of the reloader/shooter, a bullet mould has got to be one of the best bargains to be found. Given proper care and attention, they are fairly close to immortal. I still have the first and second bullet moulds I ever bought and the second remains in prime condition. The first would be, also, except that I made the unfortunate

My second bullet mould, bought about 1950 and still in fine shape. This is a Lyman double-cavity for their obsolete No. 358425 design.

error of loaning it to some other reloader/shooter and it came back hopelessly damaged. I drilled it out with a three-eighths-inch bit to convert it into a mould for cores to use in swaging .44 bullets and still have it in that capacity. In the many years since, as you might suppose, I have rarely if ever loaned out my other moulds and I commend that attitude to your attention.

The second bullet mould I bought, about '50 or '51, was for the Lyman #358425; a neat little 115-grain wadcutter for use in .38 Specials. In the years since then, it has produced about a quarter-million bullets and looks to be ready to do that again. That's about 4107 pounds of alloy and no, I didn't fire all of those, myself. Had I done so, I might be a pretty decent shot by this time. During the '50s and early '60s, I did quite a bit of commercial reloading for police departments in the upper midwest, sometimes making up loads in lots of 10,000 or so, all out of that one little double-cavity mould and going on to do the cases on my little

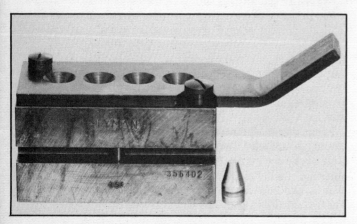

Above, a four-cavity set of Lyman blocks in No. 356402 design; a favorite for the 9mmP and others. Below, a finished, lube/sized bullet poses above half of mould, showing the cavities as well as the little lines to vent air.

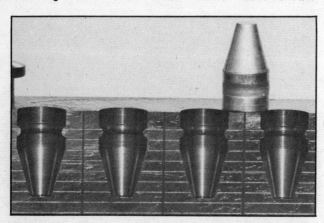

Lyman Tru-Line Junior press, without even the aid of a carbide sizing die. I got $35/thousand for the reloads in the customer's brass and plowed the meager profits back into upgrading my gear for reloading. The hourly scale was pretty chintzy but, in those days, I had exactly $6.35/week in uncommitted cash to take care of all my wants and needs. It was not until early '58 that I commenced to maul typewriters for the firearms press and get a modest trickle-down without dispensing a flake of Bullseye. At the time, I

regarded it as a wondrous break-through and still do.

My mould for the Lyman #358425 was a double-cavity and a useful time-saver. The trend in those days was toward single-cavity moulds. Today, you can't hardly find any single-cavity moulds, outside of those for hollow points. Double-cavities are the usual norm, with four-cavity blocks fairly common.

The more cavities in the blocks, the higher your production rate goes. About 1960, a friend had a six-cavity Hensley & Gibbs mould for a .38 wadcutter and used to loan it to me, occasionally. With that mould, I found, I could turn out about one hundred bullets every six minutes and I thought I had the world by the tail on a downhill drag.

Two-cavity blocks are useful, but four-cavity blocks are a good average. If you're only producing bullets for your own consumption, four-cavity blocks are about the best to get. Blocks with additional cavities are all very fine if you plan to get into producing and selling bullets, commercially. Don't lay out the price for a twenty-cavity armory mould unless you are quite certain you want a prodigious quantity of bullets in that particular design.

A bullet design may really grab your fancy by the throat when you see a photo or drawing of it. The actual bullet may shoot well or, again, it may not. It is not at all a bad idea to buy a double-cavity mould for the given design, so as to try it out and see if it performs as well as you'd hoped it might. If it does, you may be able to get a mould for the

NEI produces only the mould blocks or, as they prefer to spell it, mold, for use with Lyman or RCBS handles.

Three stages of casting a bullet with a Lee mould. Alloy has been poured into the sprue cutter to harden. Next, the sprue cutter is struck aside, releasing the sprue. After that, the blocks are parted to deliver the cast bullet. Like NEI, Lee uses aluminum alloy for their mould blocks.

same design, with four cavities or more and perhaps you'll be able to sell the smaller mould to a shooting buddy to help defray the cost of the bigger job.

Some mouldmakers offer complete moulds and sets of mould blocks that can be installed on the handles/tongs you already have. That provides a useful saving in cash output, at some slight amount of bother in changing the blocks. NEI, with the largest offering of mould designs in the field at present, makes mould blocks only and does not offer handles at all. The two-cavity NEI blocks, as I recall, are used with RCBS handles. NEI started out with blocks in aluminum alloy, more recently offering brass as an extra-cost option. NEI also makes several mould designs that are marketed exclusively by SSK Industries; J.D. Jones' outlet.

Lee Precision uses a aluminum alloy for their mould blocks in no more than two-cavity versions. Aluminum has certain advantages in the matter of resisting rust and corrosion, but they must be rendered utterly grease-free before they perform well. J.D. Jones suggests removing the steel components such as the sprue cutter and boiling the aluminum blocks in a stainless steel pot on the stove for an hour or so, with a little dishwashing detergent in the water.

Hensley & Gibbs, SAECO and Lyman use ferrous alloys for their mould blocks and, as you'd suppose, the

Mould blocks of ferrous alloys will rust, if not protected. Spray-can solvents, like these, are helpful for getting the cavities free of oils and ready for the next casting session.

cavities must be protected against rust and corrosion. Just how to do that is a moot point. Merely leaving the last bullet(s) in place to keep air out of the cavities does *not* work. That much, I can state with total assurance.

Johnny Adams, recently head of SAECO — originally, the initials for Santa Anita Engineering Company — uses an electrically heated storage cabinet for his moulds and swears by that approach. The theory is that, if the moulds are kept above the ambient temperatures, moisture can't and won't condense upon the surfaces to cause corrosion problems. I have never tried that approach. The arrival of the monthly electric bill tends to be traumatic enough, without that.

My approach has long been one of applying a reliable rust-preventive to the vulnerable surfaces inside the mould cavities and over the sprue cutter. When I want to put the mould back into use, I give the oiled surfaces a liberal dousing with a good degreasing compound. I've used many of those, down the years. Currently, my favorite is Omark/

Outers Crud-Cutter. As with all of the best of such compounds, it contains no petroleum distillates and the active ingredient is a latterday chemical cousin of carbon tetrachloride.

The chlorinated carbon compounds are highly efficient degreasers and they leave no residue upon evaporation. That's the good news. The bad news is that *you must not inhale even a little of the airborne vapors from them.* To do so is highly injurious to your health. What it does,

Eight-cavity moulds, such as this SAECO No. 371, can produce cast bullets at a gratifyingly hourly rate.

among other things, is to louse up your liver. Even a moderate intake of alcohol into a system previously polluted with carbon tet and similar compounds results in a mixture that can prove fatal or, at best, somewhat disabling. Inhaling carbon tet, by whatever fancy name known, is quite unhealthy, even if you're a teetotaller.

By all means, use such compounds, because nothing else works even a quarter as well, but do it outside and upwind of the jet stream, holding your breath, if need be. At the same time, avoid excessive wetting of the skin with the stuff, as it can be absorbed that way, also.

Virtually all of the oils and rust-preventive compounds contain some amount of petroleum by-products, technically termed *hydrocarbons.* Residues of hydrocarbons tend to contain carbon and, when exposed to the heat of molten casting alloy, the carbon oxidizes and that is why your bullet doesn't fill the cavity to perfection. Instead, it comes out looking like a small silver raisin. You have to burn away the last remaining molecules of carbon before the bullets tap out of the cavities looking pretty.

At one time, several people were recommending that the cavities of aluminum mould blocks be lightly "smoked" with the yellow, sooty flame of a kitchen match or something of the sort. Soot is — you guessed it — virtually pure carbon and it reacts just as you'd expect.

Down the years, I've received samples of many different miracle compounds bearing cutesy-poo names such as Kavity-Koter — I made that one up — alleged to go onto cavity surfaces and make moulds produce castings exquisite in their perfection. I am still awaiting appearance of one of these that performs as glowingly advertisied.

In my own gathering experience, nothing makes a bullet mould work as well as cavity surfaces that are clean and grease-free, likewise properly brought up to working temperature.

If I were to catch some do-gooder applying miracle-glop to the cavities of one of my pet moulds, I would probably chastise the blighter with the fat end of a pool cue, provided I could keep my temper under sufficient control. That also includes the sooty smoke from kitchen matches and suchlike.

I've tried a few mould blocks made of brass and my impressions have been highly favorable. It's true you have to treat them with reverent care, but that is at least equally true of ferrous-alloy blocks and even more true of aluminum-alloy blocks. I've tried out one set of blocks in stainless steel and found it an utter joy and delight to use. Brass, aluminum and stainless steel blocks are put away dry, although it's a good idea to swaddle aluminum blocks in a few layers of aluminum foil because, as a glance at the kitchenware will attest, aluminum will tarnish in time.

There is a compound called *Rust Free* which, applied with a cotton swab and lots of patience, will do wonders for getting thin layers of rust and corrosion from the cavity surfaces of ferrous-alloy blocks. Unfortunately, it also serves to deposit a rust-preventive coating and that coating, when you commence casting, will bother you until you get it all cooked off. There aren't many simple solutions in this mad world of ours and yes, it's a great pity. Rust Free is made by: MJL Industries, Box 122, McHenry, IL 60050.

Here are the three designs offered by RCBS for use in reloading the 9mmP cartridge. The center one takes a gas check, to minimize barrel fouling at higher velocities.

9mm	9mm	9mm
.356″	.356″ ‡	.356″
#09-115-RN Part 82026 (L) 358345	#9mm-124-RN Part 82062 (L) 358242	#09-124-CN Part 82027 (L) 356402
.356″ dia. Part 82221	.356″ dia. Part 82221	.356″ dia. Part 82221
#115 Part 82504	#401 Part 82521	#402 Part 82522

ata only and does not imply exact likeness of bullets

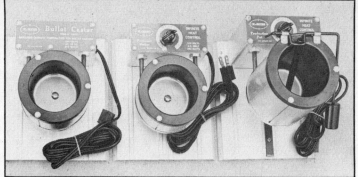

Left, Rust Free is an effective rust-remover that won't harm blued steel finishes. Applied with a cotton swab, it is useful for cleaning minor rust out of mould cavities. Right, Lee Precision offers these three melting pots, at attractively modest prices. Two at left require dippers. Center and right ones have thermostatic heat controls. One at right and in lower photo is of the bottom-delivery type, for convenience; it's termed the Production Pot.

MELTING POTS

In order to cast bullets, you need a suitable container and a heat source that can boost the temperatures up to around 750°F/399°C, preferably with the ability to regulate the heat to somewhat lower levels, as desired. Sustained operation much above 700°F will cause the absolutely vital and expensive tin content of the alloy to oxidize and get lost from the mixture, so the objective is to cast at the lowest temperature that results in satisfactory castings.

For quite a lot of years, when I started out, I cast my bullets out of an old frying pan, atop a burner on the kitchen stove, dipping the alloy off the top and decanting it into the moulds with a ladle. For several reasons, I do not recommend that approach, at all.

For one thing, you subject yourself and other family members to the foul-smelling and somewhat toxic vapors of the bullet casting process. If you are recycling old wheel weights, not to mention fragments of lead/tin mixtures purchased from a friendly local plumber, the aromas can get incredibly gamey.

One evening, I picked up the old frying pan by the han-

Control panel of the RCBS Pro-Melt casting furnace: White pointer on the knob is between 650 and 700, my usual running temperature. On/off labels were added because the indicator light is hard to see in bright light.

The top half on an old stainless steel GI mess kit makes a great device for casting bullet alloy for storage and later use. It turns out two kidney-shaped pigs weighing about six pounds apiece and they can be fed back into the Pro-Melt quite handily. I've long since gotten into the habit of casting out on my driveway, for the sake of the good ventilation it affords.

dle, only to find that the wooden handle turned freely on the steel spine. It dumped several pounds of seething-hot molten alloy onto the kitchen linoleum — a patterned blue to that moment and a sullen brown, ever after — and, as I had the abysmal stupidity to be wearing a pair of bedroom slippers, I also obtained some impromptu castings of the space between the inner surface of the slipper and my bare foot. I'd like to request that you refrain from even imagining what my comments were.

If you propose to make up cast bullets, you are going to save a substantial amount of money over the cost of store-bought bullets, assuming you do a reasonable amount of shooting. After all, you're supplying the man-hours, rather than paying for someone else's. With that in mind, the purchase of an electrically heated, thermostatically controlled, bottom-delivery bullet casting furnace is worth whatever it costs and then some. The friendliest prices on such things can be found in the catalog you get by sending one buck to Lee Precision, 4275 Highway U, Hartford, WI 53027. SAECO makes a fine casting furnace and RCBS makes another, called the Pro-Melt. I have one apiece of the latter, usually using the Pro-Melt but often putting the SAECO on the line in its stead. As a usual thing, I keep typical pot-luck bullet casting alloy in the RCBS Pro-Melt and pure lead in the SAECO. When it comes to making up cores for swaging bullets, the SAECO gets plugged in, saving the kilowatts it would take to melt the harder alloy out of the Pro-Melt and get it going with straight lead. I'm not urging you to buy one of each, merely commenting that it can offer handy aspects.

The Pro-Melt has a somewhat greater capacity and thus gets the nod for uses such as reclaiming quantities of wheel weight metal (WWM) every now

and again. It is a messy, malodorous, patience-trying chore, but it turns out pigs of metal that can be alloyed into pretty decent bullets at a cash outlay well short of exorbitant. You will need an old metal spoon or something of the sort for scooping out all the little steel clips that float to the surface as the lead alloy melts away.

Several manufacturers offer neat little ingot moulds for solidifying reclaimed metal into tiny pigs weighing perhaps as much as a pound or half-pound apiece. If you scrounge about among the war surplus stores, you might be able to latch onto an old stainless steel GI mess kit for a paltry pittance. The upper half of such an artifact makes the best of all possible ingot moulds for bullet metal. Each half, filled to the brim, turns out a more or less kidney-shaped pig weighing about six pounds. Such a pig of WWM, added to the pot with a one-pound ingot of linotype alloy (LTA), melts down into the most thoroughly satisfactory casting alloy I've been able to formulate to the present. Even the proprietary casting alloys, offered now and then by commercial suppliers, don't work as well as 1:6 LTA/WWM and the store-bought stuff costs quite a bit more.

Lacking an old mess kit, various makers offer ingot moulds to cast alloys into smaller pigs weighing about a pound apiece. These are by Ohaus, SAECO and Lyman.

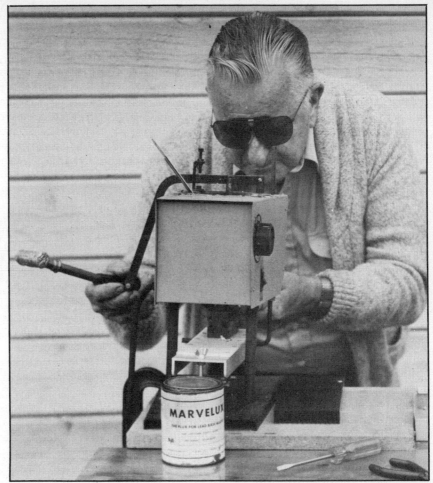

That's a lead-headed hammer in my right hand, made from a kit offered by Hensley & Gibbs. When it gets too battered, you just melt off the head and mould a new one. I'm holding the valve open and running alloy into each cavity in turn, using a Lyman mould with four cavities in this photo.

CASTING ALLOYS

Quite a bit of the pertinent details on this topic were covered in the section immediately preceding this. Nonetheless, an understanding of what works and what doesn't is good to have.

Pure lead is not overly satisfactory as a material for cast bullets to be used in centerfire guns ahead of smokeless powders. For one thing, it is a keen challenge to get a cleanly-filled casting with pure lead. Even a little bit of tin helps it to fill out the cavities much better.

There are three metallic elements, or elemental metals, that are in common usage for casting bullets: lead, tin and antimony. The presence of any other metallic elements usually poses some amount of problems. The basic threesome vary as to their melting points and density/specific gravity. Density refers to how much heavier a given volume of the metal is than an equal volume of water. Let's tabulate the three of them:

METAL	DENSITY	MELTING POINT	CHEMICAL SYMBOL
Lead	11.4	621.3°F/327.4°C	Pb
Antimony	6.62	1166.9°F/630.5°C	Sb
Tin	7.3	449.4°F/231.9°C	Sn

There is no ready figure to denote the comparative hardness of the three, but antimony is much the hardest, followed by tin and, in turn, by lead. The melting point of antimony is the highest, by a wide margin, followed by lead, and tin stays at a fluid state the longest.

Let us pause to note a curious metallurgical anomaly: Antimony melts at about 1167°F but, despite that, we can cast antimony-bearing alloys in the temperature range of 680° to 750°F, perhaps even lower. It is a curious fact that metals in alloys liquify at temperatures well below their nominal melting points in the pure state. One of the weirdest examples of that is an alloy called Wood's metal that melts at slightly below the boiling point of water, despite the fact that the elements making it up all have melting points much higher.

If you cast bullets from an alloy consisting solely of lead and antimony, as the mixture solidifies, the antimony freezes much sooner, forming crystals of antimony and the lead solidifies around the crystals, somewhat later, still in pretty much a pure state. Such bullets may seem fairly hard, by casual testing, but when fired, the pure lead will foul the bore in a highly unacceptable manner. For all the ostensible hardness, you are still rubbing pure lead against the bore surface and you will get the predictable, unpleasant, consequences.

The solution to that problem is to stir some tin into the mixture. Having a melting point much lower than lead, the tin will remain with the lead, hardening it, until the lead solidifies and bullets of such alloys, properly lube/sized, will not foul the bore to any objectionable extent.

Tin is helpful in a bullet casting alloy, up to a proportion of about one part tin to twenty parts lead. Beyond that point, it confers little further benefits, if any.

Linotype alloy, when used straight, is a most delightful mixture for casting bullets. Sad to say, LTA is an endangered species in the modern world. Every passing year sees less of it in use and more of it fired into backstops, perhaps beyond hope of eventual recovery. It was used in a now-archaic printing process, commonly termed movable type, and the Linotype machine had a keyboard, similar to but different from that of a conventional typewriter. As the keys were pressed, small brass matrices were released, going by gravity to the proper position in the line. When the line was filled, tapered spacing fingers separated the words, moving to create a justified line of even length. Molten linotype metal was forced into the aligned faces of the matrices, solidifying to form one line of type, hence the name. The freshly set line, or slug, was carried to its place in the galley and the matrices were returned to their proper places, automatically. Patented by its inventor, Ottmar Mergenthaler, in 1884, the linotype machines were technical marvels of the day and greatly helped to distribute the printed word, as one good lino operator could equal the output of a great many compositors setting type by hand — not to mention the tedious chore of redistributing the type, letter by letter, afterwards.

Today, the landslide trend is toward type that's set by computers, pasted onto layout boards, photographed on high-contrast film to produce negatives and those are used in another photochemical process to burn the plates that are put onto rotary offset presses to turn out the final copies of the printed work. No lead is used in the so-called "cold type" processes, although silver is used for the photosensitive materials and that is fairly efficiently recovered for further use.

My reason for bringing all this up is to give you a background on a key raw material for casting alloys. After use on the press, the slugs were melted down and used again, eventually reaching the point where enough tin had burned from the mixture to make it unsatisfactory for further use. Suppliers to the printing trades would take the "tired" type metal in on trade for a supply of fresh stuff, supplied in the heavy ingots with a loop on one end that were lowered by chain into the supply pot of the Linotype machine. Your friendly local printer, courteously approached, often was willing to sell you a supply of tired type metal for the same figure his suppliers allowed for it. That varied by time and place, but twenty to forty cents a pound was a reasonable average.

Another rich source of prime casting alloy at friendly prices was the local plumber. Lead pipes once were widely used in domestic plumbing systems because, once lead builds up a coating of oxide, it resists further corrosion about as adamantly as anything you'd be able to mention. Lead pipes were joined by joints of plumber's wiping solder — a 65/35 tin/lead alloy, as I recall — and molten, pure lead was used in caulking the joints between sections of steel soil pipes.

In replacing a home plumbing system, the plumber would remove the old piping and take it back to his shop. The sections of pure lead pipe sometimes were salvaged for caulked joints. The wiped joints, because of the hardening effect of their tin content, were cut free and tossed to one side. They contained too much lead to serve as wiping solder, but were too hard for caulking. An enterprising bulletmaker sometimes could become the owner of an elbow-creaking cargo of wiped joints for not much cash out of pocket and,

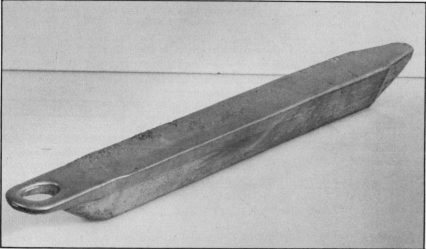

Above, as discussed in the text, it is very dangerous to try to use the plates from batteries for making up casting alloy. Left, this is an ingot of linotype alloy; an artifact seen more rarely with each passing year. It weighs roughly twenty pounds and can be used straight or mixed with reclaimed wheel weight metal to make the lovely stuff go even farther. See text for further details.

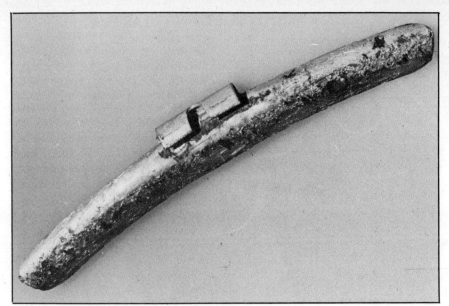

And here is the bullet caster's best friend, the humble wheel weight. This is one of the larger ones and the first step is to melt them down, skimming off and discarding all the little steel clips, along with all the road dirt and other debris, pouring into ingot moulds.

spaced out with pure lead at around one part-tin/fifteen to thirty-parts lead, it made up into lovely bullets. You can get along without antimony, but it's hard to make a decent bullet without both lead and tin.

Some have experimented with bullets cast of straight zinc, but that has never become a popular material. Its melting point is 787.1°F/419.5°C and its specific gravity is 7.14; slightly less than that of tin, but higher than antimony. It's my impression that zinc does not work well as an alloying component when used with the other three traditional bullet metals, lead, tin and antimony.

One metal source that should be avoided entirely is the salvaged plate metal from discarded automobile or marine batteries. For one thing, the plates may contain entrapped pockets of electrolyte — sulfuric acid and water — which, in melting, can detonate with savage fury, having been converted to steam before the metal softens enough to release the extremely high pressure. For yet another reason, there is a trend among battery makers to add a percentage of arsenic to the lead in the plates and that can introduce deadly toxic hazards. Assuming it doesn't blow up from entrapped fluids, the dross skimmed from the top of arsenic-bearing alloy and discarded into a trash barrel can set up a chemical reaction with small amounts of moisture to produce a gas that is fatal at a concentration of only a few parts per million. You don't want someone taking out the family trash to be exposed to such a hazard, do you? Avoid metal from old batteries!

The metal salvaged from automobile wheel weights remains the most widely available and usually least expensive source for making up casting alloys. You have to melt it down and skim off the little steel clips that rise to the surface, along with the road dirt and other debris. I've seen figures for the supposed content of wheel weight metal, but am inclined to question their accuracy in every instance. It is probable the typical wheel weight contains some amount of antimony in addition to the basic lead. Whether or not it contains any tin at all is a pretty moot point.

With that in mind, can you make decent bullets from straight, cleaned-up WWM? I'm inclined to say yes, with some reservations. Given one of the better bullet lubes, bore-fouling is not apt to be a severe problem at moderate velocities. Even a little added tin, however, improves it quite usefully.

Tin is the problem ingredient. Domestic production comes only from one small area in Texas and doesn't begin to yield enough to meet the nation's annual needs. The major tin-producing countries of the world, in descending order, are: Malaysia, China (Mainland), Bolivia, Russia, Thailand, Indonesia and Nigeria. Tin is obtained from a mineral called cassiterite and the smelting operation is moderately complex. Tin has been in recorded use by mankind since at least as long ago as 3000 B.C. Yes, you wonder how they managed to obtain it in those days.

Anyone who uses the phrase, "cheap and tinny," has not priced the stuff in recent times. Lacking a source of LTA, but faced with a driving need for tin, you can sort of uhh bite the bullet and go buy some 50/50 solder from the local hardware store. The larger bars, about five pounds in weight, are apt to be the cheapest if you can find them. I've not seen bar solder on sale in the Southern California area in many years. Prices on wire solder — the coarser diameters are the cheaper — run in the general brackets of $11 to $15/pound. Solder graded as 50/50 contains half tin and half lead. Solder with a lower tin content, such as 40/60, may be cheaper but is no bargain in the long run. Lead, you've got. It's the tin you want. Take a pocket calculator along and use it to work out the details.

Suffice to say, if you put that much cash outlay into a batch of makin's for cast bullets, you may find you aim the gun with special care. A popular theory favored by some is that the superstition about being able to bring werewolves to bag with silver bullets derives from the tendency to aim so precious a projectile with uncommon care, thus assuring a hit instead of a miss.

GENERAL PROCEDURES

Given alloy of suitable credentials, a means for melting and dispensing it, along with one or more moulds, we are (at last!) ready to commence foundering bullets, or founding them, if you prefer that verb. Other useful accessories

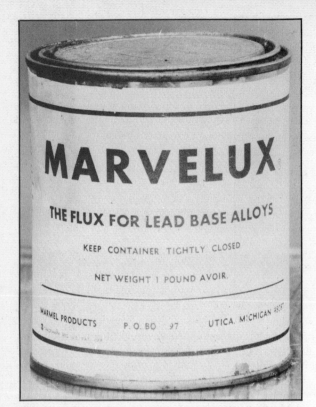

Marvelux, now to be had from Brownells, 210 S. Mill, Montezuma, IA 50171, is the all-time best stuff for cleaning up casting alloys and producing good bullets.

include such things as a stirring stick for mixing the alloy, some flux, a mallet for knocking the sprue cutter to one side and tapping the bullets free of the cavities, a small propane torch, a pair of pliers for picking up hot by-products, a screwdriver for changing blocks, perhaps a pair of welder's gloves for picking up the heavier, sizzling objects and, one more, absolutely mandatory item...

Right, a small propane-fired hand torch is handy for many applications when casting bullets. Below, a pair of heavy welders gloves is useful for handling hot items in casting.

A PAIR OF SHOOTING GLASSES!

The glasses go over your one and only pair of eyes and stay there until you've completed the operation. Molten bullet alloy is fearsomely volatile stuff. A friend related how he leaned over the pot on a hot day to examine the level and a drop of sweat fell off his face and into the pot. The sweat exploded into steam, blowing a quantity of alloy back into his face.

Casting when the clouds gather thick overhead can give you abrupt notice of the first falling water droplets. Plan to have some manner of protective roof over the pot at such times, although it's always a good idea to do your casting

This is the pair of Zeiss shooting glasses I was wearing when I really needed them, as discussed in the column at left, below. Even a cheap pair can be priceless when you need them!

outdoors under conditions of generous ventilation, due to the hazards of inhaled lead fumes and particles.

For my part, I once dumped a box of grundgy old cast and lube/sized bullets back into the pot to give them another try. The lube will smoke and stink like sixty. That's why you do it outdoors On this occasion, it erupted with a smart crack and a silvery Vesuvius came out of the pot, quite a bit of it in my face and down my open shirt collar.

I was wearing my shooting glasses and, removing them, I could see countless flecks of solidified bullet alloy over both lenses, including right where the pupils of my eyes would have been. My sole regret is that I neglected to photograph them to serve as an urgent illustration for a discussion such as this one.

Cleaning up the frightful mess that resulted, I found an empty hull from a .22 Short rimfire cartridge, but without any trace of a firing pin indentation in the rim. That suggested a live round had fallen unnoticed into the box, to be dumped in with all the reject bullets.

Since that time, I take great care to dump such boxes on a flat surface and inspect the contents keenly before dumping them into the pot. Meanwhile, I continue to be a fanatic about wearing the shooting glasses when casting or reloading. I've mentioned this incident in other books, but not all people buy all books and, if I can save the sight of even one eye by repeating it, I consider the repetition justified.

I do my casting atop a portable loading bench that I can lug out onto the driveway. It has a novel support arrangement of my own design, so that it can be leveled on a slanted surface, wobble-free, even though it has four supporting feet. I put an old piece of scrap plywood over the corner of the bench where the pot rests and use a sturdy C-clamp to secure the electric melting pot and the protective board to the top of the bench. I recognize the fact that I am a clumsy sort and prefer not to knock a pot full of molten alloy off to the ground, perhaps to slosh about my tennies. Once, long ago, a young lady was walking her St. Bernard down the street into which our little cul-de-sac tees. The pooch spotted one of our cats, ripped the chain from its owner's dainty hands and charged up our driveway with the chain cracking like a whip. The cat escaped, but it took me the rest of the afternoon to pick up all the abruptly decanted detritus of the incident. Again, I recommend clamping the pot to the bench. Mine was so secured at the time and not a drop of alloy was spilled. That was about the only thing that wasn't.

Bring out the heavy-duty extension cord and plug the pot into the three-prong socket. Turn on the little on/off switch if your pot has one. My RCBS Pro-Melt pot has a switch, but it's not marked for on/off, so I took care of that with a label-tape marker. Again, I recommend that as handy in the long haul. It does have a small red light that comes on, but it's hard to see in bright sunlight.

Set the dial of the thermostat to about 700-750°F/371-

My driveway is uneven and slopes. This bench was made to permit working surface to be level and teeter-free. Note the ingots melting in the top of the pot, which is held to the bench with C-clamp.

Brownells has this casting thermometer for use in checking alloy temperature. Insert sensing rod briefly and remove, otherwise it will break down if left under high heat for long intervals.

399°C and start loading the pot with ingots of suitable alloy you've squirreled aside previously. It's usually a good idea to leave a little metal in the pot at the close of the previous session. That will melt first and then will serve to transfer the heat efficiently to the ingots you've just added. You can hasten the melting process by firing up the propane hand torch and directing its flame down onto the added ingots or pigs.

It is not a good idea to leave casting furnaces unattended. Once, in the early '60s, I was casting in my garage, went to answer the phone and got back just in time to grab the fire-extinguisher and put out a growing blaze in some pieces of corrugated cardboard. The power cord had shorted out, burned through and the hot end had fallen onto the cardboard. Another few minutes, or less, and I'd've had a big, bad problem. Just one more hard lesson gulpingly noted and I hope to save you from the same spooky experiences. I also tend to feel the same way about case tumblers. I've never had an adventure with a case tumbler, but have heard from others who weren't as fortunate. When using either, make certain flammable materials are not nearby.

Both Brownells' and Lyman offer casting thermometers for checking the temperature of the casting alloy, independent of the thermostat, if the pot has one. The casting thermometers should be used briefly, not left in the alloy for hours on end.

Even if you booted it up to the low or middle 700s to get the alloy melted, turn it back down for routine casting. Anything much over 700 plays hob with the tin content and we've discussed the considerations that apply to that precious stuff.

Once the alloy is melted, you need to flux the mixture. In bygone years, I used to suggest beeswax because nothing was available that worked better. That is no longer true. Now, we have *Marvelux,* available from Brownells', Inc., (210 South Mill, Montezuma, IA 50171). An eighth-teaspoon or less, dumped onto the molten mix and stirred in thoroughly, works absolute wonders. What's more, it does not flare up, smoke or emit noxious vapors. It is good stuff and a little goes a long way. Nothing else fails even one-sixteenth as well.

Skim off the dross that rises to the top of the alloy? That's up to you. I tend to be casual about it. With a bottom-delivery pot, the good stuff is on the bottom and it comes out when you work the lever. A scum of black goop on the upper surface hurts little. If is offends your eye, dispose of it, but rest assured more will come along to take its place.

While all this has been going on, assuming you're using ferrous-alloy mould blocks, which you've protected with a rust-inhibitor, you will have been bringing them to readiness for further use. RIG 3 degreaser works quite well; so does Omark/Outers Crud Cutter. Either one needs to be used generously. Following that, you may wish to take the mould in and put it on the burner of the kitchen stove, set at medium heat for some few minutes before first use, to bring it up to fairly near operating temperatures. Don't let your enthusiasm go overboard. Once, I pre-warmed my blocks in such a manner, took them back out to the driveway, decanted the first load through the sprue cutter and, after a decent interval, pulled the handles apart and saw the still-molten alloy dump into the cardboard catch-box and commence smoking. Those blocks were warmed not wisely, but too well!

Bullet casting is geared for people who are, by nature, right-handed. I know of no source for left-handed bullet moulds. It makes little difference. Both hands are kept busy in the operation. Although inundated by south-paw acquaintances, I am a natural-born north-paw and I don't mind that a bit. The many procedures of reloading tend to make just about anyone ambidextrous, in the long haul.

With the alloy up to temperature, grasp the handles of the mould firmly in your left hand. Position the first opening on the sprue cutter beneath the nozzle on the mould guide. Your right hand is holding the mallet. Use the right hand to actuate the feed lever of the pot. The alloy will come dribbling down out of the delivery spout, into the opening of the cutter. If it doesn't, move the mould and cutter slightly to catch it. In a second or three, the alloy will overflow. That is your signal to move the mould to position the next opening beneath the drop tube.

We'll assume you're using a multi-cavity mould, as there aren't many singles being made these days. Whether you wish to close the valve for each cavity and open it for the next, or just let it run and move the mould, is up to you. I suggest you try it both ways and settle on the one that seems to work best for you. The procedures just described constitute what I call the "air-pour" technique, with the nozzle a fraction of an inch from the top of the sprue cutter.

The other approach is what I call "pressure-pour," in which the conical opening in the sprue cutter is held firmly in contact with the nozzle, so as to put the alloy into the cavity at whatever head of pressure may be represented by the depth of the alloy in the pot. There are advantages and disadvantages to both methods and special conditions may lead you to favor one over the other, from one particular instance to the next. I use both methods, depending upon which seems to work best at the time.

Ballpoint pen points to spot on mould tongs where you rap it with a non-marring hammer or mallet to dislodge bullet from cavity. Never hit the blocks!

At any rate, to this point, we've put molten alloy down into each of the cavities. Withdraw the mould and move it to the left, resting it in the shallow cardboard tray in which you propose to catch the sprues. Watch the surface of the exposed alloy in the top of the sprue cutter and you will see it turn from a silvery glisten to a sort of frosty grayish-white. That indicates the sprue has more or less solidified. It will take a longer interval as the mould heats up in use.

Holding the handles of the mould in your left hand, strike the rear end of the sprue cutter with the mallet, knocking that end from left to right. It may take a few whacks, so be patient.

As the sprue cutter moves to one side, it should deposit the sprue(s) in the tray. Now use your left hand to move the

mould on to the next tray to the left, in which you plan to catch the finished bullets. Pull the two mould handles apart. Quite probably, some or all of the bullets will remain in one or the other halves of the cavities. Holding the blocks slightly separated, tap gently on the front end of the right-hand tong — *not* on the mould block! — until all of the bullets are dislodged to fall into the tray.

Close the blocks firmly by squeezing the handles back together and repeat the operations, as just described.

On the first several cycles, it is unlikely that the resulting bullets will be of "keeper" grade, so be prepared to put them back in with the sprues, to be recycled back into the pot for another try.

If the alloy is none too hot, and the mould/sprue cutter still comparatively cool, the stream of alloy — if it impinges upon the metal of the sprue cutter instead of hitting the hole squarely — is apt to coagulate slightly, resulting in an incomplete fill of that cavity. Thus, at least at the start, it usually works better to close the valve after filling each cavity, opening it again for the next one and making every effort to align the hole precisely beneath the delivery spout, each time. As things warm up, it may work just as well — even better — to keep the alloy flowing and move the mould as each cavity is filled. Preferably, the nozzle or delivery spout should be within ¼-inch or a bit less above the sprue cutter.

If the air-pour method does not result in bullets that fill all of the corners of the mould cavity cleanly, try the pressure-pour technique. A second or so after you open the valve, you will probably observe a slight "squish" of alloy around the juncture between nozzle and hole. Close the valve and move on to the next. After filling all the cavities, you may wish to run a bead of additional alloy down the sprue holes to simplify removal of the sprue metal. The tiny sprues left by pressure-pouring tend to resist dislodgment, unless you do that.

As you knock the sprue cutter aside after a string of pressure-pour bullets, examine the bases of the bullets while the blocks remain held together. It is not uncommon to find a small air pocket in the bullet base, when using this approach. Should that happen, you usually can salvage the bullet(s) by swinging the sprue cutter back into place and air-pouring a stream of alloy into the particular hole(s) for a bit.

It hardly needs saying that a bullet with an off-center

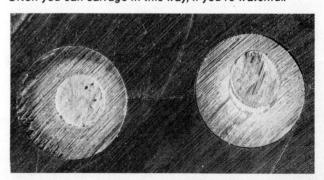

Top left, bullet at right had a hole in its base so (lower left) I ran more alloy into that side and (below) filled in the gap. Often you can salvage in this way, if you're watchful.

Sprue cutter of a four-cavity mould by Hensley & Gibbs, my favorite mouldmaker. See next photo.

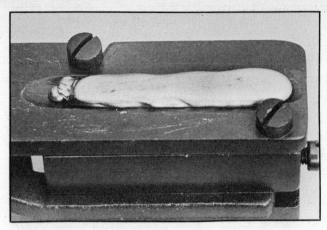

Just run alloy into the trough and allow it to cool thoroughly before knocking the sprue cutter aside.

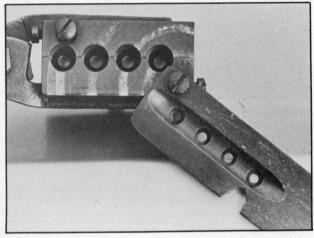

If you cut the sprues too soon, partially solidified alloy will leave silvery streaks on block and underside of cutter. This can be removed by careful use of single-edged razor, after cooling.

cavity in its base is not apt to fly with the keen accuracy you probably have in mind.

The heavier the bullet(s), the faster the mould heats up. It is quite possible and fairly common to get the mould too hot. That is indicated by several things: The exposed sprue will take progressively longer to make the shift in appearance that more or less indicates full solidification. In point of fact, it may turn "frosty," meanwhile remaining in semi-liquid state, as indicated by gently prodding it with the end of the wooden handle on the casting mallet. A further symptom is a series of silvery arcs on the under surface of the sprue cutter, indicating the sprue was cut while at least some portion of the alloy was still in liquid state. The silvery arcs can be removed by *careful* use of a single-edge razor blade. They should not be allowed to build up, as they keep the sprue cutter away from the upper surface of the blocks, resulting in lateral fins at the base of the bullets; an undesirable state of affairs.

Peter Kirker, a commercial bulletmaker, makes and markets two sizes of heat-sinks and I've found them extremely handy for keeping the running temperature of bullet moulds under control. These are finned extrusions of a special alloy of aluminum, with remarkably rapid heat-conducting properties. The smaller size is for moulds up to four cavities, the larger for moulds with more than four cavities. In use, the heat-sink is placed on the casting area, fins-down, just to the left of the pot. After filling, the base of

the mould blocks are rested on the upper surface of the heat-sink for some appropriate number of seconds, until the sprue is seen to cool and solidify. You can verify that by prodding the sprue with the end of the wooden mallet handle.

Kirker also makes the mould-guide for the RCBS Pro-Melt casting pot, shown in accompanying photos. You have to remove the support columns for the base of the Pro-Melt in order to install it, so it's best done while the pot is still cool. Once installed, it is an easy, simple matter to adjust the position of the sprue cutter in relation to the delivery nozzle to a high degree of precision. By turning and locking the support screw in front, you can get the guide dead-level — use a spirit level to check it — or you can pitch it upward or downward, as you wish. Address inquiries about either the mould-guide or heat-sinks to Peter D. Kirker, 130 E. Vista Way, Vista, CA 92083, with a self-addressed stamped envelope for current prices.

I've read the works of some who advocate plunging the over-heated mould into a bucket of water to cool it. If I caught anyone doing that to one of my moulds, I would be sorely tempted to bust a railroad tie over their solid-ivory skull. A good bullet mould is a splendid example of the machinist's gifted art and you do not subject such a noble artifact to thermal shocks of that nature; not in *my* book, you don't!

Before I got my set of Kirker heat-sinks — one of each,

as I have blocks up to eight cavities, at present — I had good results by using a small "squirrel-cage" fan that directed its air-stream across the top of the sprue cutter. That hastened the solidification of the sprue, quite nicely and tended to keep the blocks down in the comfortable range of operating temperatures. You will have more problems with over-heating mould blocks on hot days than when the temperature is at a moderate level.

A clear indication that the mould blocks are too hot is when the bullets start coming out with a distinctively "frosty" appearance. Under ideal conditions, the bullets will have a pleasing appearance, as if turned from bar silver on a jeweler's lathe.

One bad habit to avoid is that of knocking off the sprue, deciding the batch of bullets is not up to snuff and knocking them directly back into the top of the pot. That is apt to cause splashing droplets of metal that get between the two blocks and hold them apart. It will result in bullets with longitudinal fins running up and down the length on both sides of the juncture of the blocks. If that happens, use the single-edge razor blade — again, with great care! — to shave off the offending blobs and make everything shipshape, once more.

If you've followed all the procedures and recommendations and still are not producing cast bullets of good quality, the probable reasons may include one or more of the following:

    Improper alloy
    Contaminated mould cavities
    Mould blocks too cool
    Mould blocks too hot
    Sprue cutter too loose
    Mould blocks improperly aligned
    Alloy too cool
    Foreign matter between blocks
    Foreign matter at top of blocks
    Innate perversity of the Universe
    All of the above

LUBE/SIZING CAST BULLETS
You've got to have lubricant in the grooves!

That was just about the first thing I learned, when I was still the greenest neophyte reloader on the planetary crust, *circa* 1950 or so. I had my bullet mould, my loading press and dies, empty cases, primers and powder. Foosh, I said to myself, it couldn't hurt to make up just a few loads and try them out.

Another approach that works well is a heat-sink, such as this one from Peter Kirker, 130 E. Vista Way, Vista, CA 92083. It draws off excess heat and speeds cooling.

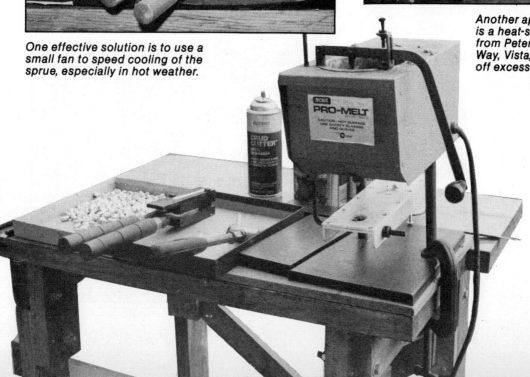

One effective solution is to use a small fan to speed cooling of the sprue, especially in hot weather.

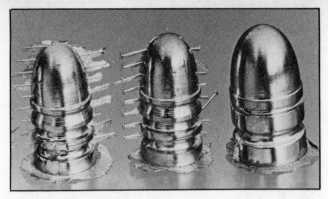

If you keep a pair of pliers handy, you can discard rejects back into the box with the sprues for recycling. Flawed base, such as the one at left, contributes to imbalance.

Well, it surely did. It took several hours, most of them deplorably profane, to get the last of the heavy coat of lead fouling out of the bore. I never made that mistake again.

The proper way to do the job is with a device called a lube/sizer. I didn't get one of those for a considerable while, but set the cast bullets base-down in a shallow tray and poured a mixture of beeswax and Vaseline around them to a depth just above the top grease groove. After the lube hardened, I cut them out, one at a time, with a tool consisting of the front end of a fired .35 Remington case, with a couple of heavy copper finger-lugs soldered, one onto each side. It wasn't great, but it worked and it kept the bore from fouling.

For the past many happy years, I've used a lube/sizer made by SAECO and I am insufferably satisfied with the work it turns out. There are faster machines — costing many times as much — but I make bullets for my own use and it's rare that I need a large quantity in a hurry, so I keep on using my pet SAECO and use the substantial difference between its cost and those of the gosh-wow machines to spend in riotous living. If you feel a driving need to lube/size thousands and thousands of bullets per day, you may

wish to explore the costlier alternatives. That's up to you.

In an earlier book, always trying to be helpful, I showed a photo of the machine that a nearby commercial bullet-maker — S&S Precision Bullets — uses for lube/sizing the output of their battery of automated casting machines. It features an automated bullet feed, is power-driven and just sits there going klunkety-chunk and processing the bullets at an awesome rate; somewhere on the order of ten per second or so. Inclusion of that photo has resulted in a few problems. Every now and again, I get a pained call from the publisher. Someone wants to know where they can get such a competent gizmo.

Well, to cut out the middlemen, I'll run that photo, or a similar one, again. If you want to know where to get one, you can call or write S&S Precision Bullets. The address is 22965 La Cadena, Laguna Hills, CA 92653. The phone is 714/768-6836. If that doesn't reach them, drop me a line at Dean Grennell, Box DG, Dana Point, CA 92629 and I'll try to put you on the trail. Please don't call the publisher, because he doesn't have the information at his fingertips.

The same firm, S&S, makes and markets a bullet lube I

A high-volume setup for lube/sizing, in the plant of S&S Precision Bullets, 22963 La Cadena, Laguna Hills, CA 92653. Bullets are fed automatically into powered lube/sizing units.

Left, my favorite SAECO lube/sizer. Above, a close look at the sizing die for 9mm bullets. Below, my collection of SAECO and homemade top punches for it.

have long since come to prefer over all others. It is composed of lithium-base grease and beeswax, in a formula originally developed by Garth Choate, of Bald Knob, Arkansas. I strongly and urgently recommend that you do not try to make it up, yourself. The reason is that the lithium-base grease has a melting point pretty close to the flash-point of the beeswax and it is not a process for the casual amateur or even the gifted amateur. It could burn your house down, and you with it. We don't want that. We can't spare a single reader.

Choate used to brew occasional batches, as needed, in his catfish cooker. The last time I ordered a fresh supply, I got a form letter saying he'd finally gotten sick and tired of eating fried catfish that tasted of bullet lube. He quoted the formula. I passed it along to Walt Stephenson, the senior S of S&S, and they've been making it, ever since. At date of writing — subject to change without notice — they sell it for a buck a stick, hollow or solid, in twelve-stick lots, plus shipping and handling. Other makes of bullet lube retail locally for at least as much at $3.60 a stick, the last time I priced some, several years ago, and they don't work nearly as well as the lithium stuff does.

Most bullet lubes today contain the miracle additive, Alox, not to be confused with Maalox, which is something else, entirely. They are generally rated to take plain-base bullets to velocities on the order of 1100 fps without appreciable problems and gas-checked bullets to perhaps 1300 fps, or so.

I really cannot say what the upper velocity for plain-base bullets may be, with the lithium-base lube. I've driven plain-base bullets to upward of 2000 fps, with excellent accuracy and no bore-fouling problems, whatsoever. Meanwhile, it's less than one-third the cost of the Alox lubes.

I plan to keep on using the lithium lubes, for the stated reasons, which strike me as ample and sufficient. The lithium mixture has never received the prestigious blessings of the National Rifle Association; the Alox has. Use whichever you prefer, but two modest suggestions: Don't try to rely on Alox at 2000 fps and don't try to brew your own lithium-base lube!

I should note that assorted research is currently being pursued into the possibilities of the so-called hard waxes. They require electrically-heated lube/sizers and there is a close-mouthed attitude as to the ingredients. They may revolutionize the world of cast bullets and yes, that would be nice. For the present, I plan to wait and see. When they become available, I will try them out and report the results.

Lyman makes a lube/sizer and so does RCBS. Both machines are quite competent and I do not mean to cast aspersions upon either, by implication or other means. Other machines include the Pitzer and the Star. The latter two push the bullet straight on through. The Lyman, RCBS and SAECO push it down into the lube/sizing chamber, then back up to be replaced by the next bullet. If there are other lube/sizers on the market, I have not become aware

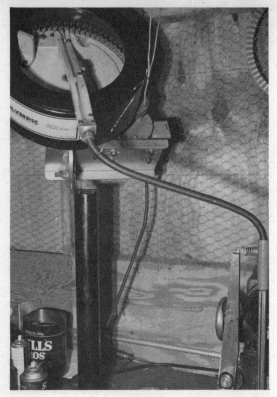

Above and left are two more looks at the automatic bullet feeder for the lube/sizer used by S&S Precision Bullets. In the photo above, you should be able to read maker's name and address, in case you want more information.

of them, to the present. I still have a Lyman unit I bought, many years ago, when Harry and Bess Truman were still in the White house. It did a decent job, but you had to give the little ratchet handle a twitch to put the lube into each bullet in turn. The SAECO machine has a spring-tensioned piston that can be turned down, enabling the lube/sizing of thirty bullets or more — depending upon the volume of lube required for each bullet — before you have to apply further tension on the spring. I regard that as an admirable feature, which is why I prefer to use it. The RCBS lube/sizer works in much the same manner as the Lyman, as I get the word, but has an automatic ratchet-twitcher. I have never owned nor used an RCBS unit, but know several other reloaders who use them with satisfaction. The Pitzer unit is a good rig. I have one, set up to two different bullets. You need to get special tooling for each given bullet and I have never bothered to extend my facilities with it. I have never owned a Star lube/sizer, for the simple reasoning that I've never been inclined to shell out the substantial price of one. As noted, I have this SAECO lube/sizer and I am happy with it.

The SAECO unit is versatile and it is a simple matter to adapt the machine to handle bullets from newly acquired moulds of any given diameter, provided you already have the basic size-dies for the diameter on hand. We can categorize lube/sizers into two groups: the in-and-outs — including the SAECO, RCBS and Lyman — or the straight-throughs, such as the Pitzer and Star. The in-and-outs have a bottom punch that goes down to a preset point and comes back up when the operating handle is reversed. All lube/sizers have a top punch that has to be contoured to the nose profile of the given bullet, although, in the example of the Pitzer, it isn't really on top.

The top punch on the SAECO is secured to the actuating head by a 5/16-24 thread. Given access to a metal lathe, it is an easy, simple operation to produce custom top punches for the SAECO in mad profusion, at little outlay of shop time. Having my own lathe, I now have more homemade SAECO top punches than I have of the elegant examples from the SAECO shops. I also have a few customized bottom punches, created to cope with cast designs having extravagant base bevels that are really closer to boat tails.

SAECO can provide top punches to fit any of their mould designs with total precision. When it comes to bullets from moulds made by others, they may or may not be able to come up with the proper hardware. I've found a couple of approaches that work extremely well. Given a semi-wadcutter, I knock out a top punch with an outside diameter that goes down into the lower sizing die, with a few thousandths of clearance. I measure the outside diameter of the portion of the bullet nose ahead of the SWC shoulder and drill a hole that size, or a few thousandths larger, in the lower tip of the top punch. The result is a fairly thin collar that engages the SWC shoulder and does not touch the bullet nose at all. Thread the upper end at 5/16-24 and you are solidly in business.

Suppose you're trying to cope with a design that has an exotic tip shape, not readily matched by anything less than super-expert machining? No big problem, really. Quite recently, I received a mould for a 9mm bullet from Hensley & Gibbs. It was their #307, with a sharp, conical point. It could have posed a real challenge, but it didn't. I made up a top punch with a cavity of suitable dimensions, then packed the cavity with a suitable mass of Kleenex, wadded together with leftover bullet lube, ran it against the tip of the first bullet and allowed the greased Kleenex to accept the shape of the pointy tip, which it did. I then proceeded to lube/size a few hundred H&G #307s, without the slightest amount of distortion of the exotic points. I will confess that I felt a trifle smug about that.

Several years ago, the late Bob Modisette — then the president of SAECO — told me he had an idea to offer a kit, by means of which any owner of a SAECO lube/sizer could make up a custom top punch that would fit the nose of any cast bullet whatsoever to total perfection. It would consist of a hollow pointed top punch, similar to the one just described, along with a small quantity of epoxy mix and release agent. The user would apply release agent to the tip of the bullet, put the epoxy mix into the open end of the punch, run them together and allow them to set up and harden. With that, the custom-fitted punch would be available for endless future use.

The customary procedure is to size cast bullets to a diameter of .001-inch larger than the groove diameter of the barrel up which you plan to launch them. My 9mm die for the SAECO unit is branded at .3565-inch groove diameter of typical 9mm barrels, but I've never had reason to complain about the performance of cast bullets I've lube/sized with it. Cast bullets tend to demonstrate a considerable degree of adaptability, which is one of the charming aspects of the wee beasties.

This discussion has exceeded its allotted space by some amount and perhaps now consists of more information on the matter than some care to acquire. Should that be the case, you have my apologies, but I continue to regard it as a complex and pertinent topic, warranting some amount of information overkill.

It's often been my chagrinful experience that major changes take place within the industry, just about the time the given book is rolling off the presses. It was bound to happen, sooner or later, and it has: Just about the time I'd gotten the bulk of this chapter onto paper, I had occasion to phone Johnny Adams and, in the course of the conversation, he mentioned that he was in the process of selling the SAECO operation to Richard Beebe, head of Redding Reloading Equipment, (114 Starr Rd., Cortland, NY 13045).

A semi-universal top punch packs a little paper and lube into the cavity to handle special noses such as this H&G No. 307. Below, the lube/sizer from Pitzer Tool Mfg. Co., Winterset, IA 50273.

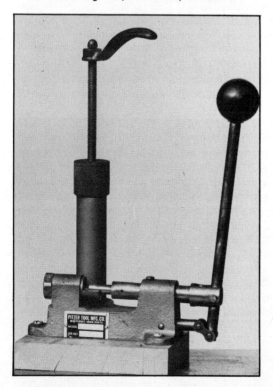

Since that time, I've talked with Beebe on the phone and was both relieved and delighted to receive his assurance that the SAECO lube/sizer will remain in production, essentially unchanged from its present format and specifications. He also plans to continue making and marketing the SAECO bullet moulds, with such manner of enhancement as he may deem fitting and proper.

As a matter of record, Wiley Clapp was on one of the other phone extensions and we had an eminently satisfying and — I'd hope — productive wide-open three-way conversation regarding things that could benefit from improvement and other things that should be left unchanged.

Beebe was aware of Modisette's concept of the custom-tailored top punch kits and we hashed various considerations of that back and forth. Even better, he said he plans and hopes to put the SAECO hardness tester back into production, again. I have had one of those incredibly useful tools for many years and would not part with it for a sum you'd hardly believe. They've been unavailable in recent times, but Beebe says he thinks he has all the necessary drawings and facilities to produce it again. It is a device that enables you to test a cast bullet, in a given alloy, determining its relative hardness and it was about the only simple and reliable approach within the price-range of typical bullet casters.

I asked Beebe if he's be interested in reviewing suggested bullet designs and he indicated that he'd like to see them, reserving the right to return them, if they did not seem commercially promising. If, on the other hand, he felt they showed commercial promise, he might add the mould to the SAECO line, with no payment for the design, other than the privilege of buying a mould for it at the regular price.

That's a much better deal than it might seem at the first casual glance. Many years ago, Lyman would produce a custom mould to your design for a flat charge, reserving the right to add it to their line if they felt so inclined. That has long gone by the boards and, up here in the upper '80s, the appearance of a new Lyman mould design is something you record on your calendar, so you can celebrate its anniversary with appropriate pagan ritual in years yet to come.

Few if any of the other mouldmakers welcome suggested new designs. Hensley & Gibbs has adopted a few of my suggestions, of which one — their #938, a conical-point for the .45 ACP at about 172 grains — has enjoyed moderate commercial success. Their #307 is a spinoff that can be used in 9mm or .38/.357, depending upon the diameter at which you lube/size it.

These and other considerations make me tend to feel grateful that SAECO has passed into good and knowledgeable hands. Redding, formerly Redding-Hunter, was a sort of also-ran in the field of reloading equipment, until Beebe took it over, some years ago. Since that time, he has demonstrated a dogged tendency to Do Things Right and I regard that as commendable.

As but one example, he has pioneered the use of titanium carbide, in place of tungsten carbide for case-resizing die inserts. Titanium carbide is about as hard as tungsten carbide, but finishes to a smoother and what can only be termed slipperier surface. It will be interesting to see what comes of all this. Personally, I'm inclined to be optimistic. — *Dean A. Grennell*

This Process Can Produce Jacketed Bullets, As Well As Unjacketed Ones Of Exotic Formats

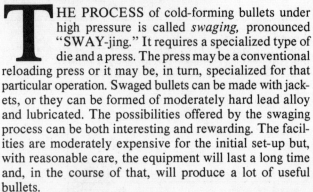

Corbin CSP-1 press, above, exerts powerful leverage. Jackets come in plastic bags of 500; here, .437-inch in length. Before drawing .38 jackets to 9mm (.355), they are rolled on a pad soaked in swaging lube.

THE PROCESS of cold-forming bullets under high pressure is called *swaging*, pronounced "SWAY-jing." It requires a specialized type of die and a press. The press may be a conventional reloading press or it may be, in turn, specialized for that particular operation. Swaged bullets can be made with jackets, or they can be formed of moderately hard lead alloy and lubricated. The possibilities offered by the swaging process can be both interesting and rewarding. The facilities are moderately expensive for the initial set-up but, with reasonable care, the equipment will last a long time and, in the course of that, will produce a lot of useful bullets.

Corbin Manufacturing & Supply, (Box 2659, White City, OR 97503; phone 503/826-5211) is the principal supplier of presses, dies, jackets and other needfuls for producing swaged bullets at the present time. They continue to add new items to their line and there may be a modest charge for a listing of the current offerings. They sell direct to the end-consumer, rather than going through jobbers, dealers and so on.

The steps for producing a jacketed bullet can be outlined briefly. First, you must produce the *core*. That can be done by at least two approaches. You can obtain lead or lead-alloy wire of suitable diameter and cut it into fairly uniform short sections by means of a core-cutter. Alternatively, you can cast bullets of suitable weight and diameter, using those castings as core blanks. Lead wire is moderately expensive and there is also the incoming freight on it. I have a four-cavity Lyman mould for their #311316 bullet and usually make up a suitable alloy and cast core-blanks

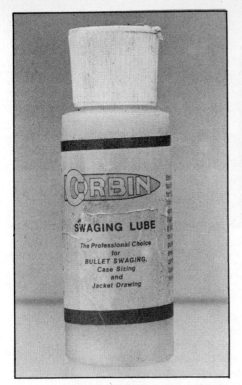

Corbin's swaging lube, above, eases effort and prevents die wear. Above, right, .38 jacket on end of punch, about to be drawn. Right, extruded lead comes from core-swage die as a .30 bullet is swaged to 9mm core.

in that for producing cores to use in the swaging of 9mm, .38 or .357 bullets. In typical alloys, that mould produces castings that weigh about 115 grains.

The stubby lead or lead-alloy cylinders, whether cut or cast, are put through the core-swage die, extruding the excess to produce a small cylinder, quite uniform in weight and dimensions. You control the weight of the core by adjusting the core-swage die in the press. Weigh it, together with the jacket, to determine the end-weight of the finished bullet.

The core is then seated in the jacket, by using the core-seating die in the press. In the process, no further core metal is extruded, but the core and jacket are pressed into an intimate fit with each other. If the proposed bullet is to be a hollow point, the open end will be at the front of the emerging bullet.

The nose-forming die is the final stage in production. Again, it is installed and adjusted to produce the desired results and, as with the previous operations, the processed bullet is ejected by reversing the operating handle.

The accompanying photos show the Corbin Swaging Press, Model CSP-1, performing these various operations. The CSP-1 operates with its own set of dies and it is

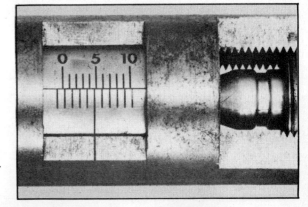

In use, SAECO hardness tester is tensioned until center line of lower scale aligns with witness line on barrel. Numbered line closest to matching is 7 or 8, here.

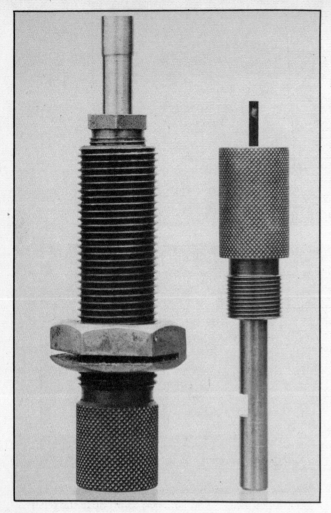

Nose-forming dies of the 9mm swaging set, disassembled at left and in use, above. LH unit moves with the ram and RH punch is held stationary in press. The pin ejects the completed bullet when the press handle moves up again.

engineered and produced specifically to cope with the fairly high stresses of the operation.

It is possible to buy dies that do much the same thing in a conventional loading press. If you propose to produce a fairly large number of bullets, I would recommend the CSP-1 press over the regular loading press. Not all that many loading presses will handle the strain of production in a satisfactory manner. The Heavyweight Champion, from C-H Tool & Die Corp., will do so, but that's one of the very few.

It is possible and quite practical to cast bullets, then lube/size them and go on to swage them into formats the mouldmaker never dreamed of. Once the lube is in the groove(s), it has no place to go during the swaging process and it remains in place. The resulting bullets can be driven to velocities limited solely by the efficiency of the bullet lube, which can be pretty respectable in the example of some lubes, With a good lithium-base bullet lube, such as the one from S&S Precision, upward of 2000 fps is obtainable without objectionable consequences, provided the cartridge and gun can do their respective parts.

One of the more interesting of such possibilities is the design I call the *Spelunker,* a sort of hollow point with delusions of grandeur. It has a polyconical nasal cavity that extends to full bullet diameter. Initially, the cavity has a broad angle that breaks to a much steeper one, with that cavity extending to nearly the base of the bullet. It is an improved variant of the hollow base wadcutter loaded backwards. It is impossible to even estimate the number of reloaders who have independently invented that particular approach. It has been in the state of the art for a great many years. As I recall, I "invented" it about early 1962, but I was far from the first to do so.

The problem with the reversed HBWC is that the skirts

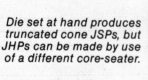

Die set at hand produces truncated cone JSPs, but JHPs can be made by use of a different core-seater.

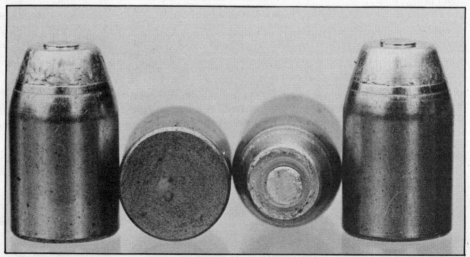

The Corbin CSP-1 press is built with castings of a special, high-strength bronze and has a toggle-link design that, as Dave Corbin puts it, delivers leverage close to infinity.

center spread at a distance of 110 yards: comfortably under the mystic minute of angle (MOA)!

Spelunkers are not especially at home in the typical autoloading pistol, although research into that continues. They perform nothing short of splendidly in revolvers, including the Model 547 Smith & Wesson in 9mmP. I'd assume they might do well in Ruger revolvers of the same chambering, although I've never gotten my hands on one of those, thus far.

To the present, in order to produce a Spelunker, you have to attend to the production of the nose-punch at the personal level. Even Corbin does not offer tooling for it, thus far. It is a highly specialized bullet design, groomed for instantaneous expansion.

They work as hopefully envisioned. They can be extremely effective. They have been employed in at least one combat confrontation to the present and, in that instance, they left nothing to be desired. — *Dean A. Grennell*

are both thin and soft. Upon impact, they will open and expand but, in so doing, they will shear off and separate, quite soon after hitting the target medium.

The Spelunker concept was engineered to provide stronger skirts that would open against even modest medium resistance, by reason of the obtuse-angled outer perimeter and then continue opening on down through the acute-angled inner cavity to produce the largest diameter of mushroom possible, meanwhile holding together as long as possible, commensurate with the velocity at hand.

One might casually assume that the basic configuration is intrinsically inaccurate, to a painful extent. As it turns out, that is not the case. Fired from handguns, the accuracy will vary, depending upon the propelling charge and the individual gun. I have fired 121-grain jacketed Spelunkers out of a Model 700 Remington Classic rifle in .350 Remington magnum at a velocity of about 3200 fps and five of them grouped into less than one inch of center-to-

Bullets of any caliber can be swaged on the CSP-1, if you have the sets of dies. Keeping track of them can be a challenge. I store mine in tagged plastic bags. Below, as you can see, the finished bullet mikes out awfully close to the desired diameter of .355-inch!

Traditional Rivals For Generations, Here Are Some Figures And Facts To Mull Over

CHAPTER 5

THE 9mmP VS. THE .45 ACP

IT WAS mentioned, in Chapter 1, that the 9mmP cartridge — particularly with the usual FMJ/RN bullet — is a penetrator and wounder. Its track record for bringing a life-threatening situation to an abrupt stop is not necessarily all that one might wistfully wish.

The Illinois State Police was one of the first large groups to adopt the 9mmP cartridge as their service load. I've heard accounts and seen rather disquieting color photos of a — the customary term — suspect who engaged their attention one night in the Illinois city of La Salle. The suspect was supercharged on PCP aka Angel Dust and thus more or less a latterday counterpart of the Norse *berserker* or the Moros who bound their abdominal region with

rawhide and proved so difficult to stop that they prompted the USA to make an abrupt transition from the .38 Long Colt to the .45 ACP cartridge.

Getting back to the suspect dealt with by the Illinois State Police that night in La Salle, he was armed with one of this country's ancient and manifestly obsolescent M1911 Colt auto pistols. He soaked up and was hardly inconvenienced at all by twenty-odd hits with 9mmP ammo from the Model 39 pistols issued to the ISP at that time. Other troopers came upon the scene and strafed him with police shotguns carrying charges of 00 buckshot. All the while, the Angel Dust sustained the suspect and, leaking from a great many punctures, he was still blithely reloading the magazine of his Colt when a really enterprising State

Opposite page: the 9mmP (left), with a .45 ACP, both with FMJ bullets. Below, Speer's 100-grain JHP offers excellent expansion, coupled with a design that helps to encourage reliable feeding. The same maker's 124-grain FMJ will feed in autoloading pistols, if any bullet will feed in them at all.

Something not seen too often is an absolutely unmodified Model 1911A1 pistol of typical military issue. The basic gun is not distinguished by its innate accuracy and it takes a lot of grim determination and dogged practice to make it shoot at its rather modest level of capability.

The Beretta Model 92SB-F, recently selected to replace the Model 1911A1 as this country's service sidearm, now is termed the Model 92-F by its maker and the M9 by the armed forces. With its fifteen-shot magazine it holds twice as many rounds as the M1911A1 and it is easier to learn to shoot the M9 with effective accuracy.

Trooper strode in close and made a butt-smash to the skull with his emptied police shotgun: end of incident, and hardly a moment too soon.

Several pistols handling the 9mmP cartridge in the modern era boast magazines with deep bottoms. Thirty-two shots at a single loading may not be the record, but it's a high average. Sixteen to twenty is closer to the upper norm. The concernable thing about the 9mmP is that you could, and just possibly might, require all the that ammo to subdue and pacify just one suspect, if the suspect happens to be in a nasty mood. You may even wish for more.

In a spirit of fair play, it should be noted that the .45 ACP cartridge is not the end-all and be-all when it comes to stopping power, either. In order to produce any hope of

useful effect, it is first necessary to score a hit. The .45 service automatic is not an easy weapon to master. The noise it makes is demoralizing and the recoil is pretty disconcerting to the neophyte shooter. A strong tendency to flinch tends to set in; at about the second shot.

Projectile weight is a factor that contributes heavily to felt recoil, and typical bullets for the 9mmP weigh about half as much as those for the .45 ACP: 115 grains compared to 230 grains, respectively. As a direct result, recoil of the 9mmP tends to be appreciably less than that of the .45 ACP, all other factors being reasonably equal.

The lower recoil of the 9mmP, in turn, makes getting acquainted with the gun substantially easier. The report is about as loud as that of the .45 ACP and, if anything,

Marlin makes their Camp Carbine in 9mmP and plans to introduce a .45 ACP version in the near future. Capable of excellent accuracy, such guns make a useful supplement to the pistols.

slightly more piercing to the ear, but the kick is quite a bit less and that should aid in overcoming the tendency to flinch, to a helpful extent.

The better 9mmP autos are quite competently accurate, as we've been discovering with a sense of pleasant surprise in the course of doing the test-firing for the book at hand. The Beretta Model 92SB-F, as recently adopted by the U.S. armed forces, is exceptionally accurate, as colleague Wiley Clapp reports upon, elsewhere here.

Having once spent several months instructing on a .45 pistol range, back in the Hitler-Tojo Fracas, I cannot in all candor say the same for the issue pistol of that era. During our free time, when we weren't processing students, the instructors spent a lot of time and consumed many rounds of ammunition in the process of attempting to learn the capabilities of the various guns on hand at the range. The pistols were by no means as uniformly capable as one might casually assume.

Eventually, I managed to isolate one that worked pretty

well and then went on to customize the trigger for a better pull. With that gun, along with expenditure of more rounds of practice ammo than I'd really care to stipulate, I finally scored something a bit better than 290X300 and qualified as Expert with the pistol, by USAAF standards of the time. A natural northpaw, I then went on to do nearly as well, firing with the left hand; well enough to rate Expert from the port-side, as well. Effective handgun firing, I learned, is more done with the brain than the hand.

You may be interested to learn that the ten-ring of those GI targets was a generous six inches in diameter. You did ten rounds of slow-fire from twenty-five yards, then moved up to fifteen yards for the timed and rapid stages. By contemporary standards, a great many readers might think — and rightly! — that it should have been easy to dot off a perfect score. Somehow, though, it didn't seem nearly so simple, with those guns, at that time. In point of rueful fact, the first time I ever fired a qualification course with the .45 in the USAAF, I turned in an ignominious thirty-three percent for a score! It was the first time I ever came to grasp with the .45 auto. I brought vast enthusiasm to the encounter, and took away profound humiliation and chagrin.

Looking back, through the mist and murk of four decades

Speer's 200-grain JHP .45 bullet has a really awesome capability for expansion on impact and often feeds well, too.

A newcomer to making handgun bullets, Nosler offers this 115-grain FMJ round nose design, along with several other diameters and types. Nosler has long been noted for their rifle bullets, including partition and solid-base types.

King-size contemporaries of the 9mmP and .45 ACP, the 9mm and .45 Winchester magnums were designed for use in the Wildey auto pistols, few of which were ever made and now thoroughly defunct. At one time, the Grizzly pistol was chambered for both loads, but the 9mm version has been dropped from production.

and some number of added years, there is little doubt in my mind that I could have wrought wonders, if only I could have gotten hands upon a Beretta Model 92SB-F and any manner of halfway decent ammo to feed it. Had some benevolent and indulgent fairy godmother managed to put such a gun in my hand, without remembering to provide the ammo, it would not have done me much good. At that time, *circa* 1944-5, in the airbase near Tonopah, Nevada, 9mmP ammo was somewhat less common than colleens in Kowloon or, comes to that, Puerto Rican leprechauns. About as frequently encountered as Genghis Khan at a Tupperware party, you could say.

A great many people have written and continue to write about firearms and their performance capabilities and they are in agreement upon one point, hardly any others. The one common consensus is that hardly anyone agrees on anything, whatsoever.

There is, for example, one school of thought that holds the theory that the most effective cartridge, in terms of stopping power, is one that throws a heavy bullet of large diameter, at no more than moderate velocity. Such a projectile, they contend, takes longer to course through the target and, as a direct result, generates a greater amount of trauma and advantageous distraction. The late Elmer Keith, rest his doughty Scottish soul, was sort of the high priest of that particular cult, although he saw nothing wrong with the .44 magnum cartridge, whose big, heavy slug stride forth rather briskly.

The partisans of the big, slow, heavy bullet tend to speak learnedly of what they term "dwell-time," quite possibly having a valid point, there. The only time in my career to date that I've been struck by a flying bullet, it was a Hensley & Gibbs cast number, and it bounced out of the .45 ACP off a hard maple bowling pin and came back to hit me in the solar plexus. It didn't break the skin, but it left an impressive bruise that lasted for a week or ten days. I was grateful it didn't hit my shooting glasses!

Several researchers have made earnest endeavors to peg down the hard facts of bullet effect, without ever coming up with anything that is readily accepted by the shooting public. One of the problems lies in what to use as a test

medium. Assuming you are interested in evaluating potential performance on a hostile human target, the first problem is that it is far different from a paper target. A hit on paper, any old place in the bullseye, scores you a ten and that's it, even if it only nicks the outer edge.

One inch, or even less of change in the point of impact upon a live target can make a world of difference in the resulting effect. A bullet that strikes a bone will behave one way; one that misses the bones will have a much different effect.

There are other subtle differences, as well. The mental/emotional state of the impactee has a major bearing upon the resulting effects. As a kid on the farm, I have watched my father slaughter a cow for the family's winter beef and I can report that an animal weighing in the vicinity of half a ton would drop instantly if shot between the eyes with a .22

Available in a choice of VHS or Beta, the Deadly Weapons video cassette offers a realistic evaluation, as discussed.

Mishapen blob of lead was once a Hensley & Gibbs #68 bullet. Fired at a hard maple bowling pin, it bounced back and hit me in the solar plexus. Most if not all of the deformation occurred when it hit the pin, and I'm glad of that!

short rimfire cartridge out of the family squirrel rifle.

On the other hand, I have read reports that a grizzly bear, shot through the heart with a high-powered rifle, can still charge a hundred yards and kill a man, before beginning to run short on steam. Any mammal, including *Homo sapiens* has adrenal glands that shoot adrenaline into the bloodstream at times of anticipated stress, as a sort of built-in supercharger. Adrenaline provides added ability to run faster or fight harder, as the situation may require.

To the present, no one has succeeded in making up a test analog capable of duplicating the heterogeneous makeup of the human body, let alone of matching the effects of a generous squirt of adrenaline. For that reason, any tests, discussions or theories on relative stopping power of a bullet or its cartridge are and probably shall always remain painfully hypothetical.

Motion picture films have had a powerful effect upon the public fancy in the matter of the overall effect of shots fired in alarm or anger. Such efforts are not always as accurate and realistic as one might wish they had been.

For one example, you may have seen a film called *Shane,* from several years ago. In it, the bad-guy, Jack Palance, shot one of his victims with a single-action revolver, presumably a .45 Long Colt cartridge and the victim was blasted backward and downward, as if struck by an invisible locomotive. If you saw the film, you are apt to recall that scene.

Several years after that picture was filmed, I had the pleasure of having lunch with the late Van Heflin, one of its stars. In the course of the conversation, I inquired as to how the scene had been filmed and he gave a candid fill-in on the details. It seems that a length of light but tough nylon line had been tied to a concealed harness on the back of the shootee. When Palance set off his blank cartridge, several members of the studio crew, holding the line, as if braced for a tug o'war, gave a mighty, concerted heave and yanked

Hornady calls these their Air Force design and turns them out in both 9mm and .45 sizes. Usually of high reliability in feeding, they also tend to offer an outstanding level of accuracy in most auto pistols.

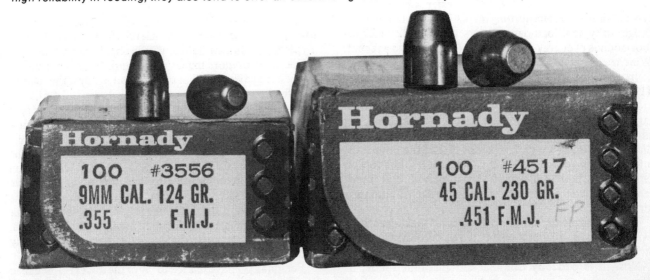

Hornady
100   #3556
9MM CAL. 124 GR.
.355   F.M.J.

Hornady
100   #4517
45 CAL. 230 GR.
.451 F.M.J.   FP

9mm (.355" Dia.)
124 GRAIN FULL METAL JACKET
#3556

CARTRIDGE OVERALL LENGTH 1.040"

POWDER	VELOCITY					
	900 fps	950 fps	1000 fps	1050 fps	1100 fps	1150 fps
BULLSEYE	3.3 gr.	3.5 gr.	3.8 gr.	4.1 gr.	4.4 gr.	
WIN 231		3.9 gr.	4.3 gr.	4.8 gr.	5.2 gr.	
UNIQUE	3.7 gr.	4.1 gr.	4.4 gr.	4.7 gr.	5.1 gr.	
HERCO	4.4 gr.	4.6 gr.	4.9 gr.	5.1 gr.	5.3 gr.	
HS-6	5.0 gr.	5.3 gr.	5.7 gr.	6.0 gr.	6.3 gr.	
BLUE DOT	6.0 gr.	6.4 gr.	6.7 gr.	7.0 gr.	7.3 gr.	7.7 gr.
WIN 630			8.0 gr.	8.6 gr.	9.3 gr.	
	223	249	275	304	333	364

Indicates maximum load • use with caution

335

Above is the table of load data from the third edition of the Hornady Handbook for their #3556 bullet in the 9mm Luger or Parabellum. The hand-lettered figures at the bottom of each column show the number of foot-pounds for what weight and velocity. HS-6 is a Hodgdon powder. Data above and on the facing page, Copyright by Hornady Manufacturing Co., and reproduced here by the kind permission of Steve Hornady.

the man off his feet, with the impressive — if starkly unrealistic — results that impressed a great many viewers quite deeply.

Within the past year, I obtained a videotape called *Deadly Weapons*, in which they tried to provide much more accurate information on a great many ballistic fantasies, including the effect of a bullet strike on a human target. When it came to the matter of the effect of bullet impact, the target donned a ballistic vest, capable of stopping a bullet from the .308 Winchester *aka* 7.62mm NATO rifle dead in its hurtling tracks. That particular cartridge, in typical loadings, musters about 2582 to 2743 foot-pounds of energy at the muzzle (according to a recent Winchester catalog). Comparable figures from the same source give the 9mmP 341-383 fpe and the .45 ACP 244-411 fpe, with 310-427 for the .38 Colt Super.

By way of underscoring the demonstration, the guy serving as the target balanced on one foot and the one with the rifle fired from hardly over ten feet away. Did the prodigious impact — up to 7.16 times that of the 9mmP or 6.67 times that of the .45 ACP — send the hapless victim pinwheeling madly for several yards? Huh-uh. But it *did* make him lower his raised foot for the sake of retaining his balance.

That, if you please, was the only effect of soaking up well over a foot-ton of kinetic energy, all at once. Makes you stop and think, doesn't it?

Now, it is perfectly true that the unarmored hide, if jabbed staunchly with a sharp pin, can cause the owner of the epidermis to react quite impressively and, in the same way, a person hit by a bullet can and may show profound reactions. That assumes the lack of armor to stop the projectile from penetrating beyond the surface. The subjective reaction can and may be quite violent.

It is possible to employ some manner of uniform test medium to assay the comparative performance of this or that bullet in various cartridges out of assorted guns and the resulting tests can prove interesting, although admittedly by no means conclusive. Common modeling clay is too soft and delicate to be useful for most such tests. Typically, handgun bullets will probably not be stopped inside of ten or more inches of the stuff. It produces highly impressive cavitation, but that's about the best that can be said for it.

Another, similar material is called duxseal or duct seal or assorted other terms. It is considerably stiffer in texture and it does not dry or harden with extended exposure to the air, although its consistency varies somewhat with the ambient temperature. You can also prepare a test medium by melting down paraffin wax and stirring in a suitable quantity of some appropriate grease to plasticize the solidified mixture and then there is ballistic gelatine. Other researchers have favored bound bundles of magazines, water-soaked telephone directories and several less-likely approaches.

Personally, I have tended to favor the duct seal, because

45 CALIBER (.451" Dia.)
230 GRAIN FULL METAL JACKET
#4518

CARTRIDGE OVERALL LENGTH 1.200"

POWDER	VELOCITY							
	600 fps	650 fps	700 fps	750 fps	800 fps	850 fps	900 fps	950 fps
HI-SKOR 700-X	3.6 gr.	3.9 gr.	4.2 gr.	4.5 gr.	4.8 gr.	5.1 gr.		
RED DOT	3.6 gr.	3.9 gr.	4.3 gr.	4.7 gr.	5.1 gr.	5.4 gr.		
BULLSEYE	3.6 gr.	4.0 gr.	4.4 gr.	4.7 gr.	5.1 gr.	5.5 gr.		
WIN 231	4.6 gr.	4.9 gr.	5.3 gr.	5.7 gr.	6.0 gr.			
UNIQUE	4.8 gr.	5.2 gr.	5.6 gr.	6.0 gr.	6.4 gr.	6.9 gr.	7.3 gr.	
HERCO	5.2 gr.	5.7 gr.	6.2 gr.	6.7 gr.	7.2 gr.	7.7 gr.	8.2 gr.	
HS-6	6.6 gr.	7.1 gr.	7.5 gr.	6.9 gr.	8.4 gr.	8.8 gr.	9.2 gr.	9.7 gr.

These loads may also be used with the 45 caliber 230 gr. RN FMJ, though overall length may vary.

Indicates maximum load • use with caution

Here, from the same source, is the .45 ACP load data for use with Hornady's #4518 bullet. The two were selected for comparison because the designs are virtually identical and both represent the upper weight of bullets used with the given cartridge. As discussed in the text, the downrange ballistics are surprising.

it does a nice job of opening up bullets that are more or less capable of expanding in the first place. After firing, you can brew up a small batch of plaster of Paris, pour it into the cavity and obtain a cast of the impact area for future reference and/or photographing.

It should be emphasized that any such research has no accurate counterpart in the Real World. It does, however, enable you to compare the performance of one bullet against that of some other bullet. By the way, avoid using melted paraffin wax for casting the impact cavities in duct seal. It always seems to find a crevice and then it proceeds to drip out and make a horrible mess!

Anyone who gives the matter much thought is apt to assume that the higher velocity and superior ballistic coefficient of the 9mmP will give it a marked edge over the .45 ACP at the longer ranges. Having a Sharp Model EL-5500II pocket computer, already programmed for the necessary work, it was a simple and fairly quick operation to set up a contest between the two cartridges, in twenty-yard increments out to two hundred yards.

I consulted the *Hornady Handbook,* primarily because it was the only work currently available that offered load data on two closely comparable bullets: Hornady's #3556 in 9mm and their #4518 in .45; both are FMJ designs with flat points, in respective weights of 124 and 230 grains. The #3556 has a sectional density (SD) of .141 and a ballistic coefficient (BC) of .152; figures for the #4518 are .162 and .148, respectively.

The highest ballistics listed in the *Hornady Handbook* for the two bullets are 1150/364 for the 9mm and 950/461 for the .45 caliber. Admittedly, that is a slightly better than average figure for the .45 ACP at that bullet weight. Typical military and commercial loadings tend to run more around the 780-860-fps levels with a 230-grain bullet: the classic ".45 Hardball" load, as it's often termed.

As a start, I ran both of the top loads in the *Hornady Handbook.* If zeroed for twenty-five yards, their .45 load was 96.12 inches low at two hundred yards. On the same basis, the 9mmP load was 63.14 inches low at the same distance: roughly three feet flatter in its trajectory.

Terminal ballistics for the 9mmP at two hundred yards were 700/134 and, for the .45 ACP, 570/165. In traveling that far, the 9mmP lost 450 fps in velocity and 230 fpe in energy. Over the same course, the .45 ACP dwindled by 380 fps and 296 fpe.

A few pertinent details, here: The 9mmP test gun used by the Hornady crew was a Model 39 Smith & Wesson, with four-inch barrel and their .45 ACP was the familiar Model 1911 Colt with five-inch barrel. For the sake of those who wish to duplicate my calculations, I was using a sight height of .750-inch, having measured that as the distance from the center of the bore to the top of the front sight. It was figured at zero degrees of elevation.

Time of flight to the two hundred-yard mark was .675-second for the 9mmP and .823-second for the .45 ACP. Wind-drift, for each one mph of crosswind, was 2.69

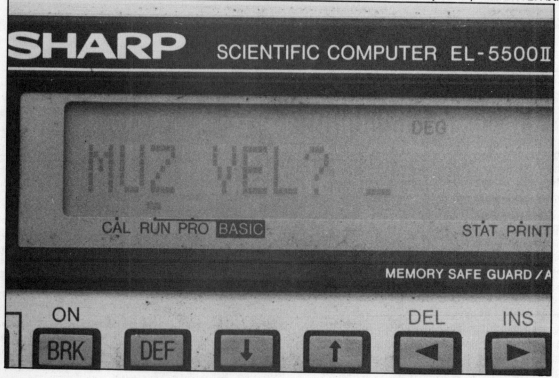

The Sharp Model EL-5500-II is a pocket-sized, battery-powered computer that is fully programmable. Mike Barnett of Renton, WA, has written programs for use with the EL-5500-II that compute trajectory, remaining velocity and energy at a given distance and wind drift, as well as time of flight to a given distance. In the photo below, the computer is asking for the muzzle velocity, having gotten to line 3013 in the program appearing on the opposite page. All you do is tap it onto the keys and press ENTER bar.

inches for the 9mmP and 3.36 inches for the .45 ACP.

Curious to see how a more typical .45 Hardball load might stack up against that 9mmP recipe, I ran another worksheet for the .45, with everything the same except for a velocity at the muzzle of 780 fps, good for 311 fpe. The difference was substantial. If zeroed for twenty-five yards, the drop at two hundred was 145.12 inches: about twelve feet and a trifle.

At that distance, the cited 9mmP load had the edge over the .45 Hardball, all the way. Quoting fps, the 9mmP had 1080 at twenty-five yards and 700 at two hundred yards.

The .45 Hardball had 731 and 468, respectively. Energy remaining was 321 and 134 for the 9mmP; 272 and a piffling 111 for the .45 Hardball.

Despite its curvaceous trajectory, the GI .45 can surprise you a little. There came a time in WWII when I had the Tonopah ground gunnery range all to myself. It was V-J Day, or perhaps the day after. The CO had decreed a gigantic victory parade on the flight line, with all — repeat: *all* — personnel participating. Someone, however, had to pull CQ (charge of quarters) duty and keep an eye on the ground range and that duty fell to me.

We had a 500-yard rifle range, although it was seldom used. I set out a few empty metal liners from crates of ammo — about the size of a silhouette target — at the 300-yard line and returned to the 500-yard line, with the liners an accurate two hundred yards away. I broke out my pet GI .45 and a generous supply of ammo, prepared to celebrate the end of the war in my own private way.

The desert floor was dry and dusty; perfect for spotting hits. I kept holding higher and ever higher, walking the dust-puffs on out toward the liners. By the time I had zeroed in upon them, I estimated that I was holding about fourteen feet high. After expending a couple of boxes at that elevation, I went out to police up the liners, lest the range officer offer some dialog about it upon his return. I didn't count the holes in the tin, little suspecting I'd want to write it all up, some day. There were, however, quite a number of punctures, all about .45-inch in diameter and,

even at 111 fpe or so, it got through the sheet metal in fine fashion.

So now I learn, forty-odd years later, that I was off in my guesstimate by nearly two feet. I consider that close enough for government work. Besides, it surely beat the heck out of marching in the parade, or so I thought.

Summing up, briefly, the 9mmP shoots faster and flatter, though not by as much margin as you'd expect. The .45 ACP can make good use of a little added velocity. The two cartridges are fairly close in kinetic energy, out to two hundred yards and neither is overly effective a lot beyond that distance. In FMJ designs, the larger diameter of the .45 bullet gives it some edge in what is often termed *knockdown power*. Let us, for the sake of accuracy, say it's apt to generate more reaction in the target. Expanding bullets will help either cartridge, but only if they feed reliably and, all too often, they may not do so. — *Dean A. Grennell*

```
PROGRAM ADDED 13 SEPT '85
3011: "L"
3012: PAUSE☐"PISTOL☐TRAJ"
3013: INPUT☐"MUZ☐VEL?☐";A
3014: INPUT☐"BAL☐COEF?☐";B
3015: D=.0001257/B
3016: INPUT☐"SCOPE☐HT?☐";E
3017: INPUT☐"ZERO☐RANGE?☐";F
3018: G=96.48/(SQU☐A*SQU☐A)
3019: H=(G*(EXP☐(6*D*F)-1-6*
       D*F)+E)/(36*F)
3020: I=0
3021: FOR☐J=1☐TO☐8
3022: I=I+25
3023: M=36*I*H-G*(EXP☐(6*D*I)-
       1-6*D*I)-E
3024: WAIT☐50
3025: PRINT☐"RANGE=☐";I
3026: WAIT☐200
3027: PRINT☐"PATH=☐";☐INT☐(100*
       M)/100
3028: NEXT☐J
3029: GOTO☐3017
3030: END
[Note: ☐ indicates a space (SPC).]
```

Reproduced from my notebook, here is the program that gives the bullet path for handgun loads — that is, below 2600 fps — in 50-yard increments, out to 200 yards. Zeros are indicated by a diagonal line through the O. Once programmed, just turn on the switch, press the CAL button once to put it in RUN mode, then press the DEF key, followed by the L key. It will ask for the needed data and, given that, will read off the bullet path for each distance. If you need more time to jot down the figures, change line 3026 to a higher number such as WAIT 300 instead of 200.

CHAPTER 6

OBSOLETE AND OBSOLESCENT
9mm PISTOLS

Noted Arms Collector Chuck Karwan Discusses Guns No Longer In Use And Those Out Of Production.

With combo holster and shoulder stock, the Mauser converts into an effective carbine. Such stocks, of original design manufacture, are now legal without federal restriction or registration, but local laws may apply. If the gun were actually being fired here, the shooter would be well advised to don shooting glasses and earmuffs — and to cock the hammer.

9mm Steyr, at left next to a 9mmP in photo below, is one of several European cartridges for a few specific guns, rarely seen over here.

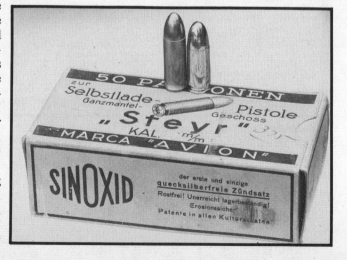

WHILE THE preponderance of this tome deals with the 9mm handguns that are currently available, this chapter will deal with the not-so-new 9mms that helped establish it as the current king of the medium-bore pistols. As in the rest of this book, our discussion in this chapter will be limited to those handguns chambering the 9mm Parabellum cartridge, also variously known as the 9mm Luger, 9x19mm, 9mm NATO, 9mm P'08 and other names. Prior to WWII, there was a plethora of other 9mms developed, including the 9mm Corto (Browning Short, Kurtz, .380 ACP), 9mm Largo (Bergmann-Bayard, Bayard Long), 9mm Steyr, 9mm Mauser, 9mm Glisenti, 9mm Browning Long, and a number of others. Since WWII, the 9mm Parabellum has reigned as king, with only the 9mm Winchester magnum being introduced as competition. As yet, even that introduction has been fruitless, since neither

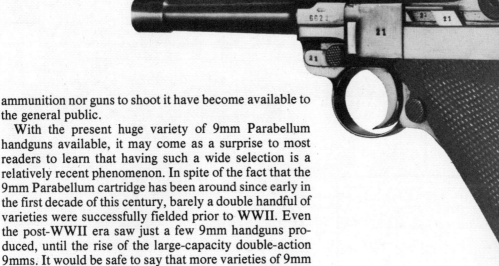

ammunition nor guns to shoot it have become available to the general public.

With the present huge variety of 9mm Parabellum handguns available, it may come as a surprise to most readers to learn that having such a wide selection is a relatively recent phenomenon. In spite of the fact that the 9mm Parabellum cartridge has been around since early in the first decade of this century, barely a double handful of varieties were successfully fielded prior to WWII. Even the post-WWII era saw just a few 9mm handguns produced, until the rise of the large-capacity double-action 9mms. It would be safe to say that more varieties of 9mm handguns have entered the market in the last ten years than in all the previous seventy-plus years.

Before we proceed it might be a good idea to define our use of the terms obsolete and obsolescent. An obsolete 9mm is one which is no longer in production, no longer in service as a police or military handgun, and/or of an outmoded design. An obsolescent 9mm would be one that is either out of production or where discontinuance is imminent, but it is still in fairly common service. It all began about 1900 with Georg Luger's redesign of the toggle-locked Borchardt pistol for DWM. He took an ugly and cumbersome pistol and redesigned it into a sleek, handsome and handy handgun.

Originally called the "Parabellum-Pistole, System Borchardt-Luger" the pistol soon became to be known as either the Parabellum or the Luger. Georg Luger followed in the footsteps of Borchardt and Mauser by chambering his new pistol for a bottlenecked high velocity caliber .30 cartridge called the 7.65mm Luger. He quickly ran into trouble when his native Germany expressed displeasure with the 7.65mm Luger cartridge, indicating an interest in a larger, more effective round. By 1902, Luger had simply necked up the 7.65mm to 9mm and reintroduced his pistol to the German military. It was an inspired bit of wildcatting for, as they say, the rest is history.

The first 9mm Luger to be adopted was the Model 1904 Marine Model by the German navy. The Navy Luger featured a grip safety, a lug for a shoulder stock, a six-inch barrel — and an adjustable rear sight. Later Navy Lugers did away with the grip safety but remain otherwise similar. To my eyes, the Navy Luger is the handsomest of all the Lugers. It was never manufactured in nearly the quantity of its Army brother and, unfortunately for collectors, most of the production ended up at the bottom of the ocean thanks to WWI and WWII. Acceptance of the Luger was wide and quick. By 1907, it had been adopted by Switzerland, Bulgaria, Netherlands, Portugal, as well as the German navy.

In 1908, the most important event in Luger history took place when the German army adopted the 9mm Luger as the Pistole '08 and the 9mm Parabellum cartridge as Pistolenpatronen '08. The P'08 differs from its sleek Navy

Traditional Pistole '08 or Luger, above, is still being produced in limited quantities and specialized modes, such as the Cartridge-Counter version, distributed in this country by Interarms of Alexandria, Virigina. In the photo below, the upper Luger is the Artillery Model, closely similar in appearance to the Navy Model, but lacking the grip safety feature of the Pistole '04 version.

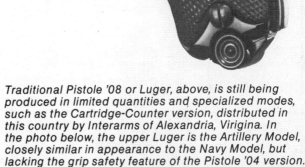

Model brother by having a stubbier four-inch barrel, no grip safety, and a mundane but serviceable fixed-notch rear sight. The P'08 is by far the most common of all Lugers encountered.

With the onslaught of WWI, the German army sought a more effective weapon than a handgun for heavy weapons crews including machine gun section leaders, artillery crewmembers, and torpedo boat crews. In these pre-submachine gun days, the answer was a Luger with an eight-inch barrel and a detachable shoulder stock. The rear sight was moved from the toggle to the barrel and consisted of a V-notch tangent arrangement similar to the one of the Mauser rifle. It was adjustable from one hundred meters to a rather optimistic eight hundred meters.

Oddly enough, the Navy or Marine Model has a slightly shorter sight radius, due to forward positioning of its adjustable rear sight, shown in photo below. Sight is graduated for up to 800 meters; about 872 yds.

ing up the tangent sight, I found that I could hit the 175 yard silhouette four out of five shots without much trouble.

The Luger remained in continuous production until 1942, when production ceased to allow manufacture of the P'38. The vast majority of the 9mm Lugers encountered will fit one of the three categories outlined, or their com-

Walther Pistole '38's exposed hammer and DA trigger, permitted a chambered round to be fired without cocking hammer. Subsequent shots were fired SA mode as action cocked the hammer during cycle.

Although pinpoint accuracy is out of the question at such ranges, a 9mm bullet will still penetrate a WWI French helmet at eight hundred meters, making it decidedly lethal even at that range. This model has been called a number of names including the Model 1914, the Model 1908/14, the Artillery Luger, and the Model 1917 (some authorities claim it wasn't introduced until 1917). Collectors usually use the term Artillery Luger.

An interesting accessory that was developed for the Artillery Luger was a 32-round drum magazine. With the stock and drum attached, a crew member had a semi-automatic equivalent of a submachine gun. I can personally attest to the long-range effectiveness of the Artillery Luger. Shooting some years ago in a unique combat match in Canada that used silhouette targets out to 175 yards, I used an Artillery Luger without a stock. By crank-

mercial equivalents, although there are hundreds of variations recognized by collectors. It has been manufactured in Germany by Deutsche Waffen und Munitionsfabriken (DWM), Erfurt Arsenal, Simpson and Company, Mauser Werke, and Heinrich Krieghoff Waffenfabrik. It was also manufactured in Switzerland at the Waffenfabrik Bern and in England by Vickers Limited.

Though it has long ceased to be a viable service pistol and its design has been outmoded since before WWI, the Luger refuses to die. For a number of years the modern Mauser Company of Germany has made a limited number of assorted Luger variations, much as various Colt Single Actions still come out of the Colt Custom Shop. Also, like Colt's SAA, they are expensive. For information on the modern Lugers, contact the current importers, Armes de Chasse, P.O. Box 827, Chadds Ford, PA 19317 or

Interarms, Number 10 Prince Street, Alexandria, Virginia 22313.

To me, the Luger is like a beautiful woman who cannot cook and is inadequate in bed. She may be good to look at and fondle, but she is only marginal for the purposes she was designed. Admittedly, without exception the Lugers are beautifully made. They virtually have to be, because of their intricate and delicate mechanism. Because of close tolerances, they are quite accurate. However, this is often difficult to prove due to the usually poor trigger pull. Though the mechanism is strong, it is far too susceptible to malfunctions from dirt, ice, sand, etc., to be a satisfactory service pistol. Invariably they will not feed modern hollow pointed ammunition reliably, though they are reasonably reliable with round nosed full jacketed ammunition if the pistol is clean.

The short-barreled Lugers also suffer from a poor, muzzle-light balance. Often touted as a natural pointer, this is only true when hip shooting, where the Luger's barrel lines up well with the shooter's forearm. When the Luger is fired from the shoulder level, as is the accepted modern practice, the preferred locked-wrist grip tends to point the Luger extremely high. One must consciously bend the wrist down to bring the pistol to bear on target. However, one cannot deny the mystique that has followed the Luger thoroughout its career, in spite of several markedly superior designs having surfaced by 1911.

One legacy of the Luger that will live on as long as there are handguns is its magazine release. It is a little known fact that, in the U.S., pistol trials of the early 1900s, the test board found the Luger magazine release to their liking. As a result they requested that future pistols to be submitted have a magazine release like the Luger if at all possible. Colt complied on what was subsequently to become the M1911 .45 auto. Many European auto pistols are often criticized for not having "a magazine release like the superior one of our M1911" when in fact the Luger should get the credit.

With the adoption of the 9mm in 1908, several German manufacturers tried unsuccessfully to follow suit with their own 9mms. The first was Dreyse with an enlarged version of their .32 auto. This ugly monstrosity was even more complicated than the Luger, in spite of operating as a totally unlocked straight blowback. First introduced around 1910, manufacture ceased during WWI. Examples are rarely found. Mauser also enlarged its M1910 pocket pistol to handle the 9mm Parabellum. A handsome pistol, it also suffered from being a straight blowback and from its limitations with so powerful a cartridge as the 9mmP. Little more than prototype quantities were manufactured and examples are extremely rare. Walther made the same mistake as Dreyse and Mauser by bringing out an enlarged

As Karwan discusses in test, the Luger had magazine release on LH side of the frame, behind trigger. The Luger was among guns in tests to select the U.S. service pistol and the board liked that feature so well that they requested it be incorporated on the Colt Model 1911 pistol that actually was adopted. Thus, the Colt owed one of its many admirable features to a rival design originally submitted for the competitive tests!

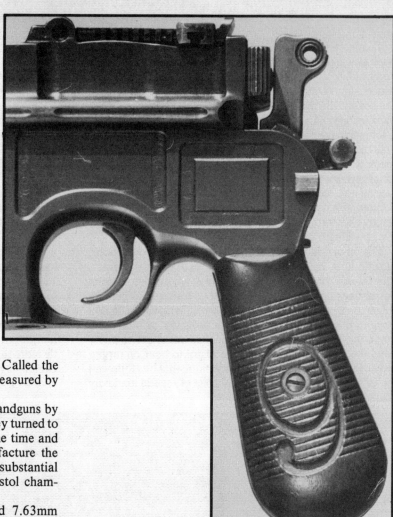

At various times during Germany's turbulent history, military pistols have been in short supply and one expedient involved chambering the Broomhandle Mauser in 9mmP. Such guns were distinctively identified by a red figure 9, carved on both sides of the handle and filled in with red paint. The common term for such pistol is Red Nine Broomhandle.

version of one of its pocket pistols in 9mmP. Called the Model 6, few were made and examples are treasured by collectors.

When the German army was pressed for handguns by the demands of the trench fighting in WWI, they turned to the Mauser company. Rather than going to the time and expense of having Mauser tool up to manufacture the Luger, in 1915 it was decided instead to place a substantial contract for the standard Mauser M1912 pistol chambered for the 9mm Parabellum cartridge.

Normally chambered for the bottlenecked 7.63mm Mauser cartridge, the M1912 was just an updated version of the M1896 Mauser, commonly called the Mauser Broomhandle in the U.S. Minor modifications to the magazine, and of course to the barrel, were all that were necessary to convert the Mauser design to handle the 9mm Parabellum cartridge. It sported a 5½-inch barrel and a tangent rear sight graduated from fifty to five hundred meters and a slot to take a combination shoulder stock/holster. It is commonly called the Model 1916. Production ceased with the end of the war in 1918, with a total production of about 150,000 pieces.

Since some standard 7.63mm Mausers had been pressed into service or personally purchased for use by individuals, it was necessary to mark the M1916 prominently to show its 9mm chambering. This was done by carving a conspicuous figure nine in each grip and staining the carving red. From these features, collectors commonly refer to this model as the "Red Nine" Broomhandle.

The Red Nine was actually simpler, more reliable, and more rugged than the Luger it supplemented. On the other hand, it is considerably larger and somewhat more awkward to handle. The Mauser uses a ten-shot fixed magazine, loaded by means of ten-shot stripper clips. Though not as handy as a detachable magazine, a trained operator can reload a Mauser quickly. I've never found the Mauser to be particularly accurate, though they are far from inaccurate.

One of the main problems for fine accuracy is the long,

jarring hammer fall and the barleycorn sights. Like the Artillery Luger, thoroughly respectable work can be done with the Mauser out to two hundred meters or so, particularly with a shoulder stock attached.

Although not nearly as common as the 7.63mm Mausers, the 9mm M1916 Broomhandles are not exactly rare either. However, demand for them is high from collectors, as are prices for good specimens.

Up to the 1950s, the Mauser Broomhandle in 7.63mm was the most popular handgun in China, from which large quantities of Mausers have recently been imported. Many suffer from bad bores as a result of corrosive ammunition and neglect. The importer is offering these rebuilt with all parts inspected and replaced where necessary, all new springs, and the barrel relined to either 9mm Parabellum or 7.63 Mauser. These are offered at a price of one-third to one-half of that of a more collectible all-original Red Nine Mauser. If you are interested in such a shooting Mauser Broomhandle in 9mm Parabellum, drop the importer a line at Antique Arms Arsenal Sporting Goods Export, P.O. Box 948, Rutherfordton, N.C. 28139. They also offer a full line of parts and accessories, as well as reconditioning services for customer-owned guns.

There is no question that the Mauser Broomhandle has a deadly charismatic look about it that offers a great deal of appeal to many people. The Red Nine variation has even more appeal, because it uses readily-available ammunition. It also doesn't hurt that Mausers are well made and finished.

One of the better handguns of WWI, the Steyr M12 was originally chambered for the powerful 9mm Steyr cartridge. It was also called the Steyr-Hahn (hammer Steyr) to differentiate it from an earlier hammerless Steyr pistol. It was the official pistol of the Austro-Hungarian and Romanian armies in WWI, as well as the army of Chile.

When the Austrian army was assimilated into the German *Wehrmacht* in 1938, it was decided to rebarrel the M12 to 9mm Parabellum rather than issue the Austrians Lugers or to try to cope with the non-standard 9mm Steyr cartridge in the supply system. The Austrians got the better of the deal since the M12 is considerably simpler, more robust, and reliable than the Luger. Since the two cartridges differ primarily only in that the 9mm Steyr is longer, it made for a simple and effective conversion.

Approximately 250,000 M12 Steyrs were converted to 9mm Parabellum and these were stamped '08 or P'08 on the left side to signify the conversion. Only manufactured from 1911 through 1918, the M12 Steyr is, without exception, beautifully made of first-class materials. Like the Mauser, it uses a fixed magazine fed by a stripper clip. In this case, the stripper clip holds eight rounds and the magazine is housed in the pistol grip as in most auto pistols. The Steyr uses a clever rotating barrel system to lock the slide to the barrel during firing. They are generally quite accurate and reliable with round nosed ammunition. Stubbier hollow point ammunition won't always feed reliably from the already-too-long magazine.

One design flaw that has showed up on several M12s I've inspected is that the safety often develops enough play that, if engaged and the trigger is pulled it will not fire, but when the safety is subsequently disengaged, it will fire without touching the trigger. Called tolerance stack-up by gunsmiths, the same thing can happen with the Colt M1911 if the sear or hammer is modified excessively during a trigger job. The M12 seems to be chronically susceptible to this problem, however. The grip is too perpendicular to the barrel for natural pointing, but it is otherwise a most commendable handgun. The 9mm Parabellum M12 is popular with collectors and shooters but be aware that there are individuals out there who convert 9mm Steyr M12s to 9mm Parabellum complete with Nazi markings.

Between WWI and WWII there was little activity in developing 9mm Parabellum pistols until the mid-1930s. Finland decided to replace its 7.65mm Luger pistols with a more modern 9mm. A talented native Finnish arms designer, Aimo Lahti, designed a pistol that was adopted by Finland in 1935 as the L35 and by Sweden in 1940 as the M40. Interestingly, only a year earlier, Sweden had adopted the Walther P'38 as the M39 but subsequently decided, in the interest of neutrality, to go with a Scandinavian design. The L35 is exceptionally robust, well made and finished.

The M40 Swedish Lahti, more common in the U.S., has a much rougher finish. The Lahti is an interesting design although unnecessarily heavy and complicated. It uses a vertically-cammed block to lock the bolt to the barrel extension. Unique among pistols, it uses a bolt accelerator as typically found on several recoil-operated machine guns, to insure reliable operation, even under sub-zero conditions. In addition, the design is well sealed against the entrance of dirt. As a result, it has an excellent reputation for reliability and durability in adverse conditions, particularly in the extremely cold environment of the Scandinavian winter.

The Lahtis are styled much like the Luger in profile. As a result, they share the Luger's characteristics of muzzle-lightness and a tendency to point high. While field strip-

The Finnish Lahti resembles the Luger in general profile, although not in operating design. Swedish version of the Lahti, shown here, has rougher finish.

ping is simple, detail stripping will generally require a trained armorer with special tools. On the other hand, the components are so robust and well made that breakage or excess wear requiring detail stripping is highly unlikely. In operation the safety is awkward, as is the magazine release. The Finnish version is less blocky and a bit more comfortable to the hand than its Swedish counterpart. Due to the small quantities available and the better finish of the Finnish version, they will bring about double the price of the Swedish Lahti. Interestingly, both are still in regular service in both countries. If they are waiting for them to wear out they will wait a long time!

The year 1935 was definitely a peak year for 9mm pistols. Besides the aforementioned Lahti there was the Browning Hi-Power and the now obsolete but still excellent Polish Radom. Also called the VIS after the initials of the designers, the Radom has the same general size and external configuration of our own M1911A1 .45. However, it incorporates a number of innovations found on the Browning Hi-Powers. These include use of a cam lock instead of a swinging link, doing away with the barrel bushing and recoil spring plug, and the use of a recoil spring guide. Retained from the M1911 were the single-column magazine and grip safety as well as the slide and magazine releases common to both pistols. Located in the M1911 safety position is, instead, a hold-open lever used in field stripping.

Unique to the Radom is a hammer-dropping device located on the slide. Pushing down on this device when the hammer is cocked interposes a solid block between the hammer and firing pin, then releases the hammer, allowing it to fall to the forward position. The Radom has no safety in the normal sense other than the grip safety. Radoms made before the Nazi occupation of Poland are among the best fitted and finished military handguns ever made. The Nazi occupiers knew a good thing when they saw it and kept the Radom pistol line in production until the end of WWII.

Quality of manufacture dropped steadily to the point where the last Radoms made were downright crude, the takedown hold-open lever was deleted, roll pins used instead of solid pins, and other manufacturing short cuts taken. There was a great deal of Polish sabotage undertaken, so care must be taken with Nazi-marked guns, particularly the cruder late specimens. Regardless, the Radom was one of the best of the Pre-WWII 9mms. Because of its substantial size and weight, it is extremely comfortable to shoot. In general, they share the robust reliability of the Browning and Colt models. Accuracy will depend largely upon the tightness of fit of the barrel and the slide, which can vary from superb to awful, depending upon the vintage of the piece. Pre-Nazi specimens bring prices approaching triple that of Nazi-marked specimens and are treasured by collectors and handgun connoisseurs.

In 1938, the German army adopted a variation of the Walther HP as the P'38. Indications are that actual

The Model 1935 Browning Hi-Power has been used by many military services, thanks in part to its capacious magazine. Most of these were made by Fabrique Nationale d'Armes de Guerre in the Belgian city of Herstal, as was this one.

Likewise introduced in 1935, the Polish Radom combined features of both the Browning Hi-Power and Colt M1911, adding a few other design features found in neither.

military production was not accomplished till late 1939 or 1940. Though the P'38 is still very much in service in Germany (called P1), Austria, Norway and a number of other countries, it has entered the world of obsolescent 9mms. Production has virtually stopped, to make way for Walther's newer designs. Interestingly, the P'38 series was not the first double-action 9mm fielded by Walther.

Making the same mistake as they had done in WWI, Walther attempted to come up with a 9mm based on one of their blowback pocket pistols, in this case the PP. The 9mm Parabellum version was called the MP and, like its WWI brother, it was unsuccessful and is quite a rarity. The exceptionally successful P'38 was, on the other hand, one of the premier handguns of WWII. It brought the double-action mechanism to the world of locked-breech service pistols. Such a double-action mechanism allows the hammer to be forward with a round in the chamber, yet it still can be fired by a long pull of trigger, without the necessity of cocking or disengaging a safety. The merits of such a mechanism are often debated; however suffice to say it is a popular feature that has become all but mandatory on modern semiauto pistol designs. After the first shot, all shots following are fired from a cocked hammer position.

The safety is mounted on the slide and serves the dual purpose as a hammer dropping device, much like the one on the Radom. Unlike the Radom, however, there have been a number of well-documented instances of WWII specimens of the P'38 pistol firing when the safety was engaged with the hammer at full cock as a result of parts failure. I highly recommend that the hammer be lowered slowly with the thumb when the safety is engaged. The P'38 suffers from a butt release magazine catch, but is otherwise a considerably better service pistol than the Luger. It is quite reliable and robust. About the only thing that ever breaks is the extractor or the stamped slide cover. Most will not feed hollow points very well, but some do. Accuracy runs from good to excellent. Early pistols — 1941 and earlier — are beautifully fitted and finished.

As the war progressed, the fit and external finish got rougher. Manufacture was by Walther, Mauser, and Spreewerke. The last is the roughest and the Walther the

best, with the Mauser examples in between. In the post-WWII period, it has been manufactured by the relocated and reorganized Carl Walther Company, as well as Steyr in Austria for the Austrian Army. A few have also recently surfaced with French Manurhin markings. All WWII specimens have steel frames while all post-war versions have aluminum alloy frames. Total production is in the millions with plenty of variations for collectors. The commoner varieties, particularly recent German police releases, can be purchased at quite reasonable prices. New P'38s are still available from Interarms, Number Ten Prince Street, Alexandria, Virginia 22313; the current importers of Walthers. They also have a quantity of WWII-vintage P'38s on hand.

Largely because of the demands of WWII, the three major Spanish handgun manufacturers (Astra, Star and Llama) converted their 9mm Largo pistols to handle the 9mm Parabellum cartridge. The Llama offering was a part-for-part copy of the M1911A1 Colt. A version of it is still in production today and it is available from Stoeger Arms, the importer. Star's offering, the Model B, is similar to the M1911A1 in looks and operation but differs in number of internal features, including a pivoting trigger and no grip safety.

The Star B lives on today in a more compact version: the Star BM imported by Interarms. Astra fielded the M600, a slightly downsized version of its M400, which in turn is little more than an enlarged version of the Browning M1910 pocket pistol. The M600 is notable in that it is the only successful blowback 9mm Parabellum ever fielded. I have always found the Stars and Astras to be very well made with excellent fit and finish.

The Spanish Star copied the general lines and design of the Colt M1911; chambered for 9mmP, it omitted grip safety.

The Llamas, while appearing well made, often have excessively soft parts. All three were used to some extent by the Nazis as substitute handguns and can be found with Nazi acceptance markings. During the Post-WWII period, Astra fielded an improved M600 called the Condor. It differs mainly in having an external hammer and an improved grip. Examples are rarely encountered.

Llama also fielded the Model XI 9mm that resembled the Star Model B more than its regular model. It was notable only for a poor grip and the tendency for the hammer to chew up the shooter's hand. Star also introduced their Modelo Super. It appeared to be virtually identical to the Model B externally, but it featured a number of unique design features. These included a quick-takedown latch, a cam-locking barrel instead of a swinging link and a magazine safety. The Modelo Super has been discontinued for some time and examples are uncommon in the U.S., although it is a superb pistol.

The French brought out the MAC 1950 after WWII to replace their pipsqueak 7.65 Long MAC 1935s. Apart from an increase in size and caliber, the MAC 1950 is otherwise identical to the MAC 1935 which is, in turn, a spinoff of the Browning M1911 design. Still in French service, but long out of production, most MAC 1950s encountered were brought back from Vietnam. A year later, the Italians fielded the now-obsolescent M1951 9mm

The Tokagypt was a Hungarian attempt to market a 9mmP version of the 7.62mm Tokarev Model TT33. Differences are in barrel, barrel bushing, magazine, grips and thumb safety.

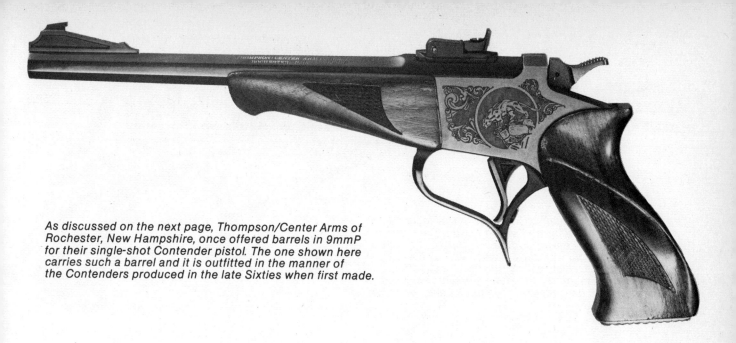

As discussed on the next page, Thompson/Center Arms of Rochester, New Hampshire, once offered barrels in 9mmP for their single-shot Contender pistol. The one shown here carries such a barrel and it is outfitted in the manner of the Contenders produced in the late Sixties when first made.

Beretta. It was sold in the U.S. as the Beretta Brigadier. It featured the classic Beretta cutaway slide look, a superb grip, a P'38-type locking system and excellent manufacture. Often they are superbly accurate. Adopted by Israel and Egypt as well as Italy, the M1951 is no longer in production in Italy, although it still may be in production in Egypt. The only poor features on the Beretta are an awkward safety and magazine release.

About the time Egypt adopted the Beretta, Hungary tried to interest them in a 9mm version of the Soviet Tokarev pistol. Called the Tokagypt 58, they are similar to the 7.62mm Russian Tokarev except for the caliber, a P'38-like grip and the addition of a thumb safety. Yugoslavia also offered a 9mm Tokarev on the world market, but it is rarely seen in the U.S.

Several 9mms have been around for a long time, but they really cannot be considered obsolescent because they are still in production and service. Most significant of these is the Browning Hi-Power of 1935 vintage. Variations of the Browning are common on the surplus military market, including even Canadian-made specimens from China and Argentinian-made specimens. All are excellent. The SIG P210 is of a somewhat outmoded design first introduced in 1947, but it refuses to go out of production. It is superbly made and even surplus specimens bring substantial prices.

That, in a nutshell, is a fairly complete picture of the obsolete and obsolescent 9mm Parabellum handguns. Extracting out all the rarely encountered specimens leaves us with only nine or ten 9mms, which isn't many, compared to the huge numbers on today's market. Few offer features such as a large magazine capacity or a double-action trigger, but many are quite serviceable in their own right, not to mention collectible. All represent a bit of history that deserves to be remembered. — *Chuck Karwan*

Here are the barrel markings on the T/CC shown at the top of the page. This is the commoner ten-inch barrel, although they once were offered in 8¾-inch lengths, later dropped as option.

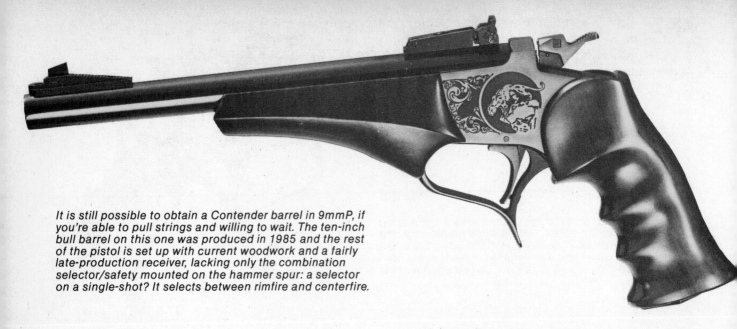

It is still possible to obtain a Contender barrel in 9mmP, if you're able to pull strings and willing to wait. The ten-inch bull barrel on this one was produced in 1985 and the rest of the pistol is set up with current woodwork and a fairly late-production receiver, lacking only the combination selector/safety mounted on the hammer spur: a selector on a single-shot? It selects between rimfire and centerfire.

A Footnote...

Friend Karwan omits mention of at least one further 9mm handgun that, by his stated standard, falls into the obsolescent category: The Thompson/Center *Contender*. This is a single-shot pistol for which interchangeable barrels are offered in a broad variety of different calibers, both rimfire and centerfire.

According to Tim Pancurak at the T/C plant, the 9mmP Contender barrel was added to the offering of barrels in 1969 and dropped in 1978. Information as to the number

of 9mmP Contender barrels produced over the nine-year interval is unavailable, as no records were kept of barrel production by caliber in those days.

Scanning back through the collection of T/C catalogs, it appears that Catalog #4 — dating from 1977 — carried the largest assortment of calibers for Contender barrels. Included were such exotics as the 5mm Remington rimfire, .22 K-Hornet, .22 Remington Jet, .218 Bee, .25-35 WCF, .30 M-1 Carbine, .38 Super, .38 Special, .357/44 Bain & David and .45 ACP. The #5 catalog, dated January 1, 1978, dropped the 9mmP, along with the .30 M-1 Carbine and .357/44 Bain & Davis. Added in #5 were the .35 Remington and .41 magnum.

Virtually all of the 9mmP Contender barrels were produced in the original, octagonal barrels and these were offered in a choice of 8¾- or 10-inch lengths. The 8¾-inch barrels apparently did not prove overly popular with Contender fans, for they were dropped fairly early. T/C Catalog #1 does not seem to carry a date of publication, but it must have appeared about 1974 or soon thereafter because it lists the ten-inch bull barrel for the .30 Herrett and I recall shooting a Texas hog with Steve Herrett's prototype in early 1973.

Speaking about the Contender calibers with Warren Center, designer of the pistol, he recalled that suggestions came thick and fast for additional chamberings after the introduction of the gun in 1967. "Everybody said we should offer it in cartridges such as the 9mm, .38 Super and .30 Carbine. When we put those in the catalog, not many were ever sold. Finally we dropped them because the sales did not warrant the expense of keeping them in the catalog."

The 9mm Winchester magnum, at right here, with a 9mmP, was developed for the somewhat stillborn Wildey auto and has not gotten far off the ground insofar as acceptance.

If you'll look closely, the old Contender at the top carries the bit of scrollwork behind the crouching puma, dropped in late Sixties. Compare it to the receiver of the lower Contender.

When the 9mm and .45 Winchester magnum cartridges appeared, initially designed for an auto pistol that never got very far off the ground, T/C added the .45 Win mag to their offering of Contender barrels and continues to list it. They never chambered for the 9mm Win mag, however, on the plausible grounds that it would not do anything the present .357 magnum barrel wouldn't do, somewhat better. I can't help but agree with that reasoning.

When they were still available in the early Seventies, I got ten-inch octagonal barrels in both 9mmP and .38 Super. I find I've used both, quite a bit, for things such as testing experimental loads and the like. The 9mmP is gratifyingly accurate, with nearly any load and the recoil is pleasantly moderate, even in the lightweight octagonal barrel.

I got my ten-inch 9mmP bull barrel for the Contender in 1985, but it was a custom operation. Within reasonable limits and safety considerations, Contender barrels can be had for almost any cartridge. When I got the 9mmP bull barrel, it was my intention to re-chamber it to 9mm Win mag for purposes of obtaining load data on that highly exotic, not to say ephemeral cartridge. I have not proceeded on that project to the present, primarily because the data would only be valid for another Contender of the same specifications and there are few of those around; none that I know of. Left in its original 9mmP chambering and fitted with a 3X scope, however, the bull barrel is capable of superb accuracy and, as with the 9mmP revolvers, you never get a crick in your back from policing up the spent cases.

The original 9mmP barrels were acid-etched 9mm, appearing over Luger in uppercase letters. The custom bull barrel is etched simply 9mm. During all the years that the barrels were listed in the T/C catalog, it appeared as, ".9M/M PARABELLUM," complete with the decimal point in front of the 9, making it, in one's imagination, at least, the ultimate smallbore. — *Dean A. Grennell*

CHAPTER 7

REVOLVERS FOR THE 9MM PARABELLUM: AN OVERVIEW

Wherein Wiley Clapp Surveys The Wheelgun Branch Of The 9mm Family

The rimmed cartridge came first. As displayed in a modern .41 magnum revolver, the rimmed case sets up against the rear face of the cylinder, where the rim positions it for correct fit in the chamber.

THE FIRST really successful metallic cartridge handguns were revolvers. It necessarily follows that the first successful handgun cartridges were typical rimmed revolver cartridges, either rimfire or center-fire. A cursory look at a revolver will give you an appreciation of why the rimmed cartridge mates with the revolver mechanism.

In a revolver, there are a number of firing chambers in the cylinder, as few as four and sometimes as many as nine, but most commonly six. Those firing chambers must be open to the rear, in order that the chambers may be manually loaded from the rear, and so that the loaded cylinder can turn on its axis. The easiest way for the cartridges to be positioned in their individual chambers is to give each of them a big fat rim, or *flange* as the British call it, which is shaped a good bit wider than the body of the cartridge. A cartridge is loaded into each chamber, stops when the integral rim contacts the rear face of the cylinder, and the

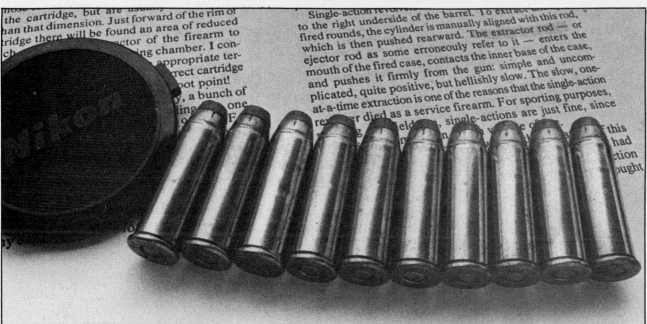

The implications of cartridge case shape are plain in these photos. Above: Rimmed cases curve when aligned as in a magazine. Right: Rimless 9mmPs are shaped to stack.

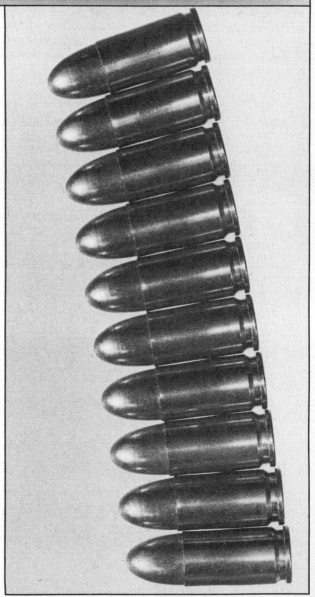

cylinder can turn to align each chamber successively with the barrel for firing. Everything should be pretty clear and straightforward up to this point, right?

As a matter of fact, it could be said that the design of the revolver dictated the shape of cartridges for the first few years of the life of the metallics. It is true that rifle development was running neck and neck with contemporary wheelguns, but rifles of the 1870s and 1880s were either single shots or repeaters equipped with tubular magazines. And the tubular magazine, which stacked cartridges end-to-end, worked quite well with the rimmed design. The cartridges with rims were also relatively easy to manufacture. All cartridges came to have those convenient rims which facilitated extraction and headspacing — there was just no need to do it any other way.

Then, on towards the end of the century, a couple of different clever fellows started fooling with new types of mechanisms that used space in the design of firearms a bit differently. Among other things, their designs called for stacking the cartridges one atop the other, and feeding them into position for chambering with a spring. In most of the handguns which concern us in this volume, this system of feeding evolved into self contained, spring-and-follower-equipped, sheet metal boxes called magazines. It was obvious right from the start that the cartridge was going to have to be shaped a bit differently, in order to work in these magazines.

The adjacent pictures tell the story pretty clearly. If you try to stack several typical rimmed cartridges, the stack curves because the rims interfere with the bodies of the cartridges snuggling up against one another. In an auto pistol magazine, this will almost invariably mean an interference in the feeding cycle — a jam. The rim, so valuable in the wheelguns and tubular magazine repeaters, was plainly in the damned way when it came to autos!

The turn of the century innovations in small arms design were automatic pistols and several types of bolt action rifles. They chambered and worked beautifully with new cartridges which featured a design that we have come to term, incorrectly I think, *rimless*.

Rimless, as it applies to auto pistol cartridges, is an erroneous term because these rounds most assuredly do have rims. Those rims are not of a greater diameter than the body of the cartridge, but are usually the same or slightly less than that dimension. Just forward of the rim of a rimless cartridge there will be found an area of reduced diameter which enables the extractor of the firearm to catch the round and pull it from the firing chamber. I confess to an inability to come up with more appropriate terminology than *rimless* — but if you use the correct cartridge in the each gun, everything will work out. Moot point!

In the first couple of decades of this century, a bunch of rimless cartridges became common, including the one which gets our attention in these pages, the 9mmP. For each cartridge, there were one or more appropriately chambered firearms. In every case where a handgun was concerned, rimless went into an auto pistol and rimmed worked in the wheelgun. That is, until 1917.

Unusual photo illustrates rimless shape. Without that projecting rim, a .45 round can be dropped into Ruger cylinder backwards. The rim is not larger than body.

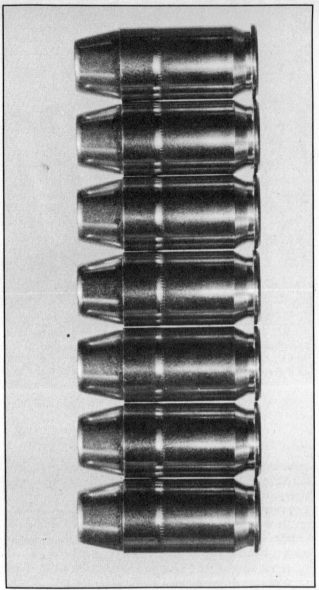

Seven .45 ACPs are aligned as in a magazine. This old auto pistol round can work successfully in revolvers.

The U.S. Army had adopted the Colt .45 automatic in 1911, but production had not caught up to demand at the time that the army exploded in size for the unpleasantness 'cross the pond — World War I. There was an immediate need for large numbers of handguns, and the service automatic could not be produced rapidly enough. Naturally, revolvers were available from both Colt and Smith & Wesson, but the army wanted to standardize on the .45 ACP cartridge. Could the existing revolver designs be modified to accept the rimless .45 cartridge? Sure, no problem.

Some unknown and unheralded designer type at one of the factories came up with the device that we now call the half-moon clip. This was a thin, sheet metal, semi-circle with three .45-size bites cut from its straight inner side. A trio of .45 rounds could be rolled into these notches, form-

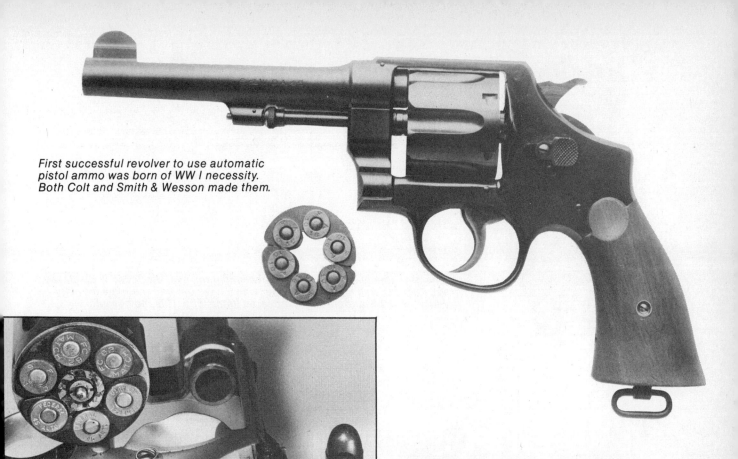

First successful revolver to use automatic pistol ammo was born of WW I necessity. Both Colt and Smith & Wesson made them.

Half-moon clips make it work. Pictured cylinder above has six rounds in a pair of clips, all ready to fire. The system made extraction of rimless ammo practical, and also served as a form of speedloader. Right: This is how you can shoot without clips. Pick out empties.

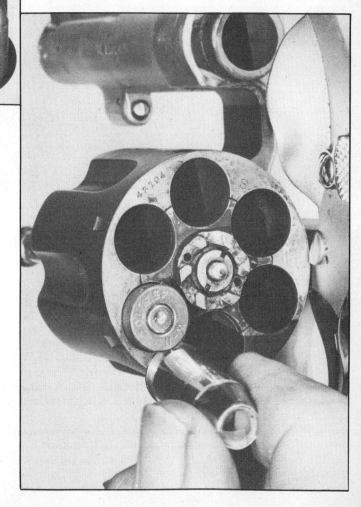

ing a single unit which was spaced so that the unit dropped easily into the cylinder of a 1917 revolver from Smith & Wesson or Colt. When you opened the cylinder and stroked the extractor rod, the star caught the underside of the half-moon clips and dumped the whole works out of the gun. It works so well that the system is still in use in the Smith & Wesson Model 25 revolver.

In a pinch, you could fire those old 1917s *without* the half-moon clip. Each chamber did have a headspacing shoulder, which effectively prevented the cartridges from entering too deeply and ending up out of reach of the firing pin. Used this way, the extractor missed the rims when the rod was depressed, forcing the shooter to use a nail or dowel to punch cartridges from the front of the cylinder. It was an eminently practical system, and buried in the back pages of the Smith & Wesson catalog, you can still find half-moon clips listed as an accessory. Most importantly, it got a lot of doughboys armed for the first big one.

One of the most commercially successful guns ever produced is displayed. Bill Ruger is well known today, but was a newcomer to the arms industry when the .22 Standard Auto appeared in the '50s. This the new MkII.

Spring-loaded single-action extractor at work. The system eases wheelgun's use of 9mmP.

With the single exception of the 1917 revolvers, no other effort is recorded by which any other truly successful wheelgun was adapted to a rimless auto pistol cartridge. There were a couple of unusual designs, like the Webley-Fosbery .38 auto revolver, and an Israeli-modified S&W revolver for the 9mmP cartridge, but no wheelgun firing an automatic cartridge came into common use. That is, until firearms and marketing genius William B. Ruger happened on the scene.

Bill Ruger, with his partner Alexander Sturm, started a small firearms manufacturing concern in the period following World War II. Their first offering was an enthusiastically received .22 auto pistol that sold for the princely sum of $37.50, a price that held for better than a decade.

When the westerns hit the TV tube in the '50s, Ruger marketed an updated Colt SAA look-alike featuring improved springs and lockwork, and .22 chambering. The gun caught on wildly, and ultimately forced Colt back into the single-action business. Ruger beefed up the main frame of their Single-Six, and offered it in .357 magnum. In short order, the Ruger Blackhawk was everywhere, and in calibers other than the original .357 magnum. The western single-action design is a rugged and simple one, easy to modify for just about any handgun cartridge, and some of the shorter rifle ones.

As we have seen thus far in this treatise, the basic difficulty in chambering a revolver for an auto pistol round lies in difficulty in extracting the fired cartridges. The rim-

This is Ruger's latest version of his updated SAA design. In the '60s, a version of this revolver in .357 magnum was adapted to the 9mmP round.

Ruger pioneered the use of two-cylinder revolvers. Shown here as .45 ACP and .45 Colt, it could also be 9mmP and .357 mag.

less rounds tend to drop beyond the reach of firing pins, and more significantly, double-action revolvers have extractors that miss the rimless cases. But if your wheelgun is a typical single-action "cowboy" type, you have the most positive extraction system ever devised for a firearm.

Single-action revolvers have a spring-loaded rod attached to the right underside of the barrel. To extract and eject fired rounds, the cylinder is manually aligned with this rod, which is then pushed rearward. The extractor rod — or ejector rod as some erroneouly refer to it — enters the mouth of the fired case, contacts the inner base of the case, and pushes it firmly from the gun: simple and uncomplicated, quite positive, but hellishly slow. The slow, one-at-a-time extraction is one of the reasons that the single-action revolver died as a service firearm. For sporting purposes, plinking and field use, single-actions are just fine, since there is no premium on a high volume of fire.

The people at Ruger were aware of the versatility of this

extraction system, and were probably aware that Colt had built a few pre-war specimens of the original Single Action Army revolver for the .45 ACP cartridge. As Ruger sought to broaden the appeal of their line of firearms in the '60s, they considered the popularity and availability of different cartridges. Two auto pistol rounds jumped out at them right away. The .45 ACP shared a common bore size with the .45 Colt cartridge, and Ruger began to offer a Blackhawk with a fitted cylinder for each of the two cartridges. For our purposes, the second cartridge is the more interesting. There's no surprises coming — it's the 9mmP!

The common bore size of 9mmP handguns is .355-inch, sometimes .356-inch. That's almighty close to the .357-inch of the .357 magnum. Ruger began to produce their versatile Blackhawk revolver with both .357 and 9mmP cylinders. The earliest reference to this revolver that I can find is in the catalog section of the 1968 edition of the *Gun Digest.* The gun is reviewed by the late George Nonte in

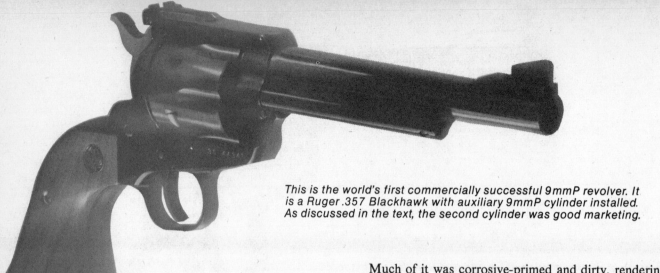

This is the world's first commercially successful 9mmP revolver. It is a Ruger .357 Blackhawk with auxiliary 9mmP cylinder installed. As discussed in the text, the second cylinder was good marketing.

the 1969 edition of the same annual publication.

At first blush, it seems an unlikely marriage of gun and cartridge. The massive cylinder of a firearm type that dates back to the last century housing a cartridge that was designed purely and simply to function through the abruptly angled magazine of a Luger pistol? Why not? It worked like a charm and the guns sold well. You could even send your old .357 Blackhawk back to Ruger and get a new 9mmP cylinder fitted for sixteen bucks. Whether you had the old gun retrofitted or bought the new type, you ended up with one of the most versatile handguns ever made. As all handgunners are certainly aware, a .357 magnum revolver will comfortably fire all types of .38 Special ammunition.

Much of it was corrosive-primed and dirty, rendering it particularly unsuitable for auto pistols and their attendant feeding problems. Nearly all of it was Berdan-primed, and therefore not reloadable. But hell's bells, it was *cheap!*

I can personally remember venturing down out of the Sierras from the Marine Base at Bridgeport about 1959, to the little village of Reno, Nevada, and finding a gun store selling European 9mmP ammo. They had a great barrel of loose rounds selling for two cents apiece, and that kept the first 9mmP that I ever owned (a pretty decent old P'38) going for a long time; even on a lieutenant's pay!

It was this market that Ruger was seeking when he brought out that first 9mmP revolver. The cheap ammo dried up in the wake of the Gun Control Act of 1968, but the popularity of the 9mmP Blackhawk continues to the present day. The current Ruger Catalog lists the .357 Blackhawk with a spare 9mmP cylinder, in 4⅝-inch and 6½-inch barrel lengths. This gun is one of the best sellers in the Ruger line, which has expanded greatly over the years.

Police and security forces in other countries rely on other guns as backups, but in the United States the cops will most often seek a good scattergun when there's real trouble. Diverter's on this one.

When Ruger added a second cylinder for the 9mmP, versatility took on a new meaning.

In the late '50s and '60s, a number of enterprising importers, principal among them Sam Cummings of Interarms, tapped a market in America that no one could have predicted. They imported literally tons of guns and ammunition from all over the world into the United States, and sold it on the open civilian market. There was some treasure there, as well as some trash, but there were enormous quantities of good, shootable 9mmP ammunition.

In this country, we enjoy a freedom of choice in regards to a great many things that is without precedent in the modern world. One of these areas is the freedom that we have over what, if any, firearms and ammunition that we will be allowed to have. It becomes a bit difficult for us to understand that the choice is so limited in much of the world that a variety of pistol calibers is unknown. Plainly stated, this

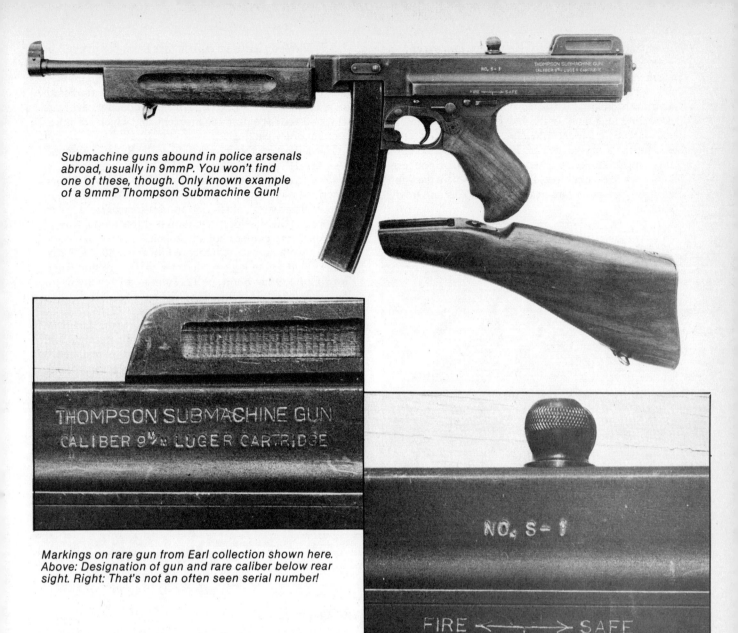

Submachine guns abound in police arsenals abroad, usually in 9mmP. You won't find one of these, though. Only known example of a 9mmP Thompson Submachine Gun!

THOMPSON SUBMACHINE GUN
CALIBER 9ᴹᴹ LUGER CARTRIDGE

NO. S-1

FIRE ← → SAFE

Markings on rare gun from Earl collection shown here. Above: Designation of gun and rare caliber below rear sight. Right: That's not an often seen serial number!

means that for many people in other nations, *pistol* means *9mmP*. For Americans, pistol would probably mean a great many things, because you can walk into any gun shop and find handguns and their ammuntiion in bewildering array.

Despite the efforts of many experts of real and imagined levels of competence to change things, American police are nearly all armed with modern double-action revolvers. In recent times, American cops have clung to their wheelguns almost universally, and have done so in the face of a steady pressure to change. Yeah, I know that the use of auto pistols increases, but for every agency that changes to an auto pistol, usually with fanfare, another agency quietly changes back. The reasons are complex, but really come down to the fact that revolvers are easier to train with, maintain, and use in a fast-developing tactical crisis.

American policemen have had to use their revolvers with sad frequency in recent times, and that use has not been lost on the security forces of the rest of the world. A world, it must be noted, where no high quality double-action revolvers are produced. Unlike mini-trucks, stereos, or champagne, we *own* DA revolver production. It has occurred to other groups that go armed routinely that this revolver that we put such store in might be a pretty fair idea.

The consequence was an interest by a number of foreign governments and police agencies in a modern double-action revolver for their use. The difficulty was that they wanted it in 9mmP.

In America, the policeman's favorite back-up weapon for real emergency conditions is the sawed-off shotgun. It is called a riot gun sometimes, or maybe a police shotgun, but it comes down to a plainly finished, sporting pump shotgun with a factory barrel eighteen or twenty inches long. It's an effective tool — a good choice to augment the revolver when real trouble comes.

The comparable weapon in most of the rest of the world

is a submachine gun. With a few, damned rare exceptions, they are in 9mmP. The use of this ammo in both sidearm and emergency submachine gun has clear advantages. The chief advantage is a single ammunition supply, a consideration which has attracted police and military logisticians for a long time. In the mid-1970s, there seemed to be a market for modern double-action revolvers chambered for the 9mmP cartridge. It must be understood that this is a *world* market, pitched to nations where police and military agencies aren't very far apart and where the 9mmP cartridge is about as rare as a #3 shellholder in Oroville, California.

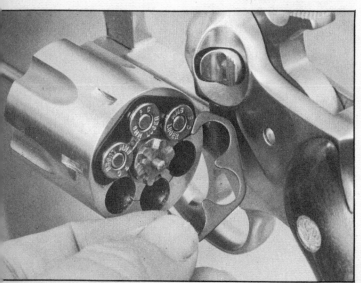

The problem, as we have seen thus far in this chapter, is the difficulty in getting the rimless 9mmP cartridge to extract from a design that favors rimmed cartridges. Colt didn't choose to get in on the act, but both Ruger and Smith & Wesson tried it. Both ended up producing revolvers which solved the extraction problem, and which are still in contemporary catalogs.

The earliest reliable information on the Ruger DA 9mmP is in the 1977 *Gun Digest,* which would have been on dealers' shelves in the summer of 1976. George Nonte described a variation of the reliable Speed-Six design, in blue steel and with both 4-inch and 2¾-inch barrels. It was rumored at the time of production that this model was an overrun from a contract for a European country, and some of them were actually chambered for the .380 ACP cartridge. That's not illogical, since the .380, (or 9mm Kurz, 9mm Corto, 9mm Short, or 9x17mm — all synonyms for the .380) is popular abroad. I don't have reliable dope on this, but the possibilities are interesting.

Those first 9mmP Speed-Sixes available to the American market handled the extraction problem in a different and unique manner. I can't, at this writing, locate a specimen to photograph in order to *picture* how the extractor worked, so you'll just have to put up with *ten thousand words.* (Oh, all right...a few less than that.)

The extractor was manufactured a bit thicker than normal in order that a groove could be cut in the edge of the extractor star. The groove housed a uniquely shaped music wire spring. Shaped somewhat like a six-pointed star, with rather blunt tips, this spring could have each tip depressed inward in sequence. Each tip of the spring projected a short

Above: 9mmP Speed-Six as delivered includes supply of half-moon clips. Above left: Another view of the clip before loading, along with another in gun. Left: Full and third-moon clips from Ranch Products really work.

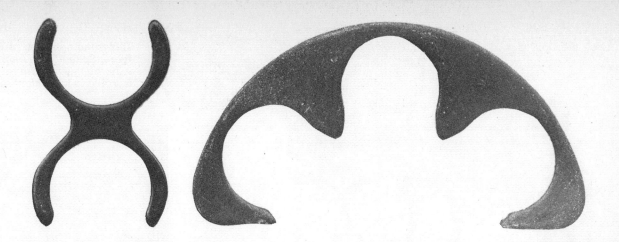

Ruger half-moon clip compared with third-moon variety from Ranch Products. Loaded third-moon type will pack flat in ammo pouch or box. Right: Full-moon clip fits in cylinder as a unit, will be ejected the same way.

distance into a semi-circular cut on the extractor. In use, a 9mmP cartridge was loaded into each chamber and, as it was settled into place past the extractor, a tip of the spring was depressed in toward the central axis of the cylinder. As the cartridge was fully seated in the cylinder, the spring tip popped into the extractor groove of that cartridge. When the revolver was to be unloaded, the extractor was lifted, and each individual cartridge was carried free of each chamber by the spring tip caught in the extractor groove. It was an exceptionally ingenious solution to a knotty problem.

Still, it was a bit fragile and, several years after the gun was introduced, the extractor system was quietly changed. The new extractor, and the one that was on the revolver we test-fired for this book, was no different than the one on contemporary Speed-Six .357s. Ruger just provided a plain brown envelope of ...half-moon clips!

Well, why not? Half-moon clips worked very well on the 1917 Colts and Smith & Wessons and they handily solve the extraction problem. As an added bonus, the half-moon clip acts as a throwaway speedloader when the gun is used in circumstances that demand rapid reloading. The clips supplied with the test gun worked perfectly, but an after-market supplier makes a pair of different versions of cartridge clips that really enhance the versatility of the gun. Ranch Products (Box 145, Malinta, OH 43535) produces third-moon clips that hold a pair of cartridges, and full-moon clips that hold six. We'll talk more about all three versions when we get to the fire-testing portion of the book.

Smith & Wesson was not idle where the 9mmP was concerned during this period. Elsewhere in this book, you can read of the many variations of the basic Model 39 Smith, which was the first domestic 9mmP. In the '60s and

This is a clever device. It makes the Ruger Speed-Six 9mmP more versatile. A sheet metal stamping, made for a few cents, the Ranch Products full-moon clip works!

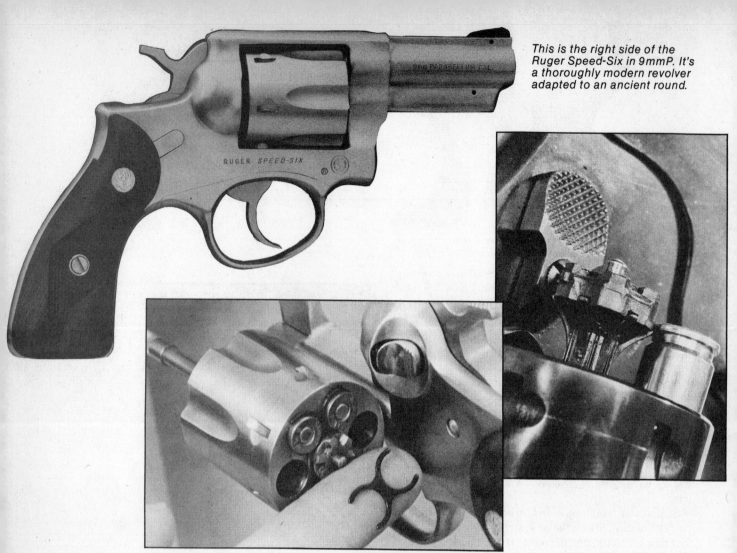

This is the right side of the Ruger Speed-Six in 9mmP. It's a thoroughly modern revolver adapted to an ancient round.

The Ranch Products third-moon clip in use. The clip solves the problem of extracting rimless cartridges. Above right: A different way of handling the problem. S&W developed a completely new extractor system for the Model 547. Fingers on extractor catch the undersides of rims to lift them out of cylinder. They are cammed inwards when rod is released.

'70s, the United States Air Force was experimenting with a number of innovations in small arms with which to arm their military police and air base security troops. They were, as I recall, the first to be armed with the M-16 rifle. At some time during this period, the USAF dropped the .45 ACP almost totally, and went to Smith & Wesson Model 15 revolvers for virtually all personnel who required a sidearm. In the face of a possible NATO-influenced change to the 9mmP round, Air Force designers began to experiment with a variety of conversion systems for their large stock of Model 15s. Some of these were well-chronicled in the firearms press.

In the long run, the design folks at Smith & Wesson attacked the extraction problems attendant to converting the reliable K-frame Military & Police revolver, and all its variants, to a cartridge for which it was never intended. Early on, they discovered a difficult peculiarity of the 9mmP cartridge.

The 9mmP, as we have noted many times, is shaped to feed in auto pistol magazines, and has a good bit more taper to its body than most revolver cartridges. Smith &

Wesson discovered that cartridges of this caliber would sometimes try to back out of their chambers when fired, due to their substantial body taper. In an autoloader that's no problem — there's a breech to hold them in place until pressure drops. But it raises hell in a revolver, which has a cylinder that's open to the rear. The result can be a revolver with its cylinder bound tightly against the recoil shield: no good!

S&W designers tried a few new wrinkles. To discourage cartridge case back-up that hampered cylinder rotation, they added a round, flat-faced pin in the recoil shield of the Model 547. It is driven forward by the hammer, simultaneously as the firing pin is driven forward. The firing pin has a small but adequate projection in the center, surrounded by a larger, flat area that prevents pierced primers. The holding pin puts a slight mark in the case head, near the primer pocket, serving to mark the case as having been fired in the Model 547, but it does no harm from the standpoint of reloading. The system works extremely well in the Model 547 and causes one to speculate upon the possible benefits with other high-energy revolver rounds.

Would a similar approach be helpful for such problem examples as the .22 Jet, the .218 Bee or the .256 Winchester magnum? Hmmmmmm......

Extraction was also handled in the Smith & Wesson DA revolver in a unique way. As the extractor of the Model 547 is raised from the surface of the cylinder, it resembles a flower blooming before your eyes! The shaft on which the extractor star is positioned also houses six petal-like fingers which engage the extractor grooves of six 9mmP cartridges. When you stroke the rod, the "petals" of the extractor flower blossom and carry the fired cases out of the chambers, where they can fall free. It works slick as the devil, making the Model 547 one of the more innovative designs that Smith & Wesson markets in the '80s. The gun is available with fixed sights only, blue steel, and in three-inch round-butt, as well as four-inch square-butt versions.

Is there a need for a 9mmP revolver? In the United States, probably not. But in the rest of the world there may well be such a need. I am not privy to the sales figures on the double-action Rugers and Smiths, but I do note that the 9mmP Ruger Speed-Six has disappeared from the Ruger catalog for 1985. They may be making it for export, or the piece may be dead. In any event, if one of them comes along at a good price, I'd snap it up as an investment. They could be collector's items in the future. The single-action Blackhawk 9mmP/.357 magnum will probably be around for a long time. It offers an inexpensive option to the basic gun when surplus military ammo from abroad is once again importable.

The Smith & Wesson 547 is allegedly selling well in Europe, and will probably persist here, at least for the immediate future.

Revolvers were never intended to fire this stubby little cartridge, but they can be made to do so without major difficulty. They handle the cartridge with relative ease, and provide another interesting chapter in the virtually unending story of 9mmP firearms.

In one way, they are superior to every other 9mmP weapon examined. They do not sling precious, reloadable brass all over the firing line and environs, there to be lost amongst the dandelions or crushed by Grennell's clumsy feet! — *Wiley M. Clapp.*

Both guns date to the same period. The Smith & Wesson M&P was first made around the same time as the Luger. But using the 9mmP round in a revolver is a new idea.

The positioning pin in the recoil shield of the Smith design leaves its signature. Frontier case is marked as shown. The mark is innocuous, case is reloadable.

Arrow points out the pin mounted in the frame of Model 547 which prevents cartridge setback. That's the firing pin next to it. Details in text.

This S&W Model 547 is dressed with wood factory grips. Professionals often choose the Pachmyar rubber grip as replacement. There's an example on 547 at top of page.

Chuck Karwan's Thoughts And Comments On His Ruger, How Much He Likes It And Why

Handgun authority Chuck Karwan favors the stainless Steel Ruger Speed-Six in the unusual 9mmP chambering. Choice is based on detailed evaluation of the gun itself as well as careful consideration of the diverse variety of available ammunition.

SO OFTEN when I sing the praises of my Ruger Speed-Six revolver in 9mm, the response is one of skepticism. Most gun people, who seem to be conservative by nature anyway, feel that the 9mm Parabellum cartridge is for auto pistols only and if you want a revolver you are better off with a revolver cartridge like .38 Special or .357 magnum. Though I have a high esteem for the various rimmed revolver cartridges, I've found that the rimless 9mm Parabellum, in many cases, actually makes a better revolver cartridge than its counterparts, particularly in the Ruger series of double-action revolvers. Longtime friends and readers that know my affection for the Colt .45 Automatic must think I've gone bonkers to recommend a 9mm for anything, let alone a 9mm *revolver,* but let me assure you my reasons are well thought out.

I've owned and used my Ruger Speed-Six 9mm for about four years. In that time it has become one of my favorite handguns. The reason centers around two factors. The first is the sheer excellence of the Ruger revolver design. The second is the considerable advantages the 9mm cartridge offers in a revolver of this type. Unfortunately, these advantages go largely unnoticed by the shooting public.

First, a bit about the Ruger revolver itself: My specimen is the stainless steel Speed-Six 9mm with a 2¾-inch barrel. The Speed-Six is characterized by fixed sights and a smaller round butt as opposed to the square butt of its other Ruger brethren, the Security-Six and the Service-Six. It also sports the optional Ruger factory spurless hammer, and Pachmayr compact grips. The latter are also available as an option or accessory from Ruger complete with Ruger

It's not a common marking, at least on revolvers, but Ruger makes one and spells out the designation fully.

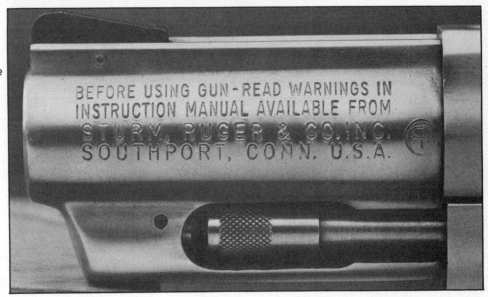

Alaskans have a standing joke that says you can spend most of an Arctic night reading a Ruger. Ruger will send you a manual if you lose your copy.

medallions. The Ruger double-action revolvers are unique in that they are readily disassembled with nothing more than a screwdriver to remove the grip screw and a pin to trap the mainspring. The latter is supplied under the factory grip and the factory grip screw can be removed with a cartridge rim. There is no side plate and the action is quite simple and rugged. Indeed, the Ruger is the least likely of any of the double-action revolvers I've worked with to go out of time. Combine this excellent rugged design with the corrosion resistance of stainless steel and you have one of the most foolproof and reliable revolvers ever made. The addition of the factory optional spurless hammer also makes the Speed-Six one of the easiest revolvers to slide in or out of a pocket, or to draw from concealment under a jacket, as it is devoid of sharp projections to snag on clothing. All the above is also true if you buy the Speed-Six in

.38 Special or .357 magnum, so what is so special about the 9mm specimen? I thought you would never ask!

First let's look at ballistic performance. Obviously the 9mm will not out-perform the .357, but in a revolver, particularly a short-barreled revolver, it will come closer than most people think. It will also consistently out-perform .38 Special +P loads right down the line. When we talk barrel lengths and ballistics between revolvers and auto pistols, we traditionally do a peculiar thing. The barrel on an automatic is measured from the breech face to the muzzle and includes the cartridge chamber, while the barrel of a revolver is measured from the cylinder face to the muzzle and does not include the chamber. This obviously puts the automatic at a disadvantage in a side-by-side comparison and it confuses comparison considerably if the auto cartridge is fired in a revolver. For example, take a look at the enclosed manufacturer's ballistic chart extract. All loads are given as having been fired in a four-inch barrel. In the bullet weight of 95 grains, the 9mm out-performs the .38 +P by 255 fps velocity and 132 fpe. There is no 95-grain .357 load for comparison. In the 110-grain bullet weight the closest 9mm equivalent is 115 grains. As you can see, 9mm out-performs .38 +P by 235 fps velocity and 129 fpe. Interestingly, the 110-grain .357 only beats the 9mm by 40 fps velocity and 37 fpe. In the 125-grain bullet weight, 9mm out-performs the .38 +P by 175 fps and 97 fpe. However the .357 125-grain out-performs the 9mm 125-grain substantially. Clearly, from the above, the 9mm out-performs .38 +P substantially in all bullet weights through 125 grains and stays right with the .357 110-grain.

Things get more interesting when you realize the difference in the way the barrels are measured for 9mm compared to .38 and .357. Taking the Ruger Speed Six 2¾-inch 9mm and measuring from the breech face to the muzzle gives an effective barrel length of 4⅜ inches. Since there is some small pressure loss from the cylinder barrel gap, the Ruger should give performances equal to the 4-inch barrel of the chart or only slightly less. However, a Speed-Six 2¾-inch firing .38 +P or .357 would be expected to give close to 100 fps less velocity than the four-inch barrel of the chart.

Taking that into consideration puts the 9mm way ahead of the .38 +P in all bullet weights and even puts it ahead of, or at least equal to, the 110-grain .357. Though the 125-grain .357 out-performs the 9mm substantially, few would choose it for a defense load in a short-barreled revolver because of its heavy recoil and massive muzzle blast and flash. Thus, in a four-inch or a 2¾-inch revolver such as the Ruger Speed-Six, the 9mm gives the best ballistics without resorting to .357 125-grain or heavier bullet loads.

The 9mm cartridge offers a number of other substantial advantages in a revolver. Since the 9mm Parabellum cartridge is rimless, there is nothing for the revolver's ejector star to push against for ejection. Ruger solved this problem in the same way S&W did when it supplied revolvers in .45 ACP to the Army during WWI with half-moon clips. Each clip holds three 9mm cartridges. Ranch Products has improved on this by offering full-moon clips that hold an entire cylinder full in one package.

Using the Ranch Products full-moon clips, one can load all six chambers in one motion much as one would using a speed loader with .38s or .357s. In the case of the 9mm, there is no button to push or knob to turn and the bullets do not have to be pointed down as is required for most speed loaders. In addition, two 9mm full-moon clips of twelve rounds will fit in the same space in a speed loader pouch as one speed loader full of six .38s. Not only does the 9mm offer advantages in the speed and convenience of loading, it also offers a substantial advantage in ejection.

The 9mm cartridge is considerably shorter than the .38 Special or the .357. Consequently the ejector stroke clears the 9mm cases by a substantial margin. A .38 or .357 in the same revolver *does not* clear the chamber on a full stroke, nor does it in many short-barreled revolvers of other makes. If one requires a fast reload, the 9mm offers a clear advantage in ejecting the empties and in reloading the chambers.

Ranch Products offers another item that can come in handy for a person carrying a 9mm Ruger revolver. These are called third-moon clips and hold two 9mm rounds apiece. These can be used for those circumstances where a person needs to carry his extra ammunition in a flat configuration such as a plainclothes or undercover cop, or a uniform cop required to use belt loops for extra ammunition. Both the third-moon and the full-moon clips by Ranch Products are of extremely high quality blued spring steel and usable over and over again.

In Jack Mitchell's experienced grasp, a Ruger Speed-Six points and handles like a dream. The rounded butt contour is perfect for the shooter's smallish hands. Mitchell, and other combat handgunners, also have come to appreciate the placement of the cylinder latch. It rocks inwards, and is out of the way until the situation demands reloading.

The 9mm Ruger offers one more advantage — which applies primarily to a person traveling abroad, but could come in handy sometime — and that is adaptability to other ammunition. Some brands of .38 S&W or British .380 Revolver will chamber and fire in the Ruger, as will .38 Short Colt. Using half-moon clips, 9mm Glisenti, 9mm Ultra (9x18 mm) and .380 ACP (9x17 mm) will all chamber and fire, although the latter two will swell at the base. Even 9mm Makarov, the soviet pistol cartridge, will chamber, but the bullet is somewhat oversize at .363. None of the above can be recommended by myself, Ruger or the publishers, but is included as an interesting observation.

Functionally, my Ruger Speed-Six 9mm has a crisp 3½-pound single-action pull and a remarkably smooth ten-pound double-action pull. It is untouched and just as it left the factory. Accuracy varies considerably between different brands of ammunition, but the better loads go under three inches at twenty-five yards with some approaching two inches. The only problems encountered were with some old WWII submachine gun ammunition with which I had a few misfires. I'm sure these were no fault of the revolver as I've never had any misfires with modern 9mm ammunition of known quality.

This is one 9mmP handgun that will never have a feeding problem. The shooter displays a handful of cartridges. As discussed in the text, a simple clip will hold six of them in position to be inserted into the revolver's cylinder.

One of author Karwan's perennial pets, the Ruger Speed-Six frequently goes along when he ventures afield. Most commonly, his piece wears rubber stocks for first-rate control.

BALLISTICS TABLE

Caliber	Bullet Wt. (grains)	Muzzle Velocity (fps)	Muzzle Energy (fpe)	Barrel Length
9mm	95	1355	387	4
.38 +P	95	1100	255	4
9mm	115	1255	383	4
.38 +P	110	1020	254	4
.357	110	1295	410	4
9mm	125	1120	345	4
.38 +P	125	945	248	4
.357	125	1450	583	4

All in all, I am quite taken with the Ruger Speed-Six 9mm. It has become my favorite handgun to toss in my kit for defense and protection when I go backpacking or camping. It is an excellent choice for a house gun to be kept loaded for defense purposes. If I were a police chief and required to issue revolvers to my officers, I believe that the Ruger Speed Six 9mm stainless with a four-inch barrel for patrolmen and 2¾-inch barrel for detectives would be nearly ideal.

Ranch Products, P.O. Box 145, Malinta, OH 43535 is the source for the third-moon and half-moon clips. Inquire from them as to the current prices. — *Chuck Karwan*

Smith & Wesson's Model 547 — Further Thoughts And Comments

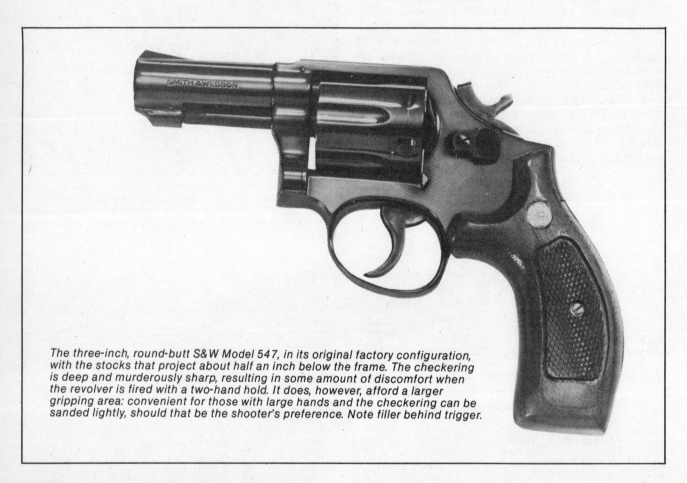

The three-inch, round-butt S&W Model 547, in its original factory configuration, with the stocks that project about half an inch below the frame. The checkering is deep and murderously sharp, resulting in some amount of discomfort when the revolver is fired with a two-hand hold. It does, however, afford a larger gripping area: convenient for those with large hands and the checkering can be sanded lightly, should that be the shooter's preference. Note filler behind trigger.

SO WE'VE HEARD from Wiley Clapp, painting the broad picture of 9mmP revolvers of all sorts; likewise from Chuck Karwan on his personal experiences and impressions of the Ruger 9mmP revolvers. To all of that, I'd like to add my own two cents' worth of notes and comments on the Smith & Wesson Model 547 revolver in 9mmP.

It saddens me to say that I've never had the chance to work with the Ruger 9mmP revolver but, a few years ago, Smith & Wesson loaned me one of their Model 547s, with three-inch barrel and round butt, to write up for GUN WORLD. By the time I'd worked with it long enough to write it up, I had become so deeply and hopelessly enamoured with it that I ended up buying it. Buying all the guns I test and write up in a given year could put a strain on the check stubs of a J. P. Morgan, were that doughty gent still around. I don't buy many of them and, from that, you

may rightfully infer that the Model 547 semi-snubbie impressed me most favorably.

The only modification I've made to my Model 547, to the present, is to replace the set of stocks with which it was supplied. The original set extended about half an inch below the steel of the receiver, which was not the problem. What was the problem was that that particular set was checkered so deeply and sharply that — when fired with my customary two-handed hold — the checkering tended to mill the fingerprints off my left-hand fingertips.

Earlier, I had purchased a 2.5-inch barreled Smith & Wesson Model 19, also with round butt. I'd yearned to own one of those for many years and, as sometimes happens, when the dream comes true, it isn't half as great as anticipated. I ended up sending the Model 19 down to the best custom revolversmith I know: Chuck Ward, in Raymore, Missouri. Ward fitted it with a four-inch Douglas

Premium barrel and added other touches of his unique wizardry. When it came back, I decided that a pair of Bianchi Lightning stocks was what really resonated with it. They shroud the hammer spur quite handily. They feel just great in my hand. They are the only set of rubber stocks I've ever encountered that didn't trigger instinctive nausea at first sight; for one thing, they're brown, not black. I have come to regard the Wardified Model 19 with warm, misty-eyed fondness.

Cap'n Clapp of the Foot Marines — my cohort in the enterprise at hand — refers to the gun as "Grennell's Abortion." Different strokes for different folks, *de gustibus* and all that...

At any rate, tacking back to the primary topic, the left-over stocks from the Model 19, when installed on the Model 547, tickle my fancy far better than the original iron maiden set ever did. In fact, they feel a darned sight better than they did on the original Model 19; they are subtly just-just-right for this particular revolver, in my humble opinion.

There are a great many things I like all to heck and gone about this particular Model 547, now that I have fitting woodwork on it. The trigger is smooth-surfaced on the front and only .3040-inch in width. In my book, that's a righteous and proper trigger to put on a double-action revolver. It is superbly well adapted for DA firing and it suffers no handicap at all for single-acton work.

The hammer spur is pleasantly vestigial and unobtrusive. I really wouldn't mind if it were absent, altogether. The action has that utterly incomparable, silky-slick, uniquely Smith & Wesson double-action pull, than which nothing has ever been whicher. Given an action such as this, I feel, it's a downright insult to the designer to cock the hammer in the first place. Milking the trigger DA, with a two-handed hold, the sight picture remains as motionless as Gibraltar on a windless day.

The barrel is — not in the Wall Street context — rather bullish, measuring .7947-inch, side-to-side just ahead of the receiver and .7760-inch at the muzzle. That figures out to a thickness of barrel wall on the rough order of .2105-inch: more than ample for any need.

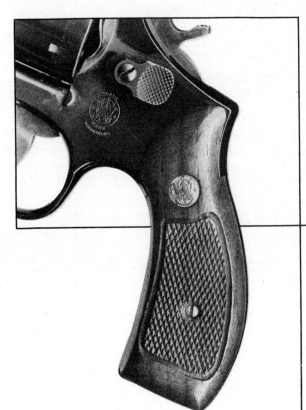

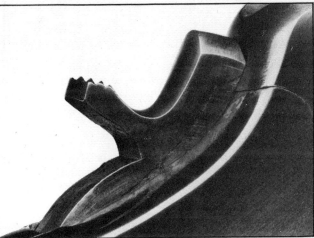

Above left, I installed these stocks from a round-butt M19 S&W on my M547 and have come to like them quite well. Above, hammer spur is rather short and the same width as the hammer, itself. Left, the trigger is fairly narrow and the front surface is smooth; ideal for double-action.

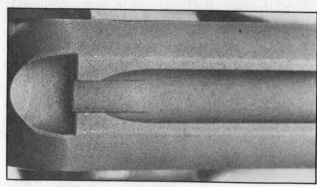

Upper surface of receiver and barrel rib have been glass-beaded to kill glare and reflections. Rear sight is fixed: a square notch milled into the upper rear of the receiver.

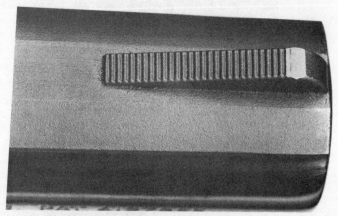

Left, as discussed in the text, the barrel of the Model 547 has a generous amount of metal around the muzzle. Here you can see the distinctive S&W-type rifling, with lands and grooves of equal width, five of each, so that a land is always opposite a groove. Right, front sight of the Model 547 is matted and snag-proof in contours.

John D. Ellison — a friend, correspondent and fellow handgun buff who lives in Devonshire, England — advises me that some of the Model 547s over there tend to recoil pretty savagely on some of the 9mmP ammo available locally. I am still looking for a load here that bothers my Model 547 in the slightest degree. With any load I've tried through mine to the present, it is purely a purring pussycat to fire. Recoil is not any problem worth worrying about with this one.

The sights are fixed, adequate, and acceptably close to the money with nearly any typical load. Put it this way: If you are out to nick dimes at twenty-five yards, some other handgun may serve you better. A U.S. dime is about .706-inch in diameter; at least the one I got out of pocket change

and miked, just then, measured that big. The Model 547 is not an all-out, world-class, Olympic-grade, target pistol. Let's face it: You can't have everything. Typical groups for five shots, fired in SA mode off a sandbag resting on the bench at twenty-five yards may show center-to-center spreads of three, four, maybe as much as five inches; sometimes a little less than three.

The basic 9mmP cartridge shows startling target capabilities no more than rarely. Old Georg Luger did not design it for potting field mice at fifty meters. By any reasonable stand, the Model 547 handles the cartridge with better than average competence. It has other intriguing virtues, as well.

For one thing, the Model 547 — and, presumably, the

Ruger 9mmP Speed-Six, which I've never fired — are totally relieved of the problem posed to any and all auto-loading 9mmP pistols: They do not require a minimum recoil impulse to function and that means you can fire some ridiculously squibby loads with no fuss, no problems. The versatility runs in both directions. The cylinder on my Model 547 measures about 1.675 inches, front to back. Deduct the nominal .754-inch/19.15mm case length and that means the nose of the seated bullet could jut ahead of the case mouth for about .921-inch before it might pose problems by interfering with cylinder rotation. You could make up some really ludicrous loads for the Model 547 and, presumably, you could fire them, no-sweat, provided you selected the powder charge to fit the situation.

Within fairly recent times, motivated by reflections that the supply of linotype metal is an ever-shrinking thing in the world of today, tomorrow and tomorrows that follow, I designed a cast bullet for which Hensley & Gibbs pro-

Above, three of the bullets cast from Hensley & Gibbs' #333 mould, at a weight of 66.5 grains each. Below and left are H&G #333 bullets lube/sized to .356-inch and loaded into the 9mmP cartridge. While it's rather rare for this bullet to feed well in autoloaders, it presents no problem in the M547 and affords an excellent approach for light recoil or high velocity, as the reloader/shooter's preference may run.

With a charge of 5.1 grains of Hercules Bullseye powder, the 66.5-grain Hensley & Gibbs cast wadcutter bullet comes out of the Model 547's three-inch barrel at about 1530 feet per second, packing a useful 346 foot-pounds of energy, every bit of which is being absorbed by the block of duct seal clay, here. Impact cavity measured about 2½ inches in diameter and penetration was about the same distance. Considerably tougher than modeling clay, it works well as a medium for testing bullet expansion, penetration and the like. This would be an effective, short-range defense load.

duced a mould. They call it their #333. It turns out a tiny wadcutter that can be lube/sized to .358-inch for use in .38 Specials or .357 magnums. Or you can size it on down to .356-inch and load it into cases such as the 9mmP. The bullet measures .258-inch from base to nose and weighs about 66.5 grains in typical casting alloys. I think of it as the Fly-Swatter. Preliminary work with bullets from that mould have been generally rewarding and encouraging. With the proper powder charge for the given case, it's capable of dotting in gratifyingly clannish groups. The recoil is like zilch-minus; about on a par with standard-velocity .22 LR ammo.

I lube/size my bullets with lithium-base bullet lube, having found that it gives no bore-fouling problems at velocities upward of 2000 fps. I get my lube from S&S Precision

Bullets, listed in the directory at the rear of this book.

Consulting various tables of load data, I came up with a powder charge of 5.1 grains of Hercules Bullseye behind the .356-inch H&G #333 for use in the 9mmP cartridge. That is well under load data offered in several contemporary and reliable manuals and handbooks. Even so, the chronographed velocities of that particular load, out of the three-inch barrel of the Model 547, average about 1530 fps. With a bullet weight of 66.5 grains, that's good for 346 fpe; by no means a trifling dollop.

Surprisingly enough, the point of impact for such an off-the-wall load is fairly close to that of more conventional loads. The Model 547 is a remarkably good-natured and anxious-to-please little revolver. It feeds anything and absolutely everything, provided the overall length is a trifle

Serial number and model number are stamped on the receiver ahead of the cutout for the cylinder. The serial number is also stamped on the butt of the receiver. A different number: 29182, appears on the facing surface of the crane, as well as C12. Several years ago, S&W also stamped the serial number on the rear face of the cylinder, but no longer does so.

Left caliber markings and patent number appear on the RH side of the barrel. Below, extended extractor of the M547 bears vague resemblance to Seattle's famed Space Needle. You can see the small fingers that engage the extraction groove of the 9mmP.

less than 1.675 inches. Load the H&G #333 ahead of 1.8 grains of Bullseye and it'd still come out the muzzle, without making a whole lot of noise and I doubt if you'd even *notice* the recoil.

Yes, in the area of experimental reloads, the Model 547 is the ultimate omnivore. It will gobble and digest almost anything a reasonably prudent reloader might care to try through it. Experience to the present suggests that it will deliver anything and everything, pretty close to the point of aim. It will handle bullets of designs so weird and *outre* that they'd never function through any autoloader, no sweat, no flap at all.

Much of the foregoing comments might well apply with approximately equal validity to the Ruger Speed-Six in 9mmP. I can't say for sure because I've never been able to put my hands upon one of those to try it out. Nevertheless, I feel I should give the Ruger the benefit of every reasonable doubt. As to Smith & Wesson's Model 547, all my doubts have been put to rest, a long while back down the road. I really like this funny little revolver. I've never even heard the sometimes dour and opinionated Wiley Clapp voice anything overly acerbic about it and that has to be some manner of super-credential. You see, he doesn't even own one.

I do, and I'm happy about that. — *Dean A. Grennell*

CHAPTER 8
THE SMITH & WESSON 9mmP AUTOS

For the GIs returning from European war in the '40s, this was the THE souvenir. The Luger is a beautifully made pistol which stimulated interest in domestic 9mmP autos.

WHEN THE WAR was over, they came home from the ETO with memories of Omaha Beach, Anzio, Bastogne and countless other now-forgotten places. It was a popular war, one that was supported by the folks at home, and one in which most veterans took pride in their service. Not surprisingly, many GIs felt the need for a remembrance of the war years. While more than a few brought home the Mauser rifle in one of its endless variations, others attempted to bring back one of the submachine guns that the Germans used in great numbers. Those who tried usually found to their sorrow that a Schmeisser, even as a wall hanger, was frowned upon by the Feds.

That left the most portable, and probably most desirable, of all souvenirs. Tens of thousands of those duffel bags and footlockers that came back from Europe contained a pistol. For many, that pistol was a Walther P'38, the standard German service automatic since 1938, the year before the war got rolling. But the real prize was the Pistole '08 or Luger, used in great numbers by the Germans and considered by most GIs to be the symbol of Teutonic engineering efficiency. I know of several veteran doughboys who will solemnly describe how they relieved an SS colonel of his sidearm; I've heard the story so often that I've come to the conclusion that about half of the German Armed Forces was composed of colonels wearing the death's-head and lightning bolt emblem.

But whether it was P'08 or P'38, most of the souvenir pistols were chambered for the 9mm Parabellum (9mmP). Now, this round was not unknown to America. For one

How The Parabellum Crossed The Pond And Got Domesticated

Service pistol ammunition compared. There's an obvious difference between the 9mmP bullet and cartridge to the left and the famous 45 ACP.

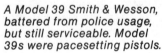

A Model 39 Smith & Wesson, battered from police usage, but still serviceable. Model 39s were pacesetting pistols.

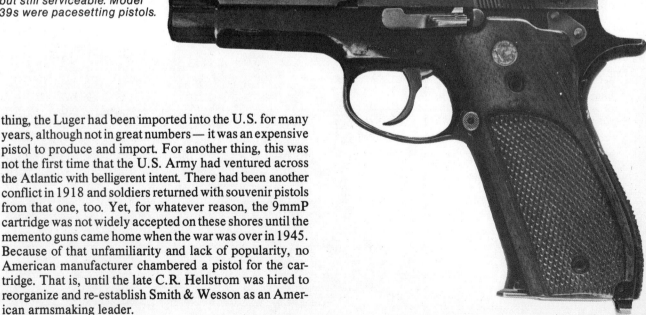

thing, the Luger had been imported into the U.S. for many years, although not in great numbers — it was an expensive pistol to produce and import. For another thing, this was not the first time that the U.S. Army had ventured across the Atlantic with belligerent intent. There had been another conflict in 1918 and soldiers returned with souvenir pistols from that one, too. Yet, for whatever reason, the 9mmP cartridge was not widely accepted on these shores until the memento guns came home when the war was over in 1945. Because of that unfamiliarity and lack of popularity, no American manufacturer chambered a pistol for the cartridge. That is, until the late C.R. Hellstrom was hired to reorganize and re-establish Smith & Wesson as an American armsmaking leader.

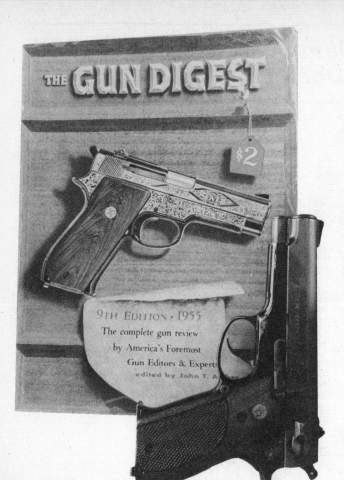

During the developmental stage of the Model 39, S&W considered a single-action version called the Model 44. There was little demand and only a few were produced.

Hellstrom set about modernizing the Smith & Wesson firm, not only in terms of its mechanical and business efficiency, but also in the sense of its product line. He wanted to appeal to every possible handgun market and soon had the Springfield, Massachusetts, plant producing target, service, and sporting handguns in greater variety than ever before. The company did not manufacture a military-style automatic pistol, however. When the U.S. joined NATO, and there was talk of our forces standardizing on the 9mmP as a pistol and submachine gun cartridge, Hellstrom turned the design people loose. The result was the pistol known as the Model 39.

The first Model 39s were produced in the early 1950s and predated the time when model numbers were assigned — that came in 1957. Hellstrom felt that there was a market for a light, compact 9mmP automatic with a feature heretofore unseen on domestic self-loaders — a double-action trigger. When the first of these guns were actually produced and advertised, they were offered in both alloy and steel frame versions, and with either double- or single-action triggers!

Pre-production prototypes had featured a double-action trigger. They were evaluated by the military, which requested a single-action trigger system. The factory complied with a pistol that they thought would get a military contract. It didn't and Smith & Wesson never put the single-action version into production. When model numbers were assigned, it was called the Model 44. An engraved, smooth-gripped Model 44 graced the cover of the 9th edition of the Gun Digest in 1955. That's really curious, since there were only ten of these unusual autos produced. That must make them one of the most desirable collector's items that you could possibly find.

It remained for the Model 39 to carry the *modern automatic* banner for Smith & Wesson. The factory settled on the alloy frame version, with double-action trigger. The familiar Model 39 of the '50s and '60s carried an eight-shot magazine and weighed twenty-eight ounces. It had a rear sight adjustable for windage only, a feature that was not popular with the users of the gun. At that time, it was unique in being the only domestic autoloader with a double-action trigger and it took the shooting public a

This is the much-maligned Model 39 rear sight, adjustable for windage but not elevation. Late in the long production life of the 39, the fault was corrected by a new rear sight.

Extractor, visible from this side of the 39, identifies it as a 39-2. The Model 39's competitor in police service was the .45, carried cocked-and-locked as seen at right.

while to get used to dropping the hammer with the safety lever. After all, we were pretty much used to expecting a *bang!* when that hammer dropped. But the 39 rolled a bar of steel between the hammer and the firing pin, preventing the gun from firing. With the hammer down on a live round, the gun was safe to carry, requiring only a long pull of the double-action trigger. After that first DA shot, the Model 39 behaved like a typical automatic, ejecting the fired case, feeding a fresh one from the magazine, and leaving the external hammer cocked for a repeat shot with a short, crisp single-action pull. The gun also featured a magazine safety for further sales appeal; the hammer-trigger linkage was disconnected with the magazine removed. The pistol achieved a modest, but well-deserved popularity as a light,

compact, reliable service automatic. Not a bad effort by Smith & Wesson — it was the first successful automatic ever made by the world's leading manufacturer of revolvers.

There were some problems with the Model 39, but they were corrected. Many shooters complained that the surface area of the safety lever was inadequate, that it was difficult to manipulate rapidly. Smith & Wesson replied by increasing the length of the part in such a way as to make it easy to wipe down and drop the hammer. Some 39s were subjected to heavy use and not infrequently the extractor broke. The first extractors were long bars of spring steel, mounted on the right side of the slide and extending into the ejection port. Smith corrected that problem by redesign-

John Browning's most durable design, the familiar Colt .45, was the other autoloader the cops tried when they needed more firepower in the '60s.

ing the extractor and tensioning it with a stubby little coil spring. This change was made in 1971; subsequent guns were called Model 39-2s. The change to a more appropriate sight, adjustable for both windage and elevation, was offered as an option late in the production life of the Model 39.

Sales of the Model 39 were steady but not really spectacular in the late '50s and '60s. Then, in the late '60s, with unrest boiling over into violence in a number of American cities, law enforcement began to cast about for a better, safer pistol to arm its officers. If that piece could produce greater firepower in the bargain, so much the better. Some agencies went to the Colt 1911A1, carrying the

When more firepower in a 9mmP handgun became a goal, the 13-shot Browning Hi-Power was sometimes chosen.

Around since the mid-'30s, the P'35 has a good record in military service. New catalog shows the DA version.

gun in "cocked and locked" mode (Condition One). Others felt that a cocked auto in an open-topped police holster was, at best, bad public relations. The Model 39, around for the best part of two decades, got a second look.

I can't find a reference to tell me when and where the first police agency adopted the Model 39, but I believe that it may have been Covina, California, about 1968. Certainly the largest agency to do so in this period was the Illinois State Police. One of the factors which influenced this de-

partment to drop the traditional revolver was the ease by which the 39 could be concealed off-duty. This was a selling point of no small magnitude, particularly in times when more and more agencies wanted to mandate an off-duty firearm.

Before long, police departments all over the nation were using the reliable Model 39. Although the gun never reached the point where it was challenging the revolver, it did make inroads in the police market. Admittedly the venerable

The long-awaited Smith & Wesson Model 59 was a marriage of the Model 39 barrel and slide unit to frame widened to handle the double column magazine similar to that of P'35.

Shown here is the 59 atop several types of modern, well-engineered 9mmP ammunition from Hornady. In the early days of the 59, the ammo wasn't so good and the reputation of the 59s suffered unfairly.

Colt .45 auto was doing just about as well. Both guns were immeasurably assisted in so doing by vastly improved anti-personnel ammunition. Then someone noticed that the "other" 9mmP, the Browning Hi-Power, had a double-column magazine that held thirteen, sometimes fourteen, shots. Could this feature be adopted to the Smith & Wesson, and still have a manageable-sized pistol? The answer was yes, and the gun was the Model 59.

For the basis of the Model 59, Smith used a previously secret military pistol made in extremely limited quantities for the Navy SEAL teams during the Vietnam War. The 59, when it was introduced in 1971, featured a newly contoured frame, onto which was grafted a regular Model 39 slide. The frame was shaped to accommodate the thicker magazine which held fifteen shots; in so doing, the voluptuous curves of the 39 backstrap gave way to a straight 59 version. The walnut grips of the 39 couldn't be comfortably thinned to fit the new frame, so high-impact black

plastic was used. The resulting pistol had a chunky, solid feel when fully loaded. Most agencies that were considering an automatic gave this new Smith & Wesson a long look. For the first few months, the guns were in such short supply as to demand premium prices. Most of them went to large police orders.

Smith & Wesson had taken a great deal of time attempting to make the new pistol as reliable as possible. Since they were aware that a variety of ammunition was going to be fed to their new automatic, they considered the various shapes of the bullets in factory and handloaded ammunition. Some of these had exposed lead tips, posing no small problem in getting them from the magazine to the chamber. The factory approach was to use a pretty radical feed ramp shape, one that was cut in such a way as to leave a crescent of brass unsupported at the head of the case, when that case was fully seated in the chamber. They had no way to predict the amount and type of reloads of dubious origin that

The Model 639 was a handgun that a lot of people really wanted. Not only was the frame steel, but stainless steel. Below: Ambidextrous safety shown.

The basic model 39 was customized by a number of gunsmiths. The ASP, seen here, was a complete rebuild project.

would be fired in the 59. The early model 59s got a bum rap from the jams and ruptured cartridges that usually could be traced to poor ammunition. Unfortunately, it also happened with factory fodder. There were also complaints concerning the length of the magazine catch, which was sometimes pressed by the tight fit of a policeman's holster. When the catch was pressed, it caused the magazine to partially eject from the magazine well, and that brought the magazine safety into play, de-activating the trigger. That's not the best of things to have happen to a handgun on which you bet your life!

One of the latest guns from Smith & Wesson is the 469. There's no denying that the design of this handgun was influenced by the work of custom 'smiths. Look at the trigger guard above and on the ASP on the facing page.

The factory responded very quickly to the complaints about the gun, from both agencies as well as individuals. In a relatively short period of time, the production guns were coming off the line up there in Massachusetts both reliable and durable. More than one handloading Model 59 user had found out that the 9mmP cartridge is *not* the easiest hull to stuff.

By the late Seventies, the two Smith & Wesson autos were sufficiently well established as to rate updating with more options. The factory had adopted a new system of designating their products. The first of three digits now described the material of the pistol's frame: 4 meant aluminum alloy, 5 meant blue steel, and 6 was the designator for the increasingly popular stainless steel. In 1981, Smith announced the models 439 and 539, updated 39s with fully adjustable rear sights. Also available were the 459s and 559s; alloy and blue steel second-generation Model 59s.

These four new models were available in nickel plate as well as blued versions. They had two very popular features: fully adjustable rear sights and ambidextrous safety levers. Their commercial success encouraged the maker to produce the pair in stainless steel and we had the 639 and 659

Here's more of the touches which came from the ideas of custom pistolsmiths: Extreme rounding of rear sight.

The safety on this model 639 has levers on both sides of the slide for ambidextrous use, a valuable feature.

The Model 469 is a compact, powerful, pocket automatic. It has found favor with any number of professional users of concealable handguns.

The Model 469 contrasted with its 9mmP ancestor, the P'08 or Luger. The Luger is fading a bit with time, but was as serviceable in its day as the 469 is now.

from which to choose. A year or so into the production of the stainless models, it became apparent that the blue steel guns were not selling well against their rust-resistant counterparts. Apparently, buyers of heavy-frame 9mmPs were willing to cough up a few more bucks for the stainless guns. The 539 and 559 were quietly dropped in 1983.

For a number of years, custom gunsmiths had been rebuilding Model 39s in such a way as to create a shorter, lighter, more concealable pocket automatic. When the Model 59 came along, it got the same treatment. The factory saw this happening and reasoned that there might be some value to a production pistol of this sort. The result was the Model 469, a variant of the 459. Featuring a shortened slide and barrel and an abbreviated butt, housing a ten-shot magazine, the 469 was an instant best-seller. From

the start, the 469 was as functionally reliable a pistol as ever left the Springfield plant.

Currently, there is considerable variety in the Smith & Wesson auto pistol line. A buyer can choose from the 439 or 459 in either blue or nickel finish, or the 639 or 659 in stainless steel. Each of these variations is available with fixed or adjustable sights, and either standard or ambidextrous safety. The concealable 469 may be had blued or frostnickeled. More recently, the stainless Model 669 made its appearance.

Just thirty years have passed since the first 9mmP Smith & Wessons were produced: not a particularly long time, but sufficiently long to give the grand old firm clear seniority in the production of these guns that are getting so much of our attention. *Wiley M. Clapp*

There is a lot of variety in the Smith & Wesson line of 9mmP automatics, more than any maker, foreign or domestic. As this was written, the current catalog displayed the guns shown. The Model 669, a stainless version of the 469 was added in mid-1985.

CHAPTER 9

HECKLER & KOCH 9mmPs: THE INNOVATORS

Unique Design Features Complement High Quality Production Standards In These Imports From Deutschland

---

Here is a latter-day version of the famous G-3 rifle, a mainstay of the Heckler & Koch line since the early days of the company. H&K makes the roller-locked gun in a number of versions with features suited to the end use for which the arm is intended. It is well known for reliability in the field.

INNOVATION! That's the hallmark of the products of a relatively new and progressive firearms manufacturing firm. The Heckler & Koch company occupies an old plant and a new place among firearms makers in this last part of the Twentieth Century. In business for a brief quarter century or so, H&K (as we'll refer to them for the remainder of this chapter — in the manner of S&W, H&R, et al) uses a site once occupied by a branch of firearms immortal — Mauser. They've been there at Oberndorf-Neckar, West Germany, since the Fifties, producing a steady stream of guns of such quality as to make them a true giant of the industry. You might say they were a Teutonic version of Sturm, Ruger & Co.!

Starting with a figurative blank sheet of paper, the H&K designers developed a full-sized military rifle as an initial offering. That was the famous G-3, which is widely used throughout the world. The basis for the G-3 is a unique roller locking system which has found its way into a number of H&K designs, and which has been imitated by others. For the first decade or so, H&K concentrated on the military and police market, and that remains the mainstay of their business. The company presently sells a variety of automatic weapons, assault rifles and light machine guns to an appreciative global market. Their submachine gun, the MP5, is popular with anti-terrorist forces all over the world. In the U.S., the gun is the standard of

The first pistol produced by the H&K firm was the HK-4. Left, pistol is seen with its multiple barrels and magazines. The HK-4 would fire four different kinds of ammo. Below: the dual-caliber version.

The VP 70Z is a fighting tool, pure and simple. Featuring a double-action only trigger as well as unique combat sights, the pistol is well suited to a purely combat role. Shaped to fit the hand, it handles well.

Butt of the VP 70Z, with catch for magazine and wide magazine floorplate. Note pebbled finish.

many police SWAT teams. The MP5 is appreciated for the fact that it is a miniaturized assault rifle firing from a closed bolt, which contributes to accuracy in a weapon of such relatively heavy weight. Design-wise, this is quite the opposite of most submachine gun models which tend to the very light and very simple. But we told you H&K was innovative, now didn't we?

For the purposes of this book, however, we are concerned with the handgun designs of the H&K firm. There have been only four designs since the beginning of the company. Not surprisingly, every one of them has some major innovation which sets it off from its contemporaries.

H&K's first effort was an update of an earlier design, the reliable and popular Mauser HSc. The H&K variant was called the HK4, and for good reason — it fired four different cartridges. They were the .22LR, .25 ACP, .32 ACP, and .380 ACP. The pistol was marketed in the U.S. as a kit complete with four barrel-and-recoil-spring units and four magazines. In a matter of a few seconds, a shooter could change from one caliber to another. It did take a little longer to change to the rimfire .22 — you had to reverse a plate in the standing breech in order to reposition the firing pin. The HK4 featured an aluminum frame and a clean new profile, and was produced with the best of modern techniques. The resemblance to the HSc was internal, the exterior being distinctively space-age.

The kits were never good sellers in the U.S.; shooters didn't want to pay for two calibers that weren't very popular. Americans have never been all that fond of the .25 and .32 auto pistol rounds. The .22 offered a low cost practice incentive to .380 purchasers. For a time, Harrington & Richardson sold an H&K-produced and dually marked (H&K and H&R) version. This gun was a .380 with an extra .22 barrel.

But for our purpose at hand, the examination of 9mmP pistols as a class, the other three H&K designs are the most interesting. All three of them are typically 9mmP handguns, with a few variants produced in other calibers. Not surprisingly, each of the three is innovative in one or more ways, and each is distinctly different from the others. Each uses the H&K "polygonal" rifling for higher pressures and less barrel wear. The three guns are the VP70Z, the P7, and the P9s.

The VP70Z is a handgun with no comparable contemporaries. It is in a class completely by itself, and you get a first inkling as to its unique character when you examine an exploded drawing. There aren't many parts in a VP70Z. The P9s has nearly half again as many parts as the VP70Z. The gun was conceived as an ultra-simple yet ultra-sturdy defensive weapon, capable of being produced and sold at a relatively low price.

The VP70Z feels bulky, yet it has a grip that is contoured so neatly as to accustom itself rather quickly to the hands of most shooters. There are no grip plates or stocks to deal with — the entire butt is a single casting of alloy with an attractive pebbled finish. And that butt houses a magazine holding a full eighteen rounds of 9mmP ammunition. To our knowledge, only the Steyr GB has a larger capacity magazine. In view of the intended use of the weapon, pure defense, that whopping big clip is a good idea. The magazine catch is heel-mounted.

Two more views of the VP 70Z. Left: With slide removed the generous feed ramp of the gun can be seen. Below: A look at the right side with cross bolt safety indicated.

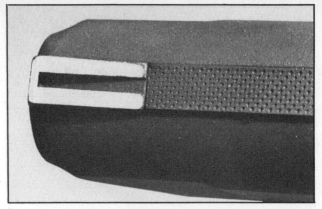

Left: Muzzle of a VP 70Z, with polygonal rifling visible. Also seen is the front edge of an unusual, but effective, front sight. Above: A top view of the VP 70Z ramp sight.

over cocking levers or hammers. The trigger pull is long and rather heavy, with a pronounced hesitation just before release — it does take a bit of getting used to. This would be an easy pistol to teach a neophyte to use, if the use was defense at relatively short range.

Sights? They're fixed and unique. The rear is a plain square notch of generous proportions. But the front sight on the VP70Z is engagingly unusual. It is a ramp, apparently cast into the slide, but finished off a bit differently. The center portion of the ramp is cut away on its rearward-facing

Controls on the VP70Z are few and simple. There is a sliding crossbolt safety on the frame just behind the trigger guard. It falls easily under the thumb on one side and the tip of the trigger finger on the other. The only other control device is the trigger, a sliding type mounted in an oversized trigger guard. The trigger can only be manipulated *double-action,* in the manner of the LeFrancais models, or some Czech designs. For a purely defense pistol, this is an excellent feature, as it obviates the need for any concern

This is the newest of the H&K handguns, the P7. It is a compact and powerful pistol, featuring two major firsts in autopistol design. Text describes each in full detail.

As seen from the front, a P7 presents trim lines, hooked trigger guard. The frontstrap is a squeeze-cocking lever.

plane, leaving an area of deep shadow. The shadow contrasts with the surrounding polished surfaces in such a way as to provide an aiming "post" — under nearly all light conditions. It looks funny, but so does a Jeep; they both work.

There is a variation of the VP70Z which harkens back to the days of the Broomhandle Mauser in its famous *schnellfeuerpistole* version. This version features a hard plastic stock which forms a holster for the pistol when removed. Attached to the pistol, a lug on the stock enters a recess on

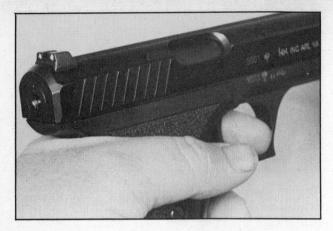

The squeeze-cocking feature at work. P7 is held loosely in shooting hand with finger on trigger. It is safe until the hand tightens around the frame in readiness to shoot.

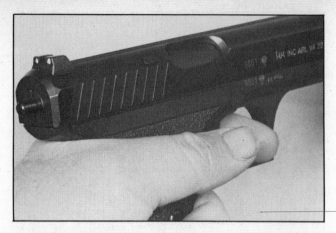

As the hand tightens, the squeeze-cocking lever is pressed inwards. Linkages inside the frame cock the pistol, which will remain cocked until the gun fires or hand relaxes.

the gun in such fashion as to alter the trigger action to a full-auto three-shot burst. In other words, a compact and effective submachine gun!

There is an obvious effort here to produce a simple gun: simple to make, maintain, and use. The VP70Z succeeds admirably in this regard — it's best described by a single word chosen by the manufacturer — *robust*.

The second H&K design that commands our attention is the P7. This is also a simple gun to use, if you know nothing about auto pistols or have been carefully re-educated. That's a statement that will require some qualification.

Most automatic pistols, fitted out with box magazines in the butt and reciprocating slides, are alike in more ways than you would realize. They may be single-action types in the manner of the Colt 1911, or double-action of the sort pioneered by Walther. But they are alike in the sense that a control of some sort is typically manipulated in order to get a hammer cocked and made ready to fire. The P7 has a box magazine in the butt and a reciprocating slide, but all that

you have to do to ready it for firing is...well, just *hold* it.

The P7 has been described as a "squeeze-cocker" and I guess that's as good a term as any. It works this way: On the front portion of the P7's grip, where the fingers of the shooting hand wrap around, there is a lever. This lever, pivoted from the bottom just above the little finger, folds inward. The lever actually constitutes the entire front surface of the grip. When the hand grasps the pistol in firing position, this lever is compressed under pressure of unseen springs. Fully compressed, the lever works internal linkages which cock the striker. The gun will now fire if a short, crisp pull on a single-action trigger is used. Repeat shots are made without changing the grip pressure, just pulling the trigger. As long as the grip is held, the gun may be fired. When pressure is relaxed, the striker is lowered and locked in place, safely away from the chambered round. The amount of pressure required to cock the pistol is about the amount needed to really get ahold of any conventional auto. To keep the gun in a cocked mode, roughly 90% less

A closer view of the German army's newest pistol. Lever would appear to be a hazard in terms of pinching the top finger, but it doesn't work that way in actual field use.

Right side of the P7 at close range. The grained finish of the plastic stocks makes the pistol easier to handle even with moist or greasy hands.

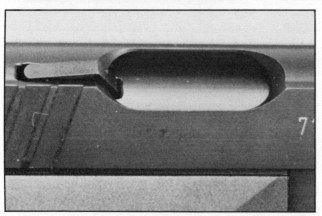

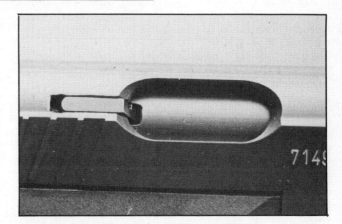

These photos show the P7's loaded chamber indicator in action. Above left: Extractor sticking out, indicates a cartridge in chamber. Above: Extractor "in" means empty.

The P7 M13, latest version of the basic design, has an even better set of sights. They are adjustable, as seen in this photo. Serrations on top of slide run to muzzle.

Heckler & Koch pioneered high visibility combat sights. The P7 uses a three-dot system. Above: A pair of glow-in-the-dark dots on rear sight. Below: Single dot front.

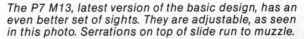

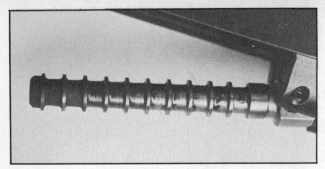

Above: The P7 uses a bit of powder gas to lock the slide shut, via plunger shown. Right: P7s will never be popular with the handloading fraternity; they screw up the brass.

pressure is needed. No safety is necessary, just relax the grip and the gun "de-cocks."

This is utter tactical simplicity, but is best taught to the tactically ignorant. Sophisticated handgunners, persons who are experienced with a variety of handguns, will have to unlearn some habits. Mostly they'll have to learn what to do with the shooting hand thumb, as it flails madly about in search of a control to manipulate. The ignorant shooter finds the system easy to learn, as he has no contradictory frame of reference.

H&K went to a great deal of obvious effort to keep the pistol trim and compact. The P7 weighs 34 ounces with a full eight-shot magazine, and is small enough to be easily concealed. A thirteen-shot version is just hitting the U.S. market in quantity as this is written. Initially accepted by several West German police agencies, the P7 reached full acceptance when the Bundeswehr chose it as the Army service pistol.

Rumors about this amazing little pistol circulated well ahead of its arrival in the United States. As discussed in the text, the P7 is a difficult handgun to master particularly if you have experience with other firearms.

The latest update of the basic P7 is this one: the P7 M13, which has a thirteen-shot double-column box magazine. It also has a magazine catch in the more desirable spot: under the tip of the right thumb.

The P9s, in several variations, H&K's other automatic, comes in calibers other than just 9mmP. The kit version, as seen here, is regarded highly for its accuracy.

The P7 is all the more unique in a technical sense. We've all heard of gas-operated weapons, where the expanding powder gases are used to manipulate the action of the arm. How about using the gas to *lock* the action? That is just what happens in the P7, by means of a small plunger just forward of the trigger guard which has gas acting on it at the instant of firing. The plunger is connected to the slide and holds the action closed until pressure drops to a level that recoil springs can handle. More innovations yet!

If the VP70Z reaches one market and the P7 makes another, then the next H&K straddles quite a few. The P9s from Heckler & Koch comes close to being "all pistols to all pistoleros."

In its various incarnations, the P9s can be either a holster-sized and reliable service pistol or a competition automatic of outstanding potential accuracy. If you buy the kit, you can have both systems in one gun. The basic pistol makes full use of the most modern manufacturing techniques. The receiver of the pistol is almost exclusively sheet steel stampings, precisely folded and welded to form a skeleton into which the various lockwork parts are fitted. The frame is covered with a wraparound grip suited to the purpose of the gun: checkered plastic for the combat piece and stippled walnut for the target version. Trigger guard, extending to the front of the frame, ...well, that's plastic. Why not? There's no stress on that portion of the gun.

The kit version, available for examination for this book, came with two slide-barrel units. The combat gun uses a shorter four-inch barrel and a slide mounted fixed sights. An inch and a half longer, the competition setup is different. While both slides are precision fitted at the plant, the match version includes a barrel weight on which the

Several notable handgun experts have rated the target P9s as one of the most accurate 9mmP pistols in the world. They will shoot!

front sight is mounted. This increases the sight radius to nearly six inches. At the rear end of the competition slide, there's a precise and repeatable micrometer rear sight. The sight picture for match work is all that you could possible ask for: clear and distinct.

As you see them pictured here, the wooden stock of the competition gun has been modified to suit the practical tastes of publisher Jack Lewis. Their original shape included about half a walnut tree more. For most purposes the modification is an improvement.

The trigger? Either double or single action, and it includes a trigger stop for the single-action mode. The single-action pull is clean and crisp. The P9s also features a cocking lever for practice firing.

This was the P9s on hand for evaluation for the book, and it was a superb shooter. Factory wooden stocks did not suit publisher Jack Lewis, were changed as shown.

These guns are not cheap, but quality seldom is. An important thing to remember is a finding of two of our best known handgun authorities, Dean Grennell and Massad Ayoob. They share an opinion that this is the most accurate out-of-the-box 9mm Parabellum in the world. Grennell has produced some groups with this same pictured pistol

Sights on the service slide in the P9s kit are seen in the pair of photos to the right. Vertical bars are used instead of dots. Most shooters queried preferred dots.

that are nothing short of phenomenal. Despite the unconventional appearance and unorthodox construction, the P9s is a fine handgun for a variety of purposes.

An additional and unusual endorsement of the P9s comes from another source. On TV's *Hunter* series, Fred Dreyer portrays a big city cop who stalks all manner of latter day black-hats. His main armament? You guessed it — a P9s, complete with photogenic barrel weight. Some of us remember Freddie from the days when he was holding forth in the blue and gold of the LA Rams. As a defensive end, he convinced more than one quarterback that he did not need a weapon — he *was* a weapon!

No manufacturer of handguns features as many different ideas as does the Heckler & Koch firm. Where pistols are concerned, they are beyond question...the innovators. — *Willey M. Clapp*

And yet another P9s variation. This one has short combat slide mounting adjustable rear and fixed front sight. Far side of the slide will show the caliber designation.

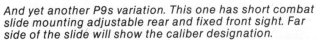

CHAPTER 10

SWEET SIGS AND SIG-SAUERS

Sophisticated target/sniper rifles are part of the lineup of weaponry from SIGARMS.

This is the SIG 210, billed as a service automatic and used by the Swiss military.

MILITANT NATIONS tend to produce the most vigorous armsmaking industries. Before World War II, the only firearms manufacturing nation in all of Asia was Japan. For the first half of this century in Europe, Germany held clear title to both militancy and armsmaking supremacy. Both of these nations suffered terrible losses in wars, but you can't fault their weaponry — it was excellent. And nowhere is that as true as it is in the case of their smallarms. It is, therefore, a little strange that one of the world's best armaments industries exists in a country that hasn't gone to war for centuries.

There are a lot of complex reasons why this situation has evolved and I wouldn't want to oversimplify and say that it's because Swiss weaponry is so far ahead of everyone else's that the world is afraid of them. But the Swiss do design and produce some of history's finest firearms. One of them is a pistol, and when you consider how little effect a pistol will have on the course of modern battle, it seems as though a nation which would produce a pistol like the SIG 210 is dead serious about their defense.

With a few rare exceptions, the authorities who evaluate and rate the automatic pistols of today's well-armed world all proclaim the SIG 210 to be the best automatic pistol produced anywhere. Whether there is merit to the argument or not is a question that we will presently address. It is

appropriate at this point to look at the reasons why the 210 is not as well known in the United States as other foreign autoloaders. And make no mistake about it, the SIG 210 is not exactly a figurative household word on the handgunning scene in America.

The 210, in all its variations is an expensive pistol to produce. The SIG standards as to fit and finish are considerably higher than most other brands of guns. Such a standard requires a great deal of precise machining and handwork in the assembly of the finished product. This tends to raise the price of the gun alarmingly. Further, the trade policies of the Swiss government are such that not

The Aristocratic Auto Pistols Of Switzerland Contrasted With Their Swiss-German Cousins

The target version of the 210 is called the 210-6. A plain service gun is shown disassembled at lower left.

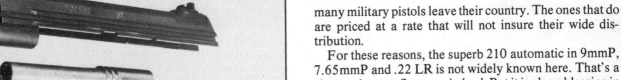

many military pistols leave their country. The ones that do are priced at a rate that will not insure their wide distribution.

For these reasons, the superb 210 automatic in 9mmP, 7.65mmP and .22 LR is not widely known here. That's a shame; they are fine guns indeed. But it is also a blessing in disguise. If it were not for the economically difficult position in which the 210 is placed, we might not have the pistols of the composite efforts of SIG (which stands for Schweizerische Industrie-Gesellschaft) and the firm of J.P. Sauer & Sohn in Germany. These guns are marketed in the United States by the SIGArms company and are called SIG-Sauers. They are available in several variations and calibers. Between the SIG 210 and the several SIG-Sauers, there are more than enough fine handguns to blanket a great many different markets.

The SIG 210 should properly be the starting point for an examination of the products imported by SIGArms. There are, by the way, several excellent long arms for military, sporting and police service also made by SIG. They aren't within the scope of a book on automatic pistols, but do merit close attention. Since so many authorities rate the 210 so highly, let's look at that firearm.

The origins of the 210 are found in the fertile imagination of one Charles Petter who obtained patents for several technical design innovations for automatic pistols. The French used some of these in developing the French service automatic of 1935. In the late thirties, the SIG firm obtained the rights to use the Petter innovations in the development of a new Swiss service pistol. Several models

Breech end of the SIG 210 barrel suggests some of the gun's ancestry. Locking lugs on top of the barrel are pure Browning, but the link system below the barrel is Petter.

were produced, but were not widely distributed. The design was essentially finalized in the late forties and the pistol which we now know as the 210 was introduced. Rather quickly, the gun was recognized as a superior design.

The reputation is a deserved one for several reasons. There are three features of the gun which are somewhat different and two of those are almost totally unique to the 210. First, it must be understood that the pistol is a straightforward 9mmP locked-breech, all-steel autoloader featuring a single column magazine holding eight rounds. The breech is locked closed at the instant of firing by the engagement of barrel locking lugs into recesses in the underside of the slide. The barrel is unlocked by the action of a cam groove on the underside of the barrel, working against a cross shaft through the receiver. This is an adaptation of the time-tested Colt-Browning system. It differs from the Colt in the sense that there is no troublesome barrel bushing to stabilize the front of the barrel. There is also no pivoting, pin-mounted link on the barrel. The cam

arrangement is far superior in the sense that much more precise fitting of the barrel to the slide is possible.

It doesn't stop there. The major portion of the firing mechanism; hammer, sear, mainspring and guide, plus related parts are mounted together as a unit. It is easier to manufacture and service them when they are together in this way. The idea works quite well, well enough that it is found on the excellent (and far less expensive) Star 28 and 30 automatics.

But the Petter-SIG technical advancements go beyond the unique modification of the Browning-designed locking system or a clever assembly of single-action lockwork. The typical automatic has a reciprocating slide mounted atop a stationary frame which is grasped in the shooter's hand. On nearly all other self-loaders, the slide is above the receiver with its rails which guide the fore and aft travel surrounding the matching rails on the frame. The slide thus rides on and around the frame.

The 210 reverses the relationship. The slide still rides above the frame, but the rails are reversed in such a way

In the center of this photo, you can clearly see the relationship between the slide and the receiver of the 210. The frame surrounds the slide. That's opposite to most automatics.

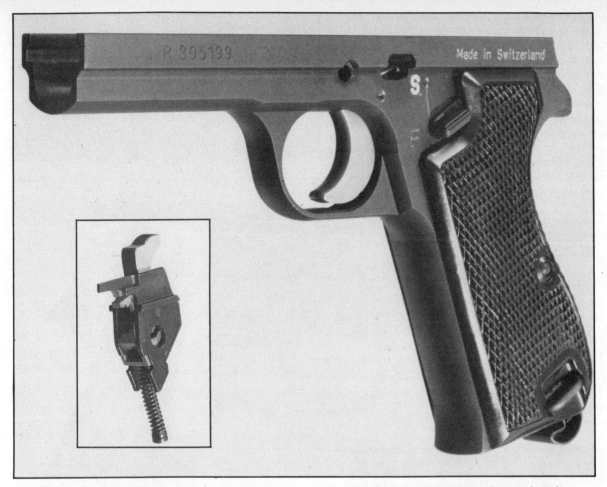

Above: The receiver of the 210. Inset photo shows the firing mechanism removed from the receiver. It lifts out of the frame as seen in the lower photo. Below left: With hammer forward and the magazine in place, the unit is ready to be removed. Right: Partially out, the precise fit is evident. Hammer, sear, hammer spring and guide are all mounted on a single block and can easily be serviced when required.

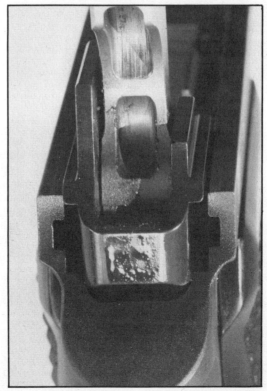

that the slide rides within the frame. The total distance that the rails extend is an inch or so greater than that found in typical competitors. The combination of the reversed rails over a greater amount of rail travel adds up to a slide that cannot go anywhere but straight forward and straight back. Retracting the slide of a 210 is an unusual experience to a shooter not used to such precision. The smoothness of the fore and aft travel of that slide cannot adequately be described or photographed — it must be experienced.

The result is a precise piece of shooting machinery. I had originally thought that there was a great deal of hand-fitting and stoning of parts in the 210, but after a conversation

The trademark of the consortium is neatly stamped into the left side of the slide of the 220, as seen in the topmost photo. The pistol, made in several calibers, is above.

with one who had visited the plant, it would seem that this is not the case. The major effort in reduced tolerances is performed by tape-controlled machinery. This means that the fitting of individual parts is reduced but the manufacturing process is still slow and expensive. In current U.S. dollars, the least expensive version of the 210 sells for well over a thousand dollars. With the plethora of excellent 9mmP handguns on the market, an essentially service automatic that costs that much will not sell in huge quantities. And that is true regardless of the unquestioned quality of the design and the execution of that design.

Those who direct the efforts of the SIG works must certainly have been aware of this harsh reality. As a matter of fact, we have tangible evidence of this awareness in the form of three automatic pistols, the SIG-Sauer Models 220, 225 and 226.

The 220 comes with a precisely checkered set of plastic stocks. It was once imported by Browning as the BDA. A reputation for great reliability is growing amongst users.

Left: All 220 series slides are made like this one: heavy sheet steel formed over a mandrel and welded in place. Below: 220s are available in the U.S. only as .45 ACPs.

The SIG company wanted to expand their line to appeal to a broader market. In the early seventies, the Germans were on the brink of a major set of test trials in which the several police agencies of West Germany would select their new service automatic pistol. An agreement was struck with the respected armsmaking firm of J. P. Sauer and Sohn. The Sauer company already had existing plant facilities which could handle the production of a new pistol. The SIG firm would provide the design guidance. The pistol, to be called the SIG-Sauer 220, would be produced in Germany from a Swiss design.

This is the often-repeated folklore as to the origins of the 220. After playing with one for quite some period of time, during which I have learned to respect the quality and simplicity of the innovative design, I think that the Swiss-designed and German-built story may be an oversimplification. What seems to me to be far more reasonable is that there was an amalgamation of ideas as to the pistol design, with the Swiss experience predominant. There are distinctly German features in the gun and the breechblock is pure Sauer. It is the Swiss experience in the design of mass-production machinery to produce a gun, rather than the design of the gun itself which shows up in the finished product. However the design was developed, the 220 and its offspring are fine automatic pistols. They are produced

in West Germany in order to avoid the prohibitive Swiss tariffs and other fees.

Of all the modern multi-shot 9mmP automatics, there are probably as many 220s in active service as any other. The SIGArms people are quite proud of the fact that in excess of one hundred thousand 220s have been produced and sold. The 220 first entered the U.S. market, it was in the form of the Browning BDA.

The gun was a much awaited pistol on these shores. The first of them had been reported by the American firearms press and interest in the gun was high. Mostly, the American market wanted the .45 ACP version and they wanted

The breech block is a separate part within the 220 slide and is visible from the underside. This is a Sauer & Sohn touch, found on other automatics from the German firm.

From the top of the slide, only part of the breech block may be seen. The block houses the extractor, firing pin firing pin spring as well as the firing pin safety system.

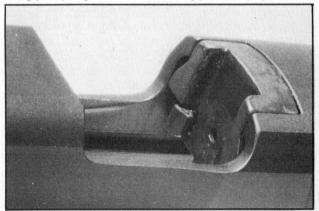

Above: Markings on the currently imported line of 220s include the importer's name and location. Right: This is one of the least desirable features of the 220. BDAs and 220s have a heel-mounted magazine catch, roundly cursed by combat shooters. 220s imported after mid-1986 are fitted with magazine catches mounted in a better spot.

Above and left: Front and rear sights on the 220 series are among the best available in the industry. The rear sight is cut in such a way as to be always in shadow.

it because it would have been one of the first double-action .45s commercially available. Browning brought the gun into the country in .45 ACP, .38 Super and 9mmP. The .45s were the most popular and the other two calibers did not sell exceptionally well. Browning ultimately dropped the BDA program for unknown reasons and other importers brought the guns into the country in somewhat limited numbers.

By the time that the present importer got into the act, there were variations on the basic 220. In any of the several calibers in which it is offered, the 220 is an excellent handgun to say the least. The pistol needs to be examined both in the sense of the technical innovations which make it unique, as well as the user-oriented features which have been universally well received.

Real diehard gun people will curl a scornful lip at the mention of sheet metal in a firearm. Guns are to be made from forged steel and walnut, and any use of stampings smacks of beer cans or cookie sheets. Tradition notwithstanding, the 220 is a durable, high quality handgun with a strong reputation for accuracy and durability — and it makes the widest possible use of sheet steel stampings.

The 220's stampings are quite thick. And they are

arranged in such a way as to be stressed in the proper plane. While some of the stampings form the small control levers and internal parts of the firing mechanism, the most original idea lies in the use of stampings for the slide itself.

In the manner of a number of other guns from the J. P. Sauer works, the 220 uses a separate breech block pinned into the slide. The block itself is a milled chunk of steel with appropriate contours to accept the firing pin and spring, plus the parts necessary to make the firing pin safety work. The remainder of the slide is a heavy piece of sheet steel formed over a mandrel and precision welded in such a way as to form the structure of the part. It requires absolute precision in the various jigs and fittings which go into producing the item, but once the necessary machinery has been designed and built, then it is really no harder to produce the slide for an automatic pistol than it is to produce — well, beer cans or cookie sheets.

The 220 is an excellent handgun, the first widely distributed auto to dispense with a safety as we commonly understand it. Instead, there is a positive firing pin block which requires a definite pull of the trigger to free it to be struck by the falling hammer. Since the gun is a first-shot double-action, the cycling slide will leave the external

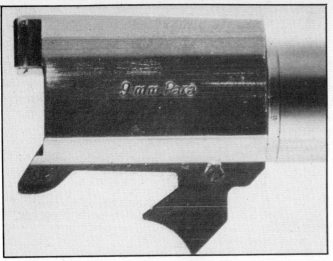

The lock-up of the 220 series pistols works by means of a barrel with a different shape. Note that the barrel is made with a large squared section at the rear and well above centerline of the bore. This is a locking lug.

Above and below: This pair of photos shows the barrel of a 220 locking up as the slide moves into the forward position. The squared section of the barrel actually fits into the ejection port. The system works extremely well.

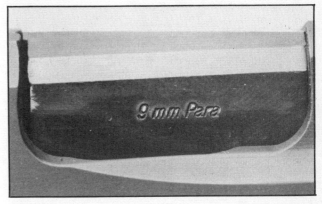

hammer cocked for subsequent single-action shots. Just above the forward-most tip of the grip plate on the left side of the gun there is a lever. When pushed down with the right thumb, the lever will "de-cock" the pistol by dropping the hammer. Since the trigger is not pulled, the firing pin is locked into place in the slide. The hammer falls, but the gun doesn't fire.

The human engineering of the 220 is good with a single exception. In the European manner, the magazine catch of the pistol is mounted in the heel of the butt. It is a little easier to make it in that way, but it is a long way from handy to use. Despite the efforts of some clever people to develop drills to use a heel-mounted catch, the fact remains that it requires two hands. If the catch is placed just aft of the trigger guard on the left side of the gun, then the thumb of the right hand can dump the expended magazine out while the left hand fetches another. SIGArms advises that the feature will be optional on 220s made after mid-1986.

One additional note on features of the 220 which favor the serious user of the gun. The rear sight is a more-or-less typical block of steel dovetailed into the top rear of the slide. It has a generous notch to match up with ramped front sight for quick and precise sighting. But the rear sight also has a semi-circular cut milled into its rear face which has the effect of placing the notch in shadow under all but a very few light conditions. It is a subtle little touch which has escaped the attention that it deserves. Some variations of the 220 series have sights which are highlighted with the

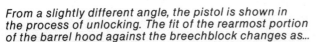

From a slightly different angle, the pistol is shown in the process of unlocking. The fit of the rearmost portion of the barrel hood against the breechblock changes as...

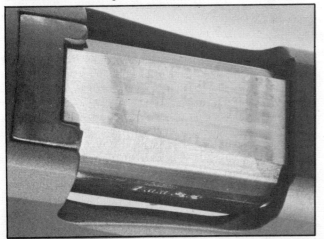

...the slide moves to the rear. The broad flat on the top of the barrel works against the front edge of ejection port; at the same time, the barrel is cammed downward.

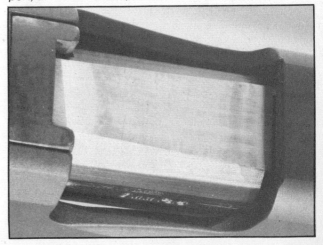

The 225 is a compact, nine-shot 9mmP pistol. Intended for use by plainclothes officers, the gun is slightly smaller than a Model 226.

The magazine catch of the 225s and 226s is located as shown here.

The SIG-Sauer 226 is a modified 220 available only in 9mmP. A magazine of fifteen shots is major difference.

Stavenhagen dots. Whenever the sight picture is augmented with the highlights, it is done on the undercut rear sight.

Before digressing from the design of the basic 220 to its descendants, it would be well to examine yet another manufacturing expedient cum technical innovation. The 220 locks by means of a Browning-type tilting barrel system. Like the 210, it avoids the pivoting link of the Colt and uses the cam groove system of the Hi-Power and derivatives. Still, the barrel pivots at the rear and is forced upwards as the slide goes forward into battery. In Brownings, Colts and countless other autoloaders, lugs on the top of the barrel mate with recesses in the underside of the slide top. The 220 uses a stamped sheet steel slide into which the recesses cannot readily be machined.

The designers solved the problem in an unusual and clever fashion. Instead of locking lugs on top of the barrel, the 220 uses a barrel with a large squared section at the rear. The greatest mass of the squared section lies above the centerline of the bore. As the slide moves forward to put the gun into battery, the barrel pivots upward and the squared section is forced into its locking recess — which is also the ejection port. It is relatively easy to make the gun work in this fashion, since the ejection port is cut entirely across the top surface of the slide. The rear surface of the ejection port is actually the front face of the breech block. A close examination of these parts on a sample pistol will make the relationship quite plain. It would seem to be a fairly easy locking system to produce, but a system that would not be prone to malfunction.

With this locking system and the other technical innovations, you'd think that the 220 would be the autoloading pistol to meet every need. It does meet a great many of them, but the fact is that some users of automatic pistols find the 220 to be excessively large for concealed carry. For that need, SIG-Sauer came up with the 225.

The 225 is a version of the 220 in which the length and height measurements have been reduced. A 225 will measure about three-quarters of an inch less in length and about a half inch less in height. Aside from the more compact dimensions, the 225 differs in the contour of the grip and trigger guard. The grip has been altered in an altogether pleasing fashion. It is slightly slimmer, but more significantly, it is attractively rounded at the lower rear of the butt. The overall impression is quite different from the 220.

The 225 trigger guard is elongated forward for use with gloves and the front face is squared and curved for a shooting grip with the index finger of the non-shooting hand. Further, it would seem that the designers got tired of the griping of combat competition shooters with respect to the placement of the magazine catch. On the 225, the catch is right where it should be — on the frame, close to the right thumb.

While the 220 and 225 are both superior pistols by any standard, they lack the feature which has been accepted as a necessity for modern times. The 220's magazine will accept nine 9mmP cartridges and the 225's will take eight. Both of them use efficient single-column designs. There are plenty of good automatics on the market which will

The magazine of the 226 uses a removable floorplate, which eases the cleaning chore. People who own more than one automatic will appreciate the clear markings.

The slightly beveled magazine well eases quick changes in a combat situation. Also note the slim, rounded shape of the butt. It can be managed by the smallest of hands.

The U.S. test trials deemed the SIG-Sauer 226 to be an acceptable handgun for American forces, but the decision went to the Beretta 92-SB-F.

226s with serial numbers above 134,000 will be made with "mud rails," recesses in the slide system which allow crud to collect without causing jams — GOOD idea.

The aristocrat of automatics, a Model 210-1 currently sells for over fifteen hundred bucks and may probably be worth it.

The SIG-Sauer lineup of high quality handguns. Above, left and right, the 220 and 225 both single column autos. Left: The redoubtable Model 226.

take as many as eighteen shots in a double column, and that's why the SIG-Sauer design people developed the 226.

The actual impetus for the 226 variation probably was the American service pistol test trials of the early 1980s. After years of discussion, the United States set about a systematic search for a new service pistol. One of the first things that was produced was a list of criteria which included a staggered-column magazine. SIG-Sauer met that requirement with the fifteen-shot magazine of the 226.

There are some other small differences, but the 226 is nothing more than a 220 with a somewhat thicker butt section. Subtly rounded like the 225's, the 226 grip houses a sturdy box magazine of fifteen shot capacity. This brings the pistol into line with the requirements of the U.S. test trials.

In that competition, the 226 was judged to be acceptable as was the Beretta 92F. All that separated the two was the price, not just of the gun, but also of spare parts, magazines and related paraphernalia. In view of the fact that the tests were quite thorough, the endorsement of the pistol as ac-ceptable is no small achievement.

The design and production of the entire family of SIG and SIG-Sauer automatic pistols is an achievement. While we are not concerned in these pages with pistols of other calibers, it is worthwhile to mention the SIG-Sauer 230, a .380 pocket automatic of impressive appearance and handling.

In 9mmPs, there are three from SIG-Sauer — the 220, 225 and 226. Each is a slightly different variation of the same basic gun and each meets a different need in the marketplace. Each handles well and produces accuracy way above the average. They are the very epitome of modern design excellence married to the best in manufacturing know-how.

But if your forte is the figurative Rolls-Royce in anything, then your hand, eye, heart and affections will go toward the SIG 210 in pistols. One of the more expensive automatic pistols in the world, the 210 sits atop the heap as the best of all 9mmP handguns. A sweet spot, to say the least! — *Wiley Clapp*

BEST BUYS IN 9MM AUTOS

CHAPTER 11

Chuck Karwan Votes These As His Top Choices, And Gives His Reasons!

AT LAST check, there were over forty different models of 9mm semi-automatic pistols available on the U.S. market. It is admittedly a tall order to pick out only two that offer best buy status. By best buy I mean those 9mms that offer the most gun for the least money. After I expound on the virtues of my two picks, I believe their excellence will become clear. When you compare their price with the rest of the market, the reason they are my choice as best buys should become obvious.

Since I did not want to waste a lot of time comparing apples with oranges, I decided to break up my choices into two broad categories. The first category is single-action autos, which are those auto pistols that must be cocked for the first shot. The other category is double-action autos, which may be fired from the hammer-down position like a double-action revolver. Without further ado, in my not so humble opinion the best buy on the U.S. market today in a single-action semi-automatic 9mm pistol is the Spanish Star BM and for a double-action 9mm it is the Brazilian Taurus PT 99. Both give performance all out of proportion to their modest purchase price.

If you will glance at the accompanying table of specifications, you can see that the Star BM is a compact pistol. In fact, it is not much bigger than a Walther PP. Because it is so flat, it is an excellent handgun to be carried concealed while at the same time it offers a full-size, comfortable grip. The Star BM is a standard sidearm in the Spanish military

The Star BM and the Taurus PT99 compared. Author sees pair as best dollar value on today's market. Lower left: the value leaders holstered in the coming thing in scabbard technology, Nylon. These holsters are from Uncle Mike's.

and Spain's National Police, the Guardia Civil. It has only recently begun to be superseded by the excellent Star Model 30 M double-action high-capacity 9mm pistol, though I am sure that the Star BM will remain favored for concealed carry. In many circles, Spanish handguns have a reputation for being poorly manufactured of inferior material. While that has been true of some Spanish handguns, it has never been true of the Star products. Over the years I have owned many Star pistols. Each and every one has been well made of excellent material. The current Star BM is no exception.

Basically a variation on the Colt Browning M1911 theme, the Star BM differs in a number of details. There is no separate mainspring housing or grip safety, the deletions of both of which many would consider as an improvement over the original M1911. In addition, it has many features which would be extra-cost gunsmith modifications on most of its competition. These include a bell-mouthed clip chute for faster reloading, a throated barrel and polished feed ramp for positive feeding of hollow point and flat nosed

SPECIFICATION TABLE

Model	cal.	finish	magazine capacity	length barrel	length overall	width	wt. oz.	suggest. retail	actual retail
Star BM	9mm	blue	8	4"	7"	1.13	35	$295	$255
BKM	Same except alloy frame						26		
Importer: Interarms **Number Ten Prince Street** **Alexandria, Virginia 22313**									
Taurus PT 99	9mm	blue	15	4.92"	8.54"	1.45	34	$341.59	$300
PT 92	9mm	Same but fixed sights						$317.46	$280
Importer: Taurus International Manufacturing, Inc. **4503 South West 71st Avenue** **P.O. Box 558567 Ludlam Branch** **Miami, Florida 33155**									

bullets, a rounded magazine follower for positive last round feeding, a captured recoil spring for smooth consistent cycling, and bold, wide fixed combat sights for fast, easy sight acquisition.

One feature of questionable value is the magazine safety. I for one feel that magazine safeties have caused more problems than they have prevented. In most cases, including the Star BM, they also inhibit magazine ejection. Fortunately, the Star magazine safety is easily removed by merely removing the grips and driving the pin-like magazine safety arm out left to right. With the magazine safety removed, the Star's magazine ejects readily, the round in the chamber may be fired with the magazine removed and the hammer may be lowered after clearing the pistol without reinserting a magazine.

The thumb safety on the Star is in the usual M1911 position, but it is actually superior in that it lifts the hammer off of the sear. Also, unlike the M1911, it may be engaged with the hammer down, though I see little use for such a feature. Like the M1911, the Star BM has an inertial firing pin, which means that when the hammer is fully forward on a chambered round the firing pin is not resting on the primer. One design feature of the Star that I truly dislike is that the firing pin is retained by a pin under the rear sight. Thus, to clean and lubricate the firing pin is a real hassle, requiring a vise to hold the slide, a brass drift and a hammer to drive off the rear sight and a pin punch to drive out the retaining pin.

The Star BM is made completely from steel except for its black plastic grips and consequently for such a compact pistol it still weighs a hefty 35 ounces. However, it has a brother called the Star BKM that is exactly the same except that it has an aluminum alloy frame which cuts nearly nine ounces off of the BM's weight, making it one of the lightest 9mms on the market. Everything else that has been said about the BM applies equally to the BKM, including best buy status. To choose between the two is strictly a matter of personal preference.

My sample Star BM has a crisp 5½-pound trigger pull. It is so crisp that it feels lighter than it is. Regardless, it is an eminently serviceable trigger, right out of the box. The Star

uses a pivoting trigger instead of the sliding trigger of the M1911. It has been my experience from a gunsmithing standpoint that is possible to get a much lighter yet totally safe and reliable pull on the pivoting trigger system of the Star than is possible with the sliding trigger of the M1911. In fact, I have in my personal collection a rare Star Model A Target 9mm which has an incredible two-pound trigger pull that is totally reliable. The slide can even be slammed on an empty chamber without the hammer falling.

From an accuracy standpoint, the sample Star BM was no target pistol, but its performance was satisfactory for a service-type arm. Best accuracy was achieved with the Remington 115-grain jacketed hollow point load with four-inch groups or better at twenty-five yards. Best of all, after trying a wide variety of ammunition of every description, including loads from 90-grain hollow points through 124-grain metal case loads including the excellent Winchester Silver Tip hollow points, the Star has yet to have a malfunction of *any* kind. It seems to have the amiable ability of feeding and firing anything you can fit in the magazine with complete reliability. That is the best trait a service or self defense pistol can have. In my book, it more than makes up for the lack of target accuracy. For example, the four-inch capability of the Star translates to eight inches at fifty yards. This in turn means that the bullet will strike within four inches of the point of aim. That makes a chest hit on a man at fifty yards easy, even on a skinny man. Accuracy better than that is pure gravy, particularly when combined with such excellent reliability.

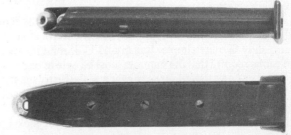

Eight shots versus fifteen. Taurus has the clear edge in capacity with its double column. Star features a single column, for a thinner magazine, and is flatter overall.

My test sample of the Taurus PT 99 shot an equally wide variety of 9mm loads with superb reliability. I have yet to have a malfunction with it of any kind. For the Taurus this should not be a surprise considering the fact that the Taurus PT 99 is a minor derivative of the super reliable Beretta Model 92, a variation of which won the recent U.S. 9mm handgun trials. For most Americans, it must seem peculiar to consider buying a quality handgun manufactured in what some people would consider as a Third World country.

First off, Brazil is not your typical developing Latin American country in that it has a strong industrial base and natural resources that approach those of the U.S. Likewise Forjas Taurus, the Brazilian company that manufacturers the PT 99, is no jungle workshop either. Instead it is an international industrial manufacturing giant that employs over 2000 workers and manufactures revolvers, pistols, submachine guns, hand tools, fishing tackle, motorcycle helmets, body armor and other consumer items to the tune of over 300,000 units annually, which are exported to over fifty-eight countries. The company was founded in 1939 and for a ten-year period was a division of Bangor-Punta, the former parent company of Smith & Wesson. Under Bangor-Punta, Taurus' handgun line was improved in quality control and manufacturing standards. In 1977, Taurus became a fully Brazilian-owned company. In 1979, Taurus purchased Beretta's Brazilian firearms manufacturing installations. One of the products of these facilities was the Beretta Model 92 9mm pistol which was being produced for the Brazilian military. Taurus continues to produce their version of the Beretta Model 92 for Brazil and for a large number of other countries as the Taurus PT 92 and PT 99 (same except adjustable sights). The Taurus 9mm has been adopted by the military forces of a number of African, Middle Eastern and other Third World countries. Interestingly, in a recent military conflict there were Taurus 9mm pistols on both sides of the fight!

Originally, the Taurus 9mm pistols were exactly like the Beretta Model 92, but just as the Beretta 92 has evolved into the improved 92 SB-F, so has the Taurus evolved into the current improved PT 92AF and PT 99AF. Both Beretta and Taurus have gone to an M1911-type magazine release, which is by far the best location and type. Both have also gone to a firing pin safety that prevents discharge except when the trigger is pulled. Likewise, they both have adopted hooked trigger guards for the finger-forward, two-handed hold and serrated front and back straps.

The only significant departure between the Beretta and the Taurus mechanically is that Taurus has retained the frame-mounted M1911-type safety of the original Beretta 92 and Beretta has changed to a slide-mounted, hammer-dropping safety.

In addition, Taurus has added a safety lever to the right side making it ambidextrous. The reason Beretta changed their safety is quite simple. Italian and U.S. military specifications require that the hammer must be able to be safely lowered without touching the trigger and the pistol must be able to be cleared — slide retracted — with the safety on. Thus Beretta went to a slide-mounted safety that safely drops the hammer automatically and does not lock the slide.

The Taurus safety is frame-mounted and located ideally for operation by the thumb: Up is on and down is off. It can

be engaged with the hammer up or down and locks the slide when engaged. In this way, with the safety on and the slide locked, the Taurus may be inserted into a tight-fitting holster without worrying about the slide being inadvertently partially retracted.

Best of all, when the Taurus safety is engaged, it does not drop the hammer, but instead gives the shooter a "cocked and locked" option. For those diehard single-action buffs, it allows you to ignore the double-action mechanism and operate the pistol just like you would an M1911.

The only other double-action auto being manufactured today that allows a true cocked-and-locked carry, to my knowledge, is the Czech CZ 75, which is virtually unavailable in the U.S. at this time. The Taurus does require extra care in lowering the hammer on a chambered round.

Personally, I believe most trained gun handlers will prefer the Taurus safety system as I do. However, I do believe the hammer-dropping safety is better for general troop issue where the training level of the respective soldier, sailor, or marine is an unknown. Actually, for most people, neither safety system offers any substantial advantage since in most cases either the Taurus or the Beretta would be carried with the hammer down and safety off anyway.

The Taurus features walnut grips as a standard feature. The ones on my sample PT 99 AF are of honey-colored slightly-figured Brazilian walnut. I have an average-sized

Look familiar? That's not surprising, as the field-stripped Star looks a lot like the Colt GM, from which it was copied. It's a little easier to disassemble, there are fewer parts.

hand and, though the grip is large, it is quite comfortable for me. I could see where a person with small hands might have some trouble with the grip, but even then the grip panels could be thinned nearly an eighth-inch on each side if necessary. My hand is fleshy between the thumb and forefinger and as a result many autos such as the Browning Hi-Power and the Colt Commander literally tear the web of my hand up with hammer-bite. The Taurus offers no such problems and is in fact one of the most comfortable pistols to shoot out-of-the-box that I have encountered. The main reason for the substantial grip of the Taurus is its staggered-column, fifteen-shot magazine, allowing a fully loaded capability of sixteen rounds. That's ten more rounds than the typical revolver and certainly a major advantage in any shooting encounter.

The Taurus has a barrel that is throated for blunt or hollow point bullets and to this day I have not had a failure to feed with any of a wide variety of ammunition that I have shot in it. It literally gobbles up anything you feed it, including hollow point loads that have given me feeding trouble in other 9mms. As I stated with the Star BM, a pistol cannot have a better or more important trait than reliability. Accuracy was quite respectable with it, being rather easy to get groups under three inches at twenty-five yards. I had a number of groups shot at fifteen yards from a supported position where three or four out of five could be covered with one-inch target paster. Some of the best groups were shot with the CCI Blazer 115-grain full metal jacket load that features a non-reloadable aluminum case. I have often found that I shoot better with the Blazers,

Field-stripped Taurus is a flat-out copy of the Beretta 92. The Beretta is an excellent design and the Taurus provides a low-cost option. Reliability is excellent.

because I can concentrate better on my shooting and not worry about where my precious reloadable brass is ending up. Too often, I've caught myself squeezing off a round and following through with a quick turn of the head to see where the empty case was landing.

The fit and finish of my sample Taurus PT 99 is most pleasing. The top, rear, and front area of the slide, as well as the side flats of the frame, have a fine matte black finish, while the front and rear area of the frame and the side flats of the slide have a shiny black finish. I find the contrasts to be esthetically pleasing as well as practical. The slide-to-frame fit is excellent. The single-action trigger pull of my specimen is a stiff but crisp 6½ pounds, while the double-action pull is thirteen pounds. The double-action pull is

quite smooth. I found that I could get consistent first-round center hits firing double-action, particularly when using a two-hand Weaver stance.

The Taurus 9mm comes in two basic flavors: The PT 92 AF and the PT 99 AF. They differ only in that the PT 99 model has a higher front sight and a well protected and low-mounted, fully adjustable rear sight. The sight even features the three-dot system in that it has a white dot on each side of the rear notch and a red dot on the front blade. If you like plain black sights, as I do, the dots are easily blacked out. While both Tauruses deserve best buy status, my choice is the PT 99 for the adjustable sight, since the price difference is only twenty dollars or so.

Since the Taurus is manufactured in a developing country, one of the first thoughts is the specifications of the materials used in manufacture. Taurus uses the same 4140 drop-forged steel favored by the U.S. manufacturers. The frames of the Taurus 9mm are made from the same high-strength aluminum alloy used by Beretta in the recently adopted U.S. 9mm. Quality of materials is no problem with any Taurus firearm. Taurus believes in the quality of their product so much that they offer a unique *lifetime* free repair policy. To quote Taurus "Without extending our normal warranty, we will repair *free of charge* (my italics), any weapon manufactured or distributed by Taurus International." I don't know where you can find a better deal than that!

The international monetary situation is such that the U.S. dollar is so strong that it often purchases more abroad than it does here at home which, in turn, puts an unfair bias pricewise in favor of many foreign products over their U.S. competition. This is certainly true of 9mm pistols, so it should be no surprise that my two picks for best buy are of foreign manufacture. The dollar is so strong that the importers of the Star and Taurus pistols have passed this price advantage along to their distributors who have, in turn, passed it along to the dealers who, in most cases, do the same to their customers. Since the former suggested retail prices have not been adjusted to reflect this situation, I have shown two retail prices in the specification tables, the suggested retail and the current actual retail that reflects the current strong dollar situation. I arrived at the actual retail price by adding a full normal mark up to the average actual dealer price and double-checked that against actual gun shop prices. As you can see, both the Star BM and the Taurus PT 92/99 are nearly the lowest-priced 9mm pistols in their respective classes (single-action and double-action). Yet they offer performance on par with the most expensive. You can nearly buy two Star BMs for the price of one Colt Combat Commander. The same holds true for the Taurus compared to the Beretta 92SB-F. Are the Star and the Taurus better? No, but for all practical purpose they are just as good and at a much lower price. That is why I rate them best buys. Are there other top buys? Surely. One that deserves mention is TZ-75, which is imported by F.I.E. It is priced about the same as the Taurus PT92 and is well made and of excellent design. The Taurus got my pick over the TZ-75 chiefly because of Taurus's Lifetime free repair policy and I like some of the Taurus features better. The point of all this is that it is possible to get top performance in a 9mm auto at a moderate price. For most of us that is important! The Star BM and the Taurus PT99-AF are excellent examples of just that. — *Chuck Karwan*

The new service pistol is the Beretta 92F. Evolved from the 951 of the early 1950s, it features a magazine which holds fifteen shots. There's also a double-action trigger and other new features. A new face to get used to...

CHAPTER 12

OLD COLTS AND NEW BERETTAS

A Comparative Look At Service Pistols: 1911A1 .45s and 92F 9mmPs

"SKIPPER, WE got six new .45s, and I fixed this one up for you, with that funny trigger and all," said the company armorer as he handed me a 1911A1. It was May of 1965, and our company of the Seventh Marines was leaving Camp Pendleton for an uncertain future in Vietnam. The supply system was dumping vast quantities of stuff on us in anticipation of wartime service, the new .45 being but one such item. In actuality, the youthful corporal was wrong on two counts, in that the piece in question was not new, and the trigger was damned sure not funny.

The pistol was an entirely typical Pistol, Caliber .45, M1911A1 which had been through the arsenal rebuild program. The gun was, as I recall, a Colt that had been given a replacement slide made by Remington-Rand and a new coat of parkerizing, along with several other new parts. It did not appear to have been fired since the rebuild, hence the "new" tag. Knowing my preference for the 1911-style long trigger and flat mainspring housing, the armorer had removed those parts from my old issue pistol and substituted them in the new gun. The resulting trigger pull was acceptable, and I took custody of my new armament.

Nearly twenty months later, I left Vietnam and surrendered a by-now battered and worn .45 to my successor, as is the custom. There was bloody little of the parkerized finish left, but the gun functioned perfectly. It had not left my side for that entire time, except for an R&R to Hong Kong and infrequent trips to showers. The gun had survived more than a few total immersions in river and rice paddy, and had been cleaned so many times that I knew

every part by its first name. It would be very warlike if I could relate how the old gun saved my butt in countless firefights, but the truth is that the gun was fired "in anger" exactly once, with no effect sufficiently dramatic as to warrant the recounting.

But it was damned obvious that the gun could have been called on at any time to defend me and I have every confidence that the .45 would have performed as well as any other one of its type that ever graced a GI's holster. It was not my first .45, nor would it be my last. I have fired both formally and informally, respected, trusted, admired, and I suspect probably loved, John Browning's greatest invention for just about three decades. I *like* this gun.

But this little piece is not to wring every last bit of emotion from a bunch of middle-aged veterans nostalgic for a great firearm. As all handgunners must be aware, the armed services have decided to change to a new pistol. The decision is made, and no keening and wailing for remembrances of the Argonne, Anzio, or An Hoa will change it.

The new service automatic is the Beretta Model 92F. It was designed, and initial quantities of the gun were produced, in Italy. That aspect of the pistol is sufficiently controversial, but there's even more to talk about. The Beretta is a 9mmP. Those big chunky cartridges with the 230-grain bullets will eventually fade out of the supply system, as the .45 ACP round has been supplanted as our service pistol cartridge by the 9mm.

For the sake of all those who have ever carried and used the Browning-designed, Colt-produced, and generally admired M1911A1, let's take a look at the new, innovative

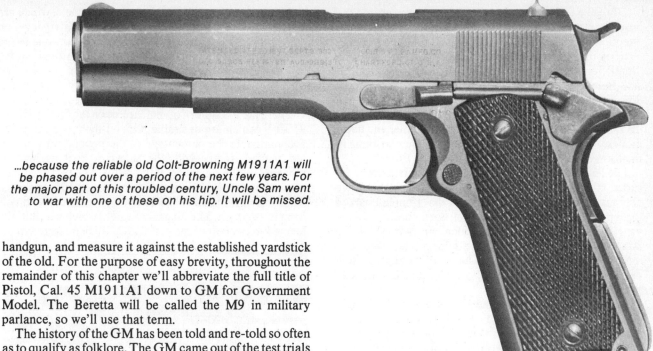

...because the reliable old Colt-Browning M1911A1 will be phased out over a period of the next few years. For the major part of this troubled century, Uncle Sam went to war with one of these on his hip. It will be missed.

handgun, and measure it against the established yardstick of the old. For the purpose of easy brevity, throughout the remainder of this chapter we'll abbreviate the full title of Pistol, Cal. 45 M1911A1 down to GM for Government Model. The Beretta will be called the M9 in military parlance, so we'll use that term.

The history of the GM has been told and re-told so often as to qualify as folklore. The GM came out of the test trials of the early part of this century. Those trials were mandated by the Department of the Army and sought to develop both a new handgun and new ammunition. After the legendary failings of the .38 rounds against charging Moro bolomen, the Army wanted a new handgun that would hit harder, hold more rounds and reload more quickly than the available revolvers.

After consideration of a number of guns, the winner was declared. It was the Colt firearms entry, a Browning-designed automatic. Seven-plus decades of service later, and after more than three million of them were made by Colt and other manufacturers, the GM was deemed to be

obsolete. The fact that the original manufacturer and other copy-cat types are doing a brisk business in selling them has little to do with the decision.

The M9 has a shorter and less colorful history. It had its conceptual origins in Mussolini's Italy of the late 1930s. The designers at one of that nation's leading firearms manufacturers, Pietro Beretta, saw that times were changing and that the service pistol for military use was changing with them. Instead of the holster versions of essentially pocket auto pistols, the service automatic for most nations was evolving to a larger, heavier and more capable battle pistol. The designers began work on the handgun which would evolve ultimately into the Beretta 92 series and, most recently, into the M9. Their efforts were interrupted by World War II.

Even the holsters will change. The two service pistols, shown here "At Ease" with their respective scabbards. A completely new nylon design from Bianchi will house the Beretta. It would have been welcomed long, long ago.

The biggest difference is immediately apparent. The 92F is chambered for the 9mmP cartridge. There's a world of difference between that and the forty-five-caliber bore of the M1911A1. Ammo will change to the NATO standard.

When the Italian arms industry came back to life in the post-war era, one of the first weapons to get developmental attention was the full-sized military pistol. By now, it was obvious that the trend in military pistols was toward the 9mmP version, so the factory followed suit. The first full-size Beretta of the post-war production was the Model 951. For the several decades that the gun was made, the 951 achieved a reputation for considerable reliability. In the U.S., the 951 came to be called the Brigadier and had a modest following. Its most impressive credential came in the form of selection by the Israeli Armed Forces.

The 951 was the major pistol used by the Israelis in the series of wars and other military expeditions that have characterized the modern history of that troubled part of the world. It served with distinction, not inconsiderable in view of the rocky, sandy, salt-ridden climes in which the Israelis must fight. During these same years, American forces were using the GM. The sturdy old Browning design served with reliability to match the Beretta's in Korea and Vietnam.

Still, by the mid 1970s, the 951 was a dated design. Although dependable, the gun lacked two of the features which were being included as "musts" on modern service autos — double-action trigger and a high-capacity magazine. Using the basic shape and locking system of the 951, the Beretta designers incorporated those missing two features and called the resulting pistol the 92. It is a slightly modified version of this gun that was given a flat black finish to become the M9.

The modifications to the original 92 to produce the M9 are slight but they are significant. Their significance is that they were incorporated into the basic gun in response to a growing awareness of the practical value of a pistol as a battle weapon. Most combat shooters of the Cooper/Gunsite line of reasoning would welcome one of the two major modifications, the movement of the magazine catch from the base of the butt where it had to be manipulated with the off hand, to the left side of the frame just aft of the trigger guard where it could be manipulated with the thumb of the shooting hand. This feature makes a rapid magazine change much easier.

The other feature is not so well accepted in combat shooting circles. This is the change to the basic safety system. On the original 92, the safety was mounted on the frame. When activated, by an upward motion of the thumb of the right hand, the safety worked by blocking the sear linkage to the hammer. It worked as well as the one on the GM, and was desirable in the sense that the gun could be carried "cocked-and-locked" in the modern combat shooting manner. Carried in this fashion, it was easy for a trained shooter to sweep the safety lever down and off while he was establishing the combat grip on the piece. This was exactly the way it was done with the GM.

While this system was essentially safe when used by a trained man, there arose a school of thought which held that a safety which physically blocked the firing pin was more nearly perfect. Also, while the original safety system did not preclude use of the original double-action trigger, it did not provide for the safe lowering of the hammer. For these two reasons, the Beretta designers changed the 92 pistol to include a re-designed safety, mounted on the slide.

The device was added to the later 92 models, which are sequentially called the 92S and 92SB. The safety lever on these guns pivots in the opposite direction as the one on the 92 and drops the hammer in the process. Throughout the process, the firing pin is totally blocked from contact with the hammer. It is an exceptionally safe way to do things. This system was, of course, incorporated into the M9.

There are a couple of other features on the finalized M9/92SB-F which are desirable. One of them is an effort to accommodate the percentage of the population which is left-handed. In the M9, the safety/de-cocking lever is repeated on the right side of the pistol. The two levers are mirror images of each other and are connected by a central shaft which is linked to the internal parts in order to perform its function. The magazine catch, which was initially located in the butt of the pistol and which migrated to the

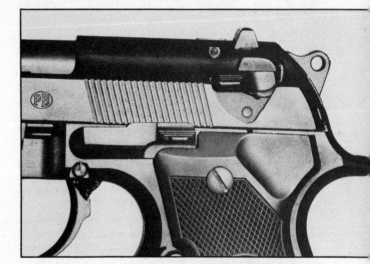

Above: The 92F will be identified as the M9 in the armed forces. It is a double-action pistol which means that it fires from a hammer-down position. A live round may be carried in perfect safety in M9's firing chamber.

Below: After the first shot, the slide cycles, ejecting the fired round from the chamber. As the recoil spring forces the slide forward, a new cartridge is fed and the hammer is left cocked. Following shots are single action.

Lefties will appreciate this feature. The safety lever is repeated on the right side of the pistol for convenient use by southpaws. Not visible in this photo is a magazine catch which can be reversed for even more convenience.

area where the trigger guard abuts the grip, is reversible. This means that the soldier to whom the pistol is issued may, at his discretion, change the catch around in such a way as to make it work left-handed. To do this, the catch is removed from the left side of the pistol and re-inserted in the right side. In use, the reversed catch is pushed inward with the thumb of the left or shooting hand.

This ambidextrous aspect of the M9 is no small thing. Left-handed people are adept at reconciling their differences with a backwards world, but to watch what a lefty had to go through with a right-handed GM will make you appreciate the features of the M9.

With the foregoing discussion of the design history of the two pistols completed, we can now look at them side by side. There are some pronounced similarities as well as the obvious differences. Dimensions are probably the area in which there is the most commonality.

The M9 weighs almost forty-one ounces unloaded and the GM weighs just over thirty-nine. The weight is thus very close. The barrel length of the chrome-lined M9 barrel is given at 4.92 inches and the GM is five inches; again, very close. Length of the M9 exceeds the overall

There's no great difference in the external measurements of the two autos. Both are big, hefty holster pistols. M1911A1 at the right...

...and the M9 to the left. Since the Beretta has an alloy frame, it can be bulkier in the butt section and match closely the weight of the GM.

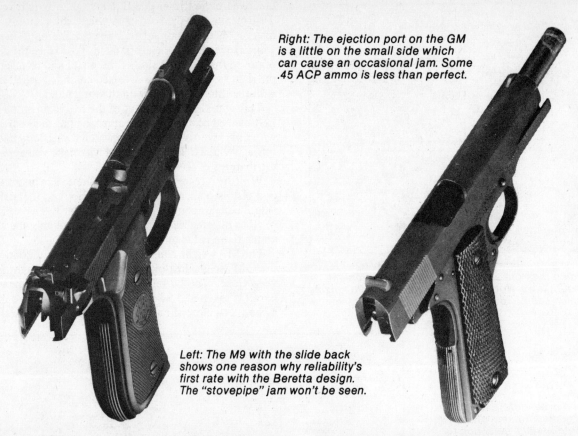

Right: The ejection port on the GM is a little on the small side which can cause an occasional jam. Some .45 ACP ammo is less than perfect.

Left: The M9 with the slide back shows one reason why reliability's first rate with the Beretta design. The "stovepipe" jam won't be seen.

length of the GM by a tiny fraction, 8.54 inches versus 8.50. In similar fashion, the height of the two guns as measured vertically is remarkably similar.

These comparisons don't tell much of the story as to how the two pistols actually compare. For example, the weights are very close, but only because the Beretta's frame is made of an aluminum alloy while the Colt's is forged steel. Had the Beretta designers made the entire gun of steel, as did the Colt, then their pistol would not have been included in the U.S. test trials. One of the standards set forth by the trial board was a maximum unloaded weight of 1300 grams (2.87 pounds). The M9 in steel would have grossly exceeded that figure.

What is more significant is the overall impression a GM-experienced shooter will have when he picks up an M9. The GM is a hefty pistol to grasp in the hand, with the weight of the all-steel piece rather evenly distributed. By comparison, however, the M9 feels downright bulky and the balance is somewhat toward the muzzle. This is due to the use of the alloy in the portion of the pistol surrounded by the hand. When the gun is fully loaded, the balance difference is far less pronounced, although the physical dimensions of the butt remain unchanged. That's because the magazine, housed in the butt section, is thicker with two columns of cartridges.

The M9 has a first shot double-action capability and the GM does not; there's nothing to compare in this regard. The single-action pulls of GMs vary widely with the amount of abuse to which they have been subjected. Well-tuned by a competent 'smith, the GM trigger can be as

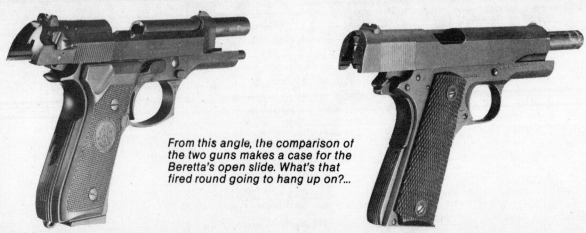

From this angle, the comparison of the two guns makes a case for the Beretta's open slide. What's that fired round going to hang up on?...

good as any. A new "issue" GM will likely have a single-action pull in the league with the M9s. Both of them have a military-type two-stage single-action pull.

It is very hard to compare reliability in an old and established design against such a relative newcomer. It becomes quite difficult in automatic pistol designs which are at the mercy of the quality of the ammunition used in them. The GM has the best part of a century of service behind it, and that has not been a time when the gun was reputed to be a problem. The record of service is, to say the least, distinguished. GMs work, when maintained with good magazines and when fed good ammunition.

The M9 is the latest pistol in the Beretta 9mmP family. That family history goes back for a lesser period of the time than the GMs, but it is a history of heavy wartime use. There is every reason to believe that the M9 will perform with great reliability when maintained, with good magazines and when fed good ammunition.

One factor in the functional reliability reputation of nearly all modern Berettas is the open slide. Berettas use a slide that is open to the top and which is not designed to have any need for an ejection port. The breech end of an M9 barrel is open to the exterior for nearly 180 degrees of the barrel's circumference. This means that the classic stovepipe jam of a GM is virtually eliminated. There is not much for the ejected round to catch against when the slide is to the rear. If there are to be jams in an M9, they are more

likely to be in the feeding and chambering cycle. That type of malfunction is almost always a function of deformed magazines or ammunition with radically contoured bullets.

Accuracy: How well does the M9 shoot as compared to the GM? Out of the box, a new M9 will probably outshoot a GM. But since the guns use different ammunition, the comparison is sort of an apples-versus-oranges thing. The margin between a GM taken from current military stocks and a new M9 would be pronounced. The difference between a new M9 and a new commercial Colt .45 version of the GM would narrow the gap considerably. And shooting the guns comparatively, with selected lots of the best available ammunition, would blur the distinction between them to the point of being inconsequential. Let it suffice to say that there is more than adequate combat accuracy in the new M9; machine rest tests with the gun prove that it will hold the ten ring of the Standard American Pistol Target with a wide variety of ammunition.

With the different type of controls on the M9, a great deal of research will have to be done on the manner of handling the pistol. The biggest single thing to be learned will be the transition from first-shot double-action to second-shot single-action. This is a problem that has plagued shooters ever since designers put the feature on automatic pistols. It is harder to overcome for some shooters than others, and hardest of all for dyed-in-the-wool GM buffs. In the M9, there is perhaps a little less difficulty than with

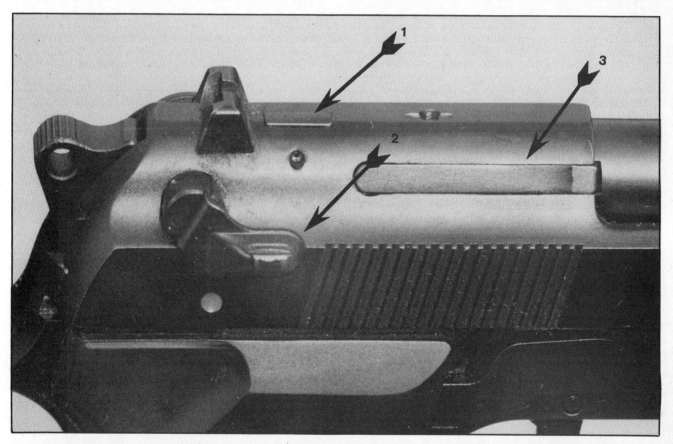

Here are some more unique features of the new M9 service pistol. #1: This bar is the tip of the firing pin block; it rises upwards from the top of the slide when the trigger is pulled. #2: The ambidextrous safety lever is a true mirror image of the one on the other side. #3: The extractor projects outwards when there's a round in the M9's chamber.

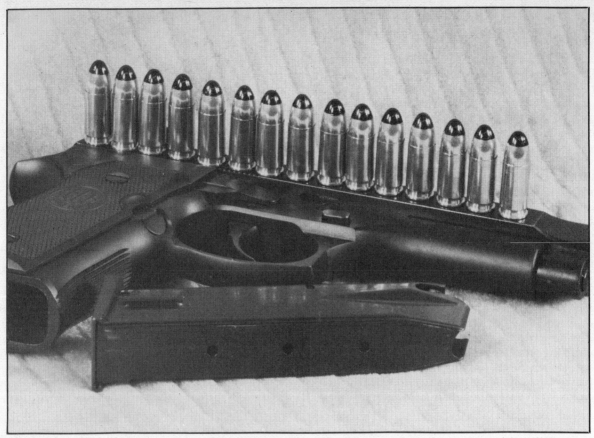

Apparently some drill instructor called a squad of fifteen 9mmP cartrdiges to attention and gave them the command "Dress right, DRESS" on top of an M9 slide. The magazine in the foreground will hold all fifteen of them, a requirement of the board which drew up the specifications. Long ago, a similar board designed…

other guns, but it is still a problem. The hand takes a certain "set" or grip to shoot double-action and a different one is needed for subsequent single-action shots. This is a tactical difficulty of no small magnitude. I hope that some clever fellow comes along with a way to teach shooters to handle it.

The GM is a sturdy and reliable pistol, perfectly safe in the hands of a man well-trained in its use. But despite the amount of ink that the GM as a combat weapon has received in the past twenty years, the fact remains that, unless a shooter is mercilessly drilled to handle the pistol properly, the GM is not safe to carry with a round in the chamber. If dropped, the GM may fire. The safety lock of the GM,

manually applied, will occasionally brush off against the holster or clothing. If everything works as designed, the M9 is a safer pistol.

But we don't have a huge body of experience yet on the functioning of the relatively complicated mechanism that is the safety system of the M9. Only time will tell. And we are not likely to know how well the thing will hold up until it has been used in battle by a variety of shooters in a variety of climes. It is intended to provide the pistol-equipped soldier with a firearm of greater firepower. With a fifteen-shot magazine, there are certainly more shots than in the GM.

At least one feature of the M9 is vastly superior to the

BIG improvement! Sights on the M9 are superior to those on the GM by a wide margin. Left: The rear sight is a wide notch highlighted as seen here. That matches up nicely with…

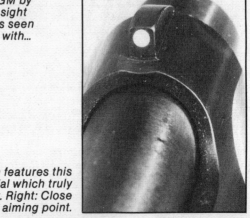

…a front sight which features this dot of luminous material which truly does glow in the dark. Right: Close up photo shows forward aiming point.

...another pistol for our Armed Forces. In those days, firepower was interpreted differently. The cartridges parading atop the M1911A1 are fewer in number, but look at how much broader their shoulders are! Seven of the chunky .45s fill the magazine. It'll take some battle data to determine the M9's value; the .45's is known.

Tucked away in the nylon holster of the future, the M9 will have a big job ahead of it. The old leather holster that carried the .45 is a big one to fill. We'll see...

GM. Every combat shooter worthy of the name took his new GM and removed the sights, to replace them with a set that were larger and easier to see. The M9 has an adequately large set of sights with a wider, deeper rear sight notch. The fact that they are highlighted with a white dot front and white bar rear is a feature that will be debated. In good light, the highlights are annoying. You won't see these sights used when the M9 goes on the line for the service pistol matches at Camp Perry. But for its battle use, that little highlight on the front sight may be enough to make the difference in aiming the pistol in a life-or-death confrontation in dim light.

The goal in developing the M9 as service pistol was to give our military a safer, more accurate handgun of greater firepower. As 9mmP automatics go, the Beretta design is one of the very best. It probably is a bit safer for most soldiers to carry due to the double-action trigger and firing pin block. It is probably a little more accurate with good ammunition.

And that leaves the firepower issue. It was a mandate of the board that the pistol be a 9mmP. Whether it should have been or not is moot; it is. Firepower, as it applies to the current line of service pistol reasoning, means more shots. The M9 has a magazine which holds fifteen rounds and which feeds them into the chamber with notable regularity. That's all well and good, and the M9 is a service pistol on which we can rely for years to come.

So was the GM. — *Wiley M. Clapp*

CHAPTER 13

The rest of the world sees it differently, but in America the cop on the beat packs a wheelgun. The 9mmPs are making some inroads, but have a long way to go in the face of competition from the likes of these quality guns from Colt, Smith & Wesson and Ruger.

NINEFIRING

IN THE COURSE of assembling the information that is reported to you in this book, we looked at a great many pistols and revolvers chambered for the 9mmP cartridge. It has been a vastly entertaining as well as an educational experience. After having done so, certain things seem clear to us.

The 9mmP cartridge and the myriad of handguns that are chambered for it have clearly occupied the attentions of a great many very clever people and they've done it for a long, long time. In the US, we tend to think of handguns in terms of the millions of double-action revolvers in .38 caliber that have left the Colt, Smith & Wesson, and more

recently, the Ruger, plants over the past many decades. We undeniably enjoy a greater freedom of choice in selecting our armament, but our selections tend to be colored somewhat by the fact that the cop on the beat packs a .38 revolver. The rest of the world just doesn't see it that way.

One of the reasons the rest of the world stays with the 9mmP cartridge is to have interchangeability with their submachine guns. Overseas, there's little ammo variety.

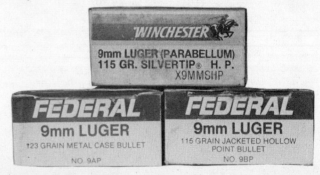

Wherein We Develop And Use A Consistent Procedure For Comparative Firing Of Everything "9" We Can Find

We had a fair variety of 9mmPs from Smith & Wesson to evaluate for this chapter. From left: Model 669, Model 639 with fancy buffalo horn stock, and an aging, service-worn Model 39.

For reasons delineated elsewhere in this book, and mostly tied up with interchangeable pistol and submachine gun ammo, the world at large chooses the 9mmP cartridge. With a few unusual variations, most of those handguns are automatic pistols. This brings us to an inescapable conclusion — more different handguns are chambered for this cartridge, and in more different places, than any other cartridge ever developed. The military and security forces of most of the Free World carry 9mmP handguns, understandable national pride causing the majority of them to choose a home-grown product.

This adds up to one hell of a lot of 9mmP handguns!

With an ambitious title such as this volume bears, it follows that you should be able to read about most, if not all, 9mmP pistols. We did our best, and you'll find our subjective and objective evaluations of a great many handguns on the followng pages.

There are some designs missing, but rest assured that if your favorite nine didn't make roll call when we headed for the range, it was because we just couldn't find an example to try out. We did get excellent support from some manufacturers and importers, and a great many of the tested guns came from our own personal collections and from those of friends.

We are satisfied that the guns we fired constitute a highly representative sampling. If, for example, we didn't get every possible Smith & Wesson automatic, we did get three: an older Model 39 and a pair of new designs in the 639 and 469. In so doing, the Springfield, Massachusetts firm is well represented with old, stainless, and double column designs. We fired all three revolver designs from Ruger and Smith & Wesson. Dean Grennell even managed to produce a 9mmP barrel for a Thompson/Center Contender. The only 9mmP that Colt ever produced is

9mmP revolvers? Better believe it, and some good ones. From top: Ruger .357 Blackhawk with 9mmP cylinder in place, Smith & Wesson Model 547, and a Stainless Steel Ruger Speed Six.

Right: The Thompson Center Contender was produced for a time in 9mmP. Dean Grennell produced this one from his selection of things Contender.

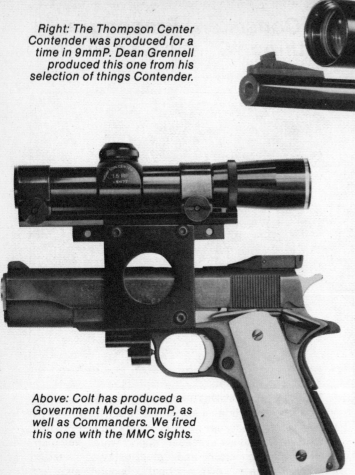

Above: Colt has produced a Government Model 9mmP, as well as Commanders. We fired this one with the MMC sights.

Customizing a Smith usually refers to the rebuilding of a revolver. Below: The ASP conversion of the Smith & Wesson M39.

Below: 9mmP automatics are made all over the world; A80 from Astra is one of several entries from the Spaniards.

reviewed. It's the familiar M1911A1, a design that dates way back to the early days of the century as does the Luger which we also fired. There's a custom 9, in the person of Grennell's ASP, and a rare one in the form of a CZ75. The P38 from Walther and the P35 from Fabrique Nationale are included. There are 9mmP designs from Spain, Germany, Italy, Switzerland and Austria. And by the time the book actually goes to press, we'll undoubtedly find a few more.

Testfiring this many guns presents major logistical problems. We wanted to use a procedure that was consistent throughout. In other words, each gun should be fired in a manner as close as possible to that used for all others. Accomplished in this way, the reports of the tests would have far greater validity for comparative purposes. Still, there are deadlines to meet and expenses to consider and we had to devise a procedure that was feasible in that light. And we also wanted to use a system that would give you a better idea of what a particular 9mmP handgun was *really* like — something more than a dreary table of tabulated data. Emphatically stated, we wanted to share our subjective impressions about the feel, the touch, the very essence of each gun.

After some consideration, we were forced to abandon the idea of doing our accuracy testing by means of Chuck Ransom's reliable machine rest. Dean Grennell and I both have Ransom Rests and did use them for certain portions of this book, those that deal with testing the new Beretta and Bar-Sto barrels. But consider that while we had many

Right: This Llama Omni is a .45 but 9mmPs are produced. Below: Chuck Ransom's plank-mounted machine rest is retained in place by a half-ton GMC pickup.

Above: Roger Combs wrings out a H&K from the bench. Right: Shooter at portable bench can place all related paraphernalia close at hand.

grip inserts for the rest, we did not have all of them. Some guns don't occur often enough for Ransom to even make inserts. Therefore, we could use the Ransom Rest for only part of the testing procedure. To operate in this way would produce distorted results. This is no indictment of the Ransom Rest, quite the contrary. Every serious handgunner should have access to one of these truly marvelous devices.

Instead of the machine rest, we used bench testing. This is a form of shooting handguns in which the gun is fired off a sturdy shooting bench. The shooter assumes a seated position behind the bench, grasping the test handgun in the shooting hand. The non-shooting mitt is used to steady the firing hand, and the underside of the handgun is rested on a sandbag. That bag is in turn rested on a solid wooden rest.

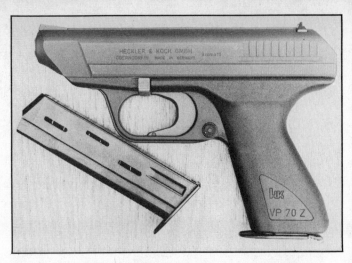

Above: This H&K was difficult to shoot from the bench in accuracy tests due to long DA-only trigger. Above left: Informal shooting sometimes gives a better feel for a gun. Below: Barricade firing can help evaluations.

Dean Grennell uses a shallow V-block, fabricated from two-inch plank stock and resembling the north end of a southbound sperm whale. As the tests wore on, I came to appreciate the value of this simple device — it's a whale of good idea.

If a shooter pays attention to the basics while using this technique, he can reach an entirely acceptable level of accuracy. But you *must* pay attention to your sight alignment and trigger control The position is sufficiently steady that your subconscious, accustomed to handguns waving around at arm's length, says "Relax buster, you can't miss." You *can* shoot crappy groups if you don't hold, align and squeeze, just as though it were an August afternoon at Camp Perry.

Inasmuch as was humanly possible, we attempted to be careful while shooting for accuracy off the bench. The results are reported for each gun in the pages that follow. You might be able to improve a bit, but I'll wager that if you do get better, it won't be by any really significant margin.

Still, shooting of this sort tells only a part of the general story of any handgun. Most 9mmPs were conceived as

This curious apparatus is the Sky Screen III from Oehler Research. Mounted on an aluminum rail, the screens sense passage of bullet over them and send signal to start and stop the clock back to a Model 33 chronograph.

defensive weapons for police or military use. To get the feel of a gun in this sense, you must do a fair amount of informal shooting at tin cans and plastic jugs and the like. Further, you should do a bit of shooting at man-sized and man-shaped silhouette targets. Informal shooting is more relaxing and more conducive to forming that subjective impression of how a gun really shoots. It further breeds confidence in the ability to use the gun in the emergency which, hopefully, will never occur. We should remain, nevertheless, *parabellum*. Or, as the Boy Scouts say, "Be Prepared."

During bench testing we also chronographed. Most of the results are via an Oheler 33 chronograph. On some days, the original Skyscreen IIs were used. Most of the time, the new Skyscreen IIIs provided excellent service.

Left: There's a lot of factory ammo to choose from. Some is seen here. Below: The test ammo from left to right: 115-grain Federal JHP, 115-grain Winchester Silvertip, and the 123-grain Federal FMJ.

The new version uses a cast plastic lens of sorts to give a greater "sensitive" area to read a bullet's passage and start or stop the clock. Under varying light conditions, the diffuser, which is the most noticeable feature of the IIIs, prevents glint from interfering with results. The Oehler system also provides a statistical summary on demand, giving highest, lowest, average and extreme spread of velocities. Finally, the 33 gives you a compound standard deviation.

What ammunition to use? That is a tough question to answer in view of the incredible variety of 9mmP ammo which may be found on dealer's shelves. We could not shoot all of it in every gun, or this book would become an encyclopedia. We selected ammo on the basis of ready availability to you, as well as past experience. The test ammo question eventually came down to a choice of three commercial rounds and three representative handloads.

The first of the commercial loads is Winchester-Western's 115-grain Silvertip hollow point. Silvertips have become nearly synonymous with high-velocity performance ammo in recent years. We weren't disappointed at all by the results that we obtained.

The second load was the Federal 115-grain JHP, the 9BP as the factory designates it. Dean Grennell has fired a good bit of this stuff, with few problems. You'll no doubt be pleased with its accuracy, as we were.

Lastly, we chose the Federal 123-grain FMJ. This load approaches the practical upper limit of bullet weight for the 9mmP. It also features a full metal jacket (FMJ) round-nosed, military-type bullet.

Handloads: Americans are handloaders and are interested in the factors in guns and ammunition components that affect handloading.

Left: The handloads fired in the test used S&W or Federal brass, CCI brand primers and Hercules powders. Bullets were, left to right, 115-grain Hornady JHP, 124-grain Hornady Flat Point FMJ, and the cast 120-grain flat point design from S&S Precision.

Above, above right, and right: These are the domestic loadings of the 9mmP used in our firing tests. They're all high quality rounds from two different manufacturers.

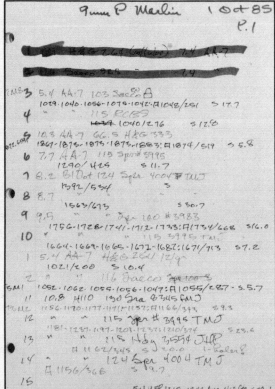

Above: Page of working data from one of Grennell's test projects hints at the nature of experimental ballistics. You can spend a lot of time working with various load combinations of the type of components shown at right.

In view of the number of guns to be tested and the number of rounds to be fired, we did not attempt to find the most accurate load for each handgun. To do so would have resulted in not just an encyclopedia, but a thirty-two volume encyclopedia. Serious load development is a subject that should be essayed on a one-gun-at-a-time basis.

We chose to assemble three representative handloads using common components available to all handloaders. Primers were the ever-present CCI-500 Small Pistol size. There is no need for Magnum primers in any sensible 9mmP load.

The brass used, at least at the start, was interesting. Grennell gave me a big plastic bag of brass from the range of the firm that did his ASP conversion of a Smith Model 39. It was presumably once-fired stuff and I first processed it by tumbling in a rotary tumbler. Once it was cleaned, I

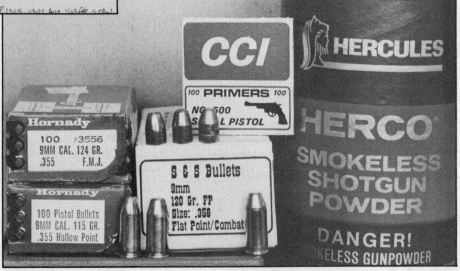

Once-fired S&W brass varied widely in overall length. The case on the left measured .738" and the one on the right was .760". Too much variation for precise loading.

sorted it and found that better than 80% was Smith & Wesson headstamp. I then culled it out for length and found an incredible variation of from .738-inch to .760-inch. That's excessive variation for good handloading performance, so I chose to use only cases running from .745-inch to .748-inch. It reduced my supply of brass by nearly forty percent, but insured that there would be greater consistency in crimp, therefore bullet pull, and consequent acceptable accuracy. I wasn't sorry, as the resulting handloads turned out to be good.

Then brass was sized in an RCBS tungsten carbide die mounted in a Rockchucker. Later on in the reloading process, I went to a new RCBS 4x4 press in order to speed things up a bit. This newest press from Oroville is a delight to use, but required care and absolutely one hundred percent consistent management. The final die used in the reloading process was an RCBS taper crimp die. That die

is required when you are assembling fodder for such a variety of chambers.

The handloads assembled in this way featured two different powders and three different bullets. Again, the idea was to produce representative ammunition, with the choice of powder and bullet combinations coming, in quiet candor, from Dean Grennell's vast experience.

The first load was the Hornady 115-grain JHP on top of 6.7 grains of Hercules Herco. The bullet is representative of designs available from all of the bullet manufacturers, its weight at about the mid-point of available weights in 9mm size. Herco is an excellent Parabellum powder.

Second, we used the 124-grain FMJ flat point bullet from Hornady, this time ahead of 5.1 grains of Herco. This is a compressed load. The bullet design is the so-called Air Force-type bullet which is shaped for maximum energy transfer, as well as reliable feeding.

Since so many handloaders cast their own slugs, we tried a cast bullet with Hercules Green Dot powder; 4.6 grains of it. The bullet is the S&S Precision Bullets 120-grain Flat Point/Combat, which resembles the Hornady design. S&S casts these bullets from an exceptionally hard alloy and we noted no leading problems.

In testing, we had surprisingly little problem with malfunctions. Those that did occur were usually attributable to the particular gun and usually to its magazine.

On succeeding pages, you'll find our impressions and objective test results. They're there for each gun and in no particular order. You may reach some conclusions of your own — compare them with ours at the end of this section. *Wiley M. Clapp*

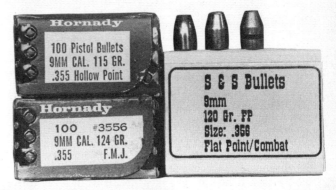

Good bullets are needed for good handloads. The ones above are as good as they come. Left: The test ammo all lined up for a family portrait, with the factory stuff placed on the left side.

CHAPTER 14

FIRING ALL AVAILABLE 9mmP HANDGUNS

BEFORE WE LAUNCH into the observations on each of the fifty handguns listed on the facing page, there's some other information that you need to have. In the previous chapter, we described the evaluation procedure is some detail, so we'll comment only so far as to say that a lot of slugs went over the chronograph screens in order to produce the data you see by each handgun. The measurements of all of those groups, by the way, was done with a ruler and we didn't try to split hairs and get them any closer than the nearest quarter inch.

There are a few handguns that aren't on the list because we couldn't turn one up to shoot. At press time, the new importer of the highly touted Bernardelli 9mmP pistols in both regular and compact form was unfortunately unable to get us a shooting sample. The Detonics Pocket 9 was another well-known pistol that just didn't find its way to us for evaluation. There are a couple of exotics, like the Korth and Korphilla, that we could not find anywhere.

In the case of some of the other guns, we didn't get every variation of the basic model. There are lots of Lugers around, but we felt that shooting one was sufficient. On the other hand, we did fire some of the revolvers in different barrel lengths, because the results of such firing are interesting to the ballisticians out there.

As noted elsewhere, there is a brand new 9mmP auto-matic on the horizon — the P85 from Ruger. The products of a manufacturer of that stature are of course immensely interesting. The P85 is no exception, but the guns are in the production prototype stage and not available for evaluation. Dean Grennell handled one at the NRA show in the spring of 1986. He reports that it was Ruger quality, just as you might expect.

There's one humorous note that I think you'd be interested in hearing about. Ninefiring Forty-One is about the Colt Government Model 9mmP in general and Dean Grennell's personal gun in particular. It seems that several years ago, someone in the Gun World offices pointed this particular pistol out to Dean when it appeared in a listing of unusual guns for sale from a major dealer. The pistol bore the inscription that you see here.

Now that's a nice touch, but a little out of place because Dean had never been presented anything from Colt. Later on, he found out that the inscription had been put on the pistol as a result of a presentation program that didn't quite come full circle. Along with a number of other odd pieces, the gun was wholesaled off to the dealer. He ended up putting up the requisite $268 and the gun was dutifully shipped to him. I couldn't resist asking why he would buy such a pistol.

"Oh," he replied with mischievous glee, "I had to buy it — it had my name on it." — *Wiley Clapp*

NINEFIRING ONE: LUGER PISTOL
NINEFIRING TWO: BROOMHANDLE MAUSER
NINEFIRING THREE: WALTHER P'38
NINEFIRING FOUR: RADOM
NINEFIRING FIVE: BROWNING HI-POWER
NINEFIRING SIX: LAHTI
NINEFIRING SEVEN: STAR MODEL B
NINEFIRING EIGHT: STAR MODEL BM
NINEFIRING NINE: STAR MODEL 28
NINEFIRING TEN: STAR MODEL 30PK
NINEFIRING ELEVEN: SMITH & WESSON MODEL 39
NINEFIRING TWELVE: SMITH & WESSON MODEL 639
NINEFIRING THIRTEEN: SMITH & WESSON MODEL 469
NINEFIRING FOURTEEN: SMITH & WESSON MODEL 669
NINEFIRING FIFTEEN: STEYR GB
NINEFIRING SIXTEEN: GLOCK 17
NINEFIRING SEVENTEEN: BJT DA
NINEFIRING EIGHTEEN: AMERICAN ARMS DERRINGER
NINEFIRING NINETEEN: EMF BISLEY
NINEFIRING TWENTY: RUGER BLACKHAWK
NINEFIRING TWENTY-ONE: SMITH & WESSON 547 (3")
NINEFIRING TWENTY-TWO: SMITH & WESSON 547 (4")
NINEFIRING TWENTY-THREE: LLAMA OMNI
NINEFIRING TWENTY-FOUR: LLAMA XI-B
NINEFIRING TWENTY-FIVE: ASP
NINEFIRING TWENTY-SIX: CONTENDER
NINEFIRING TWENTY-SEVEN: ASTRA A-90
NINEFIRING TWENTY-EIGHT: FIE TZ-75
NINEFIRING TWENTY-NINE: KASSNAR PJK 9P
NINEFIRING THIRTY: INTERARMS FEG R9
NINEFIRING THIRTY-ONE: HECKLER & KOCH P9S
NINEFIRING THIRTY-TWO: HECKLER & KOCH VP70Z
NINEFIRING THIRTY-THREE: HECKLER & KOCH P7M8
NINEFIRING THIRTY-FOUR: HECKLER & KOCH P7M13
NINEFIRING THIRTY-FIVE: SIG 210
NINEFIRING THIRTY-SIX: SIG-SAUER 225
NINEFIRING THIRTY-SEVEN: SIG-SAUER 220
NINEFIRING THIRTY-EIGHT: SIG-SAUER 226
NINEFIRING THIRTY-NINE: WALTHER P5
NINEFIRING FORTY: MAB
NINEFIRING FORTY-ONE: COLT GOVERNMENT MODEL
NINEFIRING FORTY-TWO: COLT CONVERSION UNIT
NINEFIRING FORTY-THREE: RUGER SPEED SIX (2¾")
NINEFIRING FORTY-FOUR: RUGER SPEED SIX (4")
NINEFIRING FORTY-FIVE: CZ-75
NINEFIRING FORTY-SIX: BERETTA 92F
NINEFIRING FORTY-SEVEN: TAURUS PT-99
NINEFIRING FORTY-EIGHT: NOVAK-SMITH & WESSON MODEL 469
NINEFIRING FORTY-NINE: COMPETITION BROWNING
NINEFIRING FIFTY: NOVAK COMPETITION MODEL 59

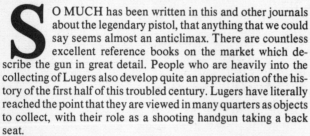

LUGER PISTOL

SO MUCH has been written in this and other journals about the legendary pistol, that anything that we could say seems almost an anticlimax. There are countless excellent reference books on the market which describe the gun in great detail. People who are heavily into the collecting of Lugers also develop quite an appreciation of the history of the first half of this troubled century. Lugers have literally reached the point that they are viewed in many quarters as objects to collect, with their role as a shooting handgun taking a back seat.

The Luger that was available to us was from the Arsenault collection. It was not one of the rare variations like, say, a Latvian Postal Service model. It is a plain Mauser-produced pistol dated 1937, all parts numbered in the customary manner. The pistol is in excellent condition with most of the original finish remaining and the aforementioned numbers matching. Still, the gun had been fired a great deal, so we weren't hesitant about putting a few more rounds through it. I mention this only to emphasize that the Luger is one of very few handguns that isn't wise to shoot if it hasn't been fired before. They are just too valuable in pristine condition.

At the risk of offending the legions of Luger lovers out there, I'll have to take exception to the alleged pointing qualities of the gun. To the hand of one who matured as a pistol shooter with a Colt .45, the steeply raked grip angle is awkward in the extreme. When the Luger is grasped with a properly firm grip, the hand is actually in an unnatural set and the shooting suffers. If the grip was so good, why hasn't it appeared on any of the numerous 9mmP pistols that have entered the marketplace in recent years? It has, on the Bennelli, and that gun is something less than an economic success.

Luger triggers have never been anything to rave about for the shooter who goes for the ten-ring. The trigger on this gun was no exception; mushy, as though a marshmallow was between the face of the trigger and the pad of the finger. Further, Luger sights are not adequate for modern shooting. The rear sight is a "V" notch. The front is a flat-topped tapered post and a precise sight picture with the two is all but impossible. In fairness to the design, it should be understood that it was developed in the days when precise shooting was done with Scheutzen rifles and handguns were for close defensive work.

This Luger, like all of them, is an ingenious mechanism. The procedure for handling the locking of the breech is a toggle action. In this design, the barrel and breech travel to the rear for a short distance locked together. A cam arrangement causes the locked unit to unlock in the manner of a human knee. The two parts hinge

Below: The Luger toggle action open for inspection. This photo suggests the amount of precise fitting that had to be done on a Luger. Superb craftsmanship.

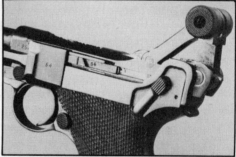

up in the middle, into the sighting plane of the shooter for one brief instant.

The original magazine had parted company with the pistol somewhere along the way. With an after-market magazine of questionable origin, we were able to get the firing evaluation accomplished. There were any number of malfunctions that would not have occurred if the proper magazine had been used. The pistol was surprisingly accurate. The Luger has a reputation for being a little choosy about ammunition, but there was no difficulty with the gun functioning with any of the six different rounds used.

The entire aspect of the Luger pistol is one of beautifully machined precision-fitted parts. The finish is a deep, polished blue-purple color. Supposedly, the pistol doesn't function well when dirty, but we had no difficulty after several boxes of shells had made their way through the toggle action.

The Luger is not a pistol which will suit the tastes of modern-day shooters. But is a fascinating handgun with a long history of wartime service. Field-stripped, the Luger is a mechanical marvel to behold. It rightfully belongs in the first-up position in this book — after all, this was the very first "9"!!

25 YD. FIRING RESULTS	AVG. VEL.	STD. DEV.	GROUP SIZE
Winchester Silvertips	1176	16	2.25"
Federal 115 JHP	1088	14	2.75"
Federal 123 FMJ	1054	8	3.25"
Handload #1	1227	24	4.0"
Handload #2	1035	17	5.0"
Handload #3	1150	26	2.25"

BROOMHANDLE MAUSER

FIRING TWO:

Broomhandle Mausers haven't been made for many years, so this sort of tangent rear sight seems out of place. The sight is graduated for ranges up to five hundred meters.

FOR THE handgunner of the eighties, accustomed to the sleek and racy lines of modern handguns, this pistol must seem to be the ugliest thing imaginable. It is an ungainly looking handgun to say the least. The prejudice continues as the shooter picks one up and attempts to shoot it; the balance is difficult to adjust to. In the Mauser 1896 Model, called the Broomhandle for obvious reasons, the magazine of ten cartridges is placed forward of the trigger guard. The balance, therefore, is all out of whack — at least in terms of what we are used to.

The Broomhandle is nevertheless one of the most beautifully made firearms that you will ever encounter. The interior surfaces of the pistol are precisely machined from forgings. In many places in the gun there is evidence of polishing and fitting that doesn't have any real need in the operational cycle of the pistol. The 1896 Mauser is recoil-operated by means of an unusual recoil system. It is also unusual in the sense that it feeds from a box magazine that isn't detachable from the pistol, at least for most of its variations. Over the several decades of production of the Broomhandle, there were a number of varying models of the basic pistol. There were also a number of copies from several Spanish firms.

The history of the Broomhandle is examined at some greater length elsewhere in this book, so we won't recap all of that material. In the early part of this century, when a great many nations were looking for a service automatic, a lot of them turned to the designer-producer of the world's best bolt-action rifle — Mauser. Mauser produced tens of thousands of the Broomhandles for other nations, as well as their own services. During World War I, when the factories could not produce Lugers fast enough, Mauser made over 150,000 Broomhandles and chambered them for the German service pistol cartridge, the 9mmP. Most of these were marked as is our shooting example — with a large red "9" carved into the grips.

The rear sight on the Broomhandle is of the tangent type, featuring a leaf which can be adjusted for increases in elevation by means of a sliding cam arrangement. Rather optimistically, the sights on this pistol are graduated for ranges to five hundred meters. That's an unlikely range for any handgun and it reflects the rifle thinking of the Mauser designers. Further evidence of that line of reasoning is found in the slot cut in the butt of the pistol. In this slot, the lug on the wooden holster-stock may be mounted. The resulting gun is sort of a pistol-carbine. Even with a stock in place, the sights aren't easy to shoot with. The rear sight is a "V" notch and the front is a tapered post with a small flat top. In

somewhat the same fashion as the Luger, the sight picture is far from the clean square notch to which most of us are accustomed.

When I got this one out to the range for the requisite session of test firing, it was my first experience with shooting a Broomhandle. I quickly found out why the original ammunition was packed in stripper clips. The pistol loads by means inserting the stripper clip into guides in the top of the opened breech and stripping the cartridges downwards into the magazine. If you don't have the clip, the breech wants to close when the first manually inserted round depresses the follower. You can load the pistol one round at a time, but it sure does make you appreciate the box magazine of other guns.

In firing the pistol, an entirely typical WWI military model in excellent and unaltered condition, I was treated to some pleasant surprises. For one thing, a tricky and elderly automatic was being fired with quite a variety of modern ammunition including a cast bullet handload. While the sights of the pistol were inadequate, the trigger pull was good, after the military-type take up was made. Functioning? Well, in the course of shooting a bunch of loads there wasn't a single malfunction of any sort.

The pistol was more than acceptably accurate as well, proving that old Mausers can be as charming to use as old Mercedes.

25 YD. FIRING RESULTS	AVG. VEL.	STD. DEV.	GROUP SIZE
Winchester Silvertips	1286	11	2.00"
Federal 115 JHPS	1213	50	1.5"
Federal 123 FMJ	1067	12	3.25"
Handload #1	1288	25	3.00"
Handload #2	1032	5	3.00"
Handload #3	1206	29	3.25"

WALTHER P'38

FIRING THREE:

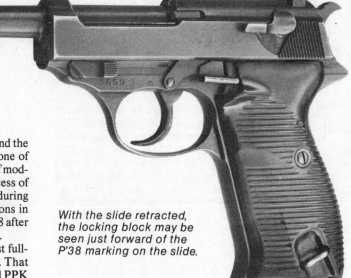

With the slide retracted, the locking block may be seen just forward of the P'38 marking on the slide.

ALONG WITH the Colt Government Model and the Browning High-Power, this reliable pistol is one of the more widely distributed military firearms of modern times. One authority has stated that in excess of one million of them were made by various manufacturers during World War II. The pistol went through several designations in the course of its development, but it's known best as the P'38 after the year of its adoption as the German service automatic.

It is unique in several ways. For one thing, it is the first full-sized military pistol to use a double-action trigger system. That system is an updated version of the one used in the PP and PPK pistols of the late Twenties and early Thirties. For its time, the DA P'38 was a radical innovation and the pistol was much prized as a wartime souvenir. That isn't particularly surprising, since it is a reliable and rugged automatic.

The locked breech system of the P'38 is different. Other than the toggle-action Luger, most military autoloaders use a version of the John Browning-designed tilting barrel system. The P'38 uses a floating locking block under the barrel. The most common pistol to compare it to is the modern Beretta 92F. The basic idea of the system is to use a block to hold the barrel and the slide in firm contact for the short initial movement of the firing cycle. After that short movement, the barrel is halted and a cam arrangement pivots the locking block down, allowing the slide to continue rearwards. In the P'38, it works as well as anything that has been developed anywhere.

The pistol was so highly regarded that it was back in production in the post-war era. It even became the service autoloader of the Bundeswehr, the West German Army. The P'38 was made in the post-war period in a number of variations. There were .22s, lightweights, short "K" guns for concealed carry and even some nicely engraved specimens. The new P5 is the current standard bearer of the Walther line, but as this is written, there are reports of a newer, multi-shot version of the P'38 called the P88.

For all its long service, the P'38 is an outmoded handgun. It has poor sights for any serious purpose, with the familiar "U" notch rear and post front. They are only drift-adjustable. The magazine is a single-column type holding eight rounds and, worse yet, the catch for the magazine is mounted in the lower rear corner of the butt.

25 YD. FIRING RESULTS	AVG. VEL.	STD. DEV.	GROUP SIZE
Winchester Silvertips	1198	24	2.50"
Federal 9BP	1164	13	5.00"
Federal 9AP	1079	24	6.00"
Handload #1	1254	20	3.25"
Handload #2	1082	21	3.00"
Handload #3	1163	37	5.75"

Back in the early Sixties, one of my favorite plinking guns was a WWII P'38 through which I cycled a good bit of dirt-cheap 9mmP surplus ammo. The gun that I used for the shooting reported here is also a veteran of that war. In shooting a P'38 once again, I am reminded of how well that butt was shaped, how light in the muzzle the pistol was, and how the god-awful DA trigger pull gave all double-action automatics a bad reputation.

POLISH RADOM

FIRING FOUR:

The Radom was a sturdy pistol that resembled the Colt Government Model.

THE POLISH Radom pistol was named after the arsenal where it was built, an arsenal which is still producing weapons, if not Radoms. The pistol is a sound design and at least the earlier examples are quite well made. In size, it is close to the Colt Government Model or the Star Model B. It is heavier than it really needs to be and that makes for an easy pistol to shoot.

Radoms were the service pistols of the Armed Forces of Poland in the period between 1935, when they were introduced, and 1939, when the Germans invaded the country. Significantly, the German weapons people thought enough of the pistol to continue production in the captured plant. If they had not done so, and significant numbers of the guns had not been sent to the Western front, the Radom might have ended up a rarity in the West. As it is, large numbers of them have found their way to the United States via GIs' dufflebags.

Design-wise, the Radom shows the influence of the Browning system. Instead of the pivoting link of the Colt, however, the Radom is more like the Browning High-Power. The barrel is locked into recesses in the underside of the slide top, just like about half of the pistols that we will discuss in this book. When the Polish government set about choosing a service pistol in the mid-Thirties, they had several guns to choose from and went with the local design effort.

It is basically a single-action automatic using a short recoil locking system to handle the pressures generated by firing. The hammer is external, with a knurled ring spur to ease thumbcocking. The magazine of the Radom is a stout sheet metal box, single column, with a self-contained follower and spring. Some versions of the Radom had cuts for stock-holsters.

There are several unusual features. One is the lever on the left side of the slide. It is shaped like, and in the same position as, the safety on a host of more modern automatic pistols. It is not a safety. It is a lever which retracts the firing pin and safely drops the hammer on a loaded chamber. In other words, it is a de-cocking lever in the same sense as the de-cocking lever on the current Sig-Sauer 220 series pistols. Those latter guns also use double-action triggers, whereas the Radom is plain single-action. Most Radoms have a Colt-type grip safety, but their hammers still have to be manually cocked for a first shot from the hammer-down position. This is quite a different feature.

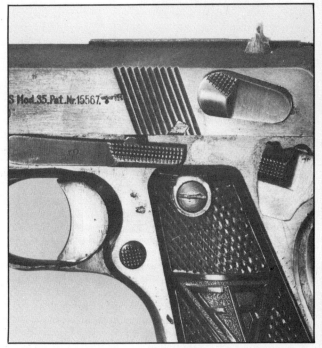

Radom controls are not what they seem. The lever on the slide isn't a safety, it's a hammer drop. And the lever on the frame is a takedown latch, not a safety.

There's another little lever that looks like a safety on the left side of the frame. It is there for no purpose other than to hold the slide back when the pistol is disassembled.

The pistol that you see pictured here is not a 9mmP, but rather has been fitted with a .30 Luger barrel. For that reason, I was forced to a bit of last minute borrowing of a battered 9mmP version from another source. That pistol was used to obtain the firing data, which would have probably been better with a different gun.

25 YD. FIRING RESULTS	AVG. VEL.	STD. DEV.	GROUP SIZE
Winchester Silvertips	1176	16	2.75"
Federal 9BP	1087	13	3.25"
Federal 9AP	1022	20	4.00"
Handload #1	1227	17	4.25"
Handload #2	1036	23	5.00"
Handload #3	1150	26	3.50"

FIRING 9 FIVE: BROWNING HI-POWER

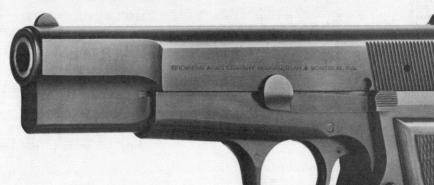

The venerable P'35, or Hi-Power, has a flawless reputation.

THERE HAVE been somewhere in the neighborhood of four million Colt Government Model pistols made and used throughout the long history of the grand old gun. Smith & Wesson has probably made even more of their reliable K-frame revolvers when you consider the endless variations of that basic gun. Both of those handguns have been in production for the best part of a century and, although it has a much shorter life span, I'll bet that the Browning Hi-Power has sold almost as many copies as either of them.

That is not surprising — this is an excellent pistol. It was John Browning's last design, worked out in concert with the designers at the FN plant in Belgium. The work was done at the behest of the French government, who paradoxically never chose to adopt it. The Hi-Power, which is also called the P'35 or GP Mle 35, was first used in the late 1930s. John Walter, author of the excellent reference *The Pistol Book,* makes the interesting point that the Hi-Power was the only pistol used in large numbers by both sides in World War II. It was due to the fact that the Germans happily occupied the FN works in Belgium and turned out many thousands of the guns for their own troops, while the Commonwealth forces were using the Hi-Powers made in the Inglis plant in Canada.

Currently, the Browning is the most widely distributed military pistol in the Western world, used by more different nations than I have the space to list. And that leads to a discussion of why.

The Browning is an excellent pistol, but it really got its foot in the door by being the first to use a double-column magazine. This single feature had a great deal to do with its immediate reputation. Much of the design philosophy of the Colt went into the Browning — the same external hammer and a very similar lock up. The magazine catch and other controls are the same. Other features are different. There is no separate barrel bushing and recoil spring plug, which aren't really necessary. The trigger is a pivoting type, one that works a drawbar on the right side of the frame and one that has been roundly cursed by a legion of gunsmiths trying to improve the trigger pull.

In an age of heavy and rather bulky double-action automatics, the Browning is a delight to handle. The slide is slim and graceful,

Brownings are a delight to shoot. The slide is slender and the pistol points and handles quite well. Joe McMahon with a late commercial gun.

the barrel and sighting plane are low and close to the hand, and the grip, while somewhat chunky, is manageable in most hands. Most of the reason for this is the design genius of John Browning and the fact that the Hi-Powers are made the old way — milled steel forgings.

One of the most eagerly awaited guns on the pistol scene is the soon-to-be-introduced DA version of the venerable thirteen-shot autoloader. I hope that the new guns have better sights than the old one. The tiny sights are about my only gripe with the Hi-Power.

25 YD. FIRING RESULTS	AVG. VEL.	STD. DEV.	GROUP SIZE
Winchester Silvertips	1261	21	3.00"
Federal 9BP	1259	19	2.00"
Federal 9AP	1113	9	2.25"
Handload #1	1261	31	3.50"
Handload #2	1071	39	2.75"
Handload #3	1162	10	3.75"

SWEDISH LAHTI

FIRING SIX:

Lahtis are massive, sturdy guns intended for wartime service.

LAHTI PISTOLS were initially designed and produced in Finland. In time, the design migrated to Sweden, where it was made by the Husqvarna works and used by the Swedish military forces. In both countries and both versions, the Lahti is a big heavy brute of a handgun. It was designed for production in the late Thirties when the use of milled steel forgings was common. Lahtis convey the impression of being nearly indestructible, which is not surprising in view of the sturdy nature of the parts.

They also end up being compared to the Luger, which is not surprising in view of the similar silhouettes of the two pistols. While Lahtis and Lugers are similar in external contour and the quality of manufacture, they are completely different handguns in the design sense. Aimo Lahti, the Finn who designed the gun, wanted to build a pistol usable in the extreme weather conditions of his native land. The major components of the Lahti are heavy and the system by which the pistol works is extremely strong.

The Lahti uses an internal bolt which moves within an enclosed barrel extension. The barrel proper is screwed into this extension. When the pistol fires, the barrel and extension are locked to the bolt, and recoil with it for a short distance. A cam arrangement on the system unlocks the locking piece of the pistol. The actual lock is a hefty steel forging in the shape of an inverted "U" and it is cammed upwards into a recess in the massive receiver of the pistol.

The Lahti operating system is further unique in that it uses an accelerator to move the recoiling parts to the rear with a bit more velocity. The reasons for the use of such a device on a handgun appear uncertain, but they may have something to do with the designer's wish to have the gun function with total reliability under the very worst of wartime conditions.

While the pistol was designed (and the first of them produced) in Finland, the Lahti eventually migrated to Sweden to be made there by Husqvarna. It was a Swedish pistol that we borrowed from the Maxwell collection for the purpose of the firing evaluation.

The Lahti weighs about thirty-six ounces, which is on the heavy side for an automatic pistol using an eight-shot single-column box magazine. It also has a catch for that magazine housed in the butt. The gun has the rather steeply raked grip angle

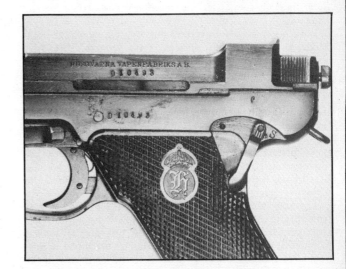

This close-up view of the Lahti receiver shows the safety lever and takedown latch. The "U" shaped locking piece is in the upper receiver.

of the Luger, a feature over which some critics become ecstatic, and which I simply cannot handle. For modern combat pistol shooting purposes, the weight of a Lahti is poorly distributed. All the mass of the pistol is above and even slightly to the rear of the hand. This makes for a somewhat awkward balance and — well, it just doesn't point very well.

But it will shoot with commendable accuracy. The listed results are pretty good for a pistol that's a half-century old. That explains why the Swedes have used it to modern times.

25 YD. FIRING RESULTS	AVG. VEL.	STD. DEV.	GROUP SIZE
Winchester Silvertips	1273	53	3.25"
Federal 9BP	1239	24	1.50"
Federal 9AP	1057	7	5.00"
Handload #1	1328	26	6.00"
Handload #2	1093	11	4.25"
Handload #3	1233	36	5.25"

STAR MODEL B

This has a familiar look, doesn't it? The Model B is styled much like that reliable Colt we all know and respect.

FOR THE CITIZENS of Spain, the Civil War which wracked their country in the 1930s was a cataclysmic event. In a far less vital sense, that war also raised hell with the efforts of arms historians. Most of the records and sometimes the physical plants of the Spanish armsmaking industry were destroyed. For that reason, there's not a great deal of information in wide circulation about one of the best of the Spanish handgun makers: *Star-Bonafacio Echeverria, SA* of Eiber, Spain. In the United States, the Star brand pistols are marketed by the importer, Interarms.

Star pistols in 9mmP which we evaluated for this book were uniformly excellent and, the present gun under consideration, the Star Model B, is one of the best that you'll find anywhere. Unfortunately, Star pistols must fight to overcome the image created by the thousands of truly poor Spanish-made automatics and revolvers that flooded the country in the early days of this century. The same unjustified bad reputation situation also troubles the other Spanish autoloaders in 9mmP which we will presently examine.

Lovers of the Colt Government model will admire the Star Model B. It is an admitted copy of the venerable Browning design. Single-action, with the typical external hammer and single-column magazine, the gun will be familiar to all of those who have handled the Colt. Still, there are differences.

There are subtle differences in the contour of the pistol. While the overall length and height are about the same, the impression is that of a slimmer, more-graceful pistol. That is due to the fact that the gun has been re-shaped in more trim lines to handle a less powerful cartridge. There is a world of difference between a Colt Government Model chambered for the 9mmP cartridge and a Star Model B for the same round; the Star is by far the more graceful handgun.

There are also a few other differences. The Star does away with the grip safety that John Browning was forced to put on the Colt and which he dispensed with on the Browning Hi-Power. This means that the rear frame of the pistol is a machined forging, contoured pleasantly for the hand. And the lower rear of the frame is finished with a checkered surface shaped to simulate the mainspring housing of the Colt. On the forward edge of the slimmer receiver, about where the little finger wraps around, there

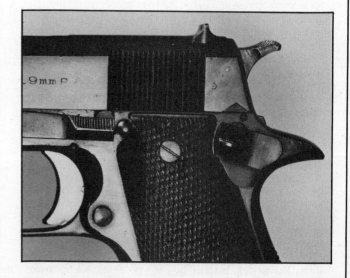

will be found a forward-projecting finger rest. It's one of those subtle little things that makes the Star B feel "right" in the hand.

In terms of actual shooting, the Star was no slouch. The gun uses a pivoting trigger system and our test sample had an acceptably clean-breaking trigger system which fired with a bit over three pounds pull. Accuracy, which ran close to two inches with a variety of loads, is made a lot easier by virtue of the sights.

The rear sight of the Star B is no longer than the Colt's, but the notch is both wider and a little deeper. With a front sight a little larger, the sight picture on a Star is excellent.

In today's double-column, double-action world of automatic pistols, there probably isn't much market for a pistol like this one. Interarms hasn't imported any of them for a long time, preferring to update the 9mmP line with the 28 and 30 series pistols. That's a shame, as this pistol is one of the nicest of the older 9s.

25. YD. FIRING RESULTS	AVG. VEL.	STD. DEV.	GROUP SIZE
Winchester Silvertips	1220	28	2.00"
Federal 9BP	1170	20	3.25"
Federal 9AP	1075	8	1.75"
Handload #1	1272	42	3.25"
Handload #2	1061	11	4.25"
Handload #3	1107	29	6.00"

FIRING EIGHT:

THE STAR MODEL BM

Star's BM is a compact, chunky little version of the Model B. This may be the smallest 9mmP auto.

I F THE STAR Model B is a shootable, graceful, well-made rendering of the basic Colt design into a 9mmP auto, then the Star Model BM is a shootable, graceful, well-made rendering of the basic Colt design into a SMALL 9mmP auto. There is a market for small auto pistols for the 9mmP round, which is approaching the point of almost universal use throughout the world. The management of the Star firm certainly realized this when they decided to produce the Model BM.

This pistol is a reduced version of the Model B. The reductions in size occur mostly in the length and height. The barrel has been reduced by about three-quarters of an inch and the height has also dropped by about the same amount. Somehow or other, the designers have been able to keep the magazine capacity at eight rounds, just one less than the full-sized Model B.

The result is a pleasing little pistol, indeed. It is virtually a three-quarter-scale version of the basic gun. It is flat and conceal-able and has received the qualified endorsement of no less an authority than Jeff Cooper. The same philosophy was used to reduce the Star Model P down to the PD in caliber .45 ACP. Mr. Cooper liked that one, too.

There are probably other places in the BM's design where dimensions were reduced, because the pistol does have a completely different subjective feel. The BM's grips are black checkered plastic instead of the checkered walnut of the pre-war Model B. In keeping with the high-speed times in which it was conceived, the grasping serrations on the slide of the BM are angled back in the racy fashion of the Colt Gold Cup version of the Government Model.

The particular pistol that was used for the firing evaluations was the one that Chuck Karwan bought from Interarms after writing the chapter on best buys in 9mmP autoloaders. He spends a great deal more time and effort in justifying the BM as a best buy than I have here. Let it suffice to say that I concur with my colleague completely; this is a charming little pistol.

The gun has all of the tactically desirable features of a Colt. The safety is the sear-blocking type, mounted on the frame of the gun. The gun can be carried in relative safety with the hammer cocked, safety on and a round in the chamber. When need arises, the pistol is drawn and readied for action by a downwards sweep of the right thumb across the safety lock. This system of gunhandling has been taught by a number of American schools, to the

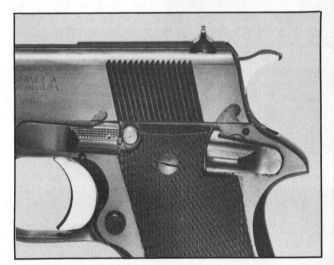

point where a European pistol which works the same way has considerable value for shooters whose duties require travel and who must carry a concealable gun in a universal caliber.

From an examination of the firing results of the Model B on the facing page and the BM on this page, it would seem that the Stars are acceptably accurate and that their preference is for ammunition with a heavier bullet.

For the weight-conscious user of the automatic pistol, there is a variation of the BM called the BKS. This gun is a BM with the frame cast from some form of weight-saving alloy. The result is a lightweight handgun which is somewhat easier to carry — and a good bit harder to shoot. The basic BM is an excellent carry gun as is. I'd stick with it.

25 YD. FIRING RESULTS	AVG. VEL.	STD. DEV.	GROUP SIZE
Winchester Silvertips	1191	23	2.25"
Federal 9BP	1086	10	2.50"
Federal 9AP	1051	14	3.00"
Handload #1	1188	37	3.25"
Handload #2	1033	16	2.75"
Handload #3	1133	24	3.25"

STAR MODEL 28

FIRING NINE:

The Star Model 28 was the company's entry in the Spanish service auto test trials — and it won!

THE FIRST that most of us heard of this pistol was when it popped up on the cover of the *Rifleman* several years ago. It was displayed with other 9mmP autos as the current crop of designs from the Spanish Arms industry. Eventually, this one was chosen as the new service pistol for the Spanish armed forces. That's not at all surprising, as this is an excellent gun.

Whoever the designers of this pistol, they did a lot of homework. The Star 28 incorporates a great many design features of a lot of other fine pistols into an all-steel, double-action automatic using a fifteen shot double-column magazine.

There are two features that are pure Charles Petter/SIG 210. One is the use of the desirable reversed rails. This system is more expensive to produce than the conventional one, but it is an idea that promotes greater accuracy. Reversed rails refers to the reversed relationship between the rails on the receiver and the matching ones on the slide. Conventional pistols, including the earlier single-action Stars, have the rails set up so that the slide moves *on* the receiver. When they're reversed, the slide rides *in* the receiver. It is a system which regulates the travel of the slide much more uniformly, and that equates to a potentially more accurate pistol.

The other SIG/Petter design feature that the Star designers used was the modular lockwork. Actually, this idea goes way back in firearms design, to the days when the term, "lock, stock and barrel" originated. It means that the major parts of the firing mechanism are grouped together on a plate of metal and can be removed from the gun as a unit. That is just what happens in the Star 28, except that the parts are fitted so that the plate that holds the parts also wedges the checkered black plastic grips in place.

Some of the first automatics on the market with double-column magazines were damned bulky guns. Most recently, the armsmakers throughout the world have found ways to reduce the bulk. The Star 28 is one of the better guns in that respect. It is a pistol with a good, solid pointable "feel" to it.

In handling the pistol, most shooters have found it to be quite controllable and accurate. The sights are good, so is the trigger pull and everything seemed to be going along pretty well for the new pistol. That is, until lots of shooters complained about the problem of getting ahold of the slide to work the action. There were some problems with this...

Above and below: Both sides of the Model 28 receiver. The left side shows the slide stop and de-cocking lever, plus magazine catch. On the right side, the safety lever is repeated. Compare the grasping grooves with the 30's.

25 YD. FIRING RESULTS	AVG. VEL.	STD. DEV.	GROUP SIZE
Winchester Silvertips	1177	21	2.25"
Federal 9BP	1160	14	2.00"
Federal 9AP	1060	18	3.5 "
Handload #1	1227	25	3.5 "
Handload #2	1034	24	3.0 "
Handload #3	1115	19	4.0 "

STAR MODEL 30PK

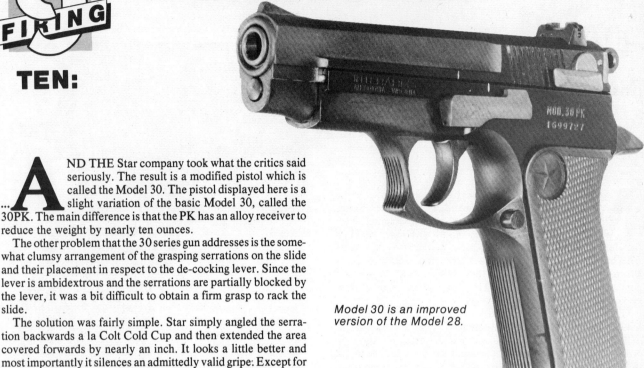

Model 30 is an improved version of the Model 28.

AND THE Star company took what the critics said seriously. The result is a modified pistol which is called the Model 30. The pistol displayed here is a slight variation of the basic Model 30, called the 30PK. The main difference is that the PK has an alloy receiver to reduce the weight by nearly ten ounces.

The other problem that the 30 series gun addresses is the somewhat clumsy arrangement of the grasping serrations on the slide and their placement in respect to the de-cocking lever. Since the lever is ambidextrous and the serrations are partially blocked by the lever, it was a bit difficult to obtain a firm grasp to rack the slide.

The solution was fairly simple. Star simply angled the serration backwards a la Colt Cold Cup and then extended the area covered forwards by nearly an inch. It looks a little better and most importantly it silences an admittedly valid gripe. Except for a small change in the extraction system, this is the only difference between the 28s and 30s. The 30 seen here is the PK, which also differs from the 28 across the page in the shorter barrel and slide.

Many shooters and writers have mentioned the difficulty arising from the handling of double-action automatics after the first shot. It is a perfectly valid point; it's hard to adjust the set of the hand and trigger finger from double to single action. The trigger system on the Star 30 is a bit better in this light than a lot of others. I didn't have a chance to take the 30PK test gun to a gunsmith for an evaluation, but the pistol has a yoke-type trigger which surrounds the magazine in the style of the Colt. I think that a good trigger man might be able to smooth up what is already an adequate trigger pull.

There are some other nice features of this gun. The front of the grip is serrated with a panel of vertical grooves that give the underside of the fingers of the shooting hand a good purchase. The sights are also good. The front is a long, sloping, snag-resistant ramp and the rear is even better. A trim little block dovetailed into the slide, the sight has rounded outer contours, a square notch and windage adjustments.

There's the ever-present recurved trigger guard, pioneered so many years ago by Armand Swenson and intended to make two-handed shooting a little easier. The magazine catch is where it belongs, on the left side of the frame. The hammer spur is the

The major improvement is the shape and placement of the grooves on the slide. You can also see the hammer and grip tang contours in this photo. They are shaped to avoid the hammer bite common to other automatics.

rounded "Commander" type, and the grip tang which extends back and over the hand is long enough to protect the hands of King Kong.

Star 28s and 30s both have a type of safety which is becoming quite common on modern DA autoloaders. It's a lever on the slide which drops the hammer and simultaneously retracts the firing pin to a locked position in the slide.

As the tables show, the 30PK's accuracy was much like the 28's.

25 YD. FIRING RESULTS	AVG. VEL.	STD. DEV.	GROUP SIZE
Winchester Silvertips	1154	18	2.50"
Federal 9BP	1064	14	2.50"
Federal 9AP	1045	13	3.00"
Handload #1	1207	21	3.75"
Handload #2	1010	22	4.00"
Handload #3	1150	18	3.25"

SMITH & WESSON MODEL 39

ELEVEN:

The Model 39 was a trend-setter when it was introduced.

MODEL 39s are history-making handguns in the fullest sense of the word. In the United States today, there are a host of double-action auto-loaders available in 9mmP and other calibers. But, for several decades, the only game in town was the Model 39. The history of the pistol dates to the first few years of the post-World War II era. At that time, the troubled Smith & Wesson company came under the control of one Carl Hellstrom, who set about modernizing the product line.

One of the things he wanted was a modern centerfire auto-loader, offered with at least the option of a double-action trigger in the style of the Walther P'38. Around the same time, the U.S. Army was in the process of evaluating handgun designs in the NATO standard 9mmP caliber. Smith & Wesson entered the consideration and produced the pistol which came to be called the Model 39; at least, it had that designation when numbers were assigned in 1957.

The rear sight of the early Model 39 was not the fully adjustable variety, which was not a good feature. The pistol was otherwise a thoroughly usable firearm. It was the first domestic 9mmP automatic pistol ever produced.

25 YD. FIRING RESULTS	AVG. VEL.	STD. DEV.	GROUP SIZE
Winchester Silvertips	1161	9	5.00"
Federal 9BP	1108	8	3.75"
Federal 9AP	1015	11	4.25"
Handload #1	1200	40	6.00"
Handload #2	994	20	5.75"
Handload #3	1137	11	4.50"

The fact that the government chose to drop the idea of a new pistol at that time did not alter the fact that the Smith & Wesson was an excellent handgun, one that a few pioneering police agencies began to adopt. Rather slowly at first, then with gathering intensity in the Sixties, revolver-minded policemen began to use the 39 and other automatics.

The pistol that they got was a good one with some minor faults. The faults centered around a sight that was adjustable only for elevation and an extractor which broke often. The latter problem was corrected pretty quickly, but the sight hung around for years. There were some options to the basic gun that did not persist, one of them a single-action-only version. Also, the steel-frame Model 39s in the original format were made in such small quantities as to now rank as collector's items.

Most 39s are alloy frame pistols made that way in order to reduce weight. They work nicely, but in the suspicious McCarthy days, the idea of a gun made from anything other than steel was radical. The early Colt Commanders took the same beating.

The basic Model 39 is a locked-breech automatic pistol feeding from a box magazine of eight rounds. The grip shape is much like the Walther P'38's, a pleasantly curved butt section that fills the hand and points well. The controls are also much like the Walther's, with a combination safety and hammer drop lever on the left side of the slide. There was also a magazine disconnect safety. The trigger pulls of the Model 39s were somewhat like those of the Walthers — long, grating and heavy.

Since the early days of the Model 39 program over thirty years ago, many of them have been made. I had to rely on a stock photo from the files for the featured portrait. Before I got a good picture of the worn veteran I fired, I traded it off — for another S&W.

SMITH & WESSON MODEL 639

9 FIRING

TWELVE:

The 639, above, is seen contrasted, below, with an early Model 39. There is no change in contour, but rear sight is offered in buyer's choice of the fixed type shown at left or fully adjustable type.

THERE'S BEEN a lot of water under the armsmaking bridge since the Model 39 was introduced so many years ago. The newest version of the old gun is called the Model 639 and it is different in several significant ways.

First of all, it is made of stainless steel. The company has been the pioneer in the stainless handgun business, starting with the Model 60, a version of the Chief's Special .38 revolver. S&W has gradually introduced a wide variety of their handguns in the miracle metal. There's nothing miraculous about the stuff. It will stain, even rust, but it is much more resistant to the ravages of weather and sweat than typical blued steel. It makes a lot of sense.

The 639 is also different in that it is available with a lot more options. It can be purchased, for example, with a fully adjustable rear sight matched to a red ramp front. The safety can be had with the lever repeated on the right side of the slide for ambidextrous use.

But the most noticeable difference between the older Model 39 and the new model 639 is the weight. There are several ounces more weight on the 639 and they are all there as a result of the steel rather than alloy receiver. It makes for a positive change in the balance and handling qualities of the newer gun. It all contributes to the fact that the 639 is a more controllable pistol with some of the hotter loadings of 9mmP ammunition.

At the time that I came by this pistol for evaluation in the book, I could have had a companion model, the 659. That pistol is the same as this one, except for a double-column magazine which holds fifteen rounds. The wider magazine makes for a thicker butt and a far less pointable and carryable pistol. Barrels, sights and other features of the guns are the same, so the ballistics are not likely to vary.

In regards to ballistic performance, consider the charts for the 39 and 639 on these two pages. The 639 was a brand new gun with only a few rounds through it when the data was taken. The 39 was an aging veteran of I don't know how many rounds. The wear shows all over the pistol — it was clearly carried in a holster for a long time.

The bore of the gun had little wear that could be seen. Still, there must be some explanation for the considerable difference in velocities. The accuracy of the 39 appears to have deteriorated markedly. I think that particular pistol needs a new barrel. If you work at it, you can wear out even a quality handgun like this one.

25 YD. FIRING RESULTS	AVG. VEL.	STD. DEV.	GROUP SIZE
Winchester Silvertips	1210	18	2.25"
Federal 9BP	1168	21	2.00"
Federal 9AP	1052	19	3.00"
Handload #1	1178	38	2.75"
Handload #2	1006	41	4.25"
Handload #3	1159	28	3.75"

SMITH & WESSON MODEL 469

FIRING THIRTEEN:

THE MODEL 39 was never a particularly expensive pistol. It was in the range of a comparable double-action revolver from the extensive Smith & Wesson line-up. The flat, alloy frame made the pistol rather easy to pack around and eventually some of the custom gunsmiths began to look at the moderately priced Model 39 with a view towards improving it. After all, if they wrecked a gun in the process, the cost of a replacement was not outrageous.

The goal was to produce a concealable pistol in a respectable caliber. This aims at the market dominated by the small revolver. If a lightweight Model 39 could be reduced in overall dimensions to the point of being in the size range of some of the pocket .380s, the result would be a desirable and marketable pistol. Several custom gunsmithing firms set about the tricky procedure of cutting them down to smaller size. In the process, they turned out some handy little guns.

Smith & Wesson watched these goings-on and saw a market of their own. When the firm's 9mmP handgun development program turned out the trouble-free Model 59 (and later the 459, 559 and 659), the company developed the 469 pistol. While the custom 39s still sell in some quantity, the 469 essentially fills the need that those custom guns handled, and does it with a relatively inexpensive out-of-the-box pistol.

The Model 469, as presently available from the S&W company, is an alloy frame, double-action, blue steel 9mmP automatic. It uses a twelve-shot double-column magazine which has a floorplate with a finger rest extension. The pistol's hammer is without a visible spur, although the tip of the stubby little hammer is grooved for thumb-cocking when that is required.

Essentially, the 469 is a modified 459. Reducing the height of the gun by cutting the butt by about three-quarters of an inch and the barrel and slide by about a half inch has a positive effect. The pistol becomes a short, blunt, easy-to-handle automatic. There is nothing else on the market that combines all of the features of this gun into such a powerful concealment piece.

One of the more usable guns from the extensive S&W line is the Model 469. This is an ultra-compact pistol made to be carried concealed and drawn without snags.

25 YD. FIRING RESULTS	AVG. VEL.	STD. DEV.	GROUP SIZE
Winchester Silvertips	1127	23	3.00"
Federal 9BP	1120	8	2.25"
Federal 9AP	1062	9	3.25"
Handload #1	1147	26	4.00"
Handload #2	1011	28	3.75"
Handload #3	1132	15	3.75"

There are certain critics of the cutting-down process that will contend that the reduction in velocity of typical ammunition makes the idea a loser. I draw their attention to the statistics derived from the test firing as printed on these pages. Compare the velocities produced by firing the six test rounds in the 469 with the same data produced by the Model 39 and 639. The barrel of the 469 is shorter by about one half inch. In most cases, the velocity difference is negligible. There are even a few times when the shorter barrel turns in higher velocities.

SMITH & WESSON MODEL 669

FIRING 9

FOURTEEN:

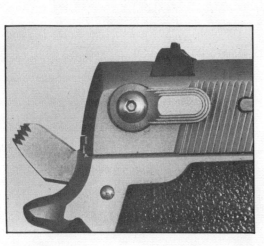

The 669 is a stainless steel mate to the 469. Left: The safety lever on the 669 is ambidextrous and the spurless hammer has serrated tip.

WITH THE 469 selling well, Smith & Wesson did the next logical thing. They made the gun of stainless steel and called it the 669. The customary practice of the company is to make their stainless models completely from the various rust-resistant steels. The 669 differs in that its frame is made of an aluminum alloy, finished in the same color as the silvery-sheened steel of the rest of the gun. All dimensions and contours of the 669 are the same as the 469's; the only difference is the material used and the color of the highlight stripe in the front sight.

Someone — or several someones — on the design staff of the 469/669 development team must have had some law enforcement experience. The 669 is clearly intended to be, first and foremost, a carrying handgun. The contours of the pistol are rounded and blended in such a way as to slip under clothing and resist snagging. Nowhere is this concept more apparent than in the shape of the safety lever.

The lever is on the slide and, on the pictured pistol, it's ambidextrous. It is shaped so as to be manipulated quickly for the intended purpose, but also to resist being caught on coat linings, pocket edges, or the like.

The rear sight, a block of steel dovetailed into the slide, is similarly rounded for the concealment function of the gun. In this case, it is the most extreme rounding that I can recall on any production handgun. The rear sight's function does not suffer in the slightest for all of the contouring. The notch is the customary one offered on most S&Ws, an eighth-incher, outlined in white.

Grips of the 669 are made of an ultra-thin plastic of some sort. They have the familiar intertwined S&W monogram moulded into them, along with the pebble-grained finish. The latter surface is just right for handling the stubby little pistol in point-and-shoot combat firing. The left panel has a bevel in its uppermost forward edge that shields the rear edge of the slide stop from snagging. There's a similar contour around the magazine catch on that same left-side panel.

Despite all the care that went into the shape of the pistol, I believe that there is a flaw in the design. That is the recurved trigger guard, wide and sharply checkered, intended for the index finger of the non-shooting hand to grasp and pull back. This feature does not belong on a pistol of this sort and partially defeats the purpose for which the gun is intended. Most major combat shooting schools don't teach this technique at all any more.

One of the more interesting options that is available for the 669 is a twenty-shot magazine. Certain elite law enforcement agencies are using these things. They stick out the bottom of the magazine well, but these guys use them after the pistol is drawn; then it doesn't matter.

25 YD. FIRING RESULTS	AVG. VEL.	STD. DEV.	GROUP SIZE
Winchester Silvertips	1155	18	2.50"
Federal 9BP	1067	15	2.75"
Federal 9AP	1046	13	1.75"
Handload #1	1208	21	2.75"
Handload #2	1012	23	3.00"
Handload #3	1140	19	4.00"

FIRING FIFTEEN:

STEYR GB

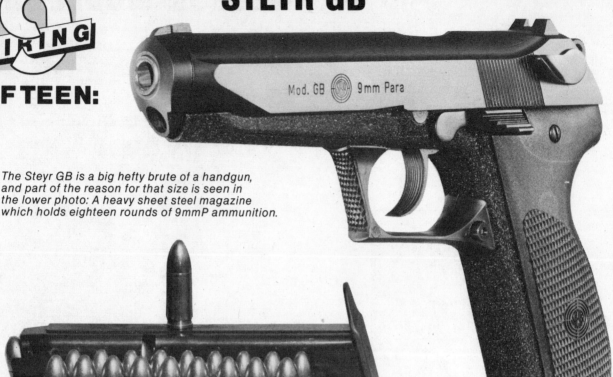

The Steyr GB is a big hefty brute of a handgun, and part of the reason for that size is seen in the lower photo: A heavy sheet steel magazine which holds eighteen rounds of 9mmP ammunition.

THIS IS ONE of those "sleepers" that comes along once in a while and steals your affections. The Steyr GB pistol is different from its peers in a host of ways, so much so that it is easy to become pre-occupied with the technical differences and overlook the fact that this is one of the best shooting, most versatile handguns made in 9mmP chambering.

It is a large pistol. The barrel is 5½ inches long and the overall length is well over nine inches. Since the double-column magazine holds eighteen shots, the pistol stands fairly high. Every effort seems to have been made to keep the butt section to manageable size, but when you put nearly a half box of cartridges into the magazine, you are going to end up with a certain bulk. The receiver of the gun is finished in a black crackle surface, while the slide is polished blue.

Controls reflect the modern trends: a slide stop on the left side of the frame, along with a magazine catch near the left lower corner of the plastic trigger guard. On the slide, there is a decocking lever, which is nicely shaped for its purpose, but unlikely to snag

25 YD. FIRING RESULTS	AVG. VEL.	STD. DEV.	GROUP SIZE
Winchester Silvertips	1229	17	3.00"
Federal 9BP	1178	24	2.50"
Federal 9AP	1063	14	2.25"
Handload #1	1272	31	3.00"
Handload #2	1088	37	2.00"
Handload #3	1174	10	3.25"

on the shooter's clothing or gear. In fact, the entire pistol is well designed for carrying, even concealed carrying — sights, rounded hammer — all radiused off.

There are two major innovative features of the gun. One is the rifling, which is a modernized form of Metford rifling and very much like the type used in a number of modern Heckler & Koch firearms. Polygonal is the term used to describe the rifling, which does not have lands and grooves cut into the barrel. The bore has a multi-sided cross section rather than a round one. The effect is to resist deformation of the bullet and to reduce gas loss. It's also easier to clean.

But the real innovation in the Steyr GB is in the locking system. Some authorities have called the GB a retarded blowback pistol because there is no mechanical lock. I suppose that this is technically correct, but the pistol is very definitely locked shut for the requisite period of time necessary to let the bullet exit the muzzle. The GB has a fixed barrel, with gas ports at about the mid-point. When fired, part of the gas bleeds into a chamber formed by annular rings around the barrel, the interior of the slide and a cap at the muzzle. The gas pressure holds firm against the muzzle cap on the slide, linked to the recoil spring. When the pressure drops and the bullet exits the muzzle, the slide is freed to travel to the rear and make the typical automatic pistol cycle. It is even self-regulating: the higher the pressure, the longer the slide stays shut. I didn't try it, but the system should allow you to shoot any kind of 9mmP ammo, even the really hot carbine stuff.

The GB is a delight to shoot, with soft, manageable recoil and commendable accuracy. The long barrel and rifling design combine to produce some of the higher velocities recorded. This is a likeable gun.

GLOCK 17

The Glock magazine is also unique in that it's made of high-impact plastic, lined in part with steel, and holding seventeen 9mmP cartridges.

Browning type and the lock-up is pretty much SIG-Sauer — into the ejection port. As they are currently imported into the country, Glocks come with adjustable sights made of plastic.

Some kind of impact resistant plastic is used to form the structure of the receiver of the pistol. It can be cast in involved contours and has sufficient strength to serve as well as steel. Even the magazine of the Glock is made of plastic. A portion of the top of the double-column box is lined with sheet steel, which extends upward to form the magazine lips. The magazine holds seventeen shots, plus one more in the chamber. There's nothing in the class that will put so much firepower into such a light, compact package.

Aside from the plastic construction, the most significant innovation in the Glock is the trigger system. I guess that the best way to describe it is semi-double-action. There is no hammer in the gun; instead, there's a spring-loaded striker housed in the steel slide. The first part of the trigger pull will cock the striker and release the integral firing pin lock. The next, and shorter, portion releases the striker which will then be driven forward by spring pressure to fire the shot.

When the slide cycles, the striker is left in what the manual calls the "half-cocked" position, wherein the striker spring is partially tensioned. There is no manual safety as we understand it, although there is a small lever on the face of the trigger which must be depressed by a deliberate pull of the trigger before the mass of the trigger can complete its arc within the trigger guard.

It might sound complicated, but it is simple to work. With a round in the chamber, pull the trigger through a short, two-stage, double-action arc. The gun will fire and the slide will cycle, chambering the first round from the magazine. Then you can do it again — seventeen times.

I F THE STEYR GB inspires appreciation for its design features, the Glock 17 has inspired a whirlwind of controversy for its construction. The clever design of the pistol tends to be overshadowed by the fact that a good bit of the pistol is made of plastic. And someone got the idea that it was an ideal tool for terrorists because it would pass undetected through airport security devices.

Bull. The pistol was designed to be a service handgun for the Austrian Army. The designer, Gaston Glock, had no background of experience in designing weapons, but had manufactured various kinds of equipment for many years. He was not, therefore, tradition minded in the slightest when he sat down to build a better gun for the troops. His approach was utterly pragmatic and the gun reflects it.

The Glock 17 is a locked-breech, recoil-operated, seventeen-shot automatic pistol. The locking system is a tilting barrel Colt/

25 YD. FIRING RESULTS	AVG. VEL.	STD. DEV.	GROUP SIZE
Winchester Silvertips	1215	16	3.00"
Federal 9BP	1245	14	2.25"
Federal 9AP	1071	5	2.25"
Handload #1	1257	21	3.00"
Handload #2	1088	36	2.75"
Handload #3	1158	33	4.00"

BJT DA DERRINGER

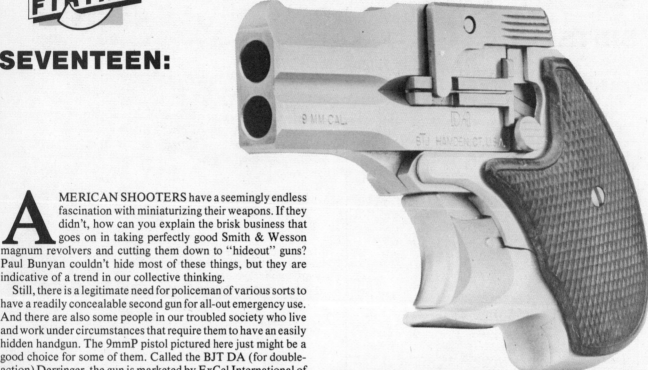

FIRING 9

SEVENTEEN:

AMERICAN SHOOTERS have a seemingly endless fascination with miniaturizing their weapons. If they didn't, how can you explain the brisk business that goes on in taking perfectly good Smith & Wesson magnum revolvers and cutting them down to "hideout" guns? Paul Bunyan couldn't hide most of these things, but they are indicative of a trend in our collective thinking.

Still, there is a legitimate need for policeman of various sorts to have a readily concealable second gun for all-out emergency use. And there are also some people in our troubled society who live and work under circumstances that require them to have an easily hidden handgun. The 9mmP pistol pictured here just might be a good choice for some of them. Called the BJT DA (for double-action) Derringer, the gun is marketed by ExCel International of Torrance, California.

Small it may be, but toylike it definitely is not. This is a high quality two-shot handgun that bears a more-than-passing resemblance to the late and lamented High Standard Double Derringer. The basic shape of the two guns is the same — superposed barrels, double-action-only trigger system, and open front trigger guard. In the BJT, however, there are some differences which place the gun in a far different category.

For one thing, the diminutive handgun is made in two serious defense pistol calibers, .38 Special and 9mmP. The BJT is necessarily a heavier, more sturdily constructed pistol. Throughout, the BJT is built from quality stainless steel, a clear intent to offer a gun that is easier to maintain when it's habitually carried next to the skin in hideaway locations. The BJT is also different in the sense that it has a positive manual safety on the left side of the receiver. The safety works like a safety should — down for "off," or ready to fire.

The drill for operating the BJT is about as simple as you can find. Open the breech for loading by pulling the latch up, which will hinge the barrels down on the pivot at the front of the frame, then drop a pair of cartridges into the chambers, close the gun and thumb the safety up to the on position. In use, the gun is drawn

Two shots is a long way from the capacity of handguns like the Steyr GB, but two shots can do the job in the hands of a careful and deliberate defensive handgunner.

and the thumb of the right hand sweeps the safety down. Since the front of the trigger guard is open, the trigger finger falls easily onto the trigger. Then you just point and pull the trigger through a double-action arc to fire one barrel. A second pull will fire the second.

Please notice that I said point the gun and not aim it. There are sights, but trying to get any accuracy from the gun is a forlorn hope. The sights are inadequate, and the gun is too small to be aimed in the true sense of the word. All of which brings us around to the conclusion that the BJT DA is a close-range last-ditch defensive handgun. It is quite good in that role.

25 YD. FIRING RESULTS	AVG. VEL.	STD. DEV.
Winchester Silvertips	1013	16
Federal 9BP	980	16
Federal 9AP	965	11
Handload #1	1079	8
Handload #2	924	13
Handload #3	1043	15

AMERICAN DERRINGER

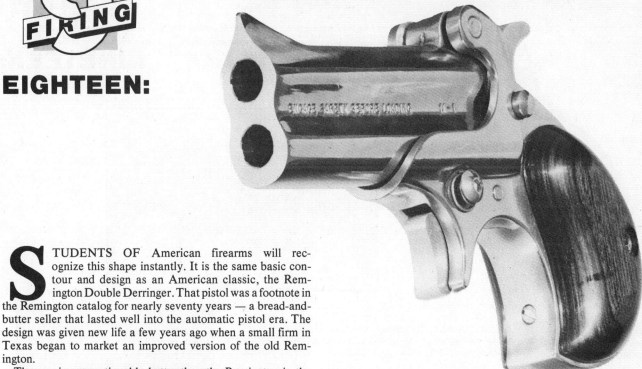

FIRING 9

EIGHTEEN:

STUDENTS OF American firearms will recognize this shape instantly. It is the same basic contour and design as an American classic, the Remington Double Derringer. That pistol was a footnote in the Remington catalog for nearly seventy years — a bread-and-butter seller that lasted well into the automatic pistol era. The design was given new life a few years ago when a small firm in Texas began to market an improved version of the old Remington.

The gun is unquestionably better than the Remington in the sense that it is chambered for cartridges as heavy as the .45 Colt and a special version of the .410 shotgun shell. The gun is better also in the sense of having improved steel throughout the construction. It's stainless and polished like a mirror in our test gun. Another attractive cosmetic touch is the use of polished rosewood in the grip of the little powerhouse.

There's a safety of sorts on this one, something missing on the original Remingtons. On this pistol, the safety is a manual hammer-block type which works like a crossbolt in the frame of the gun.

For our purposes here, we are concerned with the derringer as a 9mmP. The gun is noticably larger and heavier than the other derringer type across the page, but firing it is consequently a bit more pleasant.

Possibly the biggest drawback to the defensive use of the American Derringer is the fact that the gun has a single-action trigger system. This means you have to roll a fairly small handgun around in your hand in order to cock the hammer for each shot. It's awkward and hard to get used to.

In a book that has chapters on sophisticated automatic pistols like the SIG 210 and Heckler & Koch P9s, there's probably a tendency to look at a little gun like this one and discount it as a toy. That would be a mistake.

Not everyone can afford a $1000 target auto in 9mmP or even

The American Derringer pivots open in the manner of a classic, the Remington Double Derringer. The finish on this one is mirror-bright, with fancy rosewood stocks.

one of the lower-priced but adequate revolvers on the market. For that person, this little gun may very well be the answer. It is sturdy and strong, perfectly safe to use with the hottest 9mmP ammunition and it doesn't cost an arm and a leg.

And it is not a toy. Look at the velocities produced by the test ammunition in the three-inch barrel of this pistol. Compare them with the same data from the Smith & Wesson 469 & 669 which have 3½-inch barrels. Do you see much difference?

The American Derringer 9mmP shares a fault with the BJT DA across the page. The gun has sights, but they are almost totally useless. Because of the difficulty of shooting the gun for accuracy, I didn't include any group data.

25 YD. FIRING RESULTS	AVG. VEL.	STD. DEV.
Winchester Silvertips	1025	21
Federal 9BP	1002	18
Federal 9AP	980	17
Handload #1	1045	28
Handload #2	987	27
Handload #3	1056	29

EMF BISLEY

The EMF Bisley is a faithful rendering of the Bisley Colts of the early twentieth century. It has all of the same features, same curves and angles, and it handles the same. This one sports a 9mmP cylinder.

COLT WAS producing the Bisley Model revolver about the time that Georg Luger was getting the Borchardt pistol redesigned into what has come to be called the Luger. The latter pistol went on to achieve a great deal of notoriety as the first handgun ever chambered for the 9mmP cartridge. The Bisley is extinct — and has been so for seventy years.

Or is it? The revolver pictured is a Bisley in every line and curve — and it was manufactured in the past year or so! It's also a 9mmP, a caliber that Colt never chambered for until they made the first 9mmP Government Models in recent times. The gun is an EMF Bisley, made in Italy and imported into this country by Early and Modern Firearms of Santa Ana, California.

The original Colt Bisleys are interesting historical handguns. Collectors classify them as separate revolvers in a Colt collection, but in reality they are Colt Single Action Army revolvers with some pronounced and visible differences. The differences are the shape of the butt, hammer and trigger. All of the other parts of the gun are the same and they will interchange with corresponding parts on regular single-actions.

The Single Action Army was the first successful centerfire cartridge revolver ever made. Introduced in 1873, the gun is still in limited production via the custom shop at Colt. It took the gun world by storm in the 1870s and other revolvers were quick to get on the bandwagon. By the latter part of the century, pistol shooting had become a serious competitive sport.

The Bisley was Colt's first attempt to produce a competition revolver. Most target shooters did not care for the shape of the single-action butt. Colt re-designed it to the shape shown here, in an effort to align the shooter's hand closer to the axis of the barrel. The resulting pistol was a good bit easier to use; Colt named it after the range at Bisley, England, where international matches were held.

Since nostalgia has had such a positive effect on the firearms industry, a great many old guns have been reproduced by modern companies. That's just what happened in the case of the EMF Bisley. The company has a sixty-plus page catalog of well made guns in old styles, made of modern steels. The Bisley pictured here has all the features of an original Colt, including the smoky-hued case-hardening on the frame.

Actually, the revolver is a convertible. The 9mmP cylinder interchanges with the original in .357 magnum. The gun shoots well, and the 7½-inch barrel does interesting things for the velocities.

25 YD. FIRING RESULTS	AVG. VEL.	STD. DEV.	GROUP SIZE
Winchester Silvertips	1344	16	3.75"
Federal 9BP	1220	18	3.25"
Federal 9AP	1144	20	4.25"
Handload #1	1360	33	5.00"
Handload #2	1150	38	5.00"
Handload #3	1098	37	4.75"

RUGER BLACKHAWK

FIRING TWENTY:

Bill Ruger's first centerfire firearm was the Blackhawk revolver in .357 Magnum. It was a natural for a second cylinder in 9mmP caliber. This Blackhawk is typical.

INGLE-ACTION REVOLVERS go back a long way. The first revolver was the Patterson Colt in 1836, and it was a single-action. The basic shape of the butt on the revolver on this page was first seen on the Dragoon Colts of the Mexican War era. Overall, the Ruger Blackhawk that we are concerned with here copies quite closely the shape of one particular single action: the Colt Peacemaker.

While the Ruger differs materially from the Colt in lockwork and other details, the handling drill is the same. In a book full of sleek, multi-shot, fast-handling automatic pistols, a single-action revolver suffers somewhat by comparison. Loading cartridges through a loading gate one at a time and punching them out with a rod the same way is a far cry from stuffing an eighteen-shot magazine into a Steyr GB and emptying it in a matter of seconds.

Nevertheless, the single-action revolver in 9mmP is a sensible handgun for these times. I don't mean to imply that this is a best choice as a combat pistol, just that there is a place for it. One of the characteristics of the modern single-action is that it has great strength. Revolvers of the same size as the Blackhawk shown here will safely handle the hottest handloads. When the cylinder of a revolver is fitted to the frame with a simple axle pin, it is fairly easy to fit a second cylinder to the same gun. That is a lot harder to do when you have a swing-out cylinder revolver. This makes the single-action versatile.

Theoretically, a Ruger Blackhawk could be economically produced with extra cylinders in a diverse number of calibers that share the same bore size — everything from .380 ACP to 9mm Largo. The market for such a gun would be pretty limited and Bill Ruger and his friends are well aware of it. Therefore, what they have chosen to produce is the .357 magnum Blackhawk revolver that you see here, with an auxiliary cylinder in 9mmP.

There are two major reasons why a single-action revolver in 9mmP makes sense. One of them is the return of inexpensive surplus military ammunition from Europe. There have been some recent changes in the importation laws that make this possible, as it was in the good old days of the immediate post-war era. Cheap ammunition spells lots of cheap practice and no one practices enough.

The second reason is handloading. There are certain kinds of loads that can be more economically assembled in 9mmP cases than in the .38 Specials or .357 magnums that are used in the magnum cylinder. Like maybe a mid-velocity, light bullet load for small game?

The Blackhawk we fired for the tests performed well and the performance of the round in the nominal 6½-inch barrel was interesting.

25 YD. FIRING RESULTS	AVG. VEL.	STD. DEV.	GROUP SIZE
Winchester Silvertips	1215	19	3.00"
Federal 9BP	1117	21	2.25"
Federal 9AP	1141	12	2.75"
Handload #1	1291	40	3.00"
Handload #2	1084	37	4.00"
Handload #3	1249	35	4.25"

SMITH & WESSON MODEL 547 (3")

TWENTY-ONE:

The familiar round butt of the S&W medium sized "K" frame revolver has a big advantage over most automatics — there are many types of custom grips available. The "handle" can be tailored to the tastes of nearly everyone.

W E HAVE dealt with the subject of revolvers for the 9mmP cartridge in considerable depth in Chapter Seven, but since that portion of the book was compiled, we've turned up some more information for you that we think you'll find interesting.

This is not a marketing manager's ploy for selling more variations of a basic gun. There is a lot of logic to the idea of taking a basic revolver and chambering it for an automatic pistol cartridge. Most of that logic centers around the hard facts of ammunition availability.

Gun stores are found in many places around the world, but only in the United States are they as well stocked and as frequently encountered as we enjoy them. Within easy driving distance of where I now sit, there are stores selling nearly everything that is made throughout the world in the way of legal weapons and ammunition. The rest of the world's shooters don't have it that easy. And the indisputable fact is that the most common handgun cartridge in the Free World is the 9mmP.

If Smith & Wesson wants to sell handguns in the world, then they must offer the widest possible variety in their line. Some shooters and organizations prefer revolvers, so S&W has come up with the engaging little handgun shown here. It is called the Model 547 in the new triple-digit designation system. Outside of his beloved ASP, this revolver might very well be Dean Grennell's favorite 9mmP.

The revolver has an impressive lineage. It is simply a basic K-frame revolver, the absolute bread-and-butter piece in the S&W line. The Massachusetts firm has produced millions of these guns since they were first introduced before the turn of the century. Most of them were .38 Specials, but they were able to solve some technical difficulties and offer the gun to the world market in 9mmP.

This one is Dean Grennell's and it's a revolver that responds beautifully to carefully crafted handloads. With the popular round butt and heavy "bull" barrel, it points and handles quite well. It is also accurate and easy to shoot due to the famous Smith & Wesson trigger system.

The interesting features of the gun are ballistics out of the three-inch-in-name-only barrel and the innovative extractor, which is exactly like the one found in...

25 YD. FIRING RESULTS	AVG. VEL.	STD. DEV.	GROUP SIZE
Winchester Silvertips	1171	16	3.50"
Federal 9BP	1082	26	2.75"
Federal 9AP	1068	17	3.50"
Handload #1	1286	35	3.25"
Handload #2	1041	16	3.75"
Handload #3	1108	32	2.25"

SMITH & WESSON MODEL 547 (4")

FIRING 9

TWENTY-TWO:

Chuck Karwan has chosen to fit out his four-inch Model 547 with Pachmayr's Grippers. These moulded neoprene grips are recessed as shown for speed loader clearance. Smith & Wesson still catalogs this version of their best-selling "K" frame revolver. The engineering is unique.

CHUCK KARWAN'S Model 547, which is different in that it has a four-inch barrel and a square butt. Surprisingly, the entire subjective feel of the handgun changes with the addition of an inch more barrel and a slightly different contour to the butt.

25 YD. FIRING RESULTS	AVG. VEL.	STD. DEV.	GROUP SIZE
Winchester Silvertips	1236	10	2.50"
Federal 9BP	1256	6	1.75"
Federal 9AP	1098	17	3.00"
Handload #1	1217	48	3.00"
Handload #2	1039	14	1.75"
Handload #3	1115	28	3.25"

You also may notice that Karwan has fitted his receiver out with a set of Pachmayr Gripper grips. Moulded of a variety of neoprene rubber, the trim grips are offered by the Pachmayr firm in an assortment of sizes and styles.

This points up one of the advantages of a revolver. It is fairly easy to change the handling and feel of a revolver by changing the grips. The factory itself can provide a half-dozen or so variations in shape and checkering style on their own grips. You cannot do that, at least not as easily, with an automatic pistol.

The handling of Karwan's longer, heavier and differently shaped 547 is completely different than Dean Grennell's. For handling and carrying efficiency, I think that I'd go with the shorter gun, but the longer one will be chosen by some.

The previously mentioned technical difficulty that the factory whipped when they introduced the 547 is making a rimmed-cartridge handgun efficiently use rimless ammunition. They accomplished this by dint of a unique extractor.

The 547 extractor works by virtue of six radiused fingers which are mounted on the central shaft of the extractor within the revolver's cylinder. Spring-loaded, the fingers will blossom into the extractor cut on the body of each 9mmP round loaded into the chambers of the revolver. When you hit the extractor rod, the rimless 9mmP cartridges are lifted neatly from the chambers.

It is interesting to compare the firing data charts printed on these pages. If anyone wants to contend that you lose much of anything in velocity by using a wheelgun, here's the data that will destroy that argument completely.

FIRING

TWENTY-THREE:

LLAMA OMNI

The Llama Omni is a well-made pistol with a host of most unusual features, not the least of which is the magazine shown at left. Single column above, double below.

ALONG WITH its mates from Star and Astra, the Llama Omni was one of the automatic pistol designs that emerged from the Spanish service pistol trials held in the late Seventies and early Eighties. At least two other major powers, the United States and West Germany, as well as some smaller nations, were doing the same thing within the same general time frame. Since the guns evolved by this worldwide catharsis included the S&W 459, Beretta 92F, SIG-Sauer 226, Walther P5, H&K P7, Star 28/30, Steyr GB, Glock 17 and Astra A-80/90, the period was one of extreme interest to students of smallarms design.

The Llama design, which the factory dubbed the Omni, is the latest in a series of automatic pistols produced by Llama-Gabilondo. It is one of the first that shows much in the way of original design effort. For several decades, in the early part of this century, the company produced automatic pistols and revolvers, sometimes by sub-contracting, that are are of suspect quality. However, in the period following World War II, the Llama plant has concentrated on the quality of their products.

The Omni pistol is the first effort the company has made to come up with a high quality handgun with a completely original design. The pistol uses the Colt/Browning tilting barrel system that we see so often, but most other features are quite different.

The shape of the pistol is fairly conventional, except for the contouring of the trigger guard, where you'll find a radical upwards slope to the underside, a forward-projecting hook and a carefully shaped recess for the third finger to fit into when the hand is in firing position. The ergonomics of the gun have received a lot of attention, resulting in a funny-looking gun that shoots great.

The trigger is first-shot double-action. Within the lockwork of the pistol, there are two separate drawbars. One is for double-action and the other for single. Another unique touch is the system that uses ball bearings for the hammer pivot. Whether this feature is responsible in part for the smooth DA trigger pull or not is open to question, but the trigger is quite good.

There are several versions of the pistol in production, including single-column magazine guns in both .45 ACP and 9mmP calibers. The pistol we had to shoot was a double-column type in 9mmP. The magazine is often overlooked, but may be the most clever innovation in the entire gun. The magazine holds thirteen shots, but the upper portion of the magazine is reduced to hold the cartridges in a single column, while the lower part flairs out to typical double-column dimensions.

In firing tests, there were no jams with this arrangement. Tactically, this magazine is easy to speed-load into the pistol. You are inserting a single-column upper magazine into a double-column well. It works for the same reason that a bottle-necked case usually will feed better than a straight-sided one. This pistol deserves close attention; it's often overlooked.

25 YD. FIRING RESULTS	AVG. VEL.	STD. DEV.	GROUP SIZE
Winchester Silvertips	1183	22	2.75"
Federal 9BP	1084	14	2.50"
Federal 9AP	1029	14	3.00"
Handload #1	1195	18	3.25"
Handload #2	1054	18	4.00"
Handload #3	1163	14	3.75"

FIRING TWENTY-FOUR:

LLAMA MODEL XI-B

Unlike the Omni, this is a conventional Colt copy with typical features. It is a nicely finished handgun, which offers solid value for a relatively modest price. Llama XI-B.

THERE IS simply no way to avoid saying that this pistol is a copy. The Llama Model XI-B is a version of the standard pistol that the company has produced and sold for many years. The gun is available in three frame sizes, of which the XI-B is the middle-sized and also the newest. Indisputably, the gun is a Colt copy.

In Spain, manufacturing costs are lower and the pistol can be produced at a price that allows the importer, Stoeger, to sell it at a fraction of what a comparable Colt will cost. There's nearly a $250 difference in the prices of the 9mmP Colt Government Model and a Llama. Moreover, the copy that you get is a good quality handgun, made of modern steels and well finished.

The finish is an interesting point to examine. Llamas are available in a wide variety of finishes. The standard finish, as seen here, is polished blue with varnished, smooth walnut stocks. it is nicely done, with only a few tool marks peeping through the blue

in a couple of places. There is another market the Llama pitches to with the basic gun embellished in the extreme. You can buy stain-chromed, etched, engraved, and even gold-damascened variations of the plain guns.

Many people would prefer to have a personal piece "fancied-up" a little and Llama will be pleased to accommodate them. So will Colt, via the Custom Shop, and the real difference lies only in the quality of the embellishment and the accompanying price tag.

The XI-B is a scaled-down Colt Government Model. It is not just a shortened gun like the Commander, but a reduced model. The one place where there was no apparent reduction is in the amount of steel used. Weighing within an ounce of the Colt GM, the XI-B is a chunky pistol.

The other features are about what you would expect: a single-action-only trigger with manual safety lock, grip safety, half-cock notch on the hammer, frame-mounted magazine catch and a single-column magazine.

The slide has an integral top rib and a windage-adjustable rear sight. The grasping serrations are the racy angled ones like a Colt Gold Cup. That angle is repeated in the contour of the face of the receiver. It looks better and would probably slip back into a holster with considerable ease.

This is a rather likeable gun, chunky and solid feeling in the hand. There are some places in the design where they have improved on Colt, particularly in shape. The mainspring housing has a better shape than either of the pair offered by Colt — sort of semi-arched. It's a good gun for the money.

25 YD. FIRING RESULTS	AVG. VEL.	STD. DEV.	GROUP SIZE
Winchester Silvertips	1191	30	3.75"
Federal 9BP	1207	9	3.50"
Federal 9AP	1082	24	4.00"
Handload #1	1122	33	4.00"
Handload #2	1020	38	3.75"
Handload #3	1108	34	4.25"

FIRING

TWENTY-FIVE:

ASP

The Guttersnipe rear sight is mounted on the ASP's slide. There is no front sight. Shooter aligns target in painted center of the groove.

T HE ASP is a delightful little 9mmP automatic pistol that started life as Smith & Wesson Model 39. It has been extensively customized into a light, compact, carryable personal defense handgun. It was guns like this that prodded Smith & Wesson into introducing the Model 469/669. There are so many unique features to describe that I hardly know where to begin. How about I hit it quick and let Dean Grennell's superb photographs describe Dean Grennell's pet gun?

Here goes. It has — see-through grips and a cutaway magazine so you can tell about the ammo supply — a recontoured slide to reduce weight and bulk — trigger guard hook — spurless hammer — smooooth trigger pull — angled finger rest extensions on all three magazines — reduced clearance on right side of trigger guard for right handers — magazine pouch with magnetic retention — polished, fitted ramp on barrel — and the Guttersnipe rear sight. The latter is a tapered, trough-like groove in a block mounted on the rear of the slide.

In use, a shooter aligns the target in the groove, all the while seeing equal amounts of the yellow paint on each of the three sides.

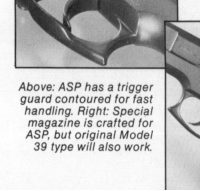

Above: ASP has a trigger guard contoured for fast handling. Right: Special magazine is crafted for ASP, but original Model 39 type will also work.

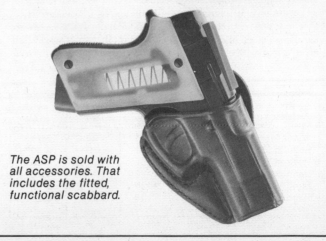

The ASP is sold with all accessories. That includes the fitted, functional scabbard.

25 YD. FIRING RESULTS	AVG. VEL.	STD. DEV.	GROUP SIZE
Winchester Silvertips	1135	19	3.50"
Federal 9BP	1158	24	3.50"
Federal 9AP	994	27	4.00"
Handload #1	1156	36	4.25"
Handload #2	1020	38	4.50"
Handload #3	1001	39	5.00"

FIRING TWENTY-SIX:

THOMPSON/CENTER CONTENDER

The close-up photo below is one of the original octagonal tubes. Though they are now out-of-print, Contender made up one special barrel, a round one at right, for Dean Grennell.

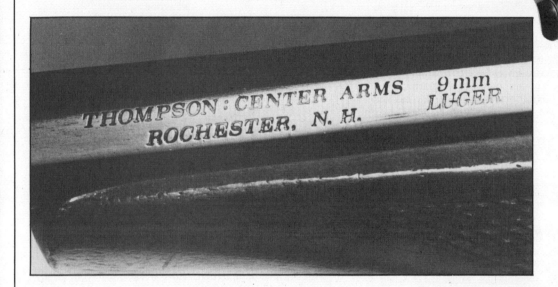

THOMPSON : CENTER ARMS
ROCHESTER, N. H. 9 mm LUGER

I CAN recall the first discussions of the Contender pistol in the firearms press sometime around 1967. That means that the pistol is coming pretty close to twenty years of service to American shooters. In that time, there have been efforts to produce competitive pistols of similar characteristics and quality. They have failed. The single-shot pistol market belongs to the Contender.

There are a lot of reasons for this. For one thing, the pistol was never particularly expensive. For another, the gun is astonishingly versatile. For about a hundred bucks (at least for most of the life of the gun) a shooter could buy an extra barrel and install it on his original frame. You could be shooting a .17 K-Hornet one minute and, within a few minutes, change barrels and be shooting a .410 shotgun.

That sort of versatility really caught on with American shooters and is still a big part of the sales appeal. While some of the reason for the health of the gun is the versatility factor, more of it hinges on accuracy. Contender may have produced some barrels that are not accurate, but I have encountered few of them. Many Contender barrels are cut for wildcat cartridges, but most are for pistol rounds.

The Contender will wring the most from the majority of pistol cartridges. The standard barrel length is now ten inches. In the case of most pistol cartridges, the capacity of the case is sufficiently limited that a barrel longer than this is wasted. The powder charge has expended its increased effort to push the bullet out of the barrel.

In the early days of the Contender, the company seemed intent on making everything in the way of barrels. The total list of cartridges must have reached fifty or so and I'm probably on the conservative side.

The barrel on this gun is a recent version, specially made for Co-author Dean Grennell. It is made in the current bull barrel contour. As the accompanying charts show, it turned in some pretty good groups as well as some impressive velocities.

25 YD. FIRING RESULTS	AVG. VEL.	STD. DEV.	GROUP SIZE
Winchester Silvertips	1397	23	2.50"
Federal 9BP	1353	6	2.00"
Federal 9AP	1306	9	3.00"
Handload #1	1432	16	1.75"
Handload #2	1226	11	2.00"
Handload #3	1542	5	2.00"

FIRING

TWENTY-SEVEN:

ASTRA A-90

WHEN THE Spanish Government held test trials to find a new service automatic in the late 1970s, the three major armsmakers of that country all submitted designs. The pistol from Astra was dubbed the A-80 and, while it did not get selected, it came close. The A-80 is an amalgamation of design features from several different guns. It is imported into this country by Interarms.

The A-80 has the tilting-barrel locking system of the Colt and Browning guns. The lockwork is that typical of the modern era, a double-action trigger with a SIG-Sauer type de-cocking lever. There's also a firing pin safety linked to the trigger. Laid out with pleasing and most shootable contours which included a relatively

The A-90 has multiple controls. There's a safety on the slide, plus slide stop and de-cocking lever on the frame. Relocating magazine catch was big change from A-80.

25 YD. FIRING RESULTS	AVG. VEL.	STD. DEV.	GROUP SIZE
Winchester Silvertips	1192	31	2.75"
Federal 9BP	1082	9	3.00"
Federal 9AP	1033	18	2.75"
Handload #1	1208	35	4.00"
Handload #2	1061	42	5.00"
Handload #3	1123	26	5.25"

slim butt section (slim for a pistol with a double-column magazine holding fifteen shots), the A-80 was a good buy. You even got a rear sight adjustable for windage, a loaded chamber indicator and an all-steel frame.

The A-80 also was available in .45 ACP with a single-column magazine holding eight shots and, in .38 Super, with a fifteen-shot type. As a fan of the latter cartridge, I bought one of them and fired it a great deal. It was a reliable and reasonably accurate pistol with sensible ammunition, and I still use it for one of my "traveling guns" in the West.

For reasons that I fail to understand, the Astra factory chose to update the A-80 to a newer version called the A-90. The major change to the pistol was put there for reasons that are no doubt adequate to the company, but might be viewed as a giant step backwards.

The A-90 now has a slide-mounted manual safety. I can only theorize that it was put there to give the pistol an ambidextrous character. The lever of the safety is mirrored on the right side of the slide to make the pistol a bit more readily usable to the twelve percent or so of the population that are left-handed.

But the left side of the pistol now has a hodge-podge of controls that can be a little confusing. There is a safety on the slide, a de-cocking lever and slide stop on the frame, plus a magazine catch adjacent to the trigger guard. That latter feature of the A-90 is an improvement; the A-80s had the accursed heel-mounted magazine catch.

The improved A-90 actually improves only in the sense of the better magazine catch location, since the ambidextrous use problem would have been better solved by some form of de-cocking lever on both sides of the pistol.

This particular A-90 was troubled by a balky pair of magazines, neither of which would feed with consistency. That's a shame, as the gun has a good balance and feel and was respectably accurate.

F.I.E. TZ-75

FIRING

TWENTY-EIGHT:

IN OTHER locations in this book, you can read about a nearly legendary automatic pistol called the CZ-75. That pistol is a Czech design and, since it's made behind the Iron Curtain, it is not well distributed in the United States. That may be changing with the importation of the pistol by Bauska Arms, but in the interim, there is a partial answer to the plight of the man who just has to have one.

The answer is an inexpensive copy of the pistol made in Italy and imported into the United States by FIE of Florida. They call their version of the gun the TZ-75. With a couple of notable exceptions, it is quite close to the dimensions and characteristics of the original Czech handgun.

The TZ-75 is a recoil-operated, tilting-barrel, double-action automatic pistol. It has a double-column fifteen-shot magazine with the magazine catch positioned on the frame adjacent to the trigger guard. Like the pistol after which it is modeled, the TZ has the desirable reversed rails in the frame/slide relationship. This means that the slide is guided somewhat more precisely in the course of its fore-and-aft travel. The gun also has the Petter-designed modular lockwork and improved Browning lock-up. All of these features are to the distinct credit of the gun.

The original CZ from the Czech designers was accepted widely due to all of the above features, but most specifically, because the pistol had a safety arranged for the modern combat shooter. On the frame of the pistol's left side, the safety lever was positioned for access to the shooter's right hand. Further, it was set to wipe down in the manner of the Colt GM. This meant that the gun could be carried quite safety in the "cocked-and-locked" mode. The safety on the TZ has migrated upwards to the slide and pivots in the opposite direction, and that is not to the benefit of the gun.

There are a couple of other differences. The CZ has slender grips of cast black plastic with a gripping pattern cast into them.

The TZ-75 is a copy of the Czech CZ-75, differing in the type of safety as well as finish details. The major selling point of both guns is the highly practical shape.

The TZ copy has beautiful polished-walnut grips which are most attractive, but serve to thicken the butt section of the pistol to an uncomfortable degree.

The other major feature of the CZ which drew much critical acclaim was the ergonomics of the of the gun. It was laid out and shaped so well that shooters who did not like double-action autos or 9mmPs were grudgingly approving. The same comments are true of the CZ copy — it is a nicely balanced and well finished pistol, much like the original CZ, with the exception of the safety.

The price tag for a TZ is down to the point that nearly any serious shooter can afford one and they are available in good quantity.

25 YD. FIRING RESULTS	AVG. VEL.	STD. DEV.	GROUP SIZE
Winchester Silvertips	1181	16	4.00"
Federal 9BP	1084	26	3.50"
Federal 9AP	1051	20	5.00"
Handload #1	1202	36	4.24"
Handload #2	1014	16	4.25"
Handload #3	1156	33	5.25"

KASSNAR PJK 9HP

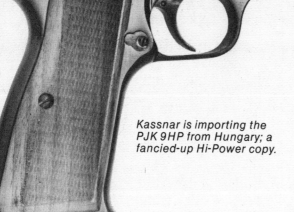

Kassnar is importing the PJK 9HP from Hungary; a fancied-up Hi-Power copy.

The PJK has controls that are the same as the original. Safety is on the frame, slide stop forward of the left grip panel and magazine catch just behind the trigger.

THE SHAPE and style of the pistol in the adjacent photo should be familiar to you. It is the Hi-Power, John Browning's last autopistol design and one of the best handguns ever made. The most sincere form of flattery is said to be imitation. The pistol shown here is an imitation of the Browning, one that never saw Belgium or the FN works, but it is an excellent and inexpensive firearm.

The pistol is imported into the United States by the Kassnar Imports Company of Harrisburg, Pennsylvania. They have chosen to give the gun the unwieldy title of Kassnar PJK 9HP, which I'll shorten to PJK for the sake of brevity.

The gun is made by FEG, the state arms plant of Hungary. None of my available references has any but the most succinct notations about this plant. Apparently the FEG works has produced good to excellent copies of many other people's designs since Hungary was joined to the Eastern bloc after World War II. Two of these guns were a lightly modified version of the Soviet Tokarev and a re-shaped Walther copy.

The pistol under consideration here is a line-for-line copy of the Browning. With some exceptions, parts will interchange between the genuine article and this copy. Copying has little stigma if you do it this well and pick something first-rate to copy in the first place.

The PJK does have some differences, though. The most immediately visible difference is that gorgeous ventilated rib added to the top of the slide. It is done in the style of the old King Gunsight Company of San Francisco, a style that appeals more to some than to others. I think that it's stylish, made more so when you look closely and realize that the rib is milled from the solid steel of the slide.

There is also a contour difference in the forward end of the slide. On the original Browning, the slide has a reduced, stepped area toward the muzzle. The PJK is straight-tapered from the rear of the slide to the front.

Two other features of the PJK which are most attractive are the bluing and the grips. The pistol is nicely polished and blued in a deep black color that is noticeably different. Some form of fancy grained walnut is the material from which the grips are crafted. They are sharply, almost uncomfortably, checkered in such a way as to eliminate the gun slipping in the hand.

Few Brownings have good trigger pulls, and this copy of a Browning does nothing to break the trend. The PJK's pull is heavy, with a grating, unpleasant creep. But, all things considered, the pistol is priced to provide most of the features of a Browning at almost half the cost.

25 YD. FIRING RESULTS	AVG. VEL.	STD. DEV.	GROUP SIZE
Winchester Silvertips	1222	10	2.25"
Federal 9BP	1208	12	2.50"
Federal 9AP	1086	11	3.25"
Handload #1	1244	25	3.00"
Handload #2	1072	17	3.25"
Handload #3	1165	9	3.25"

FEG R9

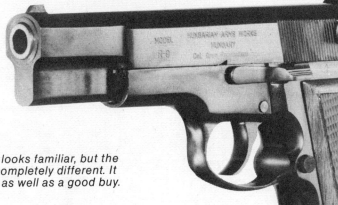

Interarms FEG R9 looks familiar, but the trigger system is completely different. It is a double-action as well as a good buy.

The trigger guard is rounded to allow the double-action trigger room to operate. Also, note the safety lever on the slide. Slide stop, magazine catch are as Browning's.

A T FIRST glance, this pistol looks much like a Browning Hi-Power. It has the same contours as the venerable Belgian design, as well as the same external dimensions. But there is a big difference between this pistol and the P'35.

This gun has a double-action trigger system. The FN works have prototypes of a DA version of their gun, a pistol which is scheduled for U.S. distribution in the fall of '86, but this pistol is available at the present time and at a reduced price.

The pistol, which we'll call the R9, is another made in Hungary in the FEG plant. Like its mate across the page, it is imported into America, but this time by Interarms. While the shape and style of this pistol are much like the PJK, there are enough differences to look at it in a separate light.

A double-action trigger system is a good bit more complicated than the single-action variety and it will take more space within the frame of the pistol to house it. The R9 has a trigger guard that is set a little lower on the frame of the gun; it's instantly apparent to the hand of a Browning user. The guard also is larger and more curved to allow room for the trigger itself to swing through a longer arc.

Most of the other cosmetic features of the PJK are here in the R9: deep polished blue-black finish and checkered walnut grips, but that exotic ventilated rib on the slide is missing. The magazines of both pistols are the same, hold thirteen 9mmP cartridges, and will in fact work in a regular Browning.

The conversion to double-action is interesting and the result is most unusual. The first-shot, double-action pull of the R9 is in two distinctly different stages. The first stage is perhaps half of the trigger-arc travel and is unbelievably harsh and grating. But the second half of the trigger arc is pleasantly smooth and light, much like that of a good quality double-action revolver. The transitional point occurs just about where the hammer is at the half-cock position. If a shooter puts the hammer on half-cock, with the intent of drawing and firing double-action, then he has one of the best two or three double-action pulls of any of the host of DA automatics featured in this book.

I haven't had the chance to deliver the gun to a good gunsmith for a technical analysis of the trigger system, but it seems to me that the pistol may very well have been designed to be carried at the half-cock. It certainly provides an easier-to-shoot option to the full double-action system.

The safety of the R9 is mounted on the slide, pivots up to the fire position, and doesn't work when the hammer is at the half-cock spot.

This is a subtly different handgun which bears close attention.

25 YD. FIRING RESULTS	AVG. VEL.	STD. DEV.	GROUP SIZE
Winchester Silvertips	1226	22	5.00"
Federal 9BP	1206	35	3.25"
Federal 9AP	1102	20	3.50"
Handload #1	1240	22	3.75
Handload #2	1069	17	3.75"
Handload #3	1165	9	5.00"

HECKLER & KOCH P9s

FIRING 9

THIRTY-ONE:

The Heckler & Koch P9s, with a combat slide in place, shows this sight picture to the shooter. The other slide has fully adjustable target sights and barrel weight. This is one of the most accurate 9mmPs.

THERE IS an entire chapter of this book given over to the innovative 9mmP handguns from the Heckler & Koch works. The pistol to be considered in this part of our Ninefiring section is the Cadillac Convertible of the H&K line. It's called the P9s and it not only has a host of technical innovations, but also the dual character of a service and target automatic.

The P9 pistol is built from a combination of sheet steel and plastic. The skeleton of the receiver is anything but the forged steel, milled-to-shape, frame of most other guns. Instead, the frame is a series of precise stampings, formed to shape over appropriate mandrels, and spot-welded in place. It looks like hell, but when grips are screwed into place, you can't see it anyway.

And it works as well as the most precisely milled receiver ever made. The entire face of the receiver, including the trigger guard, is a casting — of impact-resistant plastic.

The controls of the P9s are different, also. The pistol is double-action for the first shot like many others. But the hammer of the P9s is internal and spurless, so the designers provided a cocking indicator in the form of a pin which protrudes from the rear of the slide when the hammer is cocked. There's a safety on the slide, but the interesting feature is the little lever located at the forward edge of the left grip panel. This is a decocking lever which works like the one on the SIG-Sauers. It drops the hammer safely on a loaded round in the chamber.

But in the case of this handgun, there is even more. The lever also serves to RE-cock the hammer for single-action fire if that is what you need to do. It may have been intended for the target shooter to easily cock his hammer for repeated dry firing, but it also has advantages in the combat context.

The P9s has been called a retarded blowback pistol, but a more accurate description would probably be roller-locked. The gun uses a variation of the time-tested roller-locking principle first seen in World War II machine guns. It is a system which has been adapted for use in weapons as diverse as automatic cannons and submachine guns.

Our test pistol was a kit version. This is a cased set consisting of a single receiver and two barrel and slide units, plus two pair of grips. The basic receiver may be assembled with the fixed sight slide to produce a compact holster pistol. If target shooting is on the day's agenda, then it is the work of but a moment to assemble the target-sighted slide and match barrel with extended counterweight. The grips are a choice of checkered plastic or stippled walnut, contoured for the bulls-eye range.

My test firing was done with the service slide. Co-author Dean Grennell has fired some incredible groups with the target gun version. Either way, the P9s is one of the more accurate 9s.

25 YD. FIRING RESULTS	AVG. VEL.	STD. DEV.	GROUP SIZE
Winchester Silvertips	1264	8	2.25"
Federal 9BP	1200	17	2.75"
Federal 9AP	1191	8	2.50"
Handload #1	1332	30	1.75"
Handload #2	1134	15	2.00"
Handload #3	1179	12	2.25"

HECKLER & KOCH VP70z

The catch in the top of the trigger guard of the VP70 is a takedown latch. This is an exceptionally easy gun to handle, use and care for. It would be easy to train recruits in the use of a pistol with simplified handling.

IF THE pistol across the page, the elegantly designed P9s, is the Cadillac of the Heckler & Koch line, then this pistol must certainly be the Jeep. H&K refers to it as a sturdy defense pistol. There's not the slightest doubt that this claim is the absolute truth.

The VP70z is a pistol with an unusual trigger system. It slides fore-and-aft in the receiver and works a striker to fire the pistol. The first portion of the trigger travel retracts the striker against its spring and the final fraction of an inch of movement releases the striker to move forward and fire the cartridge. When the slide cycles in the customary fashion, the fired round is ejected and a new one fed into the chamber. The striker is not somehow cocked by this movement, unlike the hammers of most other pistols. The shooter must once again pull the trigger through the long, double-action cycle. If you are an experienced shooter, the system will drive you nuts. But if you are relatively inexperienced in the ways of handguns, there isn't anything safer and easier to learn.

There are innovative features elsewhere in the gun. The receiver is a single massive plastic casting. It houses a magazine with the astonishing capacity of eighteen shots. A simple cross-bolt safety blocks the trigger from rearwards travel. It's appropriate to mention that the magazine is retained in the butt of the pistol by a heel-mounted latch. That's usually a feature to be

criticized, but when the magazine thus retained holds eighteen shots, then changing them might be a somewhat less common occurrence.

The VP70z is also different in that it is one of the rare 9mmP handguns without a discernible locking system. The breech is held shut for the time that it takes the residual pressure to drop by a combination of the weight of the slide and the strength of the recoil spring.

One version of the VP70z used a stock which fastened to the rear of the pistol's receiver. Certain linkages on the stock worked the internal lockwork of the pistol in such a way as to give a three-shot-burst fire capability. In other words, you could snap the pistol's stock in place and have a true submachine gun. Not many of these guns were sold in the United States where they would require Federal registration, but they are interesting variations.

While the effort of the designers was to produce a usable defensive handgun, the result is a pistol that is a bit unwieldy to carry and use. The trigger is supposed to have a definite hestitation in the cycle when it's about to release, but the gun that we fired had a long trigger movement which was damned hard to get used to.

I think the potential for accuracy was much higher than the figures reported here would indicate.

25 YD. FIRING RESULTS	AVG. VEL.	STD. DEV.	GROUP SIZE
Winchester Silvertips	1130	61	4.00"
Federal 9BP	963	34	4.50"
Federal 9AP	970	19	3.50"
Handload #1	1148	31	4.00"
Handload #2	939	21	3.75"
Handload #3	1074	47	2.75"

HECKLER & KOCH P7M8

FIRING 9

THIRTY-THREE:

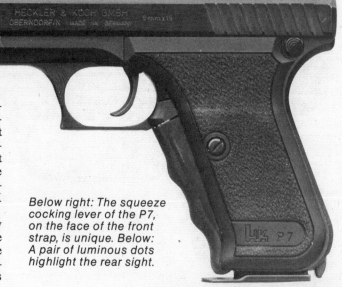

THE GERMAN service pistol trials of the early Seventies will be remembered by the historians of weaponry as a particularly interesting period. The excellent designs of SIG-Sauer were developed, as was the updated version of the venerable P'38. The most interesting designs, at least from the standpoint of pure technical innovation, were those of the new firm of Heckler & Koch. In this portion of our evaluation of 9mmP handguns, we will look at two versions of the H&K impression of a personal defense handgun.

The P7 was the first of the compact handguns produced by H&K. It is presently called the P7M8 to differentiate it from the P7M13 which is examined across the page. The two guns are quite similar in their physical appearance and the only real difference is the thirteen-shot double-column magazine which marks the M13 version.

An all-steel pistol, the P7 is blessed with a number of clever features. The sights are particularly good — wide square notch rear and plain post front. Both are marked with the luminous dots which find their way onto so many guns these days; two dots on the rear sight and a single one on the front. The gun is finished in an attractive matte-black color which isn't likely to reflect light. The grips are moulded from some form of grained plastic. It is a non-slip surface that ought to be on more guns.

As defense pistols go, the P7 is quite compact and carryable. The gun is only 6.54 inches long. Contrast that with the 8.54 inches of a Beretta 92F. The weight of the P7 is a chunky thirty-four ounces, which is within a fraction of that of the Beretta's.

None of this touches on the unique features of the pistol. One of them is purely technical, while the other is both technical and tactical. We'll look at the latter feature first.

The P7 is a single-action automatic pistol. It does not have a hammer in the sense of a Colt or Browning single-action, but rather works with a spring-driven striker in a direct line with the primer of the cartridge in the chamber of the barrel. The striker is cocked for firing in a most unusual way.

On the front face of the grip of the gun, there is a recessed lever. It actually constitutes the major portion of the frontstrap, the part of the grip covered by the fingers of the shooting hand when the gun is held in firing position. The lever is pivoted from the bottom, so that the longer and stronger fingers are grasping the lever at the top. When a shooter grasps the gun with the firm grasp of one who intends to fire, he compresses the lever. And that cocks the gun. Internal linkages are connected to the striker, retracting it in such

Below right: The squeeze cocking lever of the P7, on the face of the front strap, is unique. Below: A pair of luminous dots highlight the rear sight.

a way that a deliberate pull of the trigger will release it and fire the pistol. The slide cycles in the normal way, ejecting the fired round and feeding a new one when the recoil spring forces it forward into battery.

As long as the pistol is held in a firing grasp, it will function as a normal single-action pistol. When the grip is relaxed, the internal springs behind the cocking lever expand, forcing the lever out and the pistol is "de-cocked." There are no safeties, as there is no need for them. The gun is perfectly safe to handle as long as it is not held with the grasp of one who intends to fire. The amount of pressure required to cock the gun is reportedly about fifteen pounds, but only a pound or so of effort is required to keep it cocked.

It is bloody difficult to get used to.

25 YD. FIRING RESULTS	AVG. VEL.	STD. DEV.	GROUP SIZE
Winchester Silvertips	1150	24	3.00"
Federal 115 JHP	1098	46	3.50"
Federal 123 FMJ	1022	12	4.25"
Handload #1	1201	26	2.75"
Handload #2	994	6	2.25"
Handload #3	1133	10	2.25"

HECKLER & KOCH P7M13

THIRTY-FOUR:

The M13 version of the pistol has a larger magazine and a different trigger guard. The front sight of both guns is as seen to the left. Right: Fluted chamber's hard on brass.

A CROSS THE way, we looked at the eight-shot version of Heckler & Koch's P7 pistol. Here, we'll examine the P7M13, which is updated with a double-column magazine holding thirteen shots, plus a couple of other features. The top half of the pistol is unchanged — slide, barrel, recoil spring and sights are essentially the same as the P7M8's.

There are some pronounced differences in the receiver area, however. The most immediately noticeable difference is that the butt is far thicker. When you add another column of cartridges, this can't be avoided. On the P7M13 which we had for evaluation, the thicker butt was the first item eliciting comment from all those who had earlier handled the P7M8. There is no way to get around the fact that the butt section of the gun is boxy and awkward. When you add the complexity of the squeeze-cocking lever, you produce a pistol which can be best used by those shooters who have rather large, strong hands.

If you want those extra shots, there's no way to get them except to make the magazine long enough to hold them, an unacceptable alternative, or thick enough to use two columns, which is what nearly everyone does. The H&K magazines are better than most in the sense that they are almost straight up and down within the angled butt of the pistol. This feature promotes reliable feeding — it must work, as we had not a single malfunction of any sort with either version of the P7.

The P7M13 that we used for evaluation purposes had another unique feature which we are told is now incorporated into production M8s. It has an ambidextrous magazine catch. Better

yet, the location of the catch has been moved from the butt of the pistol to the accepted location in the vicinity of the rear of the trigger guard. The pistol is the closest thing you'll ever see to a completely ambidextrous firearm. The cocking lever actually doubles as the slide stop. With the slide locked back, a shooter has but to insert a magazine and grasp the butt, at which time the slide runs forward, chambering a round and leaving the striker cocked for an immediate first shot.

All of the foregoing is interesting and innovative material for the student of the handgun, but there is even a bit more. We have already noted that the P7s are short, compact handguns in comparison to others. Much of the reason why is because there is no locking system in the P7, at least as we commonly understand them. The P7s are blowback pistols, devoid of locking lugs, locking blocks or locking rollers. The blowback operation would be excessively violent in a pistol of this size and for a cartridge of this pressure level. That is, if it were not for the gas retarding system that the H&K people designed into this firearm.

In the P7, there is a gas bleed hole in the barrel just forward of the chamber. Part of the gas produced by firing a round enters this hole and acts against a plunger located in the underside of the frame. The plunger is connected to the slide and, within its cylinder, holds the slide closed until pressure drops when the bullet leaves the barrel. At that point in the cycle, there is enough residual inertia remaining to cause the slide to move to the rear against the tension of the recoil spring. The pistol has a self-regulating gas system which will automatically adjust to the pressure level of any ammunition that can be fired in it. It is a technical innovation of the first magnitude.

I can't regard the squeeze-cocking system in the same light. I truly believe that this system can't be readily learned by anyone used to conventional handguns. If a large group of total neophytes were taught this gun from the beginning of their weapons training, it might be a pretty fair way to go. It doesn't seem to be such a good idea for other shooters who have been taught to grasp the gun in firing position "in the leather." If you grab a P7 in that way, you have a cocked, ready-to-go pistol before it ever clears the holster. Time will tell.

25 YD. FIRING RESULTS	AVG. VEL.	STD. DEV.	GROUP SIZE
Winchester Silvertips	1137	11	2.75"
Federal 115 JHP	1067	15	3.25"
Federal FMJ	1039	12	4.00"
Handload #1	1217	24	3.75"
Handload #2	1031	17	2.00"
Handload #3	1123	10	2.50"

SIG 210

THIRTY-FIVE:

IF YOU are reading this book cover-to-cover, you've already read (some might say endured) Chapter Ten, a general discussion of the products of the SIG works of Switzerland, as well as the products of the SIG-Sauer combine of West Germany and Switzerland. On the possibility that some of you are browsing through the book, I'll repeat what I admit to be an opinion about this pistol: it is the best 9mmP made.

Sure, it has some faults. The biggest fault is the magazine catch, which is not only in the wrong place, but damned hard to work. It's a clear two-handed situation to change magazines in a SIG 210. The rear sight in at least the service pistol version of the 210 is a U notch, hopelessly out of date. And, for rough service in the field, the finely fitted parts which make the pistol so accurate might contribute to malfunctions.

Oh, and yeah, I guess you ought to know that you can buy three or four of the excellent SIG-Sauer 225s on the facing page for what one of the 210s will cost. Despite all of this, I still say that the 210 is the best you can get. Not the best buy, the most practical, or the most concealable; just the best.

The 210 is probably the most accurate, although the Browning Competition Model or target version of the H&K P9s might give it a run for its money. Look for a moment at why the 210 is so highly regarded.

First, it has an unusual slide-receiver relationship. The rails on the receiver of the 210 extend up and in, as viewed from the rear. From the same perspective, the matching rails on the moving slide extend down and out. The effect is to have the slide moving *in* the receiver. Since the rails on both components are longer than on other pistols, the slide cycles in very much the same way from shot to shot. Combined with a superior barrel, made to shoot a particular kind of ammunition, and an excellent, improved lock-up, the 210 just has to shoot better. And it does.

The 210s will not all be fired at round bullseyes; they have a combat gun potential. When you mate that silky-smooth cycle with a pointable pistol with the barrel lying a scant fraction above the hand, you've got a super "double-tapper."

The 210's trigger is clean and crisp, breaking like one of Elmer Keith's famous glass rods. No pistol, no matter how accurate, can be handled well without good trigger action. And it also follows that a shooter is more likely to get the most out of a less-than-accurate pistol if it has a good trigger.

The 210 shown is a 210-6 borrowed from the Maxwell collection. It was used to fire the tests reported here. A 210-2 was later acquired and was used for other firing sessions. If anything the latter gun is more accurate.

This photo of a SIG 210-2 shows the way that the slide and receiver interface, opposite to that used on most automatics. 210-2 has plain "U" notch rear sight. The 210-6 at the top of the page is fitted with an adjustable sight.

25 YD. FIRING RESULTS	AVG. VELOCITY	STD. DEV.	GROUP SIZE
Winchester Silvertips	1247	43	1.50"
Federal 9BP	1213	47	1.50"
Federal 9AP	1138	13	1.75"
Handload #1	1292	10	1.50"
Handload #2	1093	20	1.50"
Handload #3	1239	22	2.25"

SIG-SAUER 225

THIRTY-SIX:

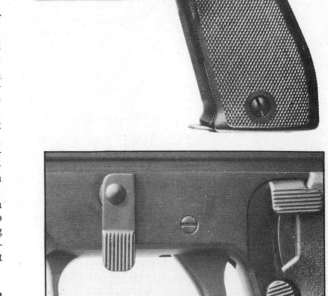

NEARLY EVERYONE who picks up the 225 has the same reaction to it. The comments usually go something like:..."chunky little brute, ain't it?" or maybe..."boy, that's a fistfull!" And all of those things are the absolute truth. The 225, from the combine of SIG-Sauer, is a compact, even blunt little 9mmP handgun. It's sort of the pit bulldog of the 9mmP automatics.

Basically, the 225 is an abbreviated version of the excellent 220, covered in detail next-up in this chapter. The overall dimensions of the 220 were reduced by about three-quarters of an inch in slide and barrel length. The butt is shorter by approximately half an inch. The dimensional changes feel like they are considerably greater when you have a 220 nearby to compare. And the reason for that is simply that the butt of the 225 is not just shorter but also rounded in an entirely pleasing fashion.

I have no reason to believe that the 225 has been made in anything but the parabellum calibers, but the gun would sell like hotcakes if it were to be made in .45 ACP or 10mm Auto, at least in the United States.

There were a few other changes made when the engineers cut a 220 down to 225 size. They moved the magazine catch over to the side where you can get to it with the thumb of the shooting hand, leaving the other mitt to grab a spare from the pouch. Combat shooters get all upset if the catch is not in this position, but damn it, they're right.

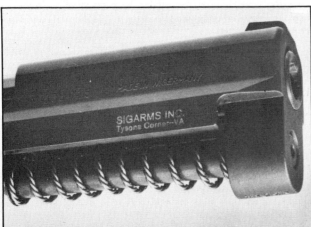

Other details of the SIG-Sauer 225 are seen in these photos. Above: The control panel of the 225 includes a magazine catch, decocking lever and takedown latch. A slide stop is out of sight. Left: Braided recoil spring of the 225 works on typical guide under the stubby barrel.

Like the other guns in the series, the 220 and 226, the 225 has those excellent, dovetailed-in sights. They are well designed to provide a clear sight picture. They were much appreciated when I got to the range to do the shooting that is reported to you in the accompanying table.

An interesting thing happens when you compare the velocities that were obtained in the 225 with those of the 226. There is no statistically significant difference. But there is about three quarters of an inch difference in the barrel length. If you need the concealability of the shorter 225, you are sacrificing nothing in the performance of typical ammunition. If you have to have the larger capacity of the 226 with its fifteen shots, so be it. Still, you could take the bottom half of a 226 (fifteen-shot magazine) and graft on the top half of a 225 (short barrel and slide) — you'd get the best of both — call it a 225½.

25 YD. FIRING RESULTS	AVG. VELOCITY	STD. DEV.	GROUP SIZE
Winchester Silvertips	1170	19	2.25"
Federal 9BP	1186	44	2.50"
Federal 9AP	1063	7	2.75"
Handload #1	1218	19	2.50"
Handload #2	1069	21	3.00"
Handload #3	1137	40	3.25"

FIRING

THIRTY-SEVEN:

SIG-SAUER 220

Sights on a combat gun should be uncomplicated and easy to see. They are just that on the 220 series of pistols. The 226 across the page had a plain rear sight, preferred by many shooters.

You might run across a SIG-Sauer 220 in one of several calibers with different markings on the pistol. In the early Seventies, the pistol was marketed by the Browning company of Morgan, Utah. Under the Browning label, they were available in the United States in 9mmP, .38 Super and .45 ACP. Not surprisingly, the .45s sold best. Only a relative few Browning-marked BDAs were imported in the other two chamberings.

The firearms press in the United States had a lot to do with the former success of the Browning BDA and the subsequent and current success of the SIG-Sauer 220. Well in advance of the introduction of the pistol in the United States, American gun writers were touting the advantages of a double-action pistol in .45 caliber. When the guns finally did enter the country in large numbers, they sold well. One of the biggest reasons for that was the combination of double-action and .45 caliber. The fact that the 220 was one of most modern and innovative 9mmPs got pushed aside in the shuffle.

In any caliber and by any name, the 220 is a fine handgun. The technical innovations which mark the 220 are unique. Described in detail in the chapter on SIGs and SIG-Sauers, they won't be recounted except in summary here. From a manufacturing standpoint, the 220 is exceptionally interesting. It uses a slide made primarily from heavy sheet steel stampings and a precisely cast alloy frame. The pistol also uses a unique locking system wherein the barrel is locked into the ejection port.

In the mid-Seventies, the controls of the 220 were revolutionary. They are still sufficiently different to warrant a great deal of attention from serious combat shooters. The 220 is a double-action pistol. It has no mechanial safety as we understand the term

safety. There is no lever or catch which may be manipulated to prevent the pistol from firing. 220s are meant to be carried with the chamber loaded and the hammer down. They do have a firing pin safety which is linked to the trigger so that the firing pin is locked in place and cannot move until the trigger is deliberately and firmly pulled.

The hammer of the gun is external and may be manually cocked. It will automatically be cocked when the slide cycles as the gun fires. A shooter in a combat situation may be faced with the need to render the pistol safe from the cocked and loaded mode. He can't lock the piece in the manner of the venerable Colt Government Model, because there is no safety. He can, however, de-cock the gun by sweeping the de-cocking lever down with the right thumb. When that is done, the hammer drops without firing the gun. It is once again as safe as can be.

Other guns have had hammer drop features for many years, but they are usually incorporated into a safety system in the manner of several Smith & Wessons and Walthers. The 220 was one of the earliest guns to feature a pure de-cocking lever. It is a simple and straightforward method by which the safety problem may be approached. In its purest form, the combination of a double-action trigger and a de-cocking lever is the same tactical approach which is common to a host of modern double-action revolvers.

The pistol shown in the photos on these pages is a .45 from SIGArms and is completely typical of the 220s in any of the three calibers. Since the barrel length is the same as the Model 226 on the facing page, you can pretty well figure the shooting to be the same.

SIG-SAUER 226

THIRTY-EIGHT:

Right: The 226 controls are, from left to right, the takedown lever, de-cocking lever and slide stop. Round button's the magazine catch.

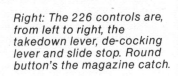

BY U.S. government standards, this pistol is acceptable as a sidearm for the armed forces of the republic. It was one of three designs that were so labeled after extensive testing conducted by the United States Army. The SIG-Sauer 226 was not chosen as the pistol of the future by our forces, but that isn't because it didn't measure up. The reason was plain economics; the SIG-Sauer gun cost a bit more to produce.

If you look across the page at the 220, you can tell where the 226 had its origins. Simply stated, the 226 is a modified and improved version of the basic 220. Since the 220 is an excellent pistol in its own right, improvements bear close examination. All of the improvements will be found on the bottom half of the pistol. The barrel and slide with associated parts are the same as the 220's. 226s lock up in the same way, use the same barrel and recoil spring, and have the same internal firing pin safety.

For combat-schooled shooters, the most immediate and vital improvement is the relocating of the magazine catch. On the 220, it is on the butt of the pistol in the European custom. This was something that most users of this and other guns deplored, because it requires two hands to remove the magazine. Further, the U.S. trials mandated the placement of the magazine catch adjacent to the trigger guard. The 226 has the catch where it belongs, at the juncture of the guard bow and the frame of the gun on the left side. A push-in button, the catch works well. The system is set up in such a way that tension from the magazine spring bearing against the follower will kick the magazine completely clear of the pistol when the catch is depressed.

The 226 is further improved in the sense that the magazine capacity has been increased to a full fifteen rounds. The increase comes by way of the inevitable double column of 9mmP cartridges. Apparently the magazine was designed with considerable care, as the gun fired without a single glitch in the course of hundreds of rounds. When the magazine design is increased to nearly double capacity, the butt becomes thicker. In the 226, the thickening of the butt section is far less objectionable than in other guns, because the butt has been subtly re-contoured. The bulk is held to a minimum and the more rounded butt actually feels better than the original 220. That is not usually the case when a single column design is altered to a double.

I fired the 226 extensively for this book. In the course of several hundred rounds downrange, I came to appreciate another feature of the pistol. The sights are excellent, among the best to be found on any of the myriad of handguns on today's market. They are big enough to be seen, with a wide, deep notch and a prominent front ramped blade. Some versions of the SIG-Sauer pistols have sights highlighted with dots for better sight acquisition in low light situations. I don't care for them.

Double-action autoloaders have traditionally poor trigger pulls, at least in the DA mode. The 226 defies tradition in that the double-action pull on this pistol is very good. Once that first double-action shot is gone, the single-action trigger action for subsequent shots is fairly light, with only a small amount of creep.

As the test results show, the 226 pistol is accurate, too.

25 YD. FIRING RESULTS	AVG. VEL.	STD. DEV.	GROUP SIZE
Winchester Silvertips	1177	39	2.25"
Federal 9BP	1140	40	2.00"
Federal 9AP	1056	4	2.75"
Handload #1	1237	47	3.25"
Handload #2	1088	42	2.75"
Handload #3	1144	49	4.25"

Walther P5

THIRTY-NINE:

THE P5 is one of three pistols produced in Germany which were evaluated extensively by German authorities in their search for an acceptable police and military automatic pistol. The trials were held in the late 1970s; the other front runners were the P6 (SIG-Sauer 225) and the Heckler & Koch P7. The P5 is presently used by many police agencies throughout Germany and the Scandanavian countries.

The resemblance to the older P'38, at least as far as butt contour, is unmistakable. The P5 is fundamentally a much-modified P'38. There isn't a thing that was changed to make the pistol that did not result in some improvement.

Certain things did not change. One of them is the locking system, a pivoting block below the breech end of the barrel. There's no reason to change it, because it works quite well just as it is. The magazine may have some minor change to it, but it is still a single-column sheet steel box holding eight rounds. The catch is still in the butt, unfortunately.

The cosmetic changes are principally a redesigned slide which surrounds the barrel clear out to the muzzle. That particular change is more than just cosmetic, since it affords better protection to the working parts of the pistol as well as positively changing the balance. The P5 is somewhat like its contemporary P6 in that it is a compact, pointable handgun. The barrel of the P5 is actually shorter than the SIG-Sauer 225's. At 3½ inches, it's the same as the Smith & Wesson's 669. The frame of the pistol is some form of weight-saving aluminum alloy.

While the pistol may feel a bit like the P'38, the handling drill is quite different. Both are first shot double-actions with exposed, spurred hammers. The P'38 had a combination safety and hammer-drop lever on the slide. The P5 uses a frame mounted decocking lever much like the SIG-Sauer's. Stroking the lever downwards will safely drop the hammer on a chambered round. The lever is also arranged to act as a slide stop. If the slide is locked back and a magazine inserted, the shooter can run the slide forward to chamber a round by depressing the de-cocking lever with his right thumb. This action will leave the hammer cocked and the shooter can lower it safely by another touch of the same button.

The safety is an ingenious one wherein the trigger and firing pin are linked in such a way that the trigger must be pulled before the rear end of the firing pin is raised to align with the flat, firing area on the hammer. If the hammer should fall without this, the pistol can't fire. It is an ingenious system.

P5s are also much different than the earlier P'38s in the smoothness of the action. The DA trigger on the test gun was easy to use. We're still at a loss to understand why the pistol ejects brass to the left, although there's no particular reason why it shouldn't.

25 YD. FIRING RESULTS	AVG. VEL.	STD. DEV.	GROUP SIZE
Winchester Silvertips	1153	11	4.75"
Federal 9BP	1144	27	3.50"
Federal 9AP	1056	12	2.50"
Handload #1	1182	28	3.25"
Handload #2	1012	36	3.50"
Handload #3	1121	80	4.00"

The Walther P5, imported into the U.S. by Interarms, is Walther's current entry in the battle pistol race. It is a considerably modified version of the P'38. One of the pistol's clever touches is the use of a single lever to close the slide and drop the cocked external hammer.

MAB P-15

FIRING
FORTY:

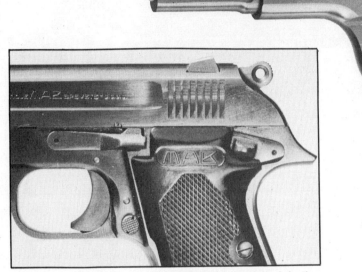

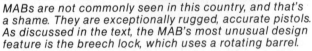

MABs are not commonly seen in this country, and that's a shame. They are exceptionally rugged, accurate pistols. As discussed in the text, the MAB's most unusual design feature is the breech lock, which uses a rotating barrel.

AT THIRTY-NINE ounces empty, the French MAB P-15 is one of the heavier pistols that we examined for this book. It is also one of the least known for reasons that completely escape me. The pistol is an exceptionally strong, serviceable and accurate gun, but several respected books skip completely over the gun or give it short shrift. Some of the reason for that may be that the gun is not widely distributed in the United States.

The MAB stands for Manufacture d'Armes de Bayonne, the plant where the pistol is made in France. The pistol is the service automatic of the French armed forces. It is a single-action, all-steel automatic with a double-column magazine of fifteen shots. The grips are checkered black plastic and the sights are a nicely contoured, plain square notch rear and ramp front. Like the Hi-Power and the Colt, controls are straightforward. There's a manual safety that goes down to the "off" position, a slide top,

and a magazine catch right where it belongs — aft of the trigger guard on the left side. No grip safety, but there is an external hammer with a ringed spur. The barrel is about 4½ inches long, rifled with a right-hand twist.

So far in this book, we haven't paid that much attention to the details of the rifling of the various guns under consideration. You have to pay attention to the MAB, because the rifling helps lock the breech shut.

Some authorities have called the MAB a retarded blowback design, but it really isn't. The barrel of the MAB is held locked into place for the brief period of time that breech pressure is high and the bullet is still in the barrel. There's a cam track inside the slide which engages a lug on the upper left side of the barrel. The barrel doesn't tilt up and down to lock, but rather uses the cam arrangement to turn another lug on the bottom of the barrel into a recess in the recoil spring guide. That initial violent rearward movement when the gun fires is somewhat slowed by the fact that the rotating barrel wants to turn to the left and the bullet passing through it wants to turn it to the right, because that's the way the rifling is cut. The two forces act to hold the locking system together for a short time.

A shooter's impression of the pistol is that it is quite strongly made, with massive slide and receiver. The butt is thick and a little awkward to handle. The pistol that we had, from the Maxwell collection, was brand new and unfired. While the accuracy was more than adequate, I can't help but speculate what would happen if this different way of locking were to get the full, hard-fitting treatment from one of our best custom gunsmiths.

One gripe. Despite what another author has recently noted about the MAB, I felt that it was a "kicker" — when that heavy slide gets all the way back, you become aware of it.

25 YD. FIRING RESULTS	AVG. VEL.	STD. DEV.	GROUP SIZE
Winchester Silvertips	1241	56	1.75"
Federal 9BP	1180	23	2.00"
Federal 9AP	1047	11	4.00"
Handload #1	1266	41	3.00"
Handload #2	1057	38	3.75"
Handload #3	1186	75	3.75"

COLT GOVERNMENT MODEL

FORTY-ONE:

THERE'S NOT been a pistol ever made that had the impact on the firearms world that this one had and continues to have. Colt — and a host of wartime contractors — have made millions of these pistols in several calibers. There's even a brisk business still under way to produce look-alikes and plain copies of the gun. In past years, Colt has licensed the production of the pistol in such diverse locations as Norway and Argentina.

Well over half of the automatic pistols covered in this Ninefiring section of the book have some form of modification of the locking system designed by John Browning for the Government Model Colt. Elsewhere in the book, you'll see photos of prototypes of the new 9mmP automatic from Bill Ruger. Those photos clearly display the pivoting link, retained with a pin, that marks the Colt.

The idea is a time- and pressure-tested one. Time-tested in the sense that it's been with us since 1911 — and pressure-tested in the sense that it has been used to contain the pressures generated by such monster cartridges as the .45 Winchester magnum. Some designers dispense with a pivoting link and use a shaped cam groove to do the same thing — lock and unlock a pistol barrel by alternately raising and lowering it at the breech end.

The system was devised by John Browning for the M1911 pistol in .45 caliber. In that form, the pistol won most of its critical acclaim. The gun in 9mmP is a fairly recent phenomenon. However, it should be noted that the gun also has been produced by Colt in several calibers: .45 ACP, .38 Super, 9mmP, 7.65mmP, 9mm Steyr, .22 LR and very likely others. There have also been experimental cartridges like the 9.8mm (.40 cal.).

Since the basic .45 had proven to be quite strong, it was not surprising that the Colt company could easily produce the gun in 9mmP caliber. The only real changes were a slightly re-shaped ejector in the frame, plus a slide and barrel unit that has a properly bored and chambered tube. There are several other differences, including a completely different magazine, but none of them are visible from the exterior. The 9mmP handles, functions and feels exactly like the .45.

25 YD. FIRING RESULTS	AVG. VEL	STD. DEV.	GROUP SIZE
Winchester Silvertips	1182	24	2.25"
Federal 9BP	1217	12	1.75"
Federal 9AP	1091	6	2.50"
Handload #1	1228	27	2.75"
Handload #2	1096	30	3.00"
Handload #3	1150	20	4.25"

Dean Grennell's pet 9mmP Colt has an MMC rear sight, fancy pearl grips. The fancy Colt shoots fancy groups.

The decision to make the pistol in 9mmP apparently was predicated on the growing popularity of the European cartridge. Colt decided to do this in the late Sixties, a time when the supply of affordable surplus 9mmP ammunition hadn't dried up. Now that changes in the law have opened the door to more of the same stuff, the 9mmP Colt is likely to sell in increasing numbers.

Still, the biggest factor in the popularity of the grand old gun, as it's produced in the series '80 version, is simply that our new service pistol cartridge will be the 9mmP. And we've always liked to have civilian versions of military caliber guns.

COLT 9mm CONVERSION UNIT

FORTY-TWO:

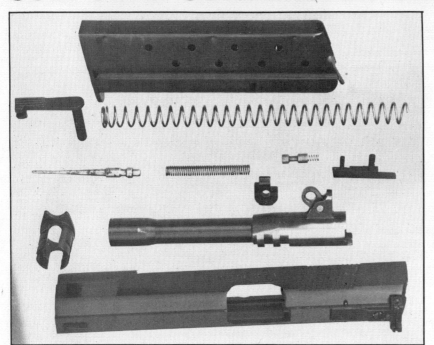

The Colt Conversion unit isn't a gun, but if you mount it onto the frame of a Colt .45, the result is a fine gun. The parts of the conversion unit are displayed to the left and the finished product is below. The Conversion Unit slide has adjustable sights and a full length rib. Accuracy is respectable.

IT WOULD be nice to say that a conversion unit for the Colt Government Model pistol was a new concept. The fact is that the idea dates back to the 1930s, at which time Colt sold a drop-in unit that converted the .45s of that era over to low-cost .22 ammunition. At the same time that Colt was selling the .22-.45 conversion units, they also were selling a pistol called the Ace. This was a Government Model chambered for the .22 round. Colt went for even more versatility when they made a .45-.22 conversion unit for the Ace that enabled the shooter to convert his .22 to a .45.

The conversion units were out-of-print for a while, but Colt returned them to production a few years ago. They really do make a lot of sense, as they literally allow a man to have a second gun at about half the cost.

With the 9mmP cartridge growing in popularity to the point that Colt was producing both the Government Model and Combat Commander Models for the cartridge, the next step was a logical one — a 9mmP-.45 Conversion Unit. Colt added that item to their catalog in the past couple of years.

The 9mmP Conversion Unit is an assemblage of parts that will change any .45 ACP Colt automatic over to the 9mmP cartridge. In the shipping carton, a shooter will find a complete 9mmP "top half" — a slide with barrel, bushing, firing pin assembly, extractor and recoil spring. He'll also find a 9mmP magazine and a slide

stop. All of the foregoing parts are easily installed with no more than the effort required to field strip the gun and substitute the different parts.

The ejector is a different story. This part is fitted to the frame of the gun, just above the magazine well on the left side of the frame. Installing the replacement ejector requires a drift punch and hammer. It is not a difficult task, but it is best to read the directions carefully before attempting it.

Also, it should be understood that the conversion unit is a Series 80. This means that the slide contains the parts that will make the firing pin safety work. If the slide is installed on a receiver that doesn't have the little lever working off of the trigger, the gun won't fire. If the conversion unit is installed on a Series 80 receiver, everything works out okay. We installed the unit on a Series 70 receiver and made it work by simply removing the plunger and spring from the slide.

The 9mmP Conversion Unit is in the current catalog at $304.50 and a 9mmP Government Model sells for $534.95. You figure it out — if you have a .45 (doesn't *everyone?*), you can have a second gun for about three hundred bucks.

25 YD. FIRING RESULTS	AVG. VEL	STD. DEV.	GROUP SIZE
Winchester Silvertips	1170	25	3.25"
Federal 9BP	1229	20	2.75"
Federal 9AP	1076	28	3.50"
Handload #1	1220	18	3.50"
Handload #2	1081	23	3.75"
Handload #3	1168	22	4.00"

RUGER SPEED SIX (2¾")

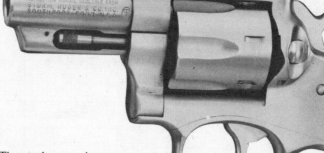

FORTY-THREE:

AMERICANS USE revolvers. The revolver was invented here, perfected here and proliferated here. There are many fine revolvers that were made in other locations around the globe, so we don't have a lock on quality. Yet when other people turned away from the wheelgun and took up the self-loading automatic pistol, we continued to use our revolvers.

Eight decades after the first commercially successful automatics were in common use, we still arm our police most commonly with revolvers. Seven decades after the best automatic ever made was introduced, our armsmaking companies introduce several new revolvers each year. Whether we are justified in our unending affair with the wheelgun or not just isn't the point. There is a huge market for revolvers and this is one the best of them.

The gun pictured here is one of the Johnny-come-latelies. It is a variation of the basic Ruger Security Six. Ruger calls the gun the Speed-Six and, yes, you can stuff the cylinder of this one with the same fodder that you use in your Steyr GB — it is a 9mmP.

The first of this basic model were .38 Specials and .357 magnums. Ruger pitched them to the police market in the early Seventies. He faced an uphill proposition in challenging Colt and S&W, but gradually the quality and unique features of the gun had their effect. Individual officers, then entire agencies, began to use the gun. It's now an established part of the American handgun scene.

For overseas sales, Ruger made the gun in other calibers. One of those calibers is the 9mmP. When this caliber was put into the first of the Ruger Speed Sixes, the company played with a different extractor system. Ultimately, this was changed to the external clip arrangement that we've pictured here.

This revolver is the shorter of the two. It has a barrel in the unusual 2¾-inch length. It also has a spurred hammer and the round butt common in the Speed Six line.

At the range, the gun demonstrated why it sells so well. It is an easily handled and shootable revolver. As we have mentioned elsewhere in the book, the theoretical velocity loss of ammunition fired in a revolver is mostly theory. Compare the velocities turned in by this gun with...

Above: There's a variety of clips made for the Ruger 9mmP revolver. You can get them that hold two, three or all six rounds. Below: This is not the true length of the barrel, at least for ballistic computation purposes. The barrel should be measured from cylinder's rear end.

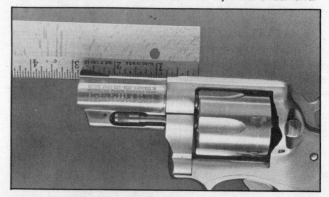

25 YD. FIRING RESULTS	AVG. VEL.	STD. DEV.	GROUP SIZE
Winchester Silvertips	1201	15	3.00"
Federal 9BP	1180	16	3.00"
Federal 9AP	1070	5	2.75"
Handload #1	1256	22	3.25"
Handload #2	1080	26	3.25"
Handload #3	1106	35	4.00"

RUGER SPEED-SIX (4")

9 FIRING

FORTY-FOUR:

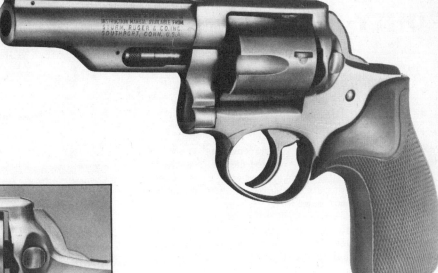

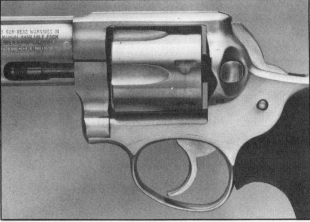

The cylinder latch on this, as well as other Ruger DA revolvers, is the best in the industry. The latch rocks inward to release the cylinder and the placement of the latch on the left side of the frame is out of the path of ammunition in clips. It is a well-designed feature.

WHAT YOU get out of Chuck Karwan's four-inch Speed-Six shown here, which were one of the higher sets of velocities of any we tested. The practical length of the barrel is not four inches, but more like 5½. This is due to the fact that we customarily measure barrel length from the face of the cylinder. Automatics are measured from the face of the closed breech. If we did that with the wheelgun we'd get a lot more realistic figures. 9mmP ammunition performance doesn't deteriorate for being fired in a revolver.

25 YD. FIRING RESULTS	AVG. VEL.	STD. DEV.	GROUP SIZE
Winchester Silvertips	1254	5	2.75"
Federal 9BP	1228	29	3.00"
Federal 9AP	1092	14	3.25"
Handload #1	1222	30	2.00"
Handload #2	1077	7	2.75"
Handload #3	1120	18	2.25"

As on his Smith & Wesson 9mmP revolver, Karwan has installed a set of Pachmayr grips. These are the wrap-around pattern that Pachmayr makes for the round butt gun.

Chuck has also added one of the spurless combat hammers to this gun. Equipped thusly, the gun takes on a different character. It has become a subtly rounded, graceful double-action gun — a superb defense revolver. With the longer barrel, the Ruger points well; much more so than almost anything in the book. It also has the combat advantage of the best cylinder latch of any of them.

This is one of the best of the many good features of the Ruger double-action revolvers. The latch, which is depressed by the right thumb in order to open the cylinder, is positioned perfectly. In both Smith & Wesson and Colt revolvers, the latch is found on the flat frame of the revolver aft of the cylinder. The Ruger positions the latch on the recoil shield at the left side. Instead of pushing forward, as in a Smith, or pulling back, like a Colt, the latch is rocked inward.

This has two advantages. One is the fact that the latch is completely away from the fingers of the shooting hand when the gun is being fired. The second is that there is no way that the latch can interfere with the movement of the clipped ammo when it goes into or comes out of the cylinder.

The clips are the key to the efficiency of the revolver. Ruger supplies half-moon clips that hold three 9mmP rounds. Ranch Products will sell you third-moon clips that hold a pair of cartridges. They also have full-moon clips that hold a cylinderful of six. They go into the cylinder clipped together as a unit, and after the rounds are fired, they eject from the gun the same way. It's sort of an instant speedloader — with no moving parts. You can fire the revolver without difficulty using no clip at all, but you have to pick out the empties with a fingernail.

Karwan will bore you at length about the efficiency of this system and how much he likes it. After playing with his gun for a couple of weeks, I'm not going to disagree.

FIRING FORTY-FIVE:

CZ 75

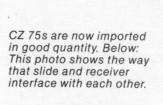

S OME OF the most highly respected authorities in the combat pistol field have rated the CZ 75 as the best available 9mmP for battle purposes. Even a cursory examination will cause anyone who knows anything about handguns to understand why.

The CZ 75 was designed and built in Czechoslovakia. Because of the Iron Curtain origins, there's a lack of information about the gun, but the design influences are quite clear. The slide/receiver relationship is that of the SIG 210, wherein the rails on the two major parts of the gun are reversed. The positive reason for this is to guide the slide's travel and the idea works quite well. The lock-up of the CZ is also the Petter-SIG modification of the Colt. Both of these features are evaluated in detail elsewhere in the book.

Most of the acclaim for the CZ doesn't turn on these features as much as it does on the layout of the controls and the general contours of the gun. It is an all-steel, double-action, fifteen-shot automatic pistol. Ten to fifteen years ago, that would have made it unique, but today the woods are full of such guns.

The CZ is different in that the safety is mounted on the frame and only works to block sear engagement when the hammer is cocked. Since the safety sweeps down to the fire position, the gun can be carried in the best approved cocked-and-locked fashion, ready to be drawn and readied for use with a downward flick of the thumb. If the shooter wants to use the double-action trigger feature, it's easy to do by manually lowering the cocked hammer. In both cases, double- or single-action, the trigger pull is good.

Gunsmith Ikey Stark has been quoted as saying that a carry pistol should feel like a well-used bar of soap. If he really did say that, he should be credited with one of the more profound observations ever made about combat handguns. You don't need sharp edges and corners on an object that you will carry and use all the time. Edges should be contoured with a gentle radius and corners rounded. Out of the box, the CZ does more of this than any other gun, including the excellent S&W Model 669. The CZ uses serrations in the metal where they are necessary to give purchase to the finger, but the edges of the parts are broken. It makes for a carryable, usable handgun with the best set of controls in the field.

CZ 75s are now imported in good quantity. Below: This photo shows the way that slide and receiver interface with each other.

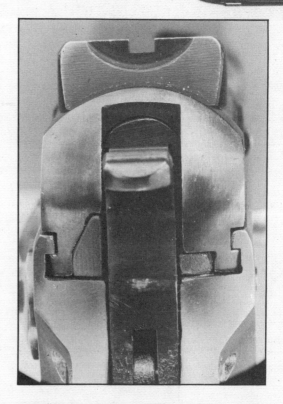

CZs currently being imported are from Bauska Arms of Kalispell, Montana. These have some form of enameled finish, apparently intended to reduce glare. Another gun was examined and fired, and this earlier specimen had the traditional polished blue finish. A new version of the pistol is pictured in the 41st edition of the Gun Digest. Called the CZ 85, this one seems to be almost completely ambidextrous. If the CZ design has any fault other than expense, it would have to be accuracy — neither pistol we fired was particularly accurate.

25 YD. FIRING RESULTS	AVG. VEL.	STD. DEV.	GROUP SIZE
Winchester Silvertips	1148	42	3.25"
Federal 9BP	1163	35	2.25"
Federal 9AP	1062	14	2.75"
Handload #1	1227	34	3.25"
Handload #2	1015	27	4.00"
Handload #3	1167	24	4.50"

M9 — BERETTA 92F

FIRING

FORTY-SIX:

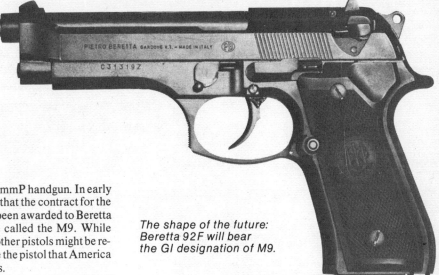

The shape of the future: Beretta 92F will bear the GI designation of M9.

IF YOU haven't heard, this is *the* 9mmP handgun. In early 1985, the government announced that the contract for the new service automatic pistol had been awarded to Beretta and that the new pistol would be called the M9. While there is some information to suggest that other pistols might be reconsidered, the Beretta is most likely to be the pistol that America takes to war for the next several decades.

It is a good gun. The Beretta 92F is the latest in a long line of 9mmP handguns that date back to the early Fifties. Moreover, the pistol has a distinguished wartime record by virtue of its use

In Joe McMahon's experienced grasp, the M9 seems to be a big handgun. It isn't the smallest, nor the most compact, and small-handed shooters may have problems.

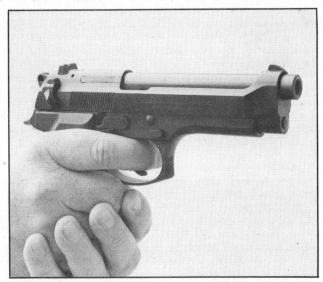

25 YD. FIRING RESULTS	AVG. VEL.	STD. DEV.	GROUP SIZE
Winchester Silvertips	1169	16	2.75"
Federal 9BP	1182	16	2.50"
Federal 9AP	1112	23	3.50"
Handload #1	1227	25	2.50"
Handload #2	1019	22	3.00"
Handload #3	1197	24	2.50"

by several armies, notably the Israelis, in the wars that have plagued the Middle East in our lifetime.

The pistol has an alloy frame and steel slide and barrel. The magazine is a fifteen-shot double-column variety. There's a combined safety and hammer drop lever on the slide; a slide stop on the frame, and a unique user-reversible magazine catch at the lower rear corner of the trigger guard. Like a number of safety-first automatic pistols of modern times, the pistol has a firing pin safety linked to the trigger in such a way as to lock the firing pin in place until the trigger is deliberately pulled. The sights of the Beretta have highlights of some luminous material that really works quite well, although the sights do not have a provision for adjustment.

In use, most shooters feel that the pistol has a decent trigger in both double- and single-action modes. The M9 points and handles well, the magazine ejects smartly from the well when the catch is pushed, and the overall character of the gun is businesslike. There are some features which are controversial.

One of them is the open slide. The barrel of the Beretta is exposed to the open for the greatest part of its length. This means that foreign matter can easily enter the action to gum up the works. In view of the mud baths and the like that the pistol was subjected to in the course of the Army testing, I doubt if this is really that much of a drawback. The open slide can be an advantage. The breech end of the barrel is open to the air when the slide is open. That means that there is no part of the pistol for fired cases in the extraction/ejection cycle can catch on.

The pistol is most reliable. Of all the guns listed in this book, this particular Beretta was fired the most. It was used for the factory ammo evaluation in Chapter Sixteen. With its Bar-Sto barrel, the pistol was fired in the production of Chapter Seventeen. The performance has been most notably free of malfunctions — it is a reliable handgun.

There are already variations of the M9/92F on the market. One is the 92FC, a compact version of the basic pistol with shortened barrel and slide plus a reduced capacity magazine in a shorter butt.

TAURUS PT-99

FIRING 9

FORTY-SEVEN:

The controls on the Brazilian import are the same as on an early Beretta 92. The safety is mounted on the frame and wipes down to "off." That makes cocked-and-locked carry possible, to the delight of most shooters trained in one of the modern schools of weaponcraft.

IF THE curves and angles of this pistol have a familiar look, it's because you have seen a lot of this shape in the firearms press in recent months. The gun under consideration here is the Taurus PT-99 and it's really a Beretta, a version of the new American service handgun.

The pistol is made in Brazil on machinery installed there and supervised by Beretta technicians. While there are differences in finish and markings, the Taurus is a Beretta 92. J.B. Wood, the gunsmith-author of the excellent *Beretta Automatic Pistols,* has said that, with certain qualifications, parts will interchange between the two brands. This fact has positive implications for the handgun buyer.

While the gun pictured is the PT-99 version, Taurus also markets the PT-92, which lacks the adjustable rear sight and corresponds pretty closely to the Beretta 92. The price differential between the two pistols is in excess of $300, according to the catalog section of the 41st Edition of the *Gun Digest.* That is a significant difference.

Curiously enough, the BT-99 actually has a pair of features which make it superior to the Beretta 92F. One is the rear sight which nearly anyone would agree is a valuable addition to the gun. On the rear of the slide of the BT-99, you will find an adjustable rear sight bearing a close resemblance to that found on most service grade Colt pistols. It is fitted into a recess milled into the slide. The front sight, matched for height, is fitted to the ringed portion of the slide which goes across the barrel near the muzzle. With this arrangement, a shooter can adjust for changes in ammo or shooting conditions.

The other feature of the PT-99 which might be superior to the Beretta is the safety. We mentioned that the Taurus is a Brazilian-made Beretta 92, not the 92S or 92SB. This simply means that the safety used is a sear-blocking, frame-mounted lever. This was the early type of safety used in the first versions of the Italian pistols. Combat shooters generally prefer this type of safety system which permits the cocked-and-locked carry.

The disadvantage is that the safety is not like that of the current Beretta, and if you are looking for an inexpensive version of the service automatic, you are not getting it in this gun. In fact, the safeties work exactly opposite to each other — *down* to fire in the Taurus and *up* in the Beretta. There's probably no problem for the one-gun man, but using them interchangeably could result in some possibly dangerous confusion.

For defense pistol use, I think I'd rather have the Taurus system. This particular pistol is Chuck Karwan's and it's easy to understand his enthusiasm for it.

25 YD. FIRING RESULTS	AVG. VEL.	STD. DEV.	GROUP SIZE
Winchester Silvertips	1236	28	3.00"
Federal 9BP	1253	26	3.50"
Federal 9AP	1096	7	3.50"
Handload #1	1218	25	4.00"
Handload #2	1027	33	5.00"
Handload #3	1176	36	4.25"

NOVAK-S&W 469

FORTY-EIGHT:

The essence of this little handgun is the sight system. Designed by custom pistolsmithing ace Wayne Novak, the contoured combat specials are state-of-the-art to improve an already excellent handgun, Smith's 469/669.

IN OPENING a discussion for this pistol, a customized Smith & Wesson Model 469, I am reminded of a long-ago conversation. It was at the Marine Corps' Western Division Matches, where I had joined several hundred other Marine pistol shooters in pursuit of the elusive "leg." I was talking to Ed Sarver, a long-time member of the Marine Corps Gold team, who was not in pursuit of a "leg." He had won his many times over.

Warrant Officer Sarver was showing me his pet softball gun, which was a much-modified Colt .45 fitted with extended sights and a host of other accurizing features, none of which made the already ugly gun any more attractive. Most of the bluing was worn off and the left grip was cracked. It looked like pure hell and I had the temerity to say so. I can still remember his response.

"When I'm shootin'," he snarled, "I don't see anything but the sights!"

The point is simply this. When you are shooting, the only things that you *should* be seeing is the sights. If your gun doesn't have a set of sights that will allow a good, clear sight picture, then your shooting will suffer. Good sights and good trigger action are essential to getting the potential accuracy from any gun.

Wayne Novak is well aware of that fact and has designed and produced the sights that you see here on the little Smith & Wesson Model 469. These are not the most accurate guns in the entire Smith & Wesson line, but they are a little easier to use with these sights.

The 469, as already discussed, is a pistol designed for concealed carry. In this role, the pistol cannot afford any sort of projection or snag-prone addition. Novak has contoured his sights to drastically reduce even the possibility of edges that might catch on clothing.

Moreover, they are better than the issue sights, because they give the shooter a little more sight radius and a more clear and distinct sight picture. Fixed sights of this sort should be adjusted for the ammo that will be used. Novak makes this a bit easier to do with locking screws in both front and rear sights.

When this particular gun was compared to the 469 pictured elsewhere in the book, it was pretty well obvious what had been achieved with the modification — a pistol that is easier to shoot.

25 YD. FIRING RESULTS	AVG. VEL.	STD. DEV.	GROUP SIZE
Winchester Silvertips	1116	29	2.75"
Federal 9BP	1115	14	2.50"
Federal 9AP	1005	24	3.25"
Handload #1	1198	29	3.75"
Handload #2	998	30	4.00"
Handload #3	1067	32	5.00"

COMPETITION BROWNING

FIRING NINE

FORTY-NINE:

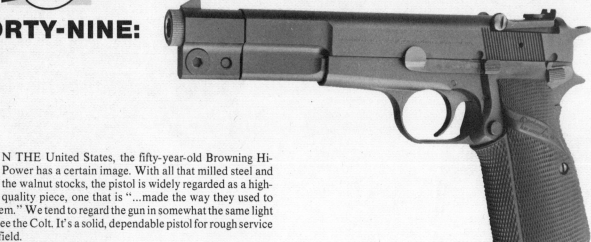

I N THE United States, the fifty-year-old Browning Hi-Power has a certain image. With all that milled steel and the walnut stocks, the pistol is widely regarded as a high-quality piece, one that is "...made the way they used to make 'em." We tend to regard the gun in somewhat the same light as we see the Colt. It's a solid, dependable pistol for rough service in the field.

We don't see the gun for the target range. It just doesn't have that sort of aura about it. For precise target work, we have to have elaborate conversions of other guns. But maybe we ought to re-think our attitude.

The pistol pictured is a Competition Model Browning Hi-Power. Several thousand of them were brought into the country several years ago, intended to be competition handguns. They have a number of features intended to increase their potential for accuracy and competition reliability.

The finish of the pistol is a sensible matte blue, dull to avoid distracting reflections. The grips are rubber Pachmayrs for an easy, non-slip hold. Both of these features make sense, but the rear sight does not. It is a sheet-metal contraption that is out of place on an otherwise excellent handgun. Competition shooters must have the capability of frequent and precise sight changes and I don't see that this sight is equal to the task.

Sights are important to any shooter and so is the trigger pull. The basic Hi-Power has confounded the best efforts of gunsmiths for years when they try to adjust the trigger for a crisp let-off. But on this Competition Hi-Power, the pull is excellent, not particularly heavy and is quite clean in release. A different type of magazine safety is part of the solution and I'd like to figure out the rest.

But the essence of a target pistol is its accuracy and this is one of the best. The barrel of the Competition Hi-Power is longer by a little more than an inch. There's a recoil-taming muzzle weight attached to the barrel which extends forward of the slide. The weight also houses the front sight. Putting the sight way out there

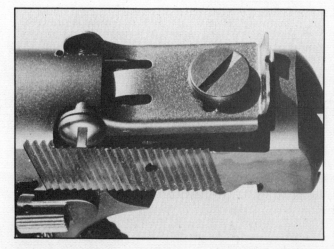

The major criticism of the Competition Browning was the rear sight. Made of lightweight stampings, the unit is not up to the standards of the rest of the gun, which are of the highest order — one of the most accurate 9s.

extends the effective sight radius which helps in the accuracy department.

Since there is no change to the basic way that the pistol functions, I have to assume that the increased accuracy may be partially due to a somewhat higher quality barrel. Most of the reason will be apparent to the experienced competition shooter when he pulls the gun apart for cleaning. The gun is more accurate, because it has been factory hand-fitted with a barrel-to-slide lock-up relationship that rivals the best of the custom shops. In other words, the gun has a factory "accurizing job" just like the ones that have been done by gunsmiths for years. This is one of the most accurate 9mmPs that we tried.

25 YD. FIRING RESULTS	AVG. VEL.	STD. DEV.	GROUP SIZE
Winchester Silvertips	1283	28	1.75"
Federal 9BP	1248	15	1.75"
Federal 9AP	1145	10	1.75"
Handload #1	1325	18	1.50"
Handload #2	1145	21	1.75"
Handload #3	1242	22	1.25"

NOVAK COMPETITION S&W

FIRING FIFTY:

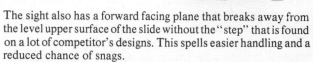

WAYNE NOVAK, the custom gunsmith from Parkersburg, West Virginia, does lots of interesting and worthwhile things to handguns. The pistol shown here is intended for certain forms of competition that feature multiple targets. One of the obvious solutions to lots of targets is lots of cartridges. Novak favors Smith & Wessons for the starting point when building up a competition handgun.

This gun uses a Model 659 stainless steel receiver on which he has installed a Model 459 slide. The photographs don't do justice to the subtle little things that have been done to edges and corners. That sort of thing is best felt. So is the trigger pull.

They claim that a double-action automatic trigger pull cannot be improved enough to make the effort worthwhile. In this case, the trigger pull — both double and single — has been smoothed and lightened to a pronounced degree. I don't know how Novak does it, but this gun has the best double-action pull of any automatic in this book.

The other feature of the gun which stands out is the sight system. These are the same sights that will be found on Smith & Wesson's new Model 745 pistol in .45 ACP. The front sight is a sturdy ramped variety with exceptionally deep serrations on the rear-facing plane. There's no way that light is going to reflect off of that surface.

But the rear sight is the showpiece of the system. It sets the notch well back on the slide, in effect lengthening the sight radius.

The sight also has a forward facing plane that breaks away from the level upper surface of the slide without the "step" that is found on a lot of competitor's designs. This spells easier handling and a reduced chance of snags.

The shape of the cavity forward of the rear sight notch itself is unique. In modern combat pistolcraft, using a two-hand hold and some form of the Weaver stance, the pistol is lifted into the plane of vision. With a rear sight shaped as this one is, there's a self-centering quality about the way the front sight blade sort of guides into the rear sight notch. It's an exceptionally easy system to shoot with.

And the pistol will shoot. I don't know everything that Wayne Novak did to get the gun to group this well, but part of it is obvious. He used a Bar-Sto barrel.

Wayne Novak slicked up this hybrid stainless-and-blued Smith & Wesson. It has fine accuracy, an incredible feel to the trigger and the new sight system of the S&W 645.

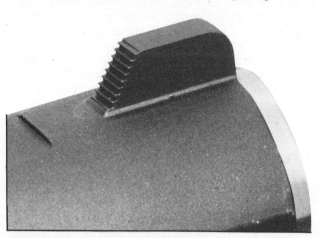

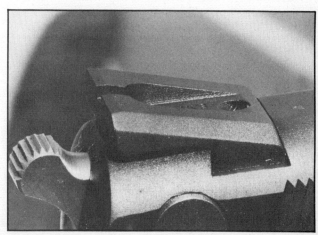

25 YD. FIRING RESULTS	AVG. VEL.	STD. DEV.	GROUP SIZE
Winchester Silvertips	1165	10	2.00"
Federal 9BP	1167	31	1.75"
Federal 9AP	1068	17	2.00"
Handload #1	1220	28	2.00"
Handload #2	1010	36	2.00"
Handload #3	1128	37	1.75"

CHAPTER 15

NINEFIRING CONCLUDED

Thoughts and Theories, Facts and Fancies, All Derived From The Firing of Four Dozen 9mmP Handguns

NOT OFTEN does a writer in the firearms field have the opportunity that came along with the preceding chapter of this book. The idea was to procure and fire as many 9mm Parabellum handguns as possible. All would be fired under the same circumstances and with the same ammunition. Since the period of time over which the book was written was in excess of a year, there was sufficient time to chase down and borrow and — in some cases, buy — many different 9mmP handguns.

The initial list of guns was about two dozen, but as things progressed, more guns became available and were fired. Every one of them got at least a hundred rounds fired through it. Many were fired by a variety of different shooters. As discussed in Chapter Thirteen, the introduction to Ninefiring, the shooting was both formal and informal. Each pistol or revolver was fired with the listed six different rounds from the bench for accuracy and simultaneously chronographed. But there were also a number of tin cans, dirt clods and stationary clay pigeons that also got nine millimetered. And we shot some silhouette targets, also.

While I did all of the bench shooting and a good deal of the informal stuff, I am indebted to friends Chris Weare and Joe Boyd, who are unselfishly ever-ready to help out by burning up someone else's ammo, and to co-author Dean Grennell, who indented more than a few 9mmP primers. The idea was to shoot the variety of guns in such a way as to reach some sort of conclusions about them. This chapter is about those conclusions.

At the outset, it should be understood that I didn't begin this procedure with any particular fondness for handguns in this caliber. I had previously loaded and fired a considerable amount of 9mmP ammunition. As a handloader's project, the 9mmP is a bit tricky to deal with, or so I thought, and I frankly felt the cartridge is underpowered for any, forgive the cliche, serious social purpose. I am willing to recant partially on one score and just a tiny bit on the other.

Handloading the 9mmP? With good dies and careful attention to detail, any handloader can produce excellent quality ammunition for any 9mmP pistol The details that must be watched are case length and overall length; these seem to be absolutely critical in view of the variety of dimensional differences in the chambers of various guns. Still, I handloaded several thousand rounds of 9mmPs in large batches and made no effort to tune to individual guns. In the early stages of that procedure, I learned what to watch for and I really had no major problems with my loads functioning well.

The test ammunition was representative of what can be handloaded and what is commercially available. A total of six different rounds were fired in each gun, three commercial and three made-to-order handloads.

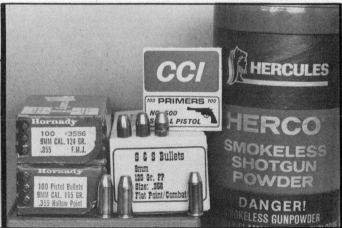

Winston Churchill armed himself with a Broomhandle Mauser for field service against the Boers, but the old guns have long since retired from active duty. Marvelous pistols to study, they're plug ugly...

As far as performance is concerned, I'll concede that the best of 9mmP ammunition in the best of 9mmP guns is a nearly unbeatable combination. For too long, Americans have knocked the round, because it was neither well known nor well liked on these shores. It can be every bit as accurate as anything we produce, and we should learn to accept that.

But all performance is not in terms of accuracy. The heaviest available bullet in 9mmP doesn't exceed 130 grains in weight and they average about 115 grains. And in no pistol that I fired did any of the 115-grain bullets produce velocities much over 1250 feet per second. That weight and that velocity don't add up to a sufficiently hard hit for defensive purposes. The problem is further compounded by the fact 9mmP ammomakers must shape their bullets for reliable feeding in a variety of pistols and even submachine guns. That means tapered round-nose slugs that slither out of magazines, up steep feed ramps and into chambers. The flat-nosed semi-wadcutter slugs that tend to stop fights are ruled out.

Modern 9mmP ammunition does tend to penetrate well and that may be a big factor in the military popularity of the cartridge. Certainly it was a factor in the recent decision to go to the round for U.S. service pistols. Nevertheless, given a choice, I would not choose any 9mmP as a primary defensive firearm. And I make the statement on the basis of inherent limitations of the cartridge, not the quality of any 9mmP pistol.

The modern trend in 9mmP handguns is toward a multi-shot pistol with a double-action trigger system. Without

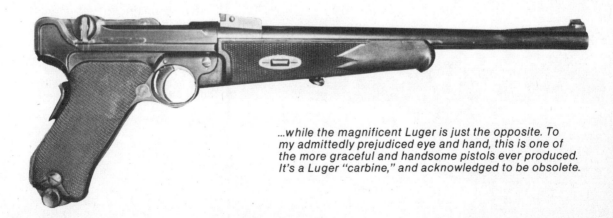

...while the magnificent Luger is just the opposite. To my admittedly prejudiced eye and hand, this is one of the more graceful and handsome pistols ever produced. It's a Luger "carbine," and acknowledged to be obsolete.

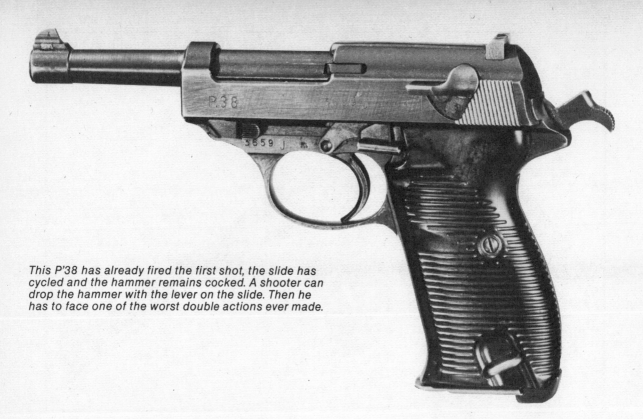

This P'38 has already fired the first shot, the slide has cycled and the hammer remains cocked. A shooter can drop the hammer with the lever on the slide. Then he has to face one of the worst double actions ever made.

exception, the means of increasing the number of shots in the pistol is to make the magazine wide enough to hold a second row of cartridges in a staggered column. The resulting pistol is thicker and harder to handle for many shooters, but the extra rounds are a worthwhile feature for handguns of this caliber. With one notable exception, all of the major battle pistols in production today were available for our review. The exception is the Bernadelli, an Italian pistol soon to be available from Springfield Armory, and a gun with an excellent reputation in Europe.

Before we get into any kind of comparative analysis of all these state-of-the-art handguns, we ought to take a shooter's look at two other classes of 9mmPs. They are first, the old ones, the obsolete and nearly obsolete, and second, the revolvers and derringers.

Lugers have been made as recently as six to eight years ago, but they are obsolete. So are the Broomhandle Mausers, Lahtis, Walther P'38s, Radoms and other elderly designs covered historically in Chapter Six. This is not to say that they won't shoot well or aren't reliable. Bob Arsenault's Luger, the lead gun in Ninefiring, was cursed with a poor after-market magazine that caused all kinds of trouble, but it was exceptionally accurate. The Broomhandle Mauser borrowed from the Maxwell collection was one of the top guns in the accuracy department; it was also most reliable. Both of these are obsolete pistols, prohibitively expensive to produce and awkward to handle. For the most part so are Lahtis, Radoms, some Astras and Stars and perhaps a few others that got overlooked.

There are several pistols in 9mmP that might be called "transitional" in that they are older designs that have persisted to modern times. The best example is the Browning

John Browning's last design was the venerable Hi-Power. It is an all-steel pistol, nicely made and finished and one of the first to use a double-column magazine. It may have been used by more people in more places than any other 9mmP...that's credentials!

Modern revolvers like the ones seen above are not likely to supplant the automatic when 9mmPs are picked.

Hi-Power, John Browning's last design, which was made first in 1935. It is widely used throughout the world and is the choice of some elite units who could have anything that they wanted. Such wide acceptance is a credential in its own right. The pistol that we fired, a recently made commercial gun, was excellent.

The P'38 dates to the late Thirties and is still used by many German agencies. I have one particular observation to make about the P'38 which will not be well received by the legion of its admirers. The double-action pull of the gun is pretty bad; a long, grating, heavy, difficult-to-manage trigger arc. Since this was the first-ever 9mmP handgun with a DA trigger — and one that is well-circulated in the U.S. via all those GI dufflebags — the P'38 formed the American impression of the full-sized DA automatic. I believe that the observation that automatics are nearly impossible to handle due to the transition from first shot double-action to subsequent shot-single action is the fault of the P'38. Most of them are far better.

Despite my pal Chuck Karwan's well reasoned argu-

The author makes a case for the SIG210 as the world's best 9mmP handgun. It is a beautifully made pistol, one of unquestionably superior design, but cursed somewhat by a ruinous price tag. Way over a thousand dollars...

For a number of years, the CZ 75 was a seldom-seen pistol. It had a reputation for excellence. Now that the pistol has been imported in quantity, you can have one of the best 9mmP autos ever built.

ment about the advantages of the 9mmP revolver, I regard them in a different light. We had the range of wheelgun 9mmPs, with two S&W 547s and two Ruger Speed-Sixes. We also had a pair of "convertible" single-actions in the Blackhawk and EMF Bisley. There's another, the Astra convertible, which we couldn't get.

Revolvers in 9mmP work exceptionally well, since the cartridge is a small and easily handled one. The only problem is the extraction and we spent a lot of time on that one in Chapter Seven. Performance notwithstanding, the main reason for the 9mmP revolver is for use in those areas of the world where there is no wide variety of ammunition available. In the U.S., there's some logic to an extra 9mmP cylinder for a .357 revolver. But the 9mmP is first and foremost an automatic pistol cartridge. Derringers for that cartridge are sometimes useful little guns, but they are fundamentally curiosities.

And that brings us around to the heart of the matter —

the large selection of modern automatic pistols chambered for the most widely used pistol cartridge in the entire world. There are a great many of them. Most come from Europe, but an increasing number are U.S.-designed and produced. Inevitably, the first question from everyone who knows of this project is: "What's the best 9mmP made?"

No suspense. The best 9mmP pistol is the SIG 210, for a variety of reasons and with only a small qualification or two. In making this claim, I know that most of the other manufacturers will not be unduly upset. They won't lose a great deal of sales to the 210. The target version of the 210 will set you back over $2000 if you buy it in California and have to pay the six percent sales tax. The expense keeps the sales down, but the quality of this gun is superb.

As discussed in Ninefiring Thirty-Five and Chapter Ten, the SIG is an exceptional pistol. I have a couple of reservations about the pistol as a defense gun. For one thing, the magazine catch is on the left side of the butt,

The Star BM is a compact 9mmP, one that reminds everyone who handles it of the Colt GM. It's a good choice for concealed carry.

awkward for a righthander and hopeless for a southpaw. The fit of the magazine is so tight in both of the guns that I tried that a fast change is virtually impossible. The rear sight of the 210 is a "U" notch, which is saved only by the fact that the "U" is pretty deep. Further, I wonder how well the 210 would perform when it gets unavoidably dirty. It would seem that the very tight fit of parts, which make the gun all that it truly is, would gum up and cause jams in extended firing sessions in rough service. Despite these considerations, I still feel that the pistol is the best in the world.

Another gun might be a better choice if you want high quality in a pure combat pistol. A seldom seen handgun from Czechoslovakia leads the pack. The CZ 75 was developed and produced in the early Seventies. In view of the gun's Iron Curtain origins, it was a firearm that was difficult to import and was therefore not well known. When Jeff Cooper brought the gun to the attention of American shooters with his endorsement, a demand of sorts developed. When the CZ 75 was used as a model for many of the design features of the BREN 10, a real demand developed. I had never seen or handled one of the CZs until this book came along and I was skeptical of all the hype.

I should not have been. The CZ 75 is a beautifully made handgun with many of the features of the SIG 210, particularly the long reversed slide rails. It has the double-action trigger of many modern guns, but this one is a good bit smoother and easier to transition to the second single-action shot. For the carefully schooled combat shooter, the most rewarding feature is the safety system, a frame-mounted manual safety which allows the gun to be carried "cocked and locked" in the manner of the beloved Colt. Most of all, every contour, plane, curve and angle of the CZ is engineered to be handled. It is one of the more usable

When the Spanish government held their own test trials to choose a new service handgun, the pistol which got the nod was the Star 28, since updated as the Model 30.

pistols that you'll ever find, right out of the box. Since the gun is now in the United States in fair quantities and at reasonable prices, the CZ 75 is a worthwhile option to consider.

In Chapter Eleven, Chuck Karwan went on at some length about best buys in 9mmP handguns. I'll go along with what he had to say about small 9mmP pistols. Chuck says his choice in this category is the Star BM. I'll agree with that, as I found this to be a truly super little pistol, a miniaturized Colt GM in 9mmP. But he went ahead with an endorsement of the Taurus BT-99 as a best buy in a DA auto; here I'll politely disagree. (It's wise to be polite about disagreeing with Karwan, a man who could hunt bears with a willow switch. He was a long-term interservice wrestling champion, and he's fond of reminding me of his record against Marines — undefeated. I was a Marine.)

At any rate, Chuck's pet BT99 is an excellent pistol. It is essentially an early-stage Beretta with the large magazine and open slide. It also has the frame-mounted "cocked and locked" safety feature of the early 92 series. Still, for just a few bucks more, you can get a Star 30. A pistol which has some of the best features of a lot of pistols, it is the current Spanish service handgun.

The 30 — and the predecessor 28 — both use the desirable reversed rails of the Petter-SIG system. The advantage of this is that it controls the travel of the slide in the backwards and forwards motion. The 30 also has the firing mechanism mounted on a plate, which is removable as a unit. Cleaning of the lockwork is considerably easier. There's also a superior set of sights, a fifteen-shot magazine, a nicely rounded butt section and one of the better double-action triggers around. The fully ambidextrous safety incorporates a de-cocking lever and a firing pin lock. That is a lot of value for a moderate price.

Early in the production of this book, I wrote a chapter

Heckler and Koch's entry in the 9mmP pistol sweepstakes was the unusual squeeze-cocked P7. There is a detailed analysis of pistol with its unique features in Chapter 9.

Custom gunsmiths used up enough S&W 39s and 59s in making ASPs and other concealed carry pieces that Smith just made their own.

about the innovative designs of Heckler & Koch. One of those pistols, the VP70, is out of print and another, the P9s, may be on the way out. That is unfortunate, as both were useful guns. The handgun fortunes of the H&K nameplate seem to be riding on the P7. Both of these pistols, the M8 and M13 versions, were checked out in detail in Ninefiring Thirty-Three and Thirty-Four. They are radical in the sense of their squeeze-cocked action. The M8 is a fairly compact and carryable handgun, already widely used in Europe. I would have a hard time learning to use the squeeze cocked action, but I think there is a use for the gun in both police and military roles.

If you are in need of a concealable 9mmP pistol, I believe your best bet is the Smith & Wesson Model 669. This chunky little derivative of the basic S&W 39s and 59s is made from mostly stainless steel, with the frame a silver-finished alloy. The pistol has a number of touches that suggest that someone who actually had carried a gun under his clothes was present on the design team of the 669. Edges

and corners are neatly rounded where they need to be.

Smith & Wesson had a version of the Model 59 in the running for the U.S. service pistol. It was not selected, to the chagrin of the company in particular and American arms industry in general. As this is written, there is some reason to believe that the findings of the board which selected another pistol might be questioned. To go much further would be speculation and it's probably better to characterize the military Model 59 as likely to be as good or better than the fully developed Model 39/59 pistols which are found in lots of U.S. police holsters.

Even the most severe critics of the test procedure agree that the gun that did get selected is an excellent pistol. The Beretta is a fine pistol. The open slide goes a long way in eliminating jams, plus the gun has an acceptable accuracy capability, a usable trigger in both modes and good sights. Of all the pistols fired, I have the most experience with this one, because of its use in the factory ammo chapter which follows this one. This particular pistol with original barrel

The government chose the Beretta as the new sevice automatic, and they picked a good handgun, one that's relatively trouble-free.

The new Ruger P85 is seen here in a company photograph. There were none available for firing, and no results to report to you.

has pretty close to 2000 rounds through it. It has yet to jam and I can't think of much more of an endorsement than that.

If there is a legitimate complaint about the Beretta, it would have to be about the pistol's size. It is a big handgun and small-handed shooters are going to have problems with this gun. In this light, consider the SIG-Sauer 226. The 226 has a fifteen-shot magazine just like the Beretta, but the contour of the butt is perceptibly slimmer. (There is detailed coverage of the pistol in Chapter Ten.) Suffice to say that the 226 has superb sights, the best DA trigger pull in the class, acceptable accuracy and a reputation for reliability. It is my personal choice as the best of the affordable and available 9mmP battle pistols.

One final note. I did everything short of ransoming my first-born son to get a Ruger P85 to test for readers of this book. The sad truth is that they just aren't available as the deadline for this book approaches. We have an extensive set of photos, some of which are reproduced nearby. The pictures — and a reading of the company's brochure — will disclose some interesting facts.

The first centerfire automatic pistol from the shop of Bill Ruger uses design features from other guns. The barrel link is the same type used in Colt Government Models, pivoting the barrel upwards into battery by a separate link. That is a proven way to do it and a good feature. So is the use of a SIG-Sauer-type squared barrel section locked into the ejection port. The Ruger P-85 seems to be nearly ambidextrous. The safety lever is repeated on both sides of the slide and there are magazine catches on both sides of the pistol. If there were an off-side slide stop, that would finish it off neatly. This is a businesslike-appearing pistol that no doubt will do well in the marketplace. Why not? Most all other Rugers have done well.

That was a lot of shooting, many rounds downrange and a lot of fun. The conclusions that we've made and reported are based on some pretty objective observations, but a certain amount of personal thinking necessarily also entered into it. I genuinely believe that you'll not go wrong with our recommendations, but you are perfectly free to go shoot forty-eight different pistols and make up your own mind. — *Wiley Clapp*

A disassembled view of the prototype Ruger P85. The final version may vary in contours, but will probably be just about like this, with features taken from other good designs and a liberal sprinkling of plain old Yankee smarts.

CHAPTER 16

COMMERCIAL AMMUNITION COMPARED

Off-The-Shelf 9mmP Ammo Exhaustively Tested

It makes quite a pile. Thirty-two different kinds of 9mmP ammunition assembled for a detailed firing test to determine the most accurate and the most consistent. Results are discussed at great length in the text.

I'M SURE you'll agree that this chapter is full of holes in the literal sense, since it is all about the firing of a lot of 9mmP ammunition into paper targets. I hope you'll agree that the chapter definitely is not full of holes in the figurative sense. The chapter reports the results of what must certainly be one of the more thorough examinations of a particular caliber of ammunition you're likely to see.

In the early stages of production of this book, I was often jokingly asked by friends and associates, "Since you're gonna be the 'expert' on 9mmPs, what is the best kind of ammo I can get for my gun?" Early on, I had formed impressions about the quality of some types of ammunition and, from those impressions, I was able to tell people confidently what was at least good ammo. Yet to answer the question as it is posed — "What's best?" — there was no choice but to shoot ALL of the 9mmP ammunition that a man could possibly buy. And that is just what I set out to do: shoot it all.

Well, I didn't shoot it all, but I did fire the overwhelming majority of commercial 9mmP ammunition. And the only reason I didn't get all of it fired was simply that some kinds were unobtainable. As the deadline for the chapter loomed on the horizon, I listed all the various rounds I had hoarded over a period of more than a year. The list totaled thirty-two different kinds of 9mmP ammunition.

On deadline day, when we did the firing from which this chapter would be produced, the package with the test ammo was a hefty bundle. It was the sheerest kind of coincidence that the actual day set for the test — deadline, or "D" day — was the sixth of June, 1986.

The first goal of the test was to determine what were the more accurate brands and loadings of ammunition. It goes without saying that such a procedure would also identify the least accurate. Another goal would be to measure the average velocity of the ammo and, if possible, its statistical consistency.

Measurements of velocity are useful in evaluating the performance of ammunition, in the sense that they can suggest how the bullet may behave terminally. Had there been a readily available medium for evaluating expansion in simulated tissue medium, I would have attempted comparison of this aspect of the ammo's performance. This sort of information is valuable in that the 9mmP cartridge is typically used in an anti-personnel role by police and military forces. Expansion comparisons would not have favored the large number of kinds of ammunition which

don't have bullets with hollow or soft points intended to induce expansion. Full metal jacket ammunition is still the most common form of 9mmP fodder.

In similar fashion, I couldn't accurately measure energy. Energy can be calculated by a rather simple formula, but the result is a calculation which may provide some easily misinterpreted information. Much ballistic information in the popular gun press is quoted and sometimes accepted as gospel when it is far from it. The purpose of calculating energy is usually to determine how hard a blow will be delivered by a particular load. Most combat shooters would like to know what hits the hardest, because they might assume that the hardest-hitting round is the best.

Calculating energy by simple multiplication of bullet weight times the square of the velocity will produce only a partial answer; there is a great deal more that goes into it, much of it tied up in terminal ballistic performance, a subject about which I am personally convinced we know little. Such esoteric data as nose shape, manner in which the hollow point opens, rate of opening, density of the object or tissue struck, amount of time that the projectile "dwells" in

Setting up for the firing session, a bench is positioned to hold a Model 33 Oehler chronograph. The cables leading to the skyscreens are seen in the foreground and up the bench.

You could look for quite a while before you find a more reliable pistol than this Beretta — zero jams!

tissue, angle of striking, armor or clothing on the target and many other things should be examined in depth.

To my knowledge, there is no consistent way to easily measure these things. At least, not until a platoon of thirty-two identical volunteers offers itself up en masse on the altar of ballistic sacrifice. What you will find reported on these pages is the data that I can measure with clearly understood instruments. To do otherwise is to invite the reader to accept comparisons of figurative apples and oranges. They are both nice, but they are unquestionably different things.

For our test, those thirty-two kinds of ammo would have to be fired, of course. And that means that we needed a consistent procedure for shooting each of them. Since there was an obvious limit to the amount of time that we could spend at the task, as well as limited supplies of some types of ammo, I discounted the firing of the ammo in a variety of guns. Instead, I decided that a single pistol would be used. Clearly, that gun should be a widely distributed pistol that was in every way typical of the modern breed of 9mm autos.

What better gun to use than the new service automatic, the M9 in military parlance, or Beretta 92F? This pistol will be with us for year to come; it is sturdy and reliable, it has excellent accuracy for a service automatic, and I had a set of Ransom rest inserts for the gun. The entire test was run with the gun in a Ransom Rest.

Below: This is how the rest is fastened to the base and how the base is fixed in its steady position. Just park a truck on it — it won't move!

With the Beretta clamped into the inserts of the Ransom Rest, the rest arm must be fully elevated to load a full magazine into the gun. The Ransom Rest reduces error.

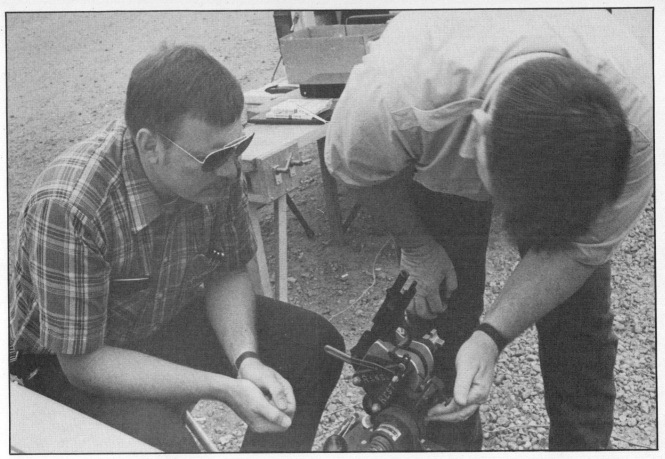

Before the test begins, the author demonstrates how to elevate the rest arm to load a magazine into the Beretta. The basic idea is to touch the pistol as little as possible to avoid disturbing fit of gun in insert.

The Ransom Rest is a handgunner's dream machine. It is a device which will hold a pistol in such a way that when the gun is fired downrange, the properly manipulated Rest will return the pistol to the same aiming point. The human error is completely eliminated and tests of guns and ammunition are far more reliable.

Consisting of a cast base and a movable carriage or arm, the Ransom Rest must be bolted securely to a solid table or bench. At the test site available to us, there was no such facility. Instead we used the base that Dean Grennell had built several years ago. This device is constructed of two-inch-thick planking. It has a table, raised some two feet above the ground, to which the Ransom Rest is securely bolted. The various support members which hold the table in place on and above the ground-level baseboard are angled in such a way as to direct the forces produced by firing the handgun down and back. In other words, the rest is designed in such a way that it wants to dig itself into the ground. And the final key to making the whole system work is the fact that the baseboard extends several feet to the right of the table and upright. To hold the whole apparatus down, you simply park a truck on it.

For the protracted session of firing necessary in this case, Grennell made a last modification to the base. He mounted a plate under the rear of the baseboard and directly behind the upright table which held the Ransom Rest. That plate was fixed to an expansion bolt which was wrenched down so as to wedge the plate between the hard-packed ground and the base. Believe me, the combination of factors delivers a system that doesn't move.

The Ransom rest is a deceptively simple device. One approach to the goal of returning a handgun to exact battery might be to use a number of heavy parts in the hopes that the sheer weight of the device would dampen the disturbing recoil. Chuck Ransom would be aghast at such an idea; he prefers sound engineering.

The bottom portion of the Ransom Rest is bolted down and immobile. The upper portion is a recoiling arm which rotates against a precisely machined friction plate in the base. A corresponding plate is machined on the arm and the two surfaces are held in constant, consistently pressured contact with each other. There is a whopping big coil spring that insures that. The arm is free to move, but only in an arc up and down.

The gun is held within a pair of inserts at the downrange end of the arm. The inserts are faced with some form of hard rubber so that the gun won't be marred when the grips are removed and the piece is placed in the inserts which are then clamped into the arm. With the inserts tightened by three of what Ransom calls star nuts, you have an absolutely rigid means of holding a gun which can only move upwards in the arc of recoil, and then against the tension and friction of the system. It works with the same monotonous efficiency as the offensive line of the Pittsburgh Steelers.

The Ransom Rest also uses an adjustable lever device

Chris Weare did the actual firing of the pistol, while the author watched the chronograph and kept records. Session went smoothly.

on the right side of the arm to actually fire the gun. In use, the arm of the Rest, in which a pistol has been mounted via the rubber-faced inserts, is tilted up. This enables the operator to insert a loaded magazine in the base of the butt. Then the arm is pushed downwards until the adjustable elevation screw indexes against the base of the rest. The operator fires a shot by using the trigger lever and the gun and arm recoil upwards. To fire again, the operator pushes the gun and arm down until the elevation screw indexes against the base. Correctly operated, the system will return the pistol to the same aiming point.

Understand that the system will only work well when it is operated properly and it's easy to do it wrong. There are three major things that an operator can do that will produce poor results. One is to push the rest arm and gun back into battery by pushing down on the barrel or slide of the pistol instead of using the shelf that Chuck Ransom provides for the purpose. Second, the operator needs to lift the recoiling arm to load new magazines into the gun by grasping the arm and not the pistol itself. Third and last, the operator usually has to trip the gun's slide stop to chamber the first round from a new magazine. He should do this before he pushes the arm back into the battery position. If he doesn't, the bounce of the slide going forward will cause the arm to bounce off of the indexed relationship between the elevation screw and the base.

All of which adds up to the fact that if the Ransom Rest is used by an inconsistent and careless operator, the results will be poor. The critical feature is the fit of the pistol in the rubber-faced inserts. If that fit is disturbed by unnecessary touching, twisting or torquing of the pistol, then the alignment of the gun in the insert will be disturbed and the barrel will not return to the same point of aim from one shot to the next. For this critical part of the test, I enlisted the services of long-time friend and shooting partner, Chris Weare — who is highly meticulous. He has to be, he takes bombs apart for a living.

With the shooting done with the gun held by means of the Ransom Rest, the measurement of velocities and statistical computation would be made with one of Dr. Ken Oehler's reliable Model 33 Chronographs. This is another device to delight the heart of experimental handgunners. The newest versions of the 33 are equipped with the Sky-Screen IIIs, which have a greater area of sensitivity and which also mount diffusers to shield the slots in the screens from the direct rays of the overhead sun.

The screens are positioned a precise distance apart, four feet in this case and the bullet fired over them. The nearest screen notes the passage of the bullet and transmits a "start the clock" signal via a cable to the control box. The far screen notes the same bullet go by and tells the electronic wizardry in the little black box on the firing line to stop the clock. After a brief moment of contemplation the device delivers an answer on a readout screen. You can read the velocity of each shot as it is electronically displayed.

The Oehler system goes a bit farther in that it will perform some statistical computations for you. After several shots, the operator pushes a button, and watches the read-

The test proceedings as viewed from the rear. Joe Boyd stands ready to change targets when twenty shots are recorded. In the lower photo, the entire test crew downrange to "C" clamp the target frame in place.

out screen deliver with each successive touch: highest velocity in the series; then the lowest; extreme spread — the difference between the highest and the lowest; the average velocity; the standard deviation; and finally the number of shots in the series. Some of this information is enormously valuable to the balistician. We'll look into this subject presently; for now suffice it to say that the Oehler gave us the data on each shot with robotic regularity.

With the Ransom Rest in place and the Beretta mounted in the proper insert, we placed the chronograph downrange so that the start screen was some twelve feet from the muzzle. Then, at a carefully measured twenty-five yards, we set up a target frame. Nobody present said it, but this is a point in time when it is pretty well understood that it's "...all ready on the firing line!"

Here's the test procedure we followed throughout the course of an extended session of shooting. As each individual type of ammunition was taken from its original container, rangemaster Joe Boyd, taking a break from schooling rookie cops in gunhandling, would head downrange and mount a fresh target to the frame. While he was there, we loaded two magazines with ten rounds each of the ammunition. Upon his return, the ammo would be loaded and fired in the gun, all twenty rounds at the same target and with the same settings on the Rest. That's correct. We fired not five- or ten-shot groups, but twenty shots each into a single group.

After the cease-fire, when the twenty rounds were in the target, Joe would put up a new one. When he returned with the old target, I'd note the statistical data from the chronograph and pass the target on to Grennell. He then would

No, Boyd is not standing in front of a loaded gun. The slide is forward so that the barrel can be changed to the Bar-Sto variety for the testing necessary to develop data for the chapter that follows this one.

measure the group, mark the target and photograph it with the partially expended box of ammunition. We followed this procedure without deviation. The only interruptions were for brushing out the bore of the pistol. Joe Boyd did the honors after about every sixty rounds.

Before proceeding to a discussion of the actual ammunition that was fired, it is appropriate to say a word about the Beretta. The contract for producing service pistols was granted to Beretta on the basis of test trials of this gun. Whatever else may have come from the Army-conducted testing of several handguns, one thing was clear. The test procedure said that the 92F is a reliable handgun. We fired about seven hundred rounds through the test pistol on "D" day, including several magazines of different loads used to settle the gun in its inserts. There was not a single malfunction of any sort whatsoever.

Considering the fact that the range of ammunition included just about every type of bullet contour possible, as well as ammo that varied almost three hundred feet per second in velocity, no malfunctions means a reliable gun. It might be well argued that other guns could have duplicated this performance. I don't doubt that a number of other pistols could have done this; the point is simply that the Beretta was chosen for the service pistol, was chosen for our ammo test, and performed as advertised.

The 9mmP ammunition? There is a hell of a variety of the stuff on the market. You can get bullets as light as 86

grains in the exotic Geco Blitz Action trauma (which we didn't have on hand to fire). Bullets are also as heavy as the 125-grain CCI Lawman. There are hollow points, soft points and a great many full metal jacket designs. Hornady produces a FMJ with a flat point. It's definitely a crowded field. Our sequence was to shoot everything produced by a single manufacturer, with the domestic makers first. The order of manufacturers was completely arbitrary; just whatever one came to hand first.

We'll start with the ammunition produced by CCI. It's also often called Speer and there are two different types of it. One is the inexpensive Blazer line. This stuff costs significantly less than other ammunition, because the case is a non-reloadable alloy that will do nicely for a single firing, but doesn't have the necessary metallurgy to be reloadable. The Good Ol' Boys make sure that you don't reload it with a crimped-in Berdan primer of a size uncommon to anything else. Both of the Blazer 9mmPs are 115 grain, a JHP and a FMJ.

In the Lawman series of ammunition, CCI offers four different kinds of 9mmP. This stuff is put up in fully reloadable cartridge cases of excellent quality. It also comes in high-quality yellow plastic boxes that find themselves used over and over for all kinds of around-the-shop purposes. The ammo is a 100-grain JHP with a huge cavity, a 115-grain FJM, a 115-grain hollow-point, and a 125-grain JSP. This latter round was the heaviest tested. The exposed

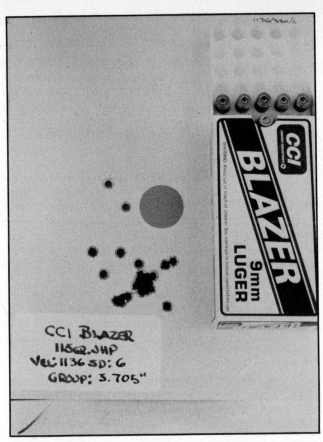

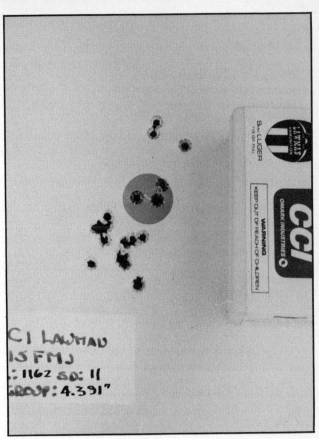

CCI Blazer JHP was the second round tested and ended up in eleventh place in accuracy. All groups are 20-shot.

Another CCI round, the reloadable Lawman 115-grain FMJ, produced this group in the new military pistol.

This form of Winchester ammunition didn't do as well as other kinds. A 5.371-inch group earned 26th place.

Had it not been for the two fliers, this Remington JHP would have shot much better than the 4.246-inch group.

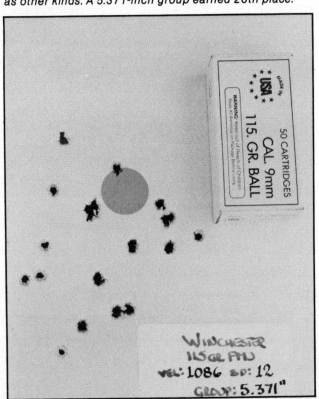

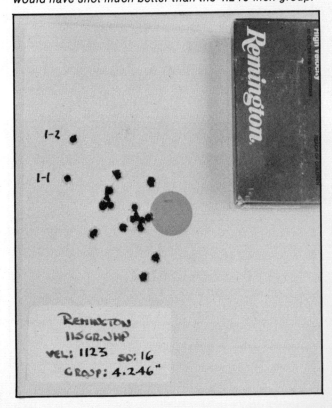

lead at the tip will often cause malfunctions in several different guns, but the Beretta ate it up.

Winchester. The familiar horse and rider logo will be found on three of the four kinds of Winchester ammo. The other one is an economically priced, plain box, military-type 115-grain FJM. The others are interesting. One bears the famous Silvertip name, a 115-grain JHP which has a repututation for excellent expansion. The other is a lightweight, high velocity JSP. My sources of information on such matters are telling me that a major West Coast police agency will use this round in their newly authorized automatics. Their feeling is that the light bullet will not tend to the over-penetration that can't be allowed to happen in a city.

Remington offers a pair of loadings in the familiar green and yellow cartons. One is a 115-grain JHP and the other is a 124-grain roundnose FMJ. I also stumbled on some of what might be the same ammo in another uniform. The ammunition looks the same and bears a similar stock number, but it is packaged in a plain brown box marked UMC with a back label that confesses to Remington origins. UMC was the Union Metallic Cartridge Company, for years part of the Remington-Du Pont scheme.

We have already seen that both Winchester and Remington have less expensive versions of their ammunition in plain wrapper. The other major manufacturer, Federal, does the same thing with the American Eagle label. This is a plain-box version of a 123-grain FJM round that looks a lot like Federal's 9AP. Along with the company's 95-grain JSP and 115-grain JHP, the 123-grain FMJ is widely distributed in the U.S. in that red and white box.

At one point in time, Hornady ammunition was marketed as Frontier, but that has changed. We fired four rounds from the Nebraska firm, each dolled up in the new white cartons with red and black trim. They were the 90-grain JHP, a 115-grain JHP, a FMJ load in the same 115-grain weight and a 124-grain FMJ. This last round uses the well known flat-nosed "Air Force" bullet. Like CCI-Speer ammo, the Hornady stuff uses bullets that the company produces primarily for handloading.

Before moving to imported ammunition, let's look at an example of what is getting to be a small industry in its own right. Black Hills Shooters Supply is one of several firms that are offering what amounts to commercial reloads. The term is something of a misnomer in that the brass is new and so are all other components. This progressive new company provided us with samples of their 115-grain FMJs and JHPs.

Ammo in 9mmP is loaded all over the world and we were able to get test quantities of ammunition from Asia, South America and Europe. The Asian ammo was PMC, two types of 115-grainers, not surprisingly a JHP and a FMJ. At least on the West Coast, PMC ammunition is widely distributed.

In a vivid yellow box from Southern Gun Distributers of Opa-Locka, Florida, we found Rio brand ammunition. Made by CBC of Brazil, this fodder is offered in 115-grain JPH and 124-grain FMJ versions. There were some sur-

American Eagle is a variety of Federal Ammunition; it would appear to be virtually identical to the red box...

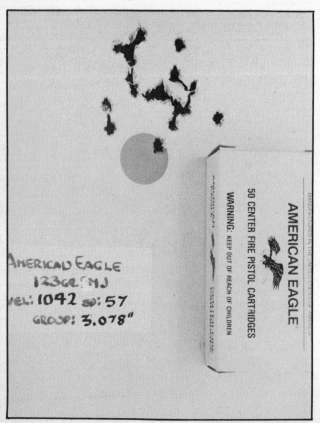

...Federal 123-grain FMJ. The stats are nearly the same and the accuracy rankings are sixth and seventh overall.

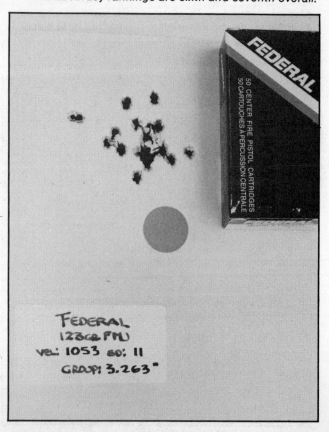

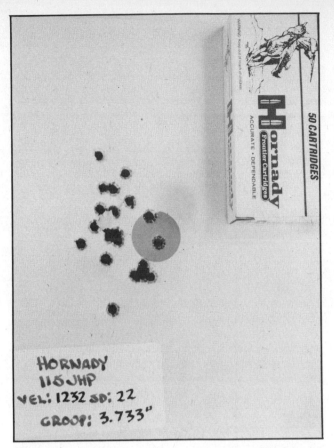

HORNADY
115 JHP
VEL: 1232 SD: 22
GROUP: 3.733"

Above: Hornady ammunition is now packaged in red-and-black-trimmed white boxes, 115-grain JHPs seen here.

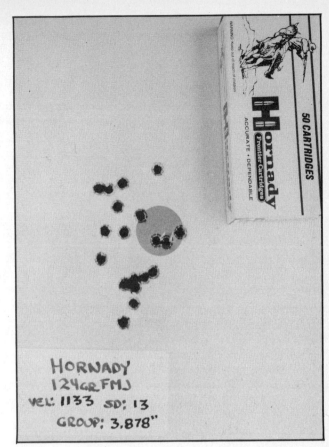

HORNADY
124gr FMJ
VEL: 1133 SD: 13
GROUP: 3.878"

Above: Another Hornady round uses the so-called "Air Force" bullet, a 124-grain FMJ with a wide, flat point.

Below: Black Hills Shooter's Supply 115-grain JHPs; a "commercial reloader" ammo that didn't need that flyer.

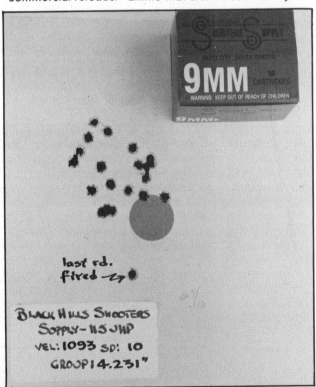

last rd.
fired

BLACK HILLS SHOOTERS
SUPPLY - 115 JHP
VEL: 1093 SD: 10
GROUP 4.231"

Below: PMC is made in Korea and sells for reasonable prices in the U.S. This ammo is in a camouflaged box.

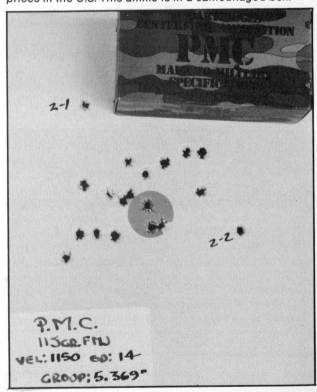

2-1

2-2

P.M.C.
115gr FMJ
VEL: 1150 SD: 14
GROUP: 5.369"

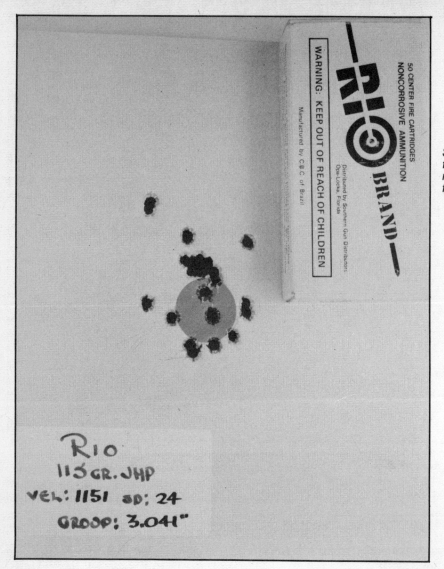

Surprise, surprise! Rio Ammo, imported from Brazil, turned in impressive group measuring a scant 3.041 inches, good for fifth place in the accuracy race.

prises in store for us with that ammunition.

This brings us to what we could find in the way of European ammunition. First was the 115-grain Fiocchi, a FMJ design in a silver box. We also tried the 115-grain FMJ load from Samson, also known as Israeli Military Industries.

The catalog from Norma of Sweden lists three different 9mmP loads. The only one that we were able to obtain was the 115-grain JHP. Hansen Cartridge Company imports Austrian Hirtenberger ammunition and sent some of their 123-grain FMJ stuff. Finally, from Dynamit Nobel of Germany, under the GECO brand name, we fired the 123-grain FMJ round.

I do not presume to say that the foregoing is a complete listing of all 9mmP ammunition, merely that it is a fairly complete listing of ammo available in the U.S. It stands to reason that, when a cartridge is the main military round of the majority of the nations of the world, then many of those

nations will make their own ammo. There is probably a wide variety of ammunition in this size produced in Europe and in other locations. For our test, I fired every type of round I could find.

At the conclusion of firing, I had a bunch of targets, quite a bit of reloadable brass and a page of tabulated data. I also had some illusions shattered. I frankly thought that much of the ammo would shoot much better than it did and I had fully expected some ammunition of known quality to go into groups under two inches. The best group measured 2.306 inches and the worst actually did not stay on the paper with a group in excess of 9.375 inches.

I have tested ammunition of various sorts in varying ways for a number of years. In recent times, I had the good fortune to be able to see some of my test firing results published. But for many years before I ever got a word into print, I've been a bit suspicious about the results of some testing that I've seen in print. There is a pronounced ten-

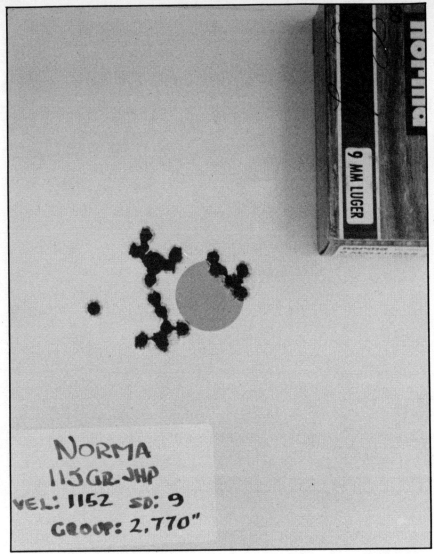

Norma of Sweden has always made good ammunition and their 115-grain JHP must be among their better loadings. This group ranked fourth in accuracy.

NORMA
115 GR. JHP
VEL: 1152 SD: 9
GROUP: 2.770"

dency on the part of some writers to portray or talk only about the best groups that they shoot, leaving many others in a sort of limbo. With this same Beretta pistol, I have personally fired, off the bench, several groups that are smaller than 2.306 inches. But those were five-shot groups, not twenty.

The testing that we did on that sunny June day in California was not calculated to put any particular brand of ammunition in a good light. There were several times when we watched good groups enlarge by those exasperating fliers that plague shooters and handloaders. The results that you see pictured and tabulated in these pages don't exclude the fliers; the measured group includes the widest shots. There are other things that we could have done to improve the grouping, like using the pistol as a single-shot or using only one magazine. Such things are departures from realism as well as from the goal of the test, which was to find out what ammunition was the most accurate in a

typical modern service automatic. The Ransom Rest was used to remove human error. The procedure was designed to be ruthless. It was.

There no doubt will be some criticism of what is reported here. I don't have any illusions about what would happen if you were to do any of the obvious things in a repeat of the test. You could possibly obtain different results if you fired one hundred shots instead of twenty. Things might change if you used a different lot of each of the rounds of ammunition. It might be different if you repeated the tests with ten identical Berettas and averaged the results.

Things might be different if any of these things were done, but I doubt if there would be any major change in the rankings. One round or another might slide up or down a few places, but not many of them would. In all fairness to some the 9mmP loadings which were eked out by a few fractions of an inch, their ranking could clearly improve with a repeat of the test — but then the round above them in

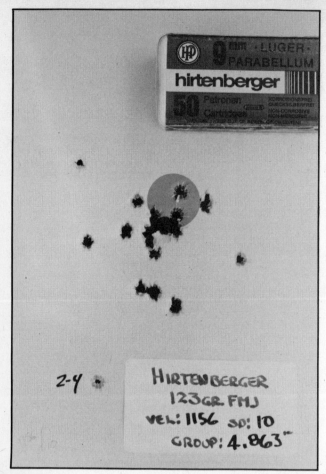

Austrian Hirtenberger ammunition is imported by the Hansen Cartridge Co. and posted the results seen here.

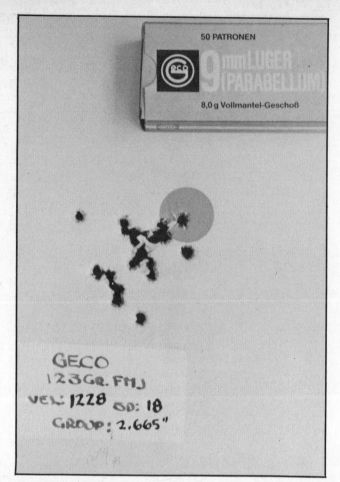

Patronen means cartridge and GECO patronen means accuracy and power. Note velocity, accuracy, weight.

the scale might improve, too.

Another goal of the test was to determine whatever I could about the consistency of the ammunition and relate that to its accuracy. I approached this goal with enthusiasm, since a test of this sort might involve enough rounds of each type that extreme spread and standard deviation might have an obvious and significant value.

These two terms have long been bandied about by experimental handloaders with confident ease. Extreme spread is the difference between the highest and lowest velocities in a series of shots. Standard deviation is a statistician's term which serves as an index of consistency. It is concisely, but not quite perfectly, described as the averge variation from the average velocity. Both are terms to which there is much deference.

The theory is that good ammunition will be consistent, that the velocities of individual fired rounds will tend to cluster together in such a way as to promote similar paths

to the target. Consistent ammunition, therefore, will tend to strike the target in close to the same spot. If the extreme spread in a series of shots was only a few feet per second, then the rounds should be pretty much alike, and they should hit in the same spot. If that were true, how do you explain what happened to Samson 115-grain ammo?

This round had the highest extreme spread of any tested — 160 feet per second — but it ranked ninth in accuracy. A couple of wild shots could run the extreme spread high, but standard deviation should take care of that. Standard deviation in this case was 31, one of the higher ones.

We had three single-digit standard deviations occur during the test. One was a 9 in the case of CCI Lawman 125 grain — which finished eighteenth in accuracy. Another was also a 9, for CCI Lawman 115-grain JHPs — eleventh in accuracy. Finally, there was a standard deviation of 6 for Norma 115-grain JHPs, high on the accuracy list at fourth. But every round which outshot the Norma had a

9mmP FACTORY AMMUNITION TEST

Firing done at measured 25 yards.

Maker	Wgt	Type	Code	ES*	Vel	SD*	Group/Rank
CCI Blazer	115	FMJ	03509	34	1135	10	6.812-31
CCI Blazer	115	JHP	03508	26	1136	6	3.705-11
CCI Lawman	100	JHP	3610	52	1223	13	4.750-22
CCI Lawman	115	FMJ	3615	47	1162	11	4.391-20
CCI Lawman	115	JHP	3614	59	1146	15	4.590-21
CCI Lawman	125	JSP	3620	35	1050	9	4.339-18
Winchester	95	JSP	X9mmJSP	75	1298	22	5.378-28
Winchester Silvertip	115	JHP	X9mmSTHP	68	1212	22	3.281- 8
Winchester	115	FMJ	X9LP	36	1075	10	5.215-25
Winchester	115	FMJ		47	1086	12	5.371-26
Remington	115	JHP	R9mm1	66	1123	16	4.246-16
Remington	124	FMJ	R9mm2	38	1096	10	4.372-19
UMC	124	FMJ	U9mm2	68	1075	19	6.425-29
Federal	95	JSP	9CP	68	1265	16	3.596-10
Federal	115	JHP	9BP	47	1150	13	2.306- 1
Federal	123	FMJ	9AP	56	1053	11	3.263- 7
American Eagle	123	FMJ	AR9AP	67	1042	57	3.078- 6
Hornady	90	JHP	9020	55	1323	11	3.849-13
Hornady	100	FMJ	9023	55	1178	13	6.662-30
Hornady	115	JHP	9025	104	1232	12	3.733-12
Hornady	124	FMJ	9027	56	1133	13	3.878-14
Black Hills Shooters'	115	FMJ		38	1076	10	5.109-24
Black Hills Shooters'	115	JHP		46	1093	46	4.231-15
PMC	115	JHP	9B	44	1167	11	9.375-32
PMC	115	FMJ	9A	51	1150	14	5.369-27
Rio	115	JHP	R9mmJHP	87	1151	24	3.041- 5
Rio	124	FMJ	R9mmL	52	1134	15	4.284-17
Fiocchi	115	FMJ		77	1208	18	2.760- 3
Samson Match	115	FMJ	9-23-A	160	1126	31	3.331- 9
Norma	115	JHP	19021	32	1152	9	2.770- 4
Hirtenberger	123	FMJ		43	1156	10	4.863-23
Geco	123	FMJ		59	1228	18	2.665- 2

* ES = Extreme Spread
* SD = Standard Deviation

higher standard deviation. You can drive yourself nutty looking for a direct relationship between the statistical factors of extreme velocity spread or its standard deviation and on-target accuracy.

I feel strongly that such factors are important particularly in much larger samplings, and contribute to the overall picture of accuracy. But I suspect that such matters as the concentricity in ammo and bullets, plus compatability of particular combinations of bullets and rifling pitch and type, are more important. If the ES and SD columns of a ballistic chart are taken too seriously, the reader is doomed to confusion in a search for relationships between those factors and accuracy. You will probably derive more precise answers from a careful study of the

entrails of a freshly slaughtered chicken.

The results of the test are published in the accompanying table. There are some surprises.

For one thing, the top five places are dominated by foreign brands of ammunition. Second through fifth places are taken by Geco, Fiocchi, Norma and Rio brands of ammunition. We've probably all heard of all of them except Rio. This excellent JHP load is produced in an all-new plant in Brazil. In a recent conversation with the importer, I was told how the assembly line of this plant is set up to produce powder as needed rather than taking the stuff from storage. That is not the way that it is done in every other plant you're likely to find.

Not surprisingly, the highest velocities came with the

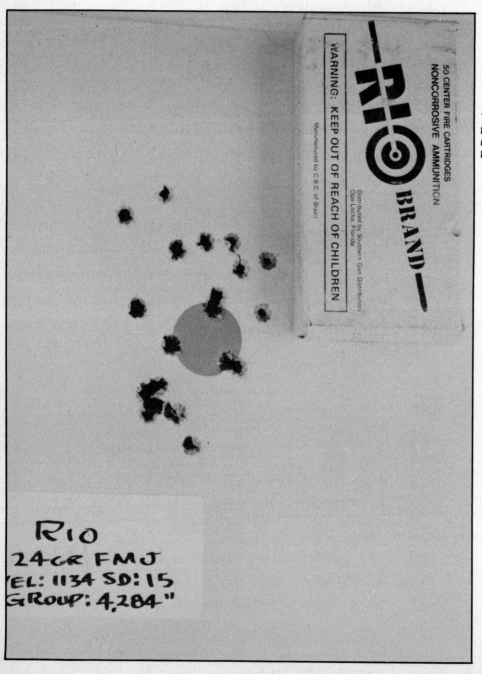

The other type of Rio ammo is the 124-grain FMJ, which ended up seventeenth in accuracy. See text for details of manufacture.

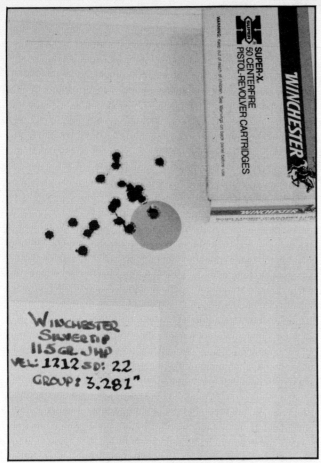

You are well armed if your 9mmP pistol is full of this stuff — the Winchester Silvertip, with an excellent "rep."

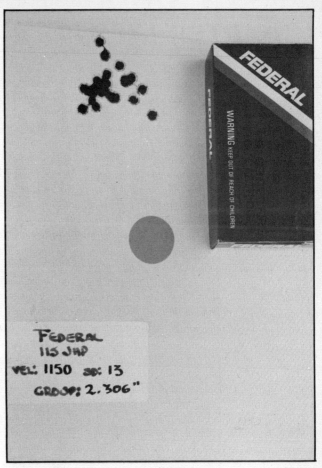

The aiming paster measures an inch and a quarter. And Federal 9BP is the most accurate ammunition tested.

lightest bullets. Hornady JHPs delivered the highest velocity at 1323 fps, followed by Winchester 95-grain JSPs (1298), Federal 95-grain JSPs (1265) and CCI Lawman 100-grain JHPs (1223). If you are concerned about overpenetration in residential settings, one of these speedy little bombs might be a good choice.

Nearly everybody makes a 115-grain load and many make one with a hollow-point and one with a full metal jacket. This is the most popular bullet weight and one which did well in the accuracy ratings. With the exception of the Speer 125 JSP, all bullets heavier than 115 grains are full metal jacket designs.

The reason for choosing a FMJ load is usually for functioning reliability and terminal penetration. In this category, there is no better choice than the German Geco. Not only is this round superbly accurate at second place in the rankings, but also is one of the faster loads at 1228 fps. When you consider that Geco uses a nicely contoured bullet of 123 grains and the highest kinetic energy developed, then you have a round which will feed smoothly and cycle the action of nearly any gun. It's the odds-on favorite

as the best of the full metal jacket ball ammo.

Also look at another factor on that list. Of all ammo listed, Federal placed first, sixth, seventh and tenth. That suggests that the guys up there in Minnesota are paying attention to what they are doing.

I guess the ultimate question is what load should you choose for a 9mmP pistol used for defensive purposes. The Winchester Silvertip has such an awesome reputation for effectiveness in real life situations that I wouldn't be thrown off by the ranking of eighth in accuracy.

Still, I have fired thousands of rounds of another type of ammunition in the course of compiling the data for this book. And my contacts in law enforcement have told me a good bit about the real life effectiveness of that round. Since it is the most accurate load in a wide variety of pistols, functions with utter reliability in everything and has a demonstrated defensive effectiveness, my unhesitating and unqualified choice for the best of 9mmP ammunition is the Federal 115-grain JHP — the 9BP. I don't believe there's anything better. — *Wiley Clapp*

CHAPTER 17

THE NICER NINES OF BAR-STO

The man himself, Irving O. Stone Jr., at work in the shop. Most of the fitting of barrels to customer's guns is done by Stone himself. An afternoon's visit with this gentleman can be a short course in automatic pistol design, if you listen to him.

SOUTHERN CALIFORNIA is the home of two institutions of the combat pistol shooting business. One of the two is the Southwest Pistol League, pioneered by Jeff Cooper in the Fifties and Sixties. The doctrine developed through this hardy and practical form of combat shooting has spread throughout the nation and even abroad. It is a form of shooting which emphasizes the combat use of a major caliber pistol with speed as well as accuracy. Therefore it was: speed — accuracy — power.

As many readers are aware, defensive pistol shooting in this light has evolved to the use of the .45 caliber Colt pistol. As Cooper and his associates worked out their techniques with the .45, they had the power assured by the legendary clout of the big gun. Speed became a function of the shooter's technique, rather than anything to do with his gun or cartridge. That left the accuracy factor and about that time along came Irving O. Stone, Jr., with the second of the two institutions of the combat pistol game; Bar-Sto barrels.

This is not to say that no one had re-built .45s for accuracy before Irv Stone. Many gunsmiths have done just that for a great many years. But their work has, for the most part, centered around the development and production of finely fitted target pistols, balanced for the use of light wadcutter loads, with little value in the rough and tumble arena of combat competition. Stone, with a great deal of experience in the aerospace industry, went about developing the

The Ultimate Accessory For Your 9mmP Handgun May Very Well Be One Of Irv Stone's Superb Barrels

Stone marks his barrels as shown above. The particular pistol is a new Browning Hi-Power, which benefited by the Bar-Sto barrel, but not as much as the other guns.

.45 as a pistol that would shoot far more accurately — and with heavy combat loads. Stone eventually formed a small company called Bar-Sto Precision.

Bar-Sto makes barrels for automatic pistols and nothing else. The beauty of the barrel from Stone's shop is that it requires little or no fitting to the individual pistol and increases accuracy to pronounced degree. While the mainstay of the company is still the production of barrels for the Government Model .45, Stone has expanded his product line in recent times to include quite a variety of barrels for some 9mmP handguns, we thought it would be appropriate to conclude the book with a discussion of the Bar-Sto barrel.

As we are all aware, there are a great many 9mmP handguns in use and more are coming. Since the Beretta was chosen to be the service pistol, a great deal of attention will focus on the accessories for the gun. Some of the accessories may be worthwhile; others won't. One that will be is the Bar-Sto barrel.

Stone presently is making 9mmP barrels for a number of guns. In addition to the Colt GM 9mmP, he can produce a barrel for the Beretta 92 and its look-alike from Taurus, the CZ 75 from the Czechs, plus the Italian copy of this gun, several Smith & Wessons in the 39/59 series, including

Laid out on a shop cloth, author's Smith & Wesson Model 639 awaits Irv Stone's attentions. This same pistol fired groups that averaged 53% improvement with the Bar-Sto.

the recently offered 669 and the Browning Hi-Power.

We had four of above 9mmP handguns for evaluation. In each case, the original barrel was retained and used interchangeably with the Bar-Sto for the sake of comparison. The guns were the same reliable Beretta used in the evaluation of factory ammo, a new Browning Hi-Power and an equally new Smith & Wesson Model 639, and finally, Irv Stone's own CZ 75. It will come as no sur-

Good old #C31319Z. This particular pistol has been fired a great deal, mostly with the original factory barrel. A Bar-Sto was installed early in 1985 and it shoots better.

prise that the Bar-Sto barrels shot better than the factory barrels in every case, but let's not get ahead of ourselves.

For a long time, back in the Seventies, Irv Stone ran a little one-inch ad in most of the popular gun magazines. The advertisement offered a drop-in replacement barrel for the Colt Government Model .45 at a cost of $39.95. People bought them through the mail, dropped them into their guns and shot better groups. Sometimes those groups were spectacularly better. In all the years that I have known about and used Bar-Sto barrels, I have never heard of any gun shooting worse groups after a Bar-Sto was installed, so they do work. The question is why.

The answer is really two-fold. Stone designs better barrels, then executes his own design with meticulous attention to detail. The result is a product that is about as nicely made as anything that you are likely to see. They cost a good bit more than the original price, but are still worth it.

Look at design first. When Irv Stone sets out to manufacture a new barrel for a new model of gun, he studies the new pistol carefully. The first thing he'll likely do is a complete disassembly and examination of every part. What he's looking for will be how the parts will interact with one another in the feeding and firing cycle. Many manufacturers produce guns with particular contours, because they are easier and cheaper to make that way. If the contour of a part in the barrel system needs to be changed for greater reliability, Stone will change it before he puts the product in the market with his name on it.

As a result of his study, Stone becomes intimately familiar with the shape and function of every part in the new gun. He usually chooses to head for the range to fire a variety of ammunition through the gun. Then, back at the shop he pulls it all apart once again. This time he studies to what degree, if any, the various parts have worn, battered or otherwise changed contour. This tells him where the stresses are being exerted on the pistol as it is fired.

Prototype barrels are roughed out in the well-equipped 29 Palms shop. He tries them in the pistol and tries them with a variety of ammunition. Eventually a design evolves and a blueprint is drawn, a veritable plan for the continued production of the pistol barrel. The end result of this careful analysis and cut-and-try fabrication is a functioning prototype barrel and a set of blueprints. From then on, it is a matter of careful quality control.

This business of understanding the functional engineering of the gun can't be overstated. I was present for a lengthy session of watching and an occasional question as Irv fitted barrels to several different handguns. At one point he snorted scornfully at the attempts of another gunsmith to fit a barrel to a Colt.

"Look at this," he muttered with barely controlled wonderment, "I see this all the time. These guys think a little tight fitting is good, so a lot must be better. The barrel link has been fitted to its pin so tightly that it won't turn. The damned thing has to pivot freely or the gun won't work; no wonder that it's jamming for the shooter." Then he fixed it.

But not all 9mmP pistols work on the basis of a pivoting link and each presents a special problem to analyze and understand. In the case of any barrel that leaves the Bar-Sto shop, you can rest assured that the homework of design was thoroughly worked out before you were ever allowed to buy the product.

All of which leads us to a need to examine an additional design characteristic of Stone's 9mmP barrels. That's the part of the barrel that does the work — the bore itself. He designs them differently.

The subject of rifling design is worth a book or two in its own right and, in fact, there have been some good books written on the subject. Stone is intimately familiar with the characteristics of good rifling. For reasons that are logical to him and which work well on the finished product, he uses a rate of twist that is quite a bit different for 9mmP barrels. Bar-Sto barrels are rifled at the rate of one turn in sixteen inches (1:16). Almost all other makers produce barrels that spin the slug at a rate of 1:10.

The rule in designing rifling has always traditionally been to use a faster twist rate as the bullet weight increases. All sorts of studies have been performed that conclusively establish the validity of the maxim. The problem to a firearms designer is to design rifling that will work well with the range of bullet weights that are found in ammunition for the particular caliber. In other words, he is forced to compromise. With a few exceptions, all rifling is a compromise.

But Stone has done his compromising with care. The Bar-Sto 9mmPs are rifled at the slower rate of 1:16, but the actual shape of the lands and grooves is different. In conventional fast-twist barrels, which tend to generate higher and less desirable pressures, the rifling groove is rather

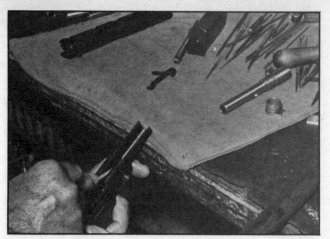

Stone is fitting one of his stainless steel barrels to the Browning Hi-Power. Note the selection of files within easy reach. They're used to make small contour changes.

narrow. In the Bar-Stos, with the slower twist, the grooves are wider. This tends to distort the bullet less as it is forced through the barrel by gas pressure. Wider groove plus slower twist add up to less deformation of the bullet and greater accuracy, at least in theory.

It's not just theory and we can prove it. Dean Grennell has a nice 9mmP Colt Government Model in his battery. At some time in the distant past, Stone graciously fitted the gun with an early barrel, rifled with a 1:10 twist. That twist was used for a brief time in the Bar-Sto plant. More recently, the gun got an updated barrel with the 1:16 twist. Dean kept the early barrel which shot like a house afire. He was unwilling to believe that any barrel could outshoot his first one.

We settled the whole thing one day at the range when the Ransom Rest was being used to test out a bunch of different guns and ammunition. With the 1:10 barrel in place, we bolted the Colt into the rest and shot several groups. Grennell was certainly correct about one thing, the barrel was accurate. Several groups were just under an inch at twenty-five yards. As usual, our beloved Federal 9BP, a 115-grain JHP, was best.

Honing barrels to the correct bore diameter. The Bar-Sto literature says they are held to .0002-inch tolerance; I saw quite a few of them honed to a miniscule .00001-inch.

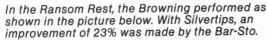

The Browning Hi-Power is readied for the test firing session in the Ransom Rest. The wooden grip scales are removed and the gun is fitted to the rubber-faced inserts.

Then we changed barrels in the gun and tried the same ammunition in the 1:16 barrel. Without exception, every single group was superior in the slow-twist barrel. While the improvement was always discernible, it was never particularly spectacular. That isn't surprising in that we are comparing a Bar-Sto to a Bar-Sto and we are also approaching the practical limits of accuracy characteristic of the ammunition.

My conclusion is just that Irv Stone can design rifling for me any way he wants to. He can manufacture them, too. I watched the entire process during my recent visit to the high desert city of 29 Palms. In the production of barrels, Stone will go as far to allow someone else to manufacture the steel for him, but that's as much as he will concede to outside contractors. This is the second of those two factors that make Bar-Sto barrels the best there is.

Bar-Stos are made from scratch, starting with long bars of premium quality stainless steel. It is a fascinating procedure to watch. After the hole that will ultimately be the bore of a pistol is drilled through a section of the stock, the barrel is cut roughly to shape. This part of the procedure produces a roughly contoured barrel blank with a under-

sized hole in same. Then the barrel is placed in a holding jig and precision-honed to an inside diameter equal to the minor, or bore, diameter of the finished tube. Incredibly, the tolerance in this critical part of the process is .0001-inch. That is a ten-thousandth of an inch!

For some reason, this part of the process really caught my fancy; I stood by and watched as one of Stone's troops honed barrels to dimensions, watching the dial indicator atop the machine. I suppose that part of my awe for what was going on is based on the fact that I am the sort of mechanical person who has a lifetime average of about three for five when it comes to driving nails straight.

Stone uses precision broaches to produce rifling in the

In the Ransom Rest, the Browning performed as shown in the picture below. With Silvertips, an improvement of 23% was made by the Bar-Sto.

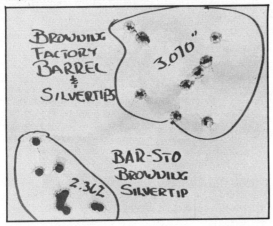

Below and right: The famous CZ75 was not particularly accurate "out-of-the-box," but Irv Stone fixed that with his barrel. The factory barrel shot a larger 4.575-inch group.

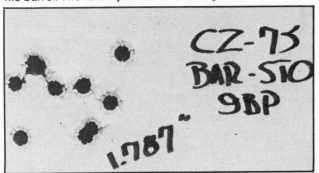

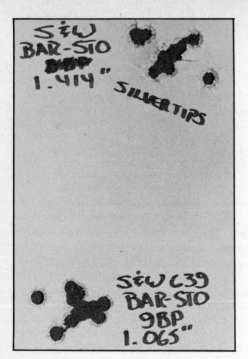

Two groups in one photo: The best two rounds fired in the Bar-Sto'ed S&W Model 639. Silvertips and Federal 9BP are superb rounds, but this is true X-ring accuracy!

bores of his barrels. For barrels as short as five or six inches, this system works as well as anything. The broaches themselves are beautifully made pieces of tooling. They are forced through the honed tubes and the end result is a barrel that is ready to be chambered and finished.

Major manufacturers of pistols and pistol barrels are plagued with the problem of production. Economics have put them in such a spot that they have to make many units and make them quick. For this reason, they cannot be expected to make a barrel the way that Irv Stone makes it. When Stone cuts a chamber into one of his rifled tubes, the chamber will be smooth, properly dimensioned and one hundred percent concentric with the bore of the barrel. This factor is one of the biggest reasons why they shoot so well.

With the barrel bored, rifled and chambered, it's ready to have the remaining exterior contours finished off in such a way that it may be fitted to whatever pistol is appropriate. Most barrels that leave the Bar-Sto plant are furnished with a set of directions on the fitting of the barrel to the pistol.

In the hands of a competent gunsmith, a Bar-Sto can be fitted to a handgun without any particular difficulty. Nevertheless, it is possible to screw it up completely. For the barrels that were fired in the course of researching this book, all were fitted by Irv Stone himself, which he will do for a small additional charge. Spend the extra few bucks to have the fitting done by the man himself, as it's well worth it.

That pretty well covers how they are made and why they are made that way, but it leaves the question of how do they shoot. For that answer, there's nothing left to do but pack up the guns and head for the range. We did just that and one of the things that went along was the Ransom Rest.

There's no point in repeating the extensive description

of the design and functioning of the Ransom Rest. That data will be found in Chapter Sixteen. Suffice to say that the device will return the pistol to the same aiming point with near perfect consistency. Good shooters can equal the Ransom Rest for short periods of time, but they can't do it all day. Chuck Ransom's invention has an infinite span of attention.

In order to keep this evaluation down to a manageable length, I decided to shoot each of the four guns, with and without the Bar-Sto barrels, using just three kinds of ammunition. In the course of producing the data reported throughout Chapter Fourteen, I fired a great deal of these three kinds of ammunition. Federal 9BP, Winchester Silvertips, and Federal 9AP all are excellent rounds, consistently accurate and functionally reliable.

Choosing good ammunition to start a comparative test is important. For one thing, if the ammo shoots better in a Bar-Sto barrel, then it has to be due to the ammo and not because of some weird inconsistency. Using the best of ammo to start with will not necessarily make the improvement as spectacular, but it will make the test results a little more credible.

The test guns were a Beretta Model 92SB-F, also called the M9; a new commercial Browning Hi-Power; a Smith & Wesson Model 639; and Irv Stone's own CZ 75. The Beretta had been fired a great deal; at least 2000 rounds. Both the Browning and the Smith were brand-new pistols when Stone fitted the barrels to them. I took the precaution of firing a couple of hundred rounds of mixed ammo through each barrel for each gun. This serves as a form of breaking in. The CZ was Stone's own pistol and it did not appear to have been worn out in use. I don't know how many shots have been fired through it.

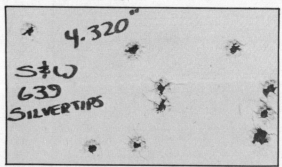

More than credible accuracy. Here's what you can expect from the same Smith & Wesson with original barrel. Compare with the groups at the top of page.

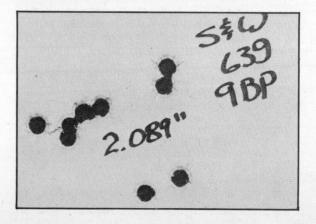

I didn't have Dean Grennell's Colt available on the day that I did the shooting or I would have included that one. As previously mentioned, this gun has barrels from Bar-Sto with two rates of twist. It would have been an interesting contrast, but the gun was away, perhaps to be fitted with a new set of *pearl* grips. (Forgive him, General Patton, for they took him away as a mere boy — for the Air Corps!)

Shooting of this sort goes pretty much as planned, particularly when using the Ransom Rest. Each gun was placed in the correct type of insert. Then a full magazine was fired to fully settle the gun into the rubber-faced blocks. The gun then was fired successively with 9BP, Silvertips and the 9AP. Then the gun was disassembled, the Bar-Sto barrel fitted into place. The firing sequence did not proceed until the Bar-Sto was settled with another magazine of hardball. The the same three rounds were fired and the results tabulated.

Each pistol was handled in an identical fashion. In every case there was at least some improvement; and sometimes the improvement was pretty considerable. Each of the groups was ten-shots in order to reduce the possibility of single extraordinary five-shot groups skewing the results.

Bar-Sto barrels unquestionably are superior. The groups are much tighter and may even get down to a point close to the practical limit of the accuracy potential of the ammunition.

Do you need it? Answer the question for yourself. Some might argue that a combat pistol doesn't need to be that accurate. Maybe not, but I need all the help that I can get. I can't see the point of rejecting anything that will improve a handgun for defense purposes. — *Wiley Clapp.*

BAR-STO BARRELS
FIRING TEST DATA TABLE

PISTOL	Federal 9BP	Winchester Silvertip	Federal 9AP
CZ 75	4.575"	5.210"	5.499"
w/Bar-Sto	1.787"	2.328"	2.911"
difference —	2.788"	2.882"	2.588"
% improved	61%	55%	47%
S&W Model 639	2.089"	4.320"	3.336"
w/Bar-Sto	1.065"	1.414"	1.804"
difference —	1.024"	2.906"	1.532"
% improved	49%	67%	45%
Browning High-Power	2.709"	3.070"	3.229"
w/Bar-Sto	2.092"	2.362"	3.018"
difference —	.617"	.708"	.211"
% improved	23%	23%	6%
Beretta Model 92-F	2.352"	2.974"	2.842"
w/Bar-Sto	1.233"	2.030"	2.114"
difference —	1.119"	.944"	.728"
% improved	48%	31%	34%

All groups were fired with the gun secured in a Ransom Rest and each measured group was a ten-shot group. Group measurements were performed with a dial caliper and are reasonably accurate. The test ammunition was selected on the basis of availability and demonstrated accuracy.

Four guns were used, with two different barrels (the original factory barrel and the Bar-Sto) in each gun. Three different kinds of ammunition were fired in each gun-barrel combination. This adds up to twenty-four different groups or twelve comparisons. In every case, there was improvement when the Bar-Sto was used. It ranged from a low of .221 inches to a high of 2.906 inches.

THE AVERAGE INCREASE IN ACCURACY WAS FORTY PERCENT.

DIRECTORY OF MANUFACTURERS

AMMUNITION (Commercial)

Alberts Corp., 519 East 19th St., Paterson, NJ 07514/201-684-1676
Cascade Cartridge Inc. (See Omark)
Dynamit Nobel of America, Inc., 105 Stonehurst Court, Northvale, NJ 07647/201-767-1660(IRWS)
Federal Cartridge Co., 2700 Foshay Tower, Minneapolis, MN 55402/612-333-8255
Frontier Cartridge Division-Hornady Mfg. Co., Box 1848, Grand Island, NE 68801/308-382-1390
Hansen Cartridge Co., 244 Old Post Rd., Southport, CT 06490/203-259-7337
Midway Arms, Inc., 7450 Old Hwy. 40 West, Columbia, MO 65201/314-445-9521
Omark Industries, Box 856, Lewiston, ID 83501/208-746-2351
Remington Arms Co., 1077 Market St., Wilmington, DE 19898
Super Vel, FPC, Inc., Hamilton Rd., Rt. 2, P.O. Box 1398, Fond du Lac, WI 54935/414-921-2652
Winchester, Shamrock St., East Alton, IL 62024

AMMUNITION (Custom)

KTW Inc., 710 Foster Park Rd., Lorain, OH 44053 216/233-6919 (bullets)
Lomont Precision Bullets, 4236 West 700 South, Poneto, IN 46781/219-694-6792 (custom cast bullets only)
Numrich Arms Corp., 203 Broadway, W. Hurley, NY 12491
Anthony F. Sailer-Ammunition, 707 W. Third St., P.O. Box L, Owen, WI 54460/715-229-2516
George W. Spence, 115 Locust St., Steele, MO 63877/314-695-4926 (boxer-primed cartridges)
The 3-D Company, Box J. Main St., Doniphan, NE 68832/402-845-2285 (reloaded police ammo)

AMMUNITION (Foreign)

Action Arms Ltd., P.O. Box 9573, Philadelphia, PA 19124/215-744-0100
Dynamit Nobel of America, Inc., 105 Stonehurst Court, Northvale, NJ 07647/210-767-1660(RWS, Geco, Rottweil)
FFV Norma, Inc., 300 S. Jefferson, Suite 301, Springfield, MO 65806
Fiocchi of America, Inc., 1308 Chase, Springfield, MO 65803/417-864-6970
Hansen Cartridge Co., 244 Old Post Rd., Southport, CT 06490/203-259-7337
Hirtenberger Patronen-, Zundhutchen-& Metallwarenfabrik, A.G., Leobersdorfer Str. 33, A2552 Hirtenberg, Austria
Paul Jaeger, Inc., P.O. Box 449, 1 Madison Ave., Grand Junction, TN 38039 (RWS centerfire ammo)
Kendall International Arms, Inc., 501 East North, Carlisle, KY 40311/606-289-7336 (Lapua)
Lapua (See Kendall International, Inc.)
PMC (See Patton and Morgan Corp.)
Patton and Morgan Corp., 5900 Wilshire Blvd., Suite 1400, Los Angeles, CA 90036/213-938-0143 (PMC ammo)
RWS (Rheinische-Westfalische Sprengstoff) (See Dynamit Nobel of America; Paul Jaeger, Inc.)

AMMUNITION COMPONENTS — BULLETS, POWDER, PRIMERS

Accurate Arms Co., Inc., (Propellents Div.), Rt. 1, Box 167, McEwen, TN 37101/615-729-5301 (powders)
Acme Custom Bullets, 5708 Evers Rd., San Antonio, TX 78238/512-680-4828
Alaska Bullet Works, P.O. Box 54, Douglas, AK 99824 (Alaska copper-bond cust.)
Alberts Corp., 519 E. 19th St., Paterson, NJ 07514/201-684-1676 (swaged bullets)
Ammo-O-Mart Ltd., P.O. Box 125, Hawkesbury, Ont., Canada K6A 2R8/613-632-9300 (Nobel powder)
Ballistic Prods., Inc., Box 488, 2105 Shaughnessy Circle, Long Lake, MN 55356
Ballistic Research Industries (BRI), 2825 S. Rodeo Gulch Rd., #8, Soquel, CA 95073/408-476-7981 (12-ga. Sabo shotgun slug)
Barnes Bullets, P.O. Box 215, American Fork, UT 84003/801-756-4222
Bell's Gun & Sport Shop, 3309-19 Mannheim Rd., Franklin Pk., IL 60131/312-678-1900
Bergman and Williams, 2450 Losee Rd., Las Vegas, NV 89030/702-642-1091 (copper tube .308 cust. bull.; lead wire i. all sizes)
Bitterroot Bullet Co., Box 412, Lewiston, ID 83501/208-743-5635 (Coin or stamps) f.50¢ U.S.; 75¢ Can. & Mex.; intl. $3.00 and #10 SASE for lit.
Black Mountain Bullets, Rte. 3, Box 297, Warrenton, VA 22186/703-347-1199 (cust.)
Milton Brynin, 214 E. Third St., Mount Vernon, NY 10550/914-664-1311 (cast bullets)
Buffalo Rock Shooter Supply (See Chevron Bullets)
CCI, (See Omark Industrico)
Chevron Bullets, R.R. 1, Ottawa, IL 61350/815-433-2471
Kenneth E. Clark, 18738 Highway 99, Madera, CA 93637/209-674-6016 (Bullets)
Clete's Custom Bullets, RR 6, Box 1348, Warsaw, IN 46580
Cooper-Woodward, P.O. Box 972, Riverside, CA 92502/714-683-4295
Corbin Mfg. & Supply, Inc., P.O. Box 2659, White City, OR 97503/503-826-5211 (bullets)

Cor-Bon Custom Bullets, P.O. Box 10126, Detroit, MI 48210/313-894-2373 (.375, .44, .45 solid brass partition bull.)
Custom Bullets by Hoffman, 2604 Peconic Ave., Seaford, NY 11783 (7mm, .308, .257, .224, .270)
Denali Bullet Co., P.O. Box 82217, Fairbanks, AK 99701/907-479-8227 (bullets)
Division Lead, 7742 W. 61 Pl., Summit, IL 60502
Du Pont, Explosives Dept., Wilmington, DE 19898
Dynamit Nobel of America, Inc., 105 Stonehurst Court, Northvale, NJ 07647/201-767-1660 (RWS percussion caps)
Eagle Bullet Works, P.O. Box 2104, White City, OR 97503 (Div-Cor.375, .224, .257 cust. bull.)
Eagle Cap Custom Bullets, P.O. Box 659, Enterprise, OR 97828/503-426-4282
Elk Mountain Shooters Supply Inc., 1719 Marie, Pasco, WA 99301 (Alaskan bullets)
Excaliber Wax, Inc., P.O. Box 432, Kenton, OH 43326/419-673-0512 (wax bullets)
Federal Cartridge Co., 2700 Foshay Tower, Minneapolis, MN 55402/612-333-8255 (nickel cases)
FFV Norma, Inc., 300 S. Jefferson, Suite 301, Springfield, MO 65806 (powder)
Fisher Enterprises, 655 Main St. #305, Edmonds, WA 98020/206-776-4365
Forty Five Ranch Enterprises, 119 S. Main, Miami, OK 74354/918-542-9307
Glaser Safety Slug, 711 Somerset Lane, P.O. Box 8223, Forest City, CA 94404
Godfrey Reloading Supply, Hi-Way 67-111, Brighton, IL 62012 (cast bullets)
Lynn Godfrey, (See: Elk Mtn. Shooters Supply)
GOEX, Inc., Belin Plant, Moosic, PA 18507/717-457-6724 (black powder)
Green Bay Bullets, P.O. Box 10446, 1486 Servais St., Green Bay, WI 54307-54304/414-469-2992 (cast lead bullets)
Grills-Hanna Bulletsmith Co., Lt., Box 655, Black Diamond, Alb. TOL OHO Canada/403-652-4393 (38, 9mm, 12-ga.)
Hansen Custom Bullets, 3221 Shelley St., Mohegan, NY 10547
Hardin Specialty Distr., P.O. Box 338, Radcliff, KY 40160/502-351-6649 (empty, primed cases)
Hercules, Inc., Hercules Plaza, Wilmington, DE 19894 (smokeless powder)
Hodgdon Powder Co. Inc., P.O. Box 2932, Shawnee Mission, KS 66201/913-362-9455
Hornady Mfg. Co., P.O. Drawer 1848, Grand Island, NE 68802/308-382-1390
Illinois Custom Bullet Mfg., R.R. 1, Dunlap, IL 61525/309-685-1392 (handgun, heavy game, silhouette)
Kendall Inernational Arms, 501 East North, Carlisle, KY 40311/606-289-7336 (Lapua bull.)
NORMA (See FFV Norma)
N.E. House Co., 195 West High St., E. Hampton, CT 06424/203-267-2133 (zinc bases in .30, .38, .44 and .45-cal. only)
Jaro Manuf., P.O. Box 6125, 206 E. Shaw, Pasadena, TX 77506/713-472-0471 (bullets)
J&J Custom Bullet, 1210 El Rey Ave., El Cajon, CA 92021 (Power-Pak)
J&P Enterprises, SR 80219, Fairbanks, AK 99701/907-488-1534 (Grizzly 4-cal. ogive 32&49 mil. bonded core tubing bull.)
Ka Pu Kapili, P.O. Box 745, Honokaa, HI 96272 (Hawaiian Special cust. bullets)
Kodiak Custom Bullets, 8261 Henry Circle, Anchorage, AK 99507
L.L.F. Die Shop, 1281 Highway 99 North, Eugene, OR 97402/503-688-5753
Lomont Precision Bullets, 4236 West 700 South, Poneto, IN 46781/219-694-6792 (custom cast bullets)
Lyman Products Corp., Rte. 147, Middlefield, CT 06455
Mack's Sport Shop, Box 1155, Kodiak, AK 99615 (cust. bull.)
Miller Trading Co., 20 S. Front St., Wilmington, NC 28401/919-762-7107 (bullets)
Morrison Custom Bullet Corp., P.O. Box 5574, Sta. Edmonton, Alb. T6C 3T5 Canada (9mm, .357 handgun)
Nosler Bullets Inc., 107 S.W. Columbia, Bend, OR 97702/503-382-5108
Ohio Shooters Supply, 7532 Tyler Blvd., Mentor, OH 44060 (cast bullets)
Old Western Scrounger, 12924 Hwy A-12, Montague, CA 96064/916-459-5445
Omark Industries, Box 856, Lewiston, ID 83501/208-746-2351
The Oster Group, 50 Sims Ave., Providence, RI 02909 (alloys f. casting bull.)
PMC Ammunition, 5400 Wilshire Blvd., Suite 1400, Los Angeles, CA 90036/213-938-3201
Pyrodex, See: Hodgdon Powder Co., Inc. (black powder substitute)
Robert Pomeroy, Morison Ave., East Corinth, ME 04427/207-285-7721 (empty cases)
Power Plus Enterprises, 6939 Macon Rd. #15, Columbus, GA 31907/404-561-1717 (12-ga. shotguns slugs; .308, .45 ACP, .357 cust. bull.)
Prospect Bullet Co., 1620 Holmes Ave., Prospect Park, PA 19076/215-586-6240 (9mm, .38 cust.)
Redwood Bullet Works, 3559 Bay Rd., Redwood City, CA 94063 (cust.)
Remington-Peters, 1007 Market St., Wilmington, DE 19898
S&S Precision Bullets, 22965 La Cadena, Laguna Hills, CA 92653/714-768-6836 (linotype cast bull.)
Sansom Bullets, 2506 Rolling Hills Dr., Greenville, TX 75401 (custom)
Sierra Bullets Inc., 10532 So. Painter Ave., Santa Fe Springs, CA 90670
Speer Products, Box 856, Lewiston, ID 83501
Supreme Products Co., 1830 S. California Ave., Monrovia, CA 91016/800-423-7159/818-357-5395 (rubber bullets)
Tallon Bullets, 1194 Tidewood Dr., Bethel Park, PA 15102/412-471-4494 (dual. diam. 308 cust.)
Taracorp Industries, 16th & Cleveland Blvd., Granite City, IL 62040/618-451-4400 (Lawrence Brand lead shot)

Traft Gunshop, P.O. Box 1078, Buena Vista, CO 81211/303-395-6034 (cust. bull.)
Winchester, Shamrock St., East Alton, IL 62024
Zero Bullet Co. Inc., P.O. Box 1188, Cullman, AL 35055/205-739-1606

BULLET SWAGE DIES AND TOOLS

C-H Tool & Die Corp., 106 N. Harding St., Owen, WI 54460/715-229-2146
Lester Coats, 416 Simpson Ave. North Bend, OR 97459/503-756-6995 (lead wire core cutter)
Corbin Mfg. & Supply Inc., P.O. Box 2659, White City, OR 97503/503-826-5211
Hollywood, 7311 Radford Ave., No. Hollywood, CA 91605/213-875-1131
Huntington Die Specialties, P.O. Box 991, Oroville, CA 95965/916-534-1210
Independent Machine & Gun Shop, 1416 N. Hayes, Pocatello, ID 83201/208-232-1264 (TNT bullet dies)
MSS Industries, P.O. Box 6, River Grove, IL 60171 (tool)
L.L.F. Die Shop, 1281 Highway 99 North, Eugene, OR 97402/503-688-5753
Rorschach Precision Products, P.O. Box 151613, Irving, TX 75015/214-790-3487
SAS Dies, (See Corbin Mfg. & Supply)
Sport Flite Mfg., Inc., 2520 Industrial Row, Troy, MI 48084/313-280-0648
TNT (See Ind. Mach. & Gun Shop)

CHRONOGRAPHS AND PRESSURE TOOLS

Benson Ballistics, Box 3796, Mission Viejo, CA 92690-1796
B-Square Co., Box 11281, Ft. Worth, TX 76110/800-433-2909
Custom Chronograph Co., Rt. 1, Box 98, Brewster, WA 98812/509-689-2004
H-S Precision, Inc., 112 N. Summit St, Prescott, AZ 86302/602-445-0607 (press, barrels)
Paul Jaeger, Inc., P.O. Box 449, 1 Madison Ave., Grand Junction, TN 38039
Oehler Research, Inc., P.O. Box 9135, Austin, TX 78766/512-327-6900
Telepacific Electronics Co., Inc., P.O. Box 1329, San Marcos, CA 92069/714-744-4415
Tepeco, P.O. Box 342, Friendswood, TX 77546/713-482-2702 (Tepeco Speed-Meter)
M. York, 5508 Griffith Rd., Gaithersburg, MD 20760/301-253-4217 (press. tool)

GUNS (Foreign)

Action Arms, P.O. Box 9573, Philadelphia, PA 19124/215-744-0100
American Arms Inc., P.O. Box 27163, Salt Lake City, UT 84127/801-972-5006
Armoury Inc., Rte. 202, New Preston, CT 06777
Bauska Arms Corp., P.O. Box 1995, Kalispell, MT 59903/406-752-2072
Benelli Armi, S.p.A., via della Stazione 50, 61029 Urbino, Italy
Beretta U.S.A., 17601 Indian Head Highway, Accokeek, MD 20607/301-283-2191
Browning (Gen. Offices), Rt. 1, Morgan, UT 84050/801-876-2711
Century Arms Co., 3-5 Federal St., St. Albans, VT 05478
E.M.F. Co. Inc., (Early & Modern Firearms), 1900 E. Warner Ave. 1-D, Santa Ana, CA 92705/714-966-0202
Firearms Imp. & Exp. Corp., (F.I.E.), P.O. Box 4866, Hialeah Lakes, Hialeah, FL 33014/305-685-5966
Glock, Inc., 500 Highlands Pkwy., Suite 190, Smyrna, GA 30080
Goncz Armament, 11526 Burbank Blvd., #18, N. Hollywood, CA 91601/818-505-0408
Gun South, Dept. Steyr, Box 6607, 7605 Eastwood Mall, Birmingham, AL 35210/205-592-7932 (Steyr, FN)
Heckler & Koch Inc., 14601 Lee Rd., Chantilly, VA 22021/703-631-2800
Interarms Ltd., 10 Prince St., Alexandria, VA 22313 (Mauser, Valmet M-62/S)
John Jovino Co., 5 Centre Market Pl, New York, NY 10013/212-925-4881 (Terminator)
Kassnar Imports, 5480 Linglestown Rd. Harrisburg, PA 17110
Llama (See Stoeger)
Magnum Research, Inc., 7271 Commerce Circle West, Minneapolis, MN 55432/612-574-1868 (Israeli Galil)
Mannlicher (See Steyr Daimler Puch of Amer.)
Manufrance, See: Armssource, Inc.
Manurhin, See: Matra-Manurhin
Matra-Manurhin International, Inc., 631 S. Washington St., Alexandria, VA 22314/703-836-8886
Mitchell Arms, 2101 E. 4th St., Suite 201A, Santa Ana, CA 92705
Osborne's, P.O. Box 408, Cheboygan, MI 49721/616-625-9626
Pachmayr Gun Works, 1220 S. Grand Ave., Los Angeles, CA 90015
Sigarms, 8330 Old Courthouse Rd., Suite 885, Tysons Corner, VA 22180/703-893-1940
Sile Distributors, 7 Centre Market Pl., New York, NY 10013/212-925-4111
Steyr-Daimler-Puch, Gun South, Inc., Box 6607, 7605 Eastwood Mall, Birmingham, AL 35210/800-821-3021 (rifles)
Stoeger Industries, 55 Ruta Court, S. Hackensack, NJ 07606/201-440-2700
Taurus International Mfg. Inc., P.O. Box 558567, Ludlam Br., Miami, FL 33155/305-662-2529

GUNS, U.S.-made

AMT (Arcadia Machine & Tool), 536 N. Vincent Ave., Covina, CA 91722/818-915-7803
American Derringer Corp., 127 N. Lacy Dr., Waco, TX 76705/817-799-9111
Armament Systems and Procedure, Inc., Box 356, Appleton, WI 54912/414-731-8893 (ASP pistol)
Arminex Ltd., 7882 E. Gray Rd., Scottsdale, AZ 85260/602-998-0443
Auto-Ordnance Corp., Box GD, West Hurley, NY 12491/914-679-7225
Browning (Gen. Offices), Rt. 1, Morgan, UT 84050/801-876-2711
Charter Arms Corp., 430 Sniffens Ln., Stratford, CT 06497
Colt Firearms, P.O. Box 1868, Hartford, CT 06102/203-236-6311
Coonan Arms, Inc., 830 Hampden Ave., St. Paul, MN 55114/612-646-6682 (.357 mag. auto.)

Detonics Mfg. Corp., 13456 S.E. 27th Pl, Bellevue, WA 98005/206-747-2100
Encom American, Inc., P.O. Box 5314, Atlanta, GA 30307/404-525-2811
Firearms Imp. & Exp. Corp., P.O. Box 4866, Hialeah Lakes, Hialeah, FL 33014/305-685-5966 (FIE)
Iver Johnson, 2202 Redmond Rd., Jacksonville, AR 72076/501-982-9491
L.A.R. Manufacturing Co., 4133 West Farm Rd., West Jordan, UT 84084/801-255-7106 (Grizzly Win mag pistol)
Magnum Sales, Subs. of Mag-na-port, 41302 Executive Drive, Mt. Clemens, MI 48045/313-469-7534
Mitchell Arms, 2101 E. 4th St., Suite 201A, Santa Ana, CA 92705
Numrich Arms Corp., W. Hurley, NY 12491
Philips & Bailey, Inc., P.O. Box 219253, Houston, TX 77218/713-392-0207 (.357/9 Ultra, rev. conv.)
Ruger (See Sturm, Ruger & Co.)
L.W. Seecamp Co., Inc., P.O. Box 255, New Haven, CT 06502/203-877-3429
Smith & Wesson, Inc., 2100 Roosevelt Ave., Springfield, MA 01101
Springfield Armory, Inc., 420 W. Main St., Geneseo, IL 61254/309-944-5138
Steel City Arms, Inc., P.O. box 81926, Pittsburgh, PA 15217/412-461-3100
Sterling Arms Corp., 211 Grand St., Lockport, NY 14094/716-434-6631
Thompson-Center Arms, P.O. Box 2426, Rochester, NH 03867/603-332-2394
Weaver Arms Corp., 115 No. Market Pl., Escondido, CA 92025/619-746-2440
Dan Wesson Arms, 293 So. Main St., Monson, MA 01057
Wilkinson Arms, Rte. #2, Box 2166, Parma, ID 83660/208-722-6771

HANDGUN ACCESSORIES

Ajax Custom Grips, Inc., 12229 Cox Lane, Dallas, TX 75244/241-6302
Bob Allen Companies, 214 S.W. Jackson St. Des Moines, IA 50302/515-283-2191
American Gas & Chemical Co., Ltd., 220 Pegasus Ave., Northvale, MJ 07467/201-767-7300 (clg. lube)
Armson, Inc., P.O. Box 2130, Farmington Hills, MI 48018/313-478-2577
Armsport, Inc., 3590 N.W. 49th St., Miami, FL 33142/305-635-7850
Assault Accessories, P.O. Box 8994 CRB, Tucson, AZ 85738/602-791-7860 (pistol shoulder stocks)
Baramie Corp., 6250 E. 7 Mile Rd., Detroit, MI 48234 (Hip-Grip)
Bar-Sto Precision Machine, 73377 Sullivan Rd., Twentynine Palms, CA 92288/619-367-2747
Behlert Custom Guns, Inc., RD 2 Box 36C, Route 611 North, Pipersville, PA 18947/215-766-8680
Bingham Ltd., 1775-C Wilwat Dr., Norcross, GA 30093 (magazines)
C'Arco (See Ransom International)
Central Specialties Co., 200 Lexington Dr., Buffalo Grove, IL 60090/312-537-3300 (trigger lock)
Dave Chicoine, d/b/a/ Liberty A.S.P., 19 Key St., Eastport, ME 04631/207-853-2327 (shims f. S&W revs.)
D&E Magazines Mfg., P.O. Box 4876, Sylmar, CA 91342 (clips)
Doskocil Mfg. Co., Inc., P.O. Box 1246, Arlington, TX 75010/817-467-5116 (Gun Guard cases)
Essex Arms, Box 345, Island Pond, VT 05846/802-723-4313 (45 Auto frames)
Frielich Police Equipment, 396 Broome St., New York, NY 10013/212-254-3045 (cases)
R.S. Frielich, 211 East 21st St., New York, NY 10010/212-777-4477 (cases)
Terry K. Kopp, Highway 13, Lexington, MO 64067/816-259-2636
Lee Precision Inc., 4275 Hwy. U, Hartford, WI 53027 (pistol rest holders)
Kent Lomont, 4236 West 700 South, Poneto, IN 46781 (Auto Mag only)
Lone Star Gunleather, 1301 Brushy Bend Dr., Round Rock, TX 78664/512-255-1805
Los Gatos Grip & Specialty Co., P.O. Box 1850, Los Gatos, CA 95030 (custom-made)
MTM Molded Prods. Oc., 3370 Obco Ct., Dayton, OH 54414/513-890-7461
No-Sho Mfg. Co., 10727 Glenfield Ct., Houston, TX 77096/713-723-0966
Harry Owen (See Sport Specialties)
Pachmayr, 1220 S. Grand, Los Angeles, CA 90015 (cases)
Pacific Intl. Mchdsg. Corp., 2215 "J" St., Sacramento, CA 95818/916-446-2737 (Vega .45 Colt comb. mag.)
Poly-Choke Div., Marble Arms Corp., 420 Industrial Park, Gladstone, MI 49837/906-428-3710 (handgun ribs)
Ransom International, P.O. Box 3845, 1040 Sandretto Dr., Ste. 1, Prescott, AZ 86302/602-778-7899 (Ransom rest)
Sile Distributors, 7 Centre Market Pl., New York, NY 10013
Sport Specialties, (Harry Owen), Box 5337, Hacienda Hts., CA 91745/213-968-5806 (.22 rimfire adapters; .22 insert bbls. f. T/C Contender, autom. pistols)
Sportsmen's Equipment Co., 415 W. Washington, San Diego, CA 92103/619-296-1501
Turkey Creek Enterprises, Rt. 1, Box 10, Red Oak, CA 74563/918-754-2884 (wood handgun cases)
Melvin Tyler, 1326 W. Britton, Oklahoma City, OK 73114/800-654-8415 (grip adaptor)

HANDGUN GRIPS

Ajax Custom Grips, Inc., 12229 Cox Lane, Dallas, TX 75234/214-241-6302
Art Jewel Enterprises Ltd., 421A Irmen Dr., Addison, IL 60101/312-628-6220
Barami Corp., 6250 East 7 Mile Rd., Detroit, MI 48234/313-891-2536
Bear Hug Grips, P.O. Box 9664, Colorado Springs, CO 80909
Bingham Ltd., 1775-C Wilwat Dr., Norcross, GA 30093
Boone's Custom Ivory Grips, Inc., 562 Coyote Rd., Brinnon, WA 98320/206-796-4330
Dave Chicoine, d/b/a/ Liberty A.S.P., 19 Key St., Eastport, ME 04631/207-853-2327 (orig. S&W 1855-1950)

Fitz Pistol Grip Co., Box 171, Douglas City, CA 96024

Gateway Shooters' Supply, Inc., 10145-103rd St., Jacksonville, FL 32210/904-778-2323 (Rogers grips)

Herrett's, Box 741, Twin Falls, ID 83301

Hogue Combat Grips, P.O. Box 2038, Atascadero, CA 93423/805-466-6266 (Monogrip)

Paul Jones Munitions Systems, (See Fitz Co.)

Russ Maloni, (See: Russwood)

Millett Industries, 16131 Gothard St., Huntington Beach, CA 92647/714-842-5575 (custom)

Monogrip, (See Hogue)

Monte Kristo Pistol Grip Co., Box 171, Douglas City, CA 96024/916-778-3136

Mustang Custom Pistol Grips, see: Supreme Products Co.

Pachmayr Gun Works, Inc., 1220 S. Grand Ave., Los Angeles, CA 90015/213-748-7271

Robert H. Newell, 55 Coyote, Los Alamos, NM 87544/505-662-7135 (custom stocks)

Rogers Grips (See Gateway Shooters' Supply)

A. Jack Rosenberg & Sons, 12229 Cox Lane, Dallas, TX 75234/214-241-6302 (Ajax)

Royal Ordnance Works Ltd., P.O. Box 3254, Wilson, NC 27893/919-237-0515

Russwood Custom Pistol Grips, 40 Sigman Lane, Elma, NY 14059/716-652-7131 (cust. exotic woods)

Jean St. Henri, 6525 Dume Dr., Malibu, CA 90265/213-457-7211 (custom)

Sile Dist., 7 Centre Market Pl., New York, NY 10013/212-925-4111

Sports Inc., P.O. Box 683, Park Ridge, IL 60068/312-825-8952 (Franzite)

Supreme Products Co., 1830 S. California Ave., Monrovia, CA 91016/800-423-7159/818-357-5359

Sergeant Violin, P.O. Box 25808, Tamarac, FL 33320/305-721-7856 (wood pistol stocks)

R.D Wallace, Star Rte. Box 76, Grandin, MO 63943

Wayland Prec. Wood Prods., Box 1142, Mill Valley, CA 94942/415-381-3543

HEARING PROTECTORS

AO Safety Prods., Div. of American Optical Corp., 14 Mechanic St., Southbridge, MA 01550/617-9711 (ear valves, ear muffs)

Bausch & Lomb, 635 St. Paul St., Rochester, NY 14602

Bilsom Interntl., Inc., 11800 Sunrise Valley Dr., Reston, VA 22091/703-620-3950 (ear plugs, muffs)

David Clark Co., Inc., 360 Franklin St., Worcester, MA 01604

Marble Arms Corp., 420 Industrial Park. Gladstone, MI 49837/906-428-3710

North Consumer Prods. Div., 16624 Edwards Rd., P.O. Box 7500, Cerritos, CA 90701/213-926-0545 (Lee Sonic ear valves)

Safety Direct, 23 Snider Way, Sparks, NV 89431/702-345-4451 (Silencio)

Smith & Wesson, 2100 Roosevelt Ave., Springfield, MA 01101

Willson Safety Prods. Div., P.O. Box 622, Reading, PA 19603 (Ray-O-Vac)

HOLSTERS & LEATHER GOODS

Active Leather Corp., 36-29 Vernon Blvd., Long Island City, NY 11106

Alessi Custom Concealment Holsters, 2465 Niagara Falls Blvd., Tonawanda, NY 14150/716-691-5615

Allen Firearms Co., 2879 All Trades Rd., Santa Fe, NM 87501/505-471-6090

Bob Allen Companies, 214 S.W. Jackson, Des Moines, IA 50315/515-283-2191

American Sales & Mfg. Co., P.O. Box 677, Laredo, TX 78040/512-723-6893

Andy Anderson, P.O. Box 225, North Hollywood, CA 91603/213-877-2401 (Gunfighter Custom Holsters)

Armament Systems & Procedures, Inc., P.O. Box 356, Appleton, WI 54912/414-731-8893 (ASP)

Rick M. Bachman (see Old West Reproductions)

Barami Corp., 6250 East 7 Mile Rd., Detroit, MI 48234/313-891-2536

Beeman Inc., 47-GDD Paul Dr., San Rafael, CA 94903/415-472-7121

Behlert Custom Guns, Inc., RD 2 Box 36C, Route 611 North, Pipersville, PA 18947/215-766-8680

Bianchi International Inc., 100 Calle Cortez, Temecula, CA 92390/714-676-5621

Ted Blocker's Custom Holsters, 409 West Bonita Ave., San Dimas, CA 91773/714-599-4415

Bo-Mar Tool & Mfg. Co., Rt. 12, Box 405, Longview, TX 75605/214-759-4784

Boyt Co., Div. of Welsh Sptg., P.O. Box 220, Iowa Falls, IA 51026/515-648-4626

Brauer Bros. Mfg. Co., 2012 Washington Blvd., St. Louis, MO 63103/314-231-2864

Browning, Rt. 4, Box 624-B, Arnold, MO 63101

J.M. Bucheimer Co., P.O. Box 280, Airport Rd., Frederick, MD 21701/301-662-5101

Buffalo Leather Goods, Inc., Rt. 4, Box 187, Magnolia, AR 71753/501-234-6367

Cathey Enterprises, Inc., 9516 Neils Thompson Dr., Suite 116, Austin, TX 78759/512-837-7150

Cattle Baron Leather Co., P.O. Box 100724, San Antonio, TX 78201/512-697-8900 (ctlg. $3)

Chace Leather Prods., Longhorn Div., 507 Alden St., Fall River, MA 02772/617-678-7556

Cherokee Gun Accessories, 4127 Bay St., Suite 226, Fremont, CA 94538/415-471-5770

Daisy Mfg. Co., P.O. Box 220, Rogers, AR 72756/501-636-1200

Davis Leather Co., G Wm. Davis, 3930 "F" Valley Blvd., Walnut, CA 91789/714-598-5620

Eugene DeMayo & Sons, Inc., 2795 Third Ave., Bronx, NY 10455/212-665-7075

DeSantis Gunhide, 140 Denton Ave., New Hyde Park, NY 11040/516-354-8000

Ellwood Epps Northern Ltd., 210 Worthington St. W., North Bay, Ont. P1B 3B4, Canada (custom made)

GALCO Gun Leather, 4311 W. Van Buren, Phoenix, AZ 85043/602-233-0596

Gunfighter (See Anderson)

Ernie Hill Speed Leather, 3128 S. Extension Rd. Mesa, AZ 85202

Hoyt Holster Co., Inc., P.O. Box 69, Coupeville, WA 98239/206-678-6640

Don Hume, Box 351, Miami, OK 74354/918-542-6604

Hunter Corp., 3300 W. 71st Ave., Westminster, CO 80030/303-427-4626

John's Custom Leather, 525 S. Liberty St., Blairsville, PA 15717/412-459-6802

Jumbo Sports Prods., P.O. Box 280, Airport Rd., Frederick, MD 21701

Kane Products, Inc., 5572 Brecksville Rd., Cleveland, OH 44131/216-524-9962 (GunChaps)

Kirkpatrick Leather Co., P.O. Box 3150, Laredo, TX 78044/512-723-6631

Kolpin Mfg. Inc., P.O. Box 231, Berlin, WI 54923/414-361-0400

Morris Lawing, 150 Garland Ct., Charlotte, NC 28202/704-375-1740

George Lawrence Co., 1435 N.W. Northrup, Portland, OR 97209/503-228-8244

Lone Star Gunleather, 1301 Brushy Bend Dr., Round Rock, TX 78664/512-255-1805

Michael's of Oregon Co., P.O. Box 13010, Portland, OR 97213/503-225-6890 (Uncle Mike's)

Mixson Leathercraft Inc., 1950 W. 84th St., Hialeah, FL 33014/305-820-5190 (police leather products)

Nordac Mfg. Corp., Rt. 12, Box 124, Fredericksburg, VA 22405/703-752-2552

No-Sho Mfg. Co., 10727 Glenfield Ct., Houston, TX 77096/713-723-5332

Kenneth L. Null-Custom Concealment Holsters. R.D. #5, Box 197, Hanover, PA 17331 (See Seventrees)

Old West Reproductions, R.M. Bachman, 1840 Stag Lane, Kalispell, MT 59901, 406-755-6902 (ctlg. $3)

Pioneer Prods. P.O. Box G, Magnolia. AR 71753/501-234-1566

Pony Express Sport Shop Inc., 1606 Schoenborn St., Sepulveda, CA 91343/818-895-1231

Red Head Brand Corp., 4949 Joseph Hardin Dr., Dallas, TX 75236/214-333-4141

Red River Outfitters, P.O. Box 241, Tujunga, CA 91042/213-352-0177

Rogers Holsters Co., Inc., 1736 St. Johns Bluff Rd., Jacksonville, FL 32216/904-641-9434

Roy's Custom Leather Goods, Hwy. 1325 & Rawhide Ln., P.O. Box G, Magnolia, AR 71753/501-234-1566

Safariland Leather Products, 1941 So. Walker Ave., Monrovia, CA 91016/818-357-7902

Safety Speed Holster, Inc., 4949 So. Vail, Montebello, CA 90640/213-723-4140

Buddy Schoellkopf Products, Inc., 4949 Joseph Hardin Dr., TX 75236/214-333-2121

Schulz Industries, 16247 Minnesota Ave., Paramount, CA 90723/213-636-7718

Seventrees Systems Ltd., R.D. 5, Box 197, Hanover, PA 17331/717-632-6873 (See Null)

Sile Dstr., 7 Centre Market Pl, New York, NY 10013/212-925-4111

Milt Sparks, Box 187, Idaho City, ID 83631/208-392-6695 (broch. $2)

Robert A. Strong Co., 105 Maplewood Ave., Gloucester, MA 01930/617-281-3300

Torel, Inc., 1053 N. South St., P.O. Box 592, Yoakum, TX 77995/512-293-2341 (gun slings)

Triple-K Mfg. Co., 568 Sixth Ave., San Diego, CA 92101/619-232-2066

Viking Leathercraft, Inc., P.O. Box 2030, 2248-2 Main St., Chula Vista, CA 92012/619-429-8050

LABELS, BOXES, CARTRIDGE HOLDERS

Milton Brynin, 214 E. Third St., Mount Vernon, NY 10550/914-667-6549 (cartridge box labels)

Corbin Mfg. & Supply, Inc., P.O. Box 2659, White City, OR 97503/503-826-5211

Del Rey Products, P.O. Box 91561, Los Angeles, CA 90009/213-823-0494

E-Z Loader, Del Rey Products, P.O. Box 91561, Los Angeles, CA 90009

Hunter Co., Inc. 3300 W. 71st Ave., Westminster, CO 80030/303-472-4626 (cartridge holders)

Peterson Label Co., P.O. Box 186, 23 Sullivan Dr., Redding Ridge, CT 06876/203-938-2349 (cartridge box labels; Targ-Dots)

LOAD TESTING and PRODUCT TESTING, (CHRONOGRAPHING, BALLISTIC STUDIES)

Accuracy Systems, Inc., 15203 N. Cave Creek Rd., Phoenix, AZ 85032/602-971-1991

Hutton Rifle Ranch, P.O. Box 45236, Boise, ID 83771/208-9841

Kent Lomont, 4236 West 700 South, Poneto, IN 45781/219-694-6792 (handguns, handgun ammunition)

Plum City Ballistics Range, Norman E. Johnson, Rte. 1, Box 29A, Plum City, WI 54761/715-647-2539

Russell's Rifle Shop, Rte. 5, Box 92, Georgetown, TX 78626/512-778-5338 (load testing and chronographing to 300 yds.)

John M. Tovey, 4710-10th Lane NE, Circle Pines, MN 55014/612-786-7268

H.P. White Laboratory, Inc., 3114 Scarboro Rd., Street, MD 21154/301-838-6550

PISTOLSMITHS

Armament Gunsmithing Co., Inc., 525 Route 22, Hillside, NJ 07205/201-686-0960

Armson, Inc., P.O. Box 2130, Farmington Hills, MI 48018/313-478-2577

Baer Custom Guns, 1725 Minesite Rd., Allentown, PA 18103/215-398-2362 (accurizing .45 autos and comp II Syst.; cust. XP100s, P.P.C. rev.)

Bain and Davis Sptg. Gds., 307 E. Valley Blvd., San Gabriel, CA 91776/213-573-4241

Bar-Sto Precision Machine, 73377 Sullivan Rd., Twentynine Palms, CA 92277/ 619-367-2747 (S.S bbls. f. .45 ACP)

Barta's Gunsmithing, 10231 US Hwy. #10, Cato, WI 54206/414-732-4472

R.J. Beal, Jr., 170 W. Marshall Rd., Lansdowne, PA 19050/215-259-1220 (conversions, SASE f. inquiry)

Behlert Custom Guns, Inc., RD 2 Box 36C, Route 611 North, Pipersville, PA 18947 215-766-8680 (short actions)

Bell's Custom Shop, 3309 Mannheim Rd., Franklin Park, IL 60131/312-678-1900

Bob's Gun & Tackle Shop, 746 Granby St., Norfolk, VA 23510/804-627-8311

F. Bob Chow, Gun Shop, Inc., 3185 Mission, San Francisco, CA 94110/415-282-8358

Brown Custom Guns, Inc., Steven N. Brown, 8810 Rocky Ridge Rd., Indianapolis, IN 46217/317-881-2771 aft. 5 PM

Leo Bustani, P.O. Box 8125, W. Palm Beach, FL 33407/305-622-2710

Dick Campbell, 1198 Finn Ave., Littleton, CO 80124/303-799-0145 (PPC guns; custom)

Cellini's, Francesca Inc., 3115 Old Ranch Rd., San Antonio, TX 78217/512-826-2584

D&D Chicoine, d/b/a Liberty A.S.P., 19 Key St., Eastport, ME 04631/207-853-2327 (rep. & rest. of early S&W prods.)

Davis Co., 2793 Del Monte St., West Sacramento, CA 95691/916-372-6789

Day Arms Corp., 2412 S.W. Loop 410, San Antonio, TX 78227/512-674-5220

Dominic DiStefano, 4303 Friar Lane, Colorado Springs, CO 80907/303-599-3366 (accurizing)

Duncan's Gunworks Inc., 1619 Grand Ave., San Marcos, CA 92069/619-727-0515

Dan Dwyer, 915 W. Washington, San Diego, CA 92103/619-296-1501

Englishtown Sptg. Gds. Co. Inc., David J. Maxham, 38 Main St., Englishtown, NJ 07726/201-446-7717

Jack First Distributors, Inc., 44633 Sierra Hwy., Lancaster, CA 93534/805-945-8961

Fountain Prods., 492 Prospect Ave., W. Springfield, MA 01089/413-781-4651

Frielich Police Equipment, 396 Broome St., New York, NY 10013/212-254-3045

Giles' 45 Shop, 8614 Tarpon Springs Rd., Odessa, FL 33556/813-920-5366

Gilman-Mayfield, 1552 N. 1st., Fresno, CA 93704/209-237-2500

The Gunworks Inc., John Hanus, 3434 Maple Ave., Brookfield, IL 60513/312-387-7888

Gil Hebard Guns, Box 1, Knoxville, IL 61448

Paul Jaeger, Inc., P.O. Box 449, 1 Madison Ave., Grand Junction, TX 38039

J.D. Jones, Rt. 1, Della Dr., Bloomingdale, OH 43910/614-264-0176

L.E. Jurras & Assoc., P.O. Box 680, Washington, IN 47501/812-254-7698

Kart Sptg. Arms Corp., 1190 Old County Rd., Riverhead, NY 11901/516-727-2719 (handgun conversions)

Ken's Gun Specialties, Rt. 1 Box 147, Lakeview, AR 72642/501-431-5606

Benjamin Kilham, Kilham & Co., Main St., Box 37, Lyme, NH 03768/603-795-4112

Terry K. Kopp, Highway 13, Lexington, MO 64067/816-259-2636 (rebblg., conversions)

John G. Lawson, The Sight Shop, 1802 E. Columbia Ave., Tacoma, WA 98404/206-474-5465

Kent Lomont, 4236 West South, Poneto, IN 46781/219-694-6792 (Auto Mag only)

Mag-na-port International, Inc., 41302 Executive Drive, Mt. Clemens, MI 48045/313-469-6727

Robert A. McGrew, 3315 Michigan Ave., Colorado Springs, CO 80910/303-636-1940

Rudolf Marent, 9711 Tiltree, Houston, TX 77075/713-946-7028 (Hammerli)

Elwyn H. Martin, Martin's Gun Shop, 937 So. Sheridan Blvd., Lakewood, CO 80226/303-922-2184

Conley E. Morris, 2135 Waterlevel Hwy., Cleveland, TN 37311/615-476-3984

Nu-Line Guns, 1053 Caulks Hill Rd., Harvester, MO 63303/314-441-4501

Pachmayr Gun Works, 1220 S. Grand Ave., Los Angeles, CA 90015

Paterson Gunsmithing, 438 Main St., Paterson, NJ 07502/201-345-4100

Ron Power, Power Custom, P.O. Box 2176, Shawnee Mission, KS 66201/816-833-3102

RPS Gunshop, 11 So. Haskell St., Central Point, OR 97502/503-664-5010

Bob Rogers Gunsmithing, P.O. Box 305, Franklin Grove, IL 61031/815-456-2685 (custom)

SSK Industries (See: J.D. Jones)

L.W Seecamp Co., Inc., Box 255, New Haven, CT 06502/203-877-3429 (DA Colt auto conversions)

Hank Shows, dba The Best, 1078 Alice Ave., Ukiah, CA 95482/707-462-9060

Silver Dollar Guns, P.O. Box 475, 10 Frances St., Franklin, NH 03235/603-934-3292 (45 ACP)

Spokhandguns Inc., Vern D. Ewer, P.O. Box 370, 1206 Fig St., Benton City, WA 99320

Sportsmens Equipmt. Co., 915 W. Washington, San Diego, CA 92103/619-296-1501 (specialty limiting trigger motion in autos)

Irving O. Stone, Jr., 73377 Sullivan Rd., Twentynine Palms, CA 92277/619-367-2747 (Bar-Sto)

Victor W. Strawbridge, 6 Pineview Dr., Dover Pt., Dover HN 03820

A.D. Swenson's 45 Shop, P.O. Box 606, Fallbrook, CA 92028

Trapper Gun, 18717 East 14 Mile Rd., Fraser, MI 48026/313-792-0134

Dennis A. "Doc" Ulrich, 2209 So. Central Ave., Cicero, IL 60650/312-652-3606

Vic's Gun Refinishing, 6 Pineview Dr., Dover, NH 03820/603-742-0013

Walters Industries, 6226 Park Lane, Dallas, TX 75225/214-691-5150

Chuck Ward, Box 610, Raymore, MO 64083/816-331-3857

RELOADING TOOLS AND ACCESSORIES

Advance Car Mover Co., Inc. Rowell Div., P.O. Box 1181, 112 N. Outagamie St., Appleton, WI 54912/414-734-1878 (bottom pour lead casting ladles)

Accessory Specialty Co., 2711 So. 84th St., West Allis, WI 53227/414-545-0879 (Reload-a-stand)

Advanced Precision Prods. Co., 5183 Flintrock Dr., Westerville, OH 43081/614-895-0560 (case super luber)

Ammo Load Inc., 1560 E. Edinger, Suite G, Santa Ana, CA 92705/714-558-8858

- C'Arco (See Ransom International)

Colorado Sutler Arsenal, 6225 W. 46th Pl, Wheatridge, CO 80033/303-420-6383

Creighton Audette, 19 Highland Circle, Springfield, VT 05156/802-885-2331 (Universal Case Selection gauge)

B-Square Eng. Co., Box 11281, Ft. Worth, TX 76110/800-433-2909

Ballistic Prods., P.O. Box 488, 2105 Shaughnessy Circle, Long Lake, MN 55356/612-473-1550

Bear Machine Co., 2110 1st Natl. Tower, Akron, OH 44308/216-253-4039

Belding & Mull, Inc., P.O. Box 428, 100 N. 4th St., Phillipsburg, PA 16866/814-342-0607

Berdon Machine Co., Box 483, Hobart, WA 98025/206-392-1866 (metallic press)

Blackhawk West, R.L. Hough, Box 285, Hiawatha, KS 66434/303-366-3659

Bonanza (See Forster Products)

Gene Bowlin, Rt. 1, Box 890, Snyder, TX 79549/915-573-2323 (arbor press)

C-H Tool & Die Corp., 106 N. Harding St., Owen, WI 54460/715-229-2146

Camdex, Inc., 2228 Fourteen Mile Rd., Warren, MI 48092/313-977-1620

Carbide Die & Mfg. Co., Inc., 15615 E. Arrow Hwy., Irwindale, CA 91706/213-337-2518

Carter Gun Works, 2211 Jefferson Pk. Ave., Charlottesville, VA 22903

Cascade Cartridge, Inc., (See: Omark)

Cascade Shooters, 60916 McMullin Dr., Bend, OR 97702/503-389-5872 (bull. seating depth gauge)

Chevron Case Master, R.R. 1, Ottawa, IL 61350

Lester Coats, 416 Simpson Ave., No. Bend, OR 97459/503-756-6995 (core cutter)

Container Devlopment Corp., 424 Montgomery St., Watertown, WI 53094

Continental Kite & Key Co., (CONKKO) P.O. Box 40, Broomall, PA 19008/215-356-0711 (primer pocket cleaner)

Cooper-Woodward, Box 972, Riverside, CA 92502/714-683-4295 (Perfect Lube)

Corbin Mfg. & Supply Inc., P.O. Box 2659, White City, OR 97503/503-826-5211

Custom Products, RD #1, Box 483A, Saegertown, PA 16443/814-763-2769 (decapping tool, dies, etc.)

Dillon Precision Prods., Inc., 7442 E. Butherus Dr., Scottsdale, AZ 85260/602-948-8009

Division Lead Co., 7742 W. 61st Pl, Summit, IL 60502

Eagle Products Co., 1520 Adelia Ave., So. El Monte, CA 91733

Edmisten Co. Inc., P.O. Box 1293, Hwy 105, Boone, NC 28607/704-264-1490 (I-Dent-A Handloader's Log)

Efemes Enterprises, P.O. Box 122M, Bay Shore, NY 11706 (Berdan decapper)

Fitz, Box 171, Douglas City, CA 96024 (Fitz Flipper)

Flambeau Prods. Corp., 15981 Valplast Rd., Middlefield, OH 44062/216-632-1631

Forster Products Inc., 82 E. Lanark Ave., Lanark, IL 61046/815-493-6360

Francis Tool Co., P.O. Box 7861, Eugene, OR 97401/503-746-4831 (powder measure)

Freechec' (See: Paco)

Geo. M. Fullmer, 2499 Mavis St., Oakland, CA 94601/415-533-4193 (seating die)

Gene's Gun Shop, Rt. 1, Box 890, Snyder, TX 79549/915-573-2323 (arbor press)

Hart Products, Rob. W. Hart & Son Inc., 401 Montgomery St., Nescopeck, PA 18635

Hensley & Gibbs, P.O. Box 10, Murphy, OR 97533/503-862-2341 (bullet moulds)

Hollywood Loading Tools, Inc., 7311 Radford Ave., No. Hollywood, CA 91605/213-875-1131

Hornady Mfg. Co., P.O. Drawer 1848, Grand Island, NE 68802/308-382-1390

Hulme see: Marshall Enterprises (Star case feeder)

Huntington, P.O. Box 991, Oroville, CA 95965/916-534-1210 (Compact Press)

Independent Mach. & Gun Shop, 1416 N. Hayes, Pocatello, ID 83201/208-232-1264

Javelina Products, Box 337, San Bernardino, CA 92402 (Alox beeswax)

Neil Jones, RD #1, Box 483A, Saegertown, PA 16443/814-763-2769 (decapping tool, dies)

Paul Jones Munitions Systems (See Fitz Co.)

King & Co., Edw. R. King, Box 1242, Bloomington, IL 61701/309-473-3558

Lee Precision, Inc., 4275 Hwy. U, Hartford, WI 53027/414-673-3075

L.L.F. Die Shop, 1281 Highway 99 N., Eugene, OR 97402/503-688-5753

Dean Lincoln, Custom Tackle & Ammo, P.O. Box 1886, Farmington, NM 87401 (mould)

Lock's Phila. Gun Exch., 6700 Rowland, Philadelphia, PA 19149/215-332-6225

Lyman Products Corp., Rte. 147, Middlefield, CT 06455

McKillen & Heyer Inc., 37603 Arlington Dr., Box 627, Willoughby, OH 44094/216-942-2491 (case gauge)

Paul McLean, 2670 Lakeshore Blvd., W., Toronto, Ont. M8V 1G8 Canada/416-259-3060 (Universal Cartridge Holder)

MSS Indstries, P.O. Box 6 River Grove, IL 60171

MTM Molded Products Co., 3370 Obco Ct., P.O. Box 14117, Dayton, OH 45414/513-890-7461

Magma Eng. Co., P.O. Box 161, Queen Creek, AZ 85242

Marshall Enterprises, 792 Canyon Rd., Redwood City, CA 94062/415-365-1230 (Hulme atom. case feeder f. Star rel.)

Merit Gun Sight Co., P.O. Box 995, Sequim, WA 98382/206-683-6127

Normington Co., Box 6, Rathdrum, ID 83858 (powder baffles)

Northeast Industrial Inc., N.E.I., P.O. Box 249, 405 N. Canyon Blvd., Canyon City, OR 97820/503-575-2513 (bullet mould)

Ohaus Scale, (See RCBS)
Omark Industries, Box 856, Lewiston, ID 83501/208-746-2351
Pacific Tool Co., P.O. Box 2048, Ordnance Plant Rd., Grand Island, NE 68801/308-384-2308
Paco, Box 17211, Tucson, AZ 85731 (Freecheck' tool for gas checks)
Pak-Tool Co., Roberts Products, 25238 S.E. 32nd., Issaquah, WA 98027/206-392-8172
4411 S.W. 100th, Seattle, WA 98146
Pitzer Tool Mfg. Co., RR #3, Box 50, Winterset, IA 50273/515-462-4268 (bullet lubricator & sizer)
Plum City Ballistics Range, Norman E. Johnson, Rte. 1, Box 29A, Plum City, WI 54761/715-647-2539
Marian Powley, Petra Lane, R.R. 1, Eldridge, IA 52748/319-285-9214
Quinetics Corp., P.O. Box 29007, San Antonio, TX 78229/516-684-8561 (kinetic bullet puller)
RCBS, Inc., Box 1919, Oroville, CA 95965/916-533-5191
Ransom International, P.O. Box 3845, 1040 Sandretto Dr., Ste. 1, Prescott, AZ 86302/602-778-7899 (Grand Master prog. loader)
Redding Inc., 114 Starr Rd., Cortland, NY 13045
Reloaders Paper Supply, Don Doerksen, P.O. box 556, Hines, OR 97738/503-573-7060 (reloader's record book)
Rifle Ranch, Rte. 10, 3301 Willow Creek Rd., Prescott, AZ 86301/602-778-7501
Rochester Lead Works, 76 Anderson Ave., Rochester, NY 14607/716-442-8500 (leadwire)
Rorschach Precision Prods., P.O. Box 151613, Irving, TX 75015/214-790-3487 (carboloy bull. dies)
Rotex Mfg. Co. (See Texan)
SSK Industries, Rt. 1, Della Drive, Bloomingdale, OH 43910/614-264-0176 (primer tool)
Sandia Die & Cartridge Co., Rte. 5, Box 5400, Albuquerque, NM 87123/505-298-5729
Shannon Associates, P.O. Box 32737, Oklahoma City, OK 73123
Shooters Accessory Supply, (See Corbin Mfg. & Supply)
J.A. Somers Co., P.O. Box 49751, Los Angeles, CA 90049 (Jasco)
Sport Flite Mfg., Inc., 2520 Industrial Row, Troy, MI 48084/313-280-0648 (swaging dies)
Star Machine Works, 418 10th Ave., San Diego, CA 92101/619-232-3216
Texan Reloaders, Inc., 444 So.Cips St., Watseka, IL 60970/815-432-5065

Trico Plastics, 590 W. Vincent Ave., Azusa, CA 91702
Tru Square Metal Products, P.O. Box 585, Auburn, WA 98002/206-833-2310 (Thumler's tumbler case polishers; Ultra Vibe 18)
Vibra-Tek, 1022 So. Tejon, Colorado Springs, CO 80903/303-634-8611 (brass polisher; Brite Rouge)
WAMADET, Silver Springs, Goodleigh, Barnstaple, Devon, England
Weaver Arms Corp, 115 No. Market St., Escondido, CA 92025/619-746-2440 (prog. loader)
Webster Scale Mfg. Co., P.O. Box 188, Sebring, FL 33870/813-385-6362
Whits Shooting Stuff, P.O. Box 1340, Cody, WY 82414
L.E. Wilson, Inc., P.O. Box 324, 404 Pioneer Ave., Cashmere, WA 98815/509-782-1328
Zenith Enterprises, 5781 Flagler Rd., Nordland, WA 98358/206-385-2142

TARGETS, BULLET & CLAYBIRD TRAPS

Amacker Products Inc., P.O. Box 1432, Tallulah, LA 71282/318-574-4903
Bulletboard Target Systems Laminations Corp., Box 469, Neenah, WI 54956/414-725-8368
Caswell Equipment Co., Inc., 1221 Marshall St. N.E., Minneapolis, MN 55413/612-379-2000 (target carriers; commercial shooting ranges)
J.G. Dapkus Co., P.O. Box 180, Cromwell, CT 06416/203-632-2308 (live bulls-eye targets)
Data-Targ. (See Rocky Mountain Target Co.)
Detroit-Armor Corp., Detroit Bullet Trap Div., 2233 N. Palmer Dr., Schaumburg, IL 60195/312-397-4070
The Dutchman's Firearms Inc, 4143 Taylor Blvd., Louisville, KY 40215/502-366-0555
Jaro Manuf., 206 E. Shaw, Pasadena, TX 77506/713-472-0417 (paper targets)
Laminations Corp. ("Bullettrap"), Box 469, Neenah, WI 54956/414-725-8368
MTM Molded Prods. Co., 3370 Obco Ct., Dayton, OH 45414/513-890-7461
Millard F. Lerch, Box 163, 10842 Front St., Mokena, IL 60448 (bullet target)
National Target Co., 4960 Wyaconda Rd., Rockville, MD 20852
Peterson Label Co., P.O. Box 186, 23 Sullivan Dr., Redding Ridge, CT 06876/203-938-2349 (paste-ons; Targ-Dots)
Rocky Mountain Target Co., P.O. Box 700, Black Hawk, SD 57718/605-787-5946 (Data-Targ)
Winchester, Olin Corp., 120 Long Ridge Rd., Stamford, CT 06904